The Economics and Ideology of Free Trade

A Historical Review

Leonard Gomes

Formerly Reader in International Economics, Middlesex University, UK

Edward Elgar
Cheltenham, UK • Northampton, MA, USA

Published by
Edward Elgar Publishing Limited
Glensanda House
Montpellier Parade
Cheltenham
Glos GL50 1UA
UK

Edward Elgar Publishing, Inc.
136 West Street
Suite 202
Northampton
Massachusetts 01060
USA

S. Husted / M. Melvin, *International Economics* – 5th Edition. (figures 6.10 and 8.1 from pages 170 and 221). © 2001 Addison Wesley. Reprinted by permission of Pearson Education, Inc.

This book has been printed on demand to keep the title in print

A catalogue record for this book
is available from the British Library

Library of Congress Cataloguing in Publication Data

Gomes, Leonard.
  The economics and ideology of free trade: a historical review / by Leonard
Gomes.
      p. cm.
  Includes bibliographical references (p.).
  1. Free trade–History. 2. Protectionism– History. 3. International trade–History.
I. Title.

HF1711.G66 2003
382'.71–dc21   2003040787

ISBN 1 84376 131 9

Printed and bound in Great Britain by Marston Book Services Limited, Oxford

Contents

Figures

Tables

Preface

Globalisation is the buzzword of our age. Much has been written and said about its opportunities, its perils and its seemingly unstoppable progress. Yet, there was a previous era of globalisation not far distant from our own, namely the late-nineteenth-century integration of the 'Atlantic Economy'. The experience of that age is sometimes forgotten or ignored in the debate on globalisation, with the result that many of the arguments over the merits of the increased interconnectedness of economies and societies lack historical perspective. However, that blind spot is likely to change. As a result of recent work by researchers into the earlier period of global integration the historical evolution of globalisation is now more widely appreciated.

Free Trade is an aspect of modern globalisation that features prominently in the debate, and one that evokes fierce emotions. But here, likewise, until very recently, intellectual perspective has been sadly lacking. Not that champions of free trade have been silent. Far from it – the so-called 'Washington consensus' and the 'Geneva consensus' have exercised enormous influence over the conduct of economic policy on the national and international levels over the past two decades. But away from the battle lines some academics, responding to the lack of historical perspective on the free trade versus protection issue, have produced intellectual histories of free trade. These doctrinal histories, plus the historical studies of actual events, have been useful contributions to the globalization debate and, hopefully, might raise somewhat the level of debate.

This book makes an additional contribution to these historical and intellectual inputs. It does so by reviewing and integrating doctrinal history and past policy debates and events bearing on the issue of free trade and protection. The book is in two parts. Part I deals with the doctrinal evolution of the economics of free trade, while Part II critically examines the debates, policies and events that marked over two centuries of fierce but intellectually stimulating controversy over the issue of Free Trade versus Protection.

In Part I, Chapter 1 is a brief account of the doctrine of state regulation of foreign trade in the Age of Mercantilism (1600s to the 1780s). Mercantilist thinking is part of our historical heritage, whether we care to be reminded of it or not. Chapters 2–5 provide a critical survey of the origin and development of comparative advantage and free-trade theories from the classical economists through the early neoclassical period (1870–90) and the

Heckscher–Ohlin–Samuelson era, right up to contemporary developments (namely the free trade implications of the 'new trade theory'). The analysis includes an assessment of the work of Friedrich List and the nineteenth-century American protectionists (Chapter 3) and four arguments for protection put forward during the period: those by Schüller, Manoilescu, and Graham and the celebrated 'Australian Case for Protection' (Chapter 4).

In Part II the economists' contributions to the great debates over Free Trade versus Protection are covered, including the pervasive role of ideology, for example, over the British Corn Laws – nineteenth century (Chapter 6), and the British Tariff Reform Debate, 1903 (Chapter 7). Keynes's support for temporary protection is included in Chapter 8 which surveys the previous era of globalisation which ended in the Great Depression of the 1930s. The book ends with some reflections on globalisation (Chapter 9).

PART I

FREE TRADE: THE ECONOMICS

1. Regulated trade – our mercantilist heritage

1.1 INTRODUCTION

Students of international economics justly claim that their subject is the oldest branch of economics. Theorems, concepts and hypotheses still currently in use were developed during the infancy of the discipline. The concept of the balance of trade, the price–specie flow mechanism, purchasing-power parity and comparative costs are examples of the ancient lineage of the concerns of international economics. In 1938 Paul Samuelson observed: 'Historically, the development of economic theory owes much to the theory of international trade.'[1] More recently, in connection with a reference to Bertil Ohlin's contribution to the theory of international trade, Samuelson repeated that 'trade theory has always been the queen realm of economic theory' (Samuelson 1981, p. 150). The economic historian Deirdre McCloskey noted in 1980: 'Since the inception of the discipline its best minds (many of them British) have put commercial policy at the centre of their thinking' (McCloskey 1980). This is so, primarily because problems of international trade and finance have always been among the most momentous and controversial of issues in economic debate.

It all started with the writers we call 'mercantilist' airing their views on pressing contemporary problems that happened to be those connected with foreign trade: monetary problems, the foreign exchanges and the balance of payments. Although they often differed in their perceptions of the problems, they shared a common assumption, namely the necessity for regulating foreign trade by the state in the interests of national power, wealth and aggrandisement.

The basic elements of mercantilist doctrine may be briefly summarised as follows:[2]

1. A favourable trade balance for the maximum accumulation of precious metals.
2. Economic policy, including foreign trade policy, must always be assessed with the above aim in mind, namely the effect such policies have on the national stock of gold and silver.

3

3. National advantage must be the overriding objective of policy. Thus the regulation of foreign trade through the promotion of exports and restriction of imports or by other indirect means are justifiable as long as they produce a net inflow of specie, namely gold and silver bullion.
4. Promotion of industry through domestic subsidies to manufacturers, the development of cheap raw materials and low interest rates to increase investment and employment.
5. Rapid population growth and a large labour force so as to keep wages and prices low and thus encourage exports.

The term 'mercantilism' originated with Adam Smith who devoted Book IV of the *Wealth of Nations* (more than 200 pages) to a wide-ranging criticism of what he called the 'commercial or mercantile system'. Ever since, the term has acquired a pejorative meaning and more often than not has been used in that sense. He attributed the various manifestations of mercantilist policy to the machinations of merchants and manufacturers, whose aim was the monopoly of the home market. The mercantile system was animated by the 'spirit of monopoly'; monopolising merchants successfully harnessed the power of the state to the pursuit of their own selfish goals to the detriment of overall economic development. Their writings were self-serving, for the most part mere 'sophistry' to justify government protection of their interests. Typical of Smith's point of view is the following:

> It cannot be very difficult to determine who have been the contrivers of this whole mercantile system; not the consumers, we may believe, whose interest has been entirely neglected; but the producers, whose interest has been so carefully attended to; and among this latter class our merchants and manufacturers have been by far the principal architects. (Smith [1776] 1976, vol. 2, p. 661)

The whole protectionist edifice was founded, he argued, on the fallacious ideas held by the mercantilists about money and the balance of payments. However effective mercantilist regulation was in promoting the interests of the commercial classes, it involved a massive misallocation of resources and was, moreover, in conflict with the 'obvious and simple system of natural liberty', namely *laissez-faire* capitalism.

The latter system – free enterprise capitalism – was, of course, what Smith proposed to erect on the ruins of the old, regulated economy. Free, competitive markets (both in foreign and domestic trades) guided by the 'Invisible Hand' would direct the employment of capital and enterprise to those trades and industries where they were likely to be most productive. This would ensure the maximum level of economic welfare and promote social harmony. Smith's powerful denunciation of mercantilist doctrine and policies, ably supported by the theoretical advances of Torrens, Ricardo and

Mill, did not, however, go unchallenged for long. In the 1860s writers of the German Historical School, sympathetic to the economic and political philosophy of mercantilism, revived the idea in opposition to the prevailing *laissez-faire* ideology of the English Classical School. For Gustav Schmoller, for example, 'Merkantilismus' was an essential part of the process of state-building. Indeed, said Schmoller, 'mercantilism in its innermost kernel is nothing but state-making'.[3] This interpretation of mercantilism was echoed in England in the 1890s in the work of Archdeacon William Cunningham, who went further than Schmoller in asserting that the rationale of mercantilism was 'the deliberate pursuit of national power'.[4]

The debate on the meaning of mercantilism was renewed with the appearance of Eli Heckscher's *Mercantilism* (Heckscher 1955). Writing from the standpoint of a free trader in the neoclassical tradition, Heckscher obviously had little sympathy for the spirit of mercantilism in any form, but his analysis of it encompassed the widest possible range of meanings: it was treated as a system of national unification, a system of power, a monetary system and a conception of society.

Adam Smith exaggerated the extent to which the mercantilists identified money and wealth and underrated their percipience. But even so, modern economists aware of the ideological motive behind Smith's attack on mercantilism find it incredible that sensible men should have espoused such views. To the English classical economists this antediluvian doctrine was the equivalent in political economy of pre-Copernican ideas in cosmology. In 1847 Richard Jones, despite his misgivings about the abstract *a priori* methodology of the economics of his day, felt obliged to label British economic writings before Adam Smith as 'primitive political economy'.[5] Primitive not only in a temporal sense, but also as being crude, naive and unsophisticated in substance.

Keynes' defence of mercantilism in the form of a coda to his *General Theory* is well known to economists (Keynes Collected Writings, VII). To the chagrin of his teachers and the corps of orthodox economists Keynes protested that the classical economists had been unfair to the mercantilists who for two hundred years had seen 'a peculiar advantage' to their countries in a favourable balance of trade. Economists were therefore guilty of 'presumptuous error in treating as a puerile obsession what for centuries had been a prime object of practical statecraft' (Keynes Collected Writings, VII, 1936, pp. 333, 339).[6] Earlier, Karl Marx objected: 'it must not be thought that these mercantilists were as stupid as they were made out to be by the later Vulgar-Freetraders'.[7]

The mercantilist literature is perhaps the best example in the history of economic thought of that wonderful combination of circumstances, theoretical development and policy recommendations, which constitutes scientific understanding in economics. That is to say, during three centuries of inquiry, we see developing (1) an interaction between theory and social–historical processes (circumstances) and (2) development in the internal structure of ideas. The early mercantilist economic ideas were attempts to explain the economic events and circumstances of the time. Inevitably, these ideas reflected to a lesser or greater extent, depending on the perceptions of the various writers, the popular prejudices or preconceptions of contemporaries. The aim of the theorising (often crude and naive) was to influence or shape these very circumstances and conditions (policy proposals). In some cases the theories were blatantly apologetic – rationalisations which sought to identify national goals with the ambitions of interest groups (overseas traders, notably). But, as economic ideas have their own internal logic, this logic began to impose its own peculiar discipline on the quality of subsequent economic thinking. The mercantilists were primarily interested in policy, and in response to perceptions of economic problems they forged analytical concepts that they required for the practical problems of policy they were discussing. The extensive English discussions on the foreign exchanges and the balance of payments in the early years of the seventeenth century is a case in point. The debate between Malynes and Misselden on the causes and consequences of the outflow of bullion during those years stimulated analytical clarity which led to the brilliant insights of Hume and the later mercantilists. In this foreign-exchange controversy Malynes not only developed a rudimentary form of the purchasing-power parity theory (PPP), but, as Schumpeter claimed, he also 'saw nearly the whole' of the automatic mechanism of international adjustment. But, of course, the analyses of pressing policy problems have always been important vehicles for the refinement and elaboration of economic theories. Thus the debate between Keynes and Ohlin over German reparations stimulated theoretical advances in the study of the 'transfer problem'. By the middle of the eighteenth century almost all the basic conceptual building blocks of the classical system had been fashioned. All that was necessary was to assemble them into a new design that permitted, for the first time, an integrated view of the rapidly emerging market economy. That, of course, was the accomplishment of Adam Smith.

Mercantilist ideas and policies developed against a background of intense national rivalries and conscious policies – economic, political and military – to enhance state power. Warfare was almost a normal relationship among the European superpowers – England, Spain, France and the Dutch Republic – as they engaged in geopolitical and dynastic struggles throughout most of the period. There was complete peace in only a single year during the period 1600 to 1667. Commercial rivalry – 'jealousy of trade', as it was called – was a frequent cause of open conflict in sixteenth-

and seventeenth-century Europe. In the seventeenth century overseas trade was still largely speculative; and a risky business too. The merchant trading overseas looked to the state for protection and the furtherance of his interests. When required, it was the duty of the state to provide military, naval or diplomatic support to the nation's commerce. Such national support was the counterpart of the personal loyalty (and taxes) one owed to the state. Effective protection depended on the power of the state, which ultimately derived from its wealth and the profitability and volume of its foreign trade.

For the ruler the activities of the overseas merchant were the very source and foundation of the nation's prosperity. A flourishing foreign trade provided him with a steady stream of tariff revenues in addition to the other sources of income derived from the sale of monopoly rights to trading companies. Less immediate and obvious, but equally important in a violent age, the activities of the overseas merchants constituted the very 'sinews of war'. The resources used by traders had important 'spin-offs'. The merchant navy was the nursery of fighting sailors: the shipbuilding and ship supplies industries produced the hardware for naval defence.

The symbiotic relationship between state and merchant, however, had to be consolidated or formalised through a system of regulated trade because in the absence of state intervention the private interests of traders were liable to clash with the national interest or the public good: for instance, when excessive imports of Eastern wares by the East India Company could drain the country of its stock of silver; or when foreign exchange dealers depreciated the currency by manipulating the exchanges so as to make speculative profits. Criteria had to be established to distinguish 'good' from 'bad' trades. In 1663 Samuel Fortrey made a distinction between 'public profit' and 'private advantage' and gave instances where the pursuit of private gain by individual merchants could work against the national interest (or 'the benefit of the whole'). On that ground he justified state regulation of foreign trade aimed at the promotion of exports, the limitation of certain types of imports (luxury goods and other non-essential consumption items) and the management of monopolies (Fortrey 1663). The mercantilist writers did not make any rigid distinction between economic and political objectives. What we would now normally regard as purely economic processes and events (business activity, consumer choice, investment decisions, the commodity composition of trade, the use of resources, and so on) were always thought of in relation to politics and strategy. Thus one of their prime concerns was to work out how exactly the merchant's gain from foreign trade was compatible with the national interest, including the security of the realm.

The reconciliation of the pursuit of private profit through foreign trade with national security was thus a matter of primary concern for these writers. It is because the mass of writings on economic subjects during the seventeenth and early eighteenth centuries have these characteristics that we call them 'mercantilist'. Economic thinking in the age of mercantilism took it for granted that international economic relations were political relations, and since international economic interaction was in large part shaped by the policies of the emerging nation-state, much of the mercantilist writing was addressed to the new state bureaucracies. Indeed, some notable mercantilists were themselves bureaucrats who wrote for the instruction of their princes. Market forces were acknowledged to have something to do with competition in international trade, but there was scant recognition of the role of an impersonal market as the arbiter of success or failure in international trade. Markets had to be won or captured from others, whether by naked force or diplomatic pressure. Conversely, markets, command of trade routes, shipping, and so on could be lost through political or military pusillanimity. There was little recognition of the possibility that nations could compete for trade by competing to create it. Trade matters were thus firmly located within the realm of statecraft. Adam Smith ridiculed this arrangement as a project which 'may at first sight appear . . . fit only for a nation of shopkeepers. It is, however, a project altogether unfit for a nation of shopkeepers; but extremely fit for a nation whose government is influenced by shopkeepers' (Smith [1776] 1976, vol. 2, p. 613). Smith's jibe, springing from a different conception of political economy, appears well-targeted; but if 'traders' were substituted for 'shopkeepers' in the above passage and notice taken of contemporary realities, Smith's remark loses much of its bite.

Mercantilists believed that wealth and power were intimately associated with possession of the precious metals; and since, for a country without gold and silver mines foreign trade was the only way to acquire treasure, the mercantilists emphasised international trade as a means of increasing the wealth and power of a nation. In particular they focused their attention on the balance of trade and the foreign exchanges as mechanisms which determine the net flow of precious metals.

The doctrine in its classic form arose in England out of the famous controversy during the early part of the seventeenth century between Malynes on one side and Mun and Misselden on the other, concerning the state of the foreign exchanges and the balance of payments.[8] The occasion was the economic and trade depression of 1619–22, and the issue under discussion was how to stop the outflow of the precious metals. The discussion ranged over a wide area of international monetary relationships, namely: the role of the exchange rate, the effects of devaluation on domestic inflation, money supply, the terms of trade (that is, the ratio of export and import prices), and so on; but there was little discussion of how commercial policy (that is, the use of trade controls) could help to restore equilibrium in the balance of payments and over the long run promote economic development.

Later writers did, however, consider the use of trade policy in the achievement of these aims. During the course of the debates on trade and the foreign exchanges Sir Thomas Mun, by then a director of the East India Company, produced a series of papers and memoranda which formed the basis of his *England's Treasure by Forraign Trade,* published posthumously by his son in 1664 (Mun 1664). For later generations it became the *locus classicus* for mercantilist thought on the role of foreign trade in the national economy, as indeed it informed popular economic thinking for over a century afterwards. Foreign trade, through the balance of trade, is assigned a crucial role in the process of wealth generation. The growth of wealth, it is asserted, depends on having an excess of exports over imports. Mun lists several methods whereby this may be achieved but how these recommendations were to be implemented so as to achieve the ultimate desirable result – a more favourable trade balance – was not discussed in any detail. Some could be put into effect by merchants themselves; others would follow from the incentives provided by the market; but much of the programme obviously depended on prudent government regulation.

Mun's programme stemmed from his model of trade and growth based on the notion that foreign trade was the source of economic 'surplus' – the sale of commodities above their purchase price (or values) – and therefore the activity that uniquely contributed to the accumulation of capital. Mun naturally envisaged this capital being reinvested in overseas trade. Mun was not consciously thinking of the principle of comparative advantage, but his model indicated a pattern of trade and development based on some such principle. Merchants would seek out domestic commodities that could profitably be sold abroad and fetch raw materials and essential commodities from foreign countries to be worked up and subsequently re-exported at increased value added. For England, foreign trade thus afforded an opportunity to diversify export lines and break away from the relatively stagnant staples of wool and woollen cloths. A cumulative process of increased profits, greater accumulation, leading to larger diversified investments would thus be set in motion. Such was the path to economic growth.

In Mun's trade model there is no recognition of the possibility of increased output from specialisation and trade. Exports can, indeed, generate growth; but the process is not automatic and self-evident. Mun emphasised one route towards growth via trade; but lacking an understanding of allocative mechanisms and a sensible view of the end of economic activity, he failed to notice some implications of his approach – the most important being the role of opportunity cost. For instance, Mun favoured the long-distance trades because these called for more expensive British ships and higher charges for insurance, freight, and so on, as if the transport resources used in these trades were costless. The greater the utilisation of domestic resources, the higher the profit to the nation, according to Mun. In general, there was no recognition of the sacrifice of resources involved in production for export – resources that alternatively could be used to produce domestic consumables. The view that exports are necessary only because they pay for imports, that is, that the sacrifice of domestic labour and resources involved in exports is worthwhile only for the sake of the consumption of foreign output it permits, would have appeared strange and deplorable to Mun and his contemporaries.

Some mercantilists later discerned a positive relationship between the quantity of money in circulation (that is, the monetary inflows associated with balance of payments surpluses) and levels of production, exports and employment. The balance of trade was, therefore, seen as being related in some certain but not yet fully understood way to the process of economic growth. Some writers perceived the growth-inducing consequences of a favourable trade balance in terms of what we would now call the 'direct multiplier effect' of exports on the income flow and hence on production, employment and profits. Thus, a favourable balance of trade (payments), instead of being an end in itself, became a means to the end of developing a manufacturing base capable of delivering manufactured exports of high value-added and secure employment to English workers. Protective measures, in so far as they are successful in producing a favourable foreign balance work by directing aggregate demand towards domestic factors of production. In this way greater resource use and production could be secured. Other mercantilists reasoned in terms of the direct liquidity influence of the positive foreign balance which draws in money to support higher levels of activity. The balance of trade was therefore a regulatory device and provided a substitute for what a later age called 'monetary policy'. Foreign trade and its regulation was the means to achieve full utilisation of resources. Increases in productive capacity and industrialisation would, in turn, lead to a more prosperous foreign trade which was the ultimate goal for many mercantilists. When Sir Francis Brewster asserted in 1702: 'That the full employment of All Hands in the Nation is the surest way and means to bring Bullion into the Kingdom' (Brewster 1702, Essay v, p. 45) he was only repeating a widely held view. A number of writers, however, who measured national well-being in terms of a flourishing foreign trade and a favourable balance of trade related this condition to further indicators of national welfare such as the possibilities for greater employment for the poor and more profit for producers and merchants. Certainly, among the later mercantilists there was a marked concern with remedying the endemic unemployment and underemployment of the times.

There is a striking parallel between the economic conditions of seventeenth- and early eighteenth-century economies and the present-day developing countries; and it is not surprising that protectionist arguments (in aid of employment and economic development) should have irresistible appeal to rational people at different times in similar conditions. The modern-day equivalent was the adoption of protectionist import-substitution development strategies by many developing countries in the 1950s designed to promote rapid industrialisation. Not many mercantilists seemed aware of the limitations of the employment argument for protection. Trade policies can increase employment in import-competing industries, but this gain is usually offset when exports fall, either because foreigners retaliate by increasing their trade restrictions or because their ability to buy domestic goods declines as a consequence of the falling off of their exports to the domestic market. In addition, of course, the associated payments surplus will not be permanent. These policies might be effective only in so far as they result in a reduction of real wages, which is again likely to be only temporary. Those who saw the alleviation of unemployment stemming from the monetary demand generated by a favourable balance of trade sometimes used the argument that increasing inflows would lower the rate of interest and increase the availability of credit. Reference was made to the prevailing low interest rates in Holland that gave the Dutch a competitive advantage in trade through a lowering of the interest cost of producing their exportables. At times of substantial unemployment of labour and idle resources the argument might be valid, but advocates of lower interest rates frequently overlooked the fact that as the economy approached full employment (or indeed long before then because of bottleneck problems and supply inelasticity of particular inputs) the rise in the price level would either leave the rate of interest unchanged or cause it to rise. In addition, the availability of credit would contract because of the reduction of the real money stock.

Keynes claimed that mercantilism was no mere puerile obsession with treasure, but was primarily a policy of employment. Later, W.D. Grampp produced evidence supporting the view that the most important economic objective of the mercantilists was the maintenance of a high level of employment (Grampp [1952] 1960, pp. 61–91). Heckscher's criticism of Keynes's interpretation was not that he was wrong to suppose that unemployment was a matter of prime concern to the earlier thinkers, but that it was a mistake to apply Keynesian analysis to mercantilist economies. The employment problem in those early days was not one of aggregate demand deficiency such as characterised the developed industrialised economies in the 1930s, but rather (as already mentioned) the structural unemployment typically found in Third World countries today. In such countries with small industrial sectors, unemployment results primarily from supply constraints, shortage of capital and technology, low productivity and high dependency ratios. In addition if we are to believe contemporary writers there was a good deal of voluntary unemployment and idleness in seventeenth-century England – 'pauperism, cheating, roaring, robbing, hanging, begging and perishing', as Mun describes it. Keynes was nevertheless justified in calling attention to an important element in mercantilist thought which the classical economists all too often ignored or explained away by appeal to Say's law of markets (that supply creates its own demand).

'It is therefore a general maxim, to discourage the importation of work, and to encourage the exportation of it.'[9] Thus Sir James Steuart summarises the essence of the employment argument for a favourable balance of trade held by a long line of mercantilist writers since Sir Thomas Smith, which by that time had achieved the status of an economic nostrum.

Concern with employment was, of course, of long standing and stemmed from the medieval prince's duty to provide employment to the poor. Later, employment was related to the balance of trade objective which was thus given additional force. Exports represent a demand for domestic labour and therefore increase employment at home. Imports, on the other hand, being the demand for foreign output, displace domestic labour. Hence, the larger the export surplus, the greater the employment of domestic labour. This was Mun's position, although it was employment in the export, or more precisely, the re-export industries that interested him. Those like Malynes and the French writer Forbonnais, conceived of the employment-generating effect as stemming from the monetary inflow associated with a favourable trade balance. Malynes claimed that 'the more ready mony . . . that our merchants should make by return . . . the more employment would they make upon our home commodities, advancing the price thereof, which price would augment the quantity by setting more people on work.'[10]

Forbonnais regarded gold and silver as 'conventional wealth' which, 'by circulating domestically, will procure a comfortable existence for a greater number of citizens'.[11] Money was seen as active, the 'great wheel of commerce and industry'. It could arouse dormant, idle resources and initiate a cumulative process of economic expansion. Part of the product of domestic labour had to be given up to foreigners, for it was only through foreign sales that the production and sale of other commodities would be accomplished. The maximisation of employment through foreign trade, therefore, led to the following policy recommendations:

1. Encourage exports of manufactured or processed goods.
2. Prohibit or restrict the export of native raw materials (raw wool, minerals, and so on).

3. Prohibit or restrict the export of machinery, tools, and so forth, and the emigration of skilled artisans.
4. Minimise imports, except in the case of essential foodstuffs and raw materials unavailable at home.

These measures were designed to enlarge the availability of raw materials, promote their further processing into fabricated manufactures and thereby increase the value added by domestic labour.[12] From these considerations there arose the 'balance of labour' doctrine as a criterion of the social welfare benefits from foreign trade. Here a favourable balance was reckoned, not in monetary terms, but in terms of the aggregate excess of labour embodied in exports over the labour content of imports. Like its monetary counterpart, the balance of labour doctrine had its corollaries, such as the division of particular trades into 'good' and 'bad' according to their actual or potential ability to stimulate or depress domestic employment.

Policy to ensure the maintenance of a favourable balance of trade took the form of what Adam Smith called the 'twin engines' of the mercantile system: one working at full speed to promote exports and import substitution, while the other was behind the encouragement of native shipping (that is, the Navigation Laws) and control of colonial commerce. In England export promotion took the form of:

1. Remission of duties on goods re-exported ('drawbacks').
2. Direct subsidies or 'bounties' on exports (for example, on corn, salt pork, linen, silk, sailcloth, and so on).
3. The retention of local raw materials through prohibitions or high duties on their export, presumably on the ground that by keeping them at home they would be made abundant and cheap, thereby increasing the rate of production of finished products for export; also keeping them at home prevented foreign manufacturers from acquiring such supplies. Wool, woollen yarn, and fuller's earth (used for cleaning raw wool) were the major items subject to export bans.
4. Import substitution measures comprised tariffs, embargoes and prohibitions on the import of goods which could be produced at home.

Bilateral commercial treaties were another weapon in the armoury of mercantilist practices. Since all European countries were pursuing broadly similar policies of self-sufficiency designed to foster the growth of the same range of industries and services, the basis for mutually beneficial trade negotiations was severely limited.

Complementary trading patterns suited the interests of the major powers, but attempts to negotiate reciprocal agreements along these lines were only successful through the exercise of *force majeure* and often resulted in trade diversion. The political implications of trade (that is, balance-of-power ramifications) were such that commercial clauses or agreements figured prominently in almost all major treaties ending international conflicts.

English woollen manufacturers pressed for the opening of the Portuguese market to British exports, which they obtained by the Methuen Treaty (1703) between England and Portugal. The result was that the Portuguese industry was stifled at birth; but Portuguese wines were admitted at two-thirds of the duty imposed on French wines. The Methuen Treaty was a masterstroke of English commercial diplomacy. Although the immediate object of the treaty was to draw Portugal away from its policy of neutrality to one of armed alliance on England's side during the War of the Spanish Succession, the agreement was long remembered for the two commercial clauses it contained. They formed the basis for England's commercial supremacy over its 'oldest ally'. The ground was prepared by a series of bilateral treaties (1642, 1654 and 1661) which opened Portuguese commerce to English merchants. The latter enjoyed special privileges, both in metropolitan Portugal and in its overseas possessions. By the end of the seventeenth century Portugal was a virtual commercial vassal of England; and what the treaty negotiated by John Methuen did was to confirm Portugal's dependency. Earlier, under the Duke of Ericeira, Portugal started its own cloth industry by means of a protective tariff, but efforts in that direction had to be abandoned; for under the 1703 treaty Portugal was forever obliged to admit duty-free the products of the English woollen industry. The English cloth industry was saved, but it ruined Portuguese industry in general. Portugal's carrying trade came into English hands, and through the permanent trade surplus with its trading partner England obtained an annual inflow of between one-half to one million pounds sterling of Brazilian gold. Between 1703 and 1760 British exports to Portugal increased by just over 260 per cent.[13]

The other main pillar of British mercantile practice was enshrined in the so-called Navigation Code, comprising a series of Acts of Trade and Navigation passed between 1651 and 1733. The important ones were those of 1660, 1663, 1673 and 1696. In the minds of Sir George Downing and other architects of the Navigation Act the legislation was clearly and directly aimed at the achievement of strategic power and wealth (relative to other states) through the control of native colonial shipping and commerce. The Dutch carrying trade was the principal target; and Downing expressed the wishes of many in England when he wrote: 'If England were once brought to a Navigation as cheap as this [Dutch] country, good night Amsterdam.'[14] To understand these motives and ambitions it is important to consider them in the context of the growing importance of colonies in the mid-seventeenth century. By the early eighteenth century England had adopted a complex system of regulating trade, the keystone of which was the Navigation Laws. In conception and practical application these laws faithfully followed Josiah Child's injunction that 'Profit and Power ought jointly to be considered'. They were the means for effectively controlling imports, keeping foreigners out of the colonial trades, undermining Dutch (and later, French) mercantile marines, ensuring the maintenance of a favourable balance of trade and the building up of naval power. Making the Navigation Acts an integral part of the Old Colonial System exhibited a clear perception, too, of the interdependence of profit and power. As is well known, Adam Smith admired the Navigation Acts, calling them 'perhaps the wisest of all the commercial regulations of England'. But Smith makes it plain that he does not support them upon economic grounds, but because, in the last resort, 'defence is much more important than opulence' (Smith [1776] 1976, pp. 464–5, 518, 522–3.)[15] The English found that war as an instrument of policy could be both effective and profitable. When the Dutch refused Cromwell's offer of union, the Rump used naval action to enforce the Navigation Acts, thus precipitating the first Dutch War. The war did not make the Dutch any more willing to accept Cromwell's improved offer (1653) to divide world trade between the two countries, but it did swell enormously the English mercantile fleet. Seventeen hundred enemy merchant vessels were seized as prizes. Practically overnight the English were equipped with carriers of bulk cargoes – the English merchant fleet almost doubled between 1660 and 1688.

The theme of 'power' and 'plenty' being mutually reinforcing joint goals of national policy echoes like a refrain throughout the mercantilist literature. In the conditions of the time the two aims were never separated in people's minds. However, the pursuit of power and wealth varied according to time, place, and the ambitions of particular regimes. There were constraints set by resource endowments, levels of economic development, administrative machinery, tradition, and so on. Opportunities were provided by favourable economic and political circumstances, extent and nature of involvement in trading relations, including colonial ties, and so on. The emphasis accorded to one or the other twin goals naturally depended on these circumstances, and the instruments chosen for their attainment also varied according to what, in particular national contexts, were thought most suitable.

When Francis Bacon accused Henry VII of 'bowing the ancient policy of this State from consideration of plenty to consideration of power' he was referring to one particular instance of fifteenth-century international economic diplomacy where the twin aims of state action (wealth and national

security) got out of proper balance.[16] Heckscher went further and suggested that, as a general rule, mercantilist policy subordinated 'plenty' to
'power'. Viner disagreed with this judgement and contended that for the
mercantilists 'power and plenty were regarded as coexisting ends of
national policy which were fundamentally harmonious.'[17] Their thinking
had an eminently practical orientation: how to use state power to achieve
economic ends, and just as importantly, how to use economic strength to
achieve political goals. In the 1620s Mun indicated how, through the
pursuit of sound commercial policies, the king and the commonwealth
would benefit as merchants increased their riches. Later in the century such
a harmonious relationship was accepted as axiomatic. Sir Josiah Child, for
one, had no doubt that the expansion of commerce produced a beneficent
cycle. 'Foreign trade', he wrote in 1681 'produces riches, riches power,
power preserves our trade and religion.'[18]

In the early modern period agriculture was, of course, the major source
of income. The landed gentry gained wealth from the sale of grain and
rising rents in the expanding home market. However, agricultural output
increased only slowly and it was difficult to export. The low value relative
to volume of agricultural produce meant high transport costs which made
exports uncompetitive in foreign markets, except at times of famine prices.
Mercantilists therefore looked to foreign trade as one of the few means of
increasing wealth and power rapidly. The fact that the king could not
effectively tax landed wealth added to the quest for other sources of royal
revenue (customs and excise). The finances of the state – hence its power
and ability to pursue foreign policy objectives – came to depend critically
on the state of its foreign trade. This was unpleasantly brought home to the
French during the Seven Years War. The disruption of French trade (particularly the valuable colonial trades) reduced the government's ability to
borrow, and with it the means of supporting allies and even the continued
prosecution of the war itself. Choiseul, French Minister for Foreign Affairs,
admitted in 1759: 'The disruption of commerce, followed by the loss of the
colonies has destroyed credit, resulting in a kind of bankruptcy. It is not a
question only of courage; one must have the means of sustaining it.'[19]

A further factor influencing the fulfilment of national ambitions in the
sphere of international economic relations was the limitations to the attainment of military and diplomatic objectives set by small armies, diplomatic
conventions, weak administrations, and so on. No one state was able to
exercise a permanent hegemony because power was nearly equally distributed and they all suffered to a lesser or greater degree from the same weaknesses. Thus foreign trade became the main area of competition and
conflict. In the conditions of the times of mutual suspicion, rivalry and
brutally competitive state-building, international economic relations were

most definitely political relations. As regards the pursuit of power, what mattered was relative strength or, as Viner puts it, 'the ratio of power, not the terms of the ratio'. Relatively minor changes could alter the overall power position of states, so if a country lost out militarily on any particular occasion it sought compensation in the international economic sphere or vice versa. Commercial treaties and regulations affecting foreign trade, including shipping and the fisheries, were made with the expectation of gaining commercial advantages by applying the same criteria used in other negotiations where military, political, dynastic or religious advantages were sought.

1.2 ECONOMIC AND INTELLECTUAL CHANGES

As the seventeenth century came to a close heterodox ideas appeared from many quarters containing statements normally associated with classical liberalism. To those imbued with the new spirit of inquiry and its successes typified by Newton's discovery of the laws of physics and Harvey's description of the circulation of the blood in the human body, mercantilist theory was vulnerable on two counts. First, protectionist policies might conceivably preserve trade for a while, but could not guarantee its expansion. The only sound basis for a thriving commerce is the accumulation and efficient utilisation of productive resources. And both commerce and the efficient employment of resources are best left to be carried on by individuals pursuing their own self-interest. Critics increasingly argued that government regulation and interference were superficial, opportunistic and often sinister. Sir Roy Porter sums up contemporary demands this way: 'Economic policy must be grounded in empirical realities not rulers' wish lists, and certainly not the machinations of monopolists' (Porter 2000, p. 386). Second (and reinforcing the first point), the indefinite accumulation of treasure must be self-defeating in the long run if the logic of the quantity theory of money was to be taken seriously.

The decline of mercantilist foreign-trade doctrines can be traced to (i) the rise of free-trade ideas, (ii) the development of the theory of international monetary adjustment (that is, the price–specie flow mechanism) and (iii) the teachings of the Physiocrats in France.

Before dealing with these developments which undermined the mercantilist programme we must briefly say something about the changes in the economic environment and attitudes of business people. Changes in economic structure and institutions occurred which (a) made the old anxiety over the adequacy of bullion supplies if not otiose, at least less pressing; and (b) strengthened attitudes antagonistic to the paternalistic view of the state and state regulation. Defoe's England was significantly different from that of Thomas Mun. By the early 1700s trade was largely multilateral and an elaborate system of international settlements or clearing had developed through the widespread use of bills of exchange. The system appears to have functioned with the minimum actual movement of specie; the specie flows that actually took place were usually activated by exchange rates moving outside the specie export and import points. Trade routes multiplied and became more complex, replacing the earlier simpler patterns of trade. The range of commodities widened and new markets were exploited. As well as the old staples, the goods moving in international trade covered a broad variety of intermediate products. Matching this growing complexity of trade was the equally marked growth in credit institutions, banking and insurance business.

These times, too, saw the rise of a new class of small businessmen who were increasingly finding that mercantile regulation was not in their best interest. These men typically rose from the ranks of the guild masters to become employers or capitalists and even moved into the fields of commerce and marketing. As the British economy became more diversified, the new entrepreneurs found their search for and exploitation of markets for their products obstructed by the corporate trading monopolies (such as the Merchant Adventurers, the Russian Company, the Hudson's Bay Company, the Levant Company and the East India Company). They resented the monopolistic privileges granted a few big financiers and City merchants and complained about the taxes levied to maintain a system of power, unrelated, as they saw it, to their individual interests. The extension of capitalist control over the processes of production and commerce stemmed from the fact that it was becoming more difficult to make large profits simply from taking advantage of price differences between different regions and countries. The path to secure profits henceforth lay in the process of production and through attention to costs and productivity.

In France, too, the rising class of small entrepreneurs felt hemmed in by Colbertian regulations. They resented the multiplicity of taxes and tolls and the privileges accorded to others. The very expression '*laissez-faire*' apparently originated in these merchants' complaints, later to be endowed with the status of an economic principle by the government inspector of trademarks, Vincent de Gourney, who, disenchanted with mercantilist regulation, extended this cry into the classic liberal phrase '*laissez faire, laissez passer*' – 'free enterprise, free trade'.[20] The origin of the classical liberal slogan, in fact, epitomises the transition to economic liberalism. The grievances of the early capitalists could easily have been dismissed as mere special pleading by vested interests (of a particular industry, region, town or port). What gave added merit to these demands, however, was the supportive voice of philosophy. The thinkers of the Enlightenment threw their weight behind the men of business who clamoured for freedom from detailed and onerous regulation by the state. Thus an ideology was born.

The ideas, attitudes and programmes of the *philosophes* and *illuminati* of the Age of Reason presented the first real intellectual challenge to mercantilism. The ideas of the men of the Enlightenment were not wholly new; some of their theories had been aired during the preceding century and others can be traced back to the Renaissance. But they were zealots for the cause of freedom, reason and the new science. They took hold of age-old concepts like Reason, Law, Nature, Liberty, Humanity, Perfectibility, invested them with new meanings and then applied them to social phenomena. Condorcet said of himself and his friends that they were 'a class of men less concerned with discovering truth than with propagating it . . . [who] find their glory rather in destroying popular error than in pushing back the frontiers of knowledge'.[21] They were greatly impressed with the mathematical and experimental methods used by Newton in his *Principia* and *Opticks*, which had shed so much light on the nature of physical reality. The discovery of the universal laws of motion and gravitation suggested to the *philosophes* the existence of similar orderly, predictable laws in society. Newton discovered the marvellous properties of light simply by playing about with a prism. Using reason as their prism, the *philosophes* felt they could discover equally wonderful truths about human society. 'What we can do for bees and beavers', said Condorcet, 'we ought to do for man.'[22] Following this injunction, thinkers set about laying the foundations of systematic work in the social sciences, writing the classics in the process. They confidently believed that rational criticism (the 'light of reason') could free the world from myth, superstition and ignorance. Oliver Goldsmith called them 'cosmopolites', citizens of the world. And indeed, it was this frame of mind – at once pacific and cosmopolitan – that confronted the chauvinism and bellicosity of the mercantilists. Voltaire's call '*Ecrasez l'infâme*' was meant to encompass all this as well as the injustice and iniquities that constricted the individual in society. Earlier, the spokesman for the Whig oligarchy in England and staunch defender of property, John Locke, gained wide acceptance for his views on political liberty and toleration. He inspired belief in the inalienable rights of the human individual in society based on the 'natural' and 'original' liberties of man. Eighteenth-century thinkers interpreted this as a plea for limited government: on the whole, things, if left to themselves, were more likely to work together for the good than if regulated by interfering governments. Governments cannot change the basic nature of individuals motivated as they are by egoistic or selfish motives. Laws and institutions walk properly with Nature when they provide an orderly social framework for the pursuit of self-interest, which is the only avenue for advancing towards national prosperity.

1.3   DEVELOPMENT OF FREE TRADE IDEAS

In the economic sphere this sort of reasoning led naturally to *laissez-faire*. Just as David Hume hoped that politics might be reduced to a science, so some of these thinkers believed that the laws of economy could be discovered by the same methods that enlightened mankind about the laws of physics. The first step in this direction was to get a proper understanding of the *motivation* rather than the *ethics* of economic behaviour, that is, to apply cause-and-effect analysis to economic activity. Here, perhaps more than in other fields of social activity, the eighteenth-century thinkers found what they expected: selfish, egoistic motives were the primary, if not the only, ones that moved people to economic endeavour. Somehow, it was believed, the pursuit of private, selfish interests would tend to promote the social and economic good. This social vision was admirably put by one of the finest poets of the age, Alexander Pope in his *Essay on Man*:

> That REASON, PASSION answer one great aim;
> That true SELF-LOVE and SOCIETY are the same.

Earlier, the same idea was expressed in rather more controversial tones by Bernard de Mandeville in his long doggerel poem *The Fable of the Bees* ([1714] 1924) and succinctly affirmed by Nicholas Barbon in 1690 thus: 'Prodigality is a vice that is prejudicial to the man, but not to trade' (Barbon 1690, p. 32).[23] Mandeville's shocking paradox – 'private vices are often public benefits' – caused a bit of a stir among his contemporaries in the early eighteenth century, and his book achieved an immediate *succès de scandale*. Mandeville's paradox outraged the sensibilities of the moralists by exposing the hypocrisy of their praise of frugality and contentment, but it was merely stating an obvious economic fact; and this latter fact was not lost on the liberal-minded writers on economics. Mandeville's argument is simply that individuals, by indulging in vices, pursuing self-love or self-interest contribute to social welfare and economic prosperity.

Turning now to the rise of free-trade ideas, we find ourselves dealing with the application by writers of the same basic principle of the self-regulatory nature of the economy to the conduct of foreign trade. The writers who pioneered various aspects of the free-trade approach to international trade before Adam Smith include Sir Dudley North, Charles Davenant and Henry Martyn who anonymously published the 1701 pamphlet *Considerations upon the East-India Trade*.

For these writers, foreign trade was in essence not different from domestic trade; businessmen engaged in it for the same reason – the prospect of making a profit. Unlike most of their contemporaries, they saw the profit motive as the regulator of orderly economic activity. There are no 'good' trades (for example, export of manufactures) and 'bad' trades (for example, export of raw materials, import of luxury items), only profitable and unprofitable ones; and whatever was profitable to private businessmen in free bargains was socially beneficial. They did not, however, like Cantillon, press the logic of the profit motive to reach a theory of the allocation of resources among alternative uses through the phenomenon of market exchanges. Neither did they consistently think, like Cantillon, of the economy as an automatically adjusting mechanism; but what they glimpsed of it convinced them of the futility of mercantilist regulation. Starting with the axiom that all men are motivated by self-interest, Dudley North (1641–91), a wealthy merchant of the Turkey Company, develops an uncompromising case for free trade in his book *Discourses Upon Trade* (North [1691] 1954). The profit motive, he maintains, must be the sole arbiter of what goods to export and import, from which sources supplies are to be obtained and to which markets goods are to be consigned. He declares 'there can be no trade unprofitable to the public; for if any prove so, men leave it off; and wherever the traders thrive, the public, of which they are a part, thrives also'. And again, 'no people ever grew rich by policies; but it is peace, industry, and freedom that brings trade and wealth and nothing else'. North went on to attack the assumption that a favourable balance of trade was necessarily desirable. The supply of money adjusts itself automatically among countries according to the needs of trade; but he did not develop this argument since evidently he did not quite grasp the quantity theory of money. He firmly denied, however, another mercantilist maxim, namely that in trade one nation's loss was another's gain. No, says North, it was the loss of all; 'for all is combined together' (North [1691] 1952, pp. 513, 543). Charles Davenant, who held the post of Inspector-General of Imports and Exports from 1703 to 1714 held much the same opinions. In his 1696 *Essays on the East-India Trade* he asserts: 'Trade is in its nature free, finds its own channel and best directeth its own course; and all laws to give it rules and directions, and to limit and circumscribe it may serve the particular ends of private men, but are seldom advantageous to the public'; and further: 'They say few laws in a state are an indication of wisdom in a people; but it may be more truly said that few laws relating to trade are the mark of a nation that thrives by traffic' (Davenant 1696, vol. I, pp. 98, 99).

In one of his official reports, Davenant wrote: 'It is utterly impossible exactly to state the balance between our country and another, all traffic have a mutual dependence one upon the other'.[24] The early mercantilists either ignored opportunity costs or had no conception of them. This neglect or ignorance of the alternative use of money and resources might

have been partly due to the fact that the economy they lived in was characterised by widespread unemployment and underemployment of labour –
then a key factor of production. This fact, however, meant that men's minds
did not turn in the direction that would have led to the discovery of the law
of comparative advantage. They therefore were bereft of any substantial
theory of the gains from trade. For them, there was a profit in foreign trade,
but this profit was realised only as a consequence of a favourable balance
of trade. Mun was quite explicit that the gain or loss to the nation from
foreign trade could be measured only by reference to the state of the
balance of trade. The classical economists' case for free trade based on
comparative advantage, by contrast, relied on the principle of specialisation and division of labour to promote the accumulation and efficient utilisation of resources which alone can make a country rich.

It was these advantages of international specialisation (ignored by mercantilists) that writers like North, Davenant and in particular Henry
Martyn (the author of the remarkable 1701 pamphlet mentioned above)
dimly saw as the source of mutually beneficial trade. In this pamphlet
Martyn, who succeeded to Davenant's job, mounted an attack on the textile
manufacturers who clamoured for protection against Indian imports. He
pointed to the advantages (increases in productivity) resulting from the use
of machinery and the practice of division of labour. The latter concept he
referred to as 'order and regularity' and applied it to international trade.
Bullion is exchanged for Indian finished cotton textiles, he declares, because
it is a cheaper way of getting textiles than by producing them at home. He
illustrates this argument by an example to show the saving in labour costs
(or labour time) that results when certain goods are obtained through trade
rather than by self-sufficient production at home:

> If nine cannot produce above three bushels of wheat in England, if by equal
> labour they might procure nine bushels from another country, to employ these
> in agriculture at home, is to employ nine to do no more work than might be done
> as well by three . . . is the loss of six bushels of wheat; is therefore the loss of so
> much value. ([Martyn] 1701, p. 55)

Martyn implies that the benefits of specialisation or gains from trade –
namely the saving of labour effort – can best be reaped under a regime of
free trade, for trade is nothing more than a voluntary exchange of marketable assets and commodities. He likened the effects of free trade to the
benefits of technical progress and the division of labour. Imports of cheap
Indian fabrics would exert a downward competitive pressure on the prices
of British textiles, and workers would be thrown out of employment as
high-cost producers contracted their output. But the real-income gain to
consumers would increase spending on other, efficiently produced English

products. These industries would expand, because of both the increased demand for their output and lower manufacturing costs brought about by the lower level of wages consequent upon the increased labour supply. Eventually he envisaged a situation where the surplus labour would be absorbed by output expansions of the remaining efficient English industries. Trade was therefore a means by which more goods could be obtained from the same amount of resources.

Both North and Davenant also made references to the international division of labour. Davenant argued against the promotion of industry in a country which is unsuitable to it by reason of either climate or availability of resources, that is, an industry should be encouraged only if it has natural advantages in a particular region. It is not clear what influence these works had on contemporaries – apparently not much. North's book was published anonymously in the year of his death. Martyn's pamphlet also came out anonymously, and both were virtually ignored at the time. Only Davenant's work was known, and a few years before the *Wealth of Nations* came out a five-volume edition of his collected works was published.

The Victorian liberals were full of praise for these writers, who they regarded as pioneers of *laissez-faire* and free-trade doctrines. However, the truth is that these writers' statements of general liberal principles were often at variance with their recommendations on specific issues. They were very much men of their time, political animals, and, in the case of Davenant and Martyn, senior public servants who had careers to safeguard and political masters to humour. Davenant and North were Tories and Martyn a Whig. Despite his liberal free-trade utterances, Martyn, for instance, was bitterly opposed to freer trade with France (for example, he joined the Whig merchants in campaigning against the proposed commercial clauses, Articles 8 and 9, of the Peace of Utrecht, 1713). Referring to the economic writings of Child, Barbon, Davenant and North, E.A. Johnson commented: 'the liberal theories of trade espoused by the Tory pamphleteer were perhaps more the result of circumstances and political sympathy than evidence of superior enlightenment' (Johnson 1937, p. 144).[25] And Leslie Stephen, the late-Victorian historian, said of them: 'For one moment they reach an elevation from which they can contemplate the planet as a whole, and at the next moment their vision is confined to the horizon visible from an English shop window'.[26] Schumpeter's opinion was that, excepting North, none of the others were thoroughgoing free traders – 'North alone was'. He had a high opinion, though, of Martyn's analytical accomplishment, referring to it as 'a technically superior formulation of the benefits from territorial division of labour' and hailed the author as 'a predecessor of Ricardo, though possibly a quite uninfluential one' (Schumpeter 1954, pp. 239, 373, 374).

However, the fact remains that economic sentiments of a distinctively 'liberal' flavour – opposed to mercantilist reasoning – did surface in the early years of the eighteenth century, for example, the explicit recognition of the essence of opportunity costs and its relevance to an understanding of the benefits of international trade in a competitive market context. Stemming from this acceptance of the principle of opportunity costs, joined with the equally relevant notion of division of labour (specialisation), there grew up a doctrine standing in uneasy rivalry with the balance-of-trade dogma – the doctrine referred to by Jacob Viner as the '18th-century rule'. The 'rule' stated that trade was beneficial to a country when it provided commodities 'which could not be produced at home at all or could be produced at home only at costs absolutely greater than those at which they could be produced abroad' (Viner [1937] 1955, pp. 439–40). It is, of course, a statement of the case for free trade based on *absolute advantages* in production and was in essence the argument put forward in the 1701 *Considerations upon the East-India Trade* in favour of the free importation of Indian calicoes. In effect, the 'rule' states that the opportunity cost of importing goods from abroad is the quantity of real resources devoted to the production of the required exports given in exchange. Whenever the resource cost of obtaining, say, commodity X (imports) in terms of commodity Y (exports) is lower when obtained through trade than when produced domestically, then trade is clearly beneficial. The advantage (or gains) from trading then exists in the amount of goods that can be produced with the resources saved. Even Adam Smith did not advance the argument beyond this point, for the 'eighteenth-century rule', while not inconsistent with the notion of *comparative* advantage is not identical with it. What remained to be further explained was how trade (in two goods, for example) could take place between two countries to the advantage of each when one country was absolutely more efficient in the production of *both* goods. In terms of the 'rule', that is, it has to be shown that it might still be profitable to import commodity X. However, what later generations of free-traders applauded was that, at any rate, the 'eighteenth-century rule' wrecked the notion that trade was a zero-sum game.

The next fatal blow to the preconceptions of mercantilism was delivered in 1752 by David Hume whose brilliant synthesis of the writings of John Locke, Jacob Vanderlint and Richard Cantillon on the monetary mechanism of international trade shattered the intellectual credibility of mercantilist doctrine (Hume [1752] 1955). Known to us as the price–specie flow mechanism (PSFM) the theory asserts that there is a natural distribution of specie (gold, international money) among countries according to their relative levels of real income or production. Thus any attempt by a country to garner more than its share of the world's stock of specie through balance of payments surpluses is self-defeating. Gold flows set in motion by such imbalances would produce equal and opposite money-supply and price-level changes in the two countries which would work to equalise prices and restore equilibrium in the balance of payments of each country. There is no doubt that Hume's analysis 'sounded the death-knell of mercantilism', as Mark Blaug puts it (Blaug 1968, p. 23). The mercantilists suffered a fatal blow since so many of their specific objectives or policy goals were premised on or relied upon a favourable balance of trade. Hume applied his sceptical and empiricist mind to the grosser contradictions of mercantilist dogma. Free international trade will not drain a country of its money. One-way gold losses are ruled out because of the specie-flow mechanism. Hence, it is futile to maintain trade controls designed to amass precious metals and to prevent their loss since 'it is impossible to heap up money, more than any fluid, beyond its proper level' (Hume [1752] 1955, p. 63). His immediate predecessors or contemporaries like Locke, Vanderlint and Gervaise were content to expound the novel monetary doctrine and make the occasional critical asides. Hume, however, pointedly and effectively deployed the quantity theory and the self-regulating mechanism in a deliberate attack on mercantilist prejudices. He was successful in this effort, inasmuch as through his friend Adam Smith it was his insights that were absorbed into the later dominant classical tradition of economic thought.

In France the most notable critics of mercantilist regulation in all its forms – guilds, state monopolies, restrictions on trade, special privileges – were the *Economistes*, better known as the Physiocrats. François Quesnay ('the guru of Versailles') was the intellectual leader of the school which included Pierre Paul Mercier de la Rivière, Pierre Samuel du Pont de Nemours and the brilliant but non-doctrinaire Anne Robert-Jacques Turgot, who served Louis XVI as comptroller-general. The Physiocrats were mainly, indeed exclusively, concerned with the problems of the French economy, the sources of its weaknesses and the conditions necessary for economic development and regeneration.

The Physiocrats traced the source of economic surplus – the *produit net* – to the agricultural sector. This net product was looked upon as the true source of real wealth, since all other incomes depended on it. It was their basic assumption that agriculture is the one and only source of productivity that separated them from the mercantilists. Trade and industry yield no disposable surplus over necessary cost; although necessary activities, they are 'sterile' in this sense. Whereas the mercantilists had located the economic surplus in the profits of foreign trade (measured by a favourable balance of trade) the Physiocrats found it in the net gain from domestic agricultural production. The means to prosperity lay not in exchange but in *production*. To the Physiocrats it was folly to indulge in an exchange of real goods for specie, as the mercantilist system dictated.

For all their fervent belief in *'laissez faire, laissez passer'* the Physiocrats (with the exception of Turgot) made no notable contributions to the development of international trade theory; but their arguments certainly challenged the assumptions on which the mercantilism of the *ancien régime* rested. Recently Turgot has been hailed as 'one of the leading theoretical economists of the eighteenth century . . . one of the major contributors to the rise of economic liberalism in Europe . . .' (Groenewegen 1983, pp. 590, 593). On international trade theory, he endorsed the 'eighteenth-century rule' in connection with the case he made for opposing protection to the iron industry:

> To persist in opposing . . . the advantages of free trade from a narrow-minded political viewpoint which thinks it is possible to grow everything at home, would be to act just like the proprietors of Brie who thought themselves thrifty by drinking bad wine from their own vineyards, which really cost them more in the sacrifice of land suitable for good wheat than they would have paid for the best Burgundy, which they could have bought from the proceeds of their wheat. (Turgot, 'Letter on the Marque des fers', quoted in Groenewegen 1983, p. 591)

In the elaboration of his case for free trade he placed particular emphasis on the gains to the domestic consumer and the stimulus to competition provided by a regime of unrestricted trade. Thus 'the general freedom of buying and selling will assure the consumer of the best merchandise at the lowest price', and there is 'no means of stipulating any trade or industry than that of giving it the greatest freedom' (Groenewegen 1983, p. 591). Turgot further argues that protection involves a welfare loss to the community, since it raises the cost structure of industry in general and so reduces demand, output and employment. This is the likely result, since protection once granted to certain favoured trades tends to be extended across the board to practically all trades. Because of the interdependence of production (that is, the input–output structure of industry) protectionism leads to an uneconomic cost structure not only in the sheltered industries, but also in the industries which use as inputs the outputs of protected industries or trades. Free trade is a spur to efficiency in other ways besides acting on costs – it also stimulates development of new products, the adoption of the latest techniques and the search for new, improved methods. Turgot's total commitment to free trade and its benefits puts him at variance with mainstream physiocratic thought. He did not view foreign trade as merely a 'necessary evil' and he, no doubt, did not go along with Adam Smith's exception of *laissez-faire* in the case of defence and shipping. He was also against the monopoly of colonial trade, including colonial preferences.

Despite Adam Smith's scathing denunciation of mercantilism and the subsequent negative stereotyping of that episode, he had no doubt in his own mind that governments during the age of mercantilism genuinely tried to enrich their subjects. They followed policies which were intended to increase national wealth. He was entirely in favour of this end; what he objected to were the *means*. Now, looking back from our own times to seventeenth- and eighteenth-century Europe with our experience of state trading, centrally-planned economies, import-substitution policies, exchange controls and such-like devices, we do not find it difficult to recognise mercantilism as an early manifestation of economic nationalism. But the politicians, merchants and publicists of the earlier age knew no other system of political economy. As far as they were concerned, economies had always been regulated. The greater involvement of merchants in economic activity and the desire of the new states to expand their wealth, population and territory called for new regulations or the adaptation of old ones to suit these needs. The doctrines they purveyed reflected ordinary, common-sense notions about the nature of wealth, how an economy should function and the proper role of the state.

We cannot just dismiss the mercantilists as a bunch of dyed-in-the-wool protectionists. On the contrary, they were full of praise of international trade and vigorously backed schemes to increase export volumes, albeit within a system of national priorities. They argued about these priorities, had their disagreements about how to deal with particular, pressing economic problems and, of course, were not immune to contradictions and confusion of reasoning. Nevertheless, they cannot be accused of anti-trade bias, but nor were they free trade liberals of the later classical sort. Although he drew attention to the analytical weaknesses of the earlier mercantilist writers, Joseph Schumpeter must have been sufficiently impressed by at least some of the later writers (for example, Henry Martyn and other Restoration liberals) when he suggested that there was no need for any spectacular break between mercantilists and classical liberals as far as economic analysis was concerned. But he stuck his neck out a bit when he continued by further surmising that if Smith and his followers had refined and developed the mercantilist hypotheses instead of throwing them away, 'a much truer and much richer theory of international economic relations could have been developed by 1848' (Schumpeter 1954, p. 376). This generalisation has not pleased some mainstream neoclassical economists, but surely Schumpeter's point is both reasonable and defensible, one that is fully endorsed by modern development economists. The mercantilist trade propositions are embedded in a total paradigm which includes a concern with international inequalities, national ambitions, growth and development. The trade theory which became associated with the classical economists – rightly or wrongly – abstracted from these real-world concerns, and this default impoverished the utility and relevance of classical theory. It triggered the repudiation of

classical trade theory by the national economists of the nineteenth century;
and that was what Schumpeter deplored. It need not have happened, since
some of the classical economists themselves were forced to recognise legitimate exceptions to the analytical core of their doctrine (that is, the free-
trade doctrine).

NOTES

1. See Paul A. Samuelson, 'Welfare Economics and International Trade', *American
   Economic Review*, 28 (June 1938), p. 261. Note also John Chipman's observation: 'The
   emergence of economic science in Great Britain in the seventeenth to nineteenth centuries was to some extent an offshoot of the development of the theory of adjustment of
   the balance of payments': J.S. Chipman, 'Balance of Payments Theory,' in J. Creedy and
   D.P. O'Brien (eds), *Economic Analysis in Historical Perspective* (London: Butterworths,
   1984), p. 186.
2. For more on mercantilist thought on foreign trade, including the historical background,
   European mercantilism and the decline of mercantilist trade doctrines, see Gomes
   (1987), chapters 1–3, pp. 3–125.
3. G. Schmoller, *The Mercantile System and its Historical Significance* (London:
   Macmillan, 1897), p. 50. This essay is a translation of Schmoller's introduction to his
   1884 work, *Studien über die wirtschaftliche Politik Friedrichs des Grossen.* Schmoller
   (professor at Berlin University) was critical of abstract economic theorising as practised
   by Menger and the Marginal Utility School and became associated with
   Kathedersozialismus (German academic socialism). Schmoller was an influential academic in Imperial Germany and was well acquainted with Bismarck and even more so
   with von Bülow.
4. W. Cunningham, *Growth of English Industry and Commerce*, 2nd ed. (London:
   Cambridge University Press 1892), vol. II, p. 16. Cunningham, a contemporary of
   Schmoller, was a nationalist sympathetic to state intervention. According to him, writers
   on economics before Adam Smith focused on the power of the state: 'Economic history
   must trace out the conscious efforts . . . to develop the resources and expand the commerce of the realm.' Ibid., 5th ed. (Cambridge, 1922), vol. I, pp. 21–2.
5. Richard Jones, 'Primitive Political Economy of England' (1847), reprinted in W.
   Whewell (ed.), *Literary Remains* (London: John Murray, 1859), pp. 291–335.
6. Keynes was not a reactionary mercantilist, neither was he a protectionist. His position
   on tariffs was pragmatic: they were 'second-best' measures appropriate when international monetary and other arrangements fail to provide a satisfactory framework for
   domestic full-employment policies.
7. K. Marx, *Theories of Surplus Value* (Moscow: Progress Publishers, 1975), vol. 1, p. 174.
8. For a good analytical discussion of the controversy, see Marian Bowley, 'Some
   Seventeenth Century Contributions to the Theory of Value', *Economica*, 30 (May 1963),
   pp. 122–39. See also B.E. Supple, *Commercial Crisis and Change in England, 1600–1642*
   (Cambridge University Press, 1959), chapter 9, pp. 197–221, and J.D. Gould, 'The Trade
   Crisis of the Early 1620s and English Economic Thought', *Journal of Economic History*,
   15 (1955), pp. 121–33. A useful supplement to Viner on the development of the balance of
   trade doctrine is Bruno Suviranta, *The Theory of the Balance of Trade in England. A Study
   jn Mercantilism* (Helsingfors, 1923), reprinted and published by A.M. Kelley (N.Y. 1967).
9. Quoted in E.A.J. Johnson, *Predecessors of Adam Smith* (Englewood Cliffs NJ: Prentice-
   Hall, 1937), p. 308.
10. Quoted in Viner ([1937] 1955), p. 54n.
11. F.V. de Forbonnais, *Eléments du Commerce*, vol. 1, Amsterdam: F. Changuion, 1755, p.
    78.

12. Although the 'infant industry' case for protection was known to mercantilists, they rarely invoked the argument. The argument, of course, is premised on production for the domestic market until the industry achieves such economies of scale and other 'learning effects' that it is able to withstand foreign competition in the open market without tariff support. Mercantilist writers rarely considered the potential of the home market, and perhaps this is why the argument was so little employed. Forbonnais was one writer who discussed it in the above sense, see Forbonnais, op. cit., p. 251.

13. The French ambassador in Madrid, the Duc de Duras, reported in 1756 that the English 'have attracted the whole trade of Brazil and India; they have destroyed the manufactures . . . of Portugal and have bought all its produce in order to introduce their own goods.' France: *Archives Nationales,* Archives de la Marine, B7, 400, 'Mémoire sur le Portugal' (1756).

14. Quoted in Violet Barbour, 'Anglo-Dutch Shipping', *Economic History Review* (1929), p. 290. Also quoted in Simon Schama, *The Embarrassment of Riches* (London: Fontana Press, 1991), p. 256.

15. Leo Amery, the British Conservative politician, in a polemical tract published in 1908 questioned the historical basis of Adam Smith's opinion of the Navigation Acts: 'Adam Smith attempts to justify the Navigation Acts on the ground that defence is better than opulence, forgetting that we had soundly drubbed both Spaniards and Dutch at sea before the Acts were passed, and were supreme in naval fighting power long before the Acts finally took effect in placing us at the head of the commercial shipping of the world. Undoubtedly, like every other sound economic measure, the Navigation Acts contributed to national defence, and, perhaps, in an exceptional degree; but their primary justification was economic and not military.' See Leopold S. Amery, *The Fundamental Fallacies of Free Trade* (London: Love and Malcomson, Ltd.) p. 123.

16. *The History of the Reign of King Henry the Seventh,* quoted in Heckscher (1955), vol. II, p. 16.

17. J. Viner, 'Power versus Plenty as Objectives of Foreign Policy in the Seventeenth and Eighteenth Centuries', first published in *World Politics,* vol. 1 (1948), reprinted in D.C. Coleman (ed.), *Revisions in Mercantilism* (London: Methuen, 1969), p. 78.

18. Viner, ibid., p. 76.

19. R. Waddington, *La Guerre de Sept Ans* (Paris, 1899), vol. III, p. 445.

20. See Eugene Daire (ed.), *Economistes-Financiers du XVIIIᵉ Siècle* (Paris: Guillaumin Libraire, 1843), p. 409.

21. Quoted in C.B.A. Behrens, *The Ancien Régime* (London: Thames & Hudson, 1967), p. 123.

22. Quoted in John Marks, *Science and the Modern World* (London: Heinemann, 1983), p. 106.

23. Mandeville, meanwhile, still urged the authorities 'above all . . . keep a watchful eye over the Balance of Trade in general and never suffer that the Foreign Commodities together, that are imported in one year, shall exceed in value what of their own growth or manufacture is in the same year exported to others.' He also repeated the popular mercantilist slogan: 'Trade is the Principal . . . Requisite to aggrandize a Nation.' See Bernard de Mandeville, *The Fable of the Bees,* ed. F.B. Kaye (London, [1714] 1924), vol. 1, p. 116.

24. See C. Davenant, *Political and Commercial Works,* ed. C. Whitworth (London, 1771), vol. v, p. 378.

25. Earlier (1897) Sir William Ashley drew attention to the Tory affiliations of North, Child, Davenant and Barbon and suggested that their politics explained their free trade opinions: 'Tory writers on trade, however sensible we may suppose them, could hardly fail to have a partisan bias in favour of liberty of commerce . . . they were likely to have their insight sharpened by party prejudice.' W.J. Ashley, 'The Tory Origins of Free Trade Policy', *Quarterly Journal of Economics,* 2 (1897), p. 338.

26. Leslie Stephen, *English Thought in the Eighteenth Century,* vol. II, 1902 edition, London: Macmillan, p. 297.

2. Classical trade theory

2.1 SMITH ON FOREIGN TRADE

The *Wealth of Nations* (1776) launched the new science of political economy. Its foundation was the maximising behaviour of individuals in free and competitive markets. Its objective was twofold: (i) to explain and interpret the workings of developing capitalism; and (ii) to advise, guide and direct policy according to the sound principles of political economy. Central to its concerns was an interest in economic growth, a topic Adam Smith placed prominently on the agenda of intellectual and political debate right from the start. Another was the role of international trade in the process of economic development. These were, of course, the very concerns of mercantilism; but the approach and perspective of the classical economists were radically different. Like Smith, they rejected blundering mercantilist (or government) regulation and placed their bets on the competitive market as the best mechanism for promoting growth. Foreign trade – which connects the national market with the wider world market – had an important role to play in this process. To be sure, these economists did not all speak with the same voice, but, in general, they had optimistic visions of prosperity and progress based on the potential of developing capitalism. Classical political economy is associated in the popular mind with domestic *laissez-faire* and international free trade. At least in respect of foreign trade this portrayal of classical orthodoxy is substantially correct. This policy preference was derived from hypotheses purporting to reveal the true nature and benefit of trade for all countries.

To trace this development of the analysis of the causes and consequences of foreign trade we start with the views of the founding father, Adam Smith. We have already referred to his famous polemic against the mercantilist system and now turn to his theory of international trade.

Economists generally do not rate Smith's contribution to international trade theory very highly. Compared with Ricardo's work his theoretical writings on foreign trade are regarded as being neither original nor brilliant. His work as a theorist (not only in matters of trade) is often said to suffer from a fuzziness and eclecticism which obscures the clarity and sharpness of his reasoning.[1] At the same time, as a policy analyst he is frequently praised for his devastating attack on mercantilist regulation. Thus modern textbooks on international economics only mention Smith's theory as an example of the meaning of *absolute* advantage and then hurry on to the more interesting case of comparative advantage associated with his successor David Ricardo.

Recently, however, as part of the resurgence of interest in Smith's economics his theorising on foreign trade has come in for closer scrutiny. The result has been a greater appreciation of the value of his work in this area which vindicates it against long-standing criticism. Typical of this rehabilitation is Professor Bloomfield's assessment: 'Smith showed profound insights as to the underlying basis and gains of trade. He analysed in greater detail than any of his predecessors the nature and benefits of international specialisation and the factors affecting them.'[2] As one who repudiated mercantilist fallacies and shifted the focus of economic discourse from exchange to production (like the Physiocrats before him) Smith saw no peculiar virtue in foreign-trade activities. Indeed, viewed from the perspective of the social returns on investment, foreign trade ranks pretty low. In terms of employment-generating effects a given amount of capital has the highest productivity when used in agriculture, followed by home trade and the lowest in foreign trade. That is, Smith believes that capital invested in either agriculture or domestic manufacturing supports a larger quantity of productive labour and raises national income more than an equal investment in foreign trade. Smith thus reverses the order of investment priorities that prevailed in mercantilist thought.

For him, foreign trade is not essentially different from domestic trade. Although greater distances are normally involved in international trade and hence higher transport costs are incurred which tend to reduce what he calls 'the frequency of returns' (stock turnover), this is not always the case. The English Channel is no great distance, hence the frequency of returns is higher in trade between the southern counties of England and France than it is in domestic trade involving the Home Counties and distant parts of Great Britain. Smith did not differentiate (as did his followers in the classical school) domestic from foreign trade in terms of differing assumptions about the mobility of productive factors – Ricardo assumed labour does not move between countries. This being the case, Smith finds the basis of international trade in the fact that both foreign and domestic industry have branches where each is more efficient; that is to say, countries have absolute advantages in the production of the goods they export. In each country imports consist of goods made more efficiently abroad (at lower real costs) and exports consist of goods made more efficiently at home (also at lower real costs). We have here an application of the concept of opportunity costs, since it is clear that a country benefits from trade because the exports required to pay for the imports cost less to produce in real terms than what

it would cost to produce the imports at home. There are thus mutual gains
(in production and consumption) from free exchange through trade – a
greater abundance and variety of goods. These gains arise from a more
efficient allocation of resources in each country (that is, international specialisation) based on inter-country differences in absolute costs. Smith puts
the principle thus:

> It is the maxim of every prudent master of a family, never to attempt to make at
> home what it will cost him more to make than to buy . . . What is prudence in
> the conduct of every private family, can scarce be folly in that of a great
> kingdom. If a foreign country can supply us with a commodity cheaper than we
> ourselves can make it, better buy it of them with some part of the produce of
> our own industry, employed in a way in which we have some advantage. (Smith
> [1776] 1976, vol. 1, pp. 456–7)

This is, of course, the 'eighteenth-century rule' (previously mentioned) for
free trade based on static allocative efficiency grounds. But Smith does not
stop here; he quickly moves on to a dynamic model and the consideration
of benefits provided by trade through the widening of markets and a more
intensive division of labour. Applying his dictum 'Division of labour is
limited by the extent of the market' to trade, he shows how it helps to overcome the narrowness of the domestic market.[3] This widening of markets
raises the level of productivity of all resources and sets in motion other
growth-inducing effects, namely: (1) economies of scale, (2) activation of
idle resources, (3) improvement of workers' skill and dexterity through
further divisions of labour, and (4) the adoption of specialised capital
equipment, and so on.

These are the dynamic benefits of trade which Smith reckons to be of a
high order. He also makes reference in several places, in connection with
the market-widening effect, to the fact that trade opens up a market for
goods produced in excess of domestic requirements (consumption or
demand). Are two themes then implied in Smith's account of the dynamic
benefits? H. Myint has for a long time maintained that this is in fact the case
and is in keeping with the general developmental orientation of Smith's
work. He detects two distinct theories implicit in the foregoing ideas: (1) a
'productivity' theory, and (2) a 'vent-for-surplus' theory.[4] Smith's own classical followers, John Stuart Mill and David Ricardo, regarded the 'vent-for-
surplus' idea as a weakness in Smith's trade theory. Mill rejected it as a
'surviving relic of the Mercantile Theory' and Ricardo more moderately
observed that it was 'at variance with all [Smith's] general doctrines on this
subject'.[5] In our own times, trade literature specialists like Haberler,
Bloomfield and Hollander find no real distinction between the two ideas
which they take to be merely two aspects of the same theory.[6]

The trouble with the vent-for-surplus idea is that while it has some relevance for Third World countries (or developed countries in the past) it obviously conflicts with much of what Smith has to say about the workings of the competitive-market mechanism in Book I of the *Wealth of Nations*. There the whole emphasis is on the clearing of markets, allocative efficiency and the way a fully employed economy adjusts to disequilibrium. How does he square these general market characteristics with the existence of a surplus which can be disposed of through foreign trade? Smith cannot obviously do this, except by making special assumptions relating to demand inelasticity and internal factor immobility. Since there is no unequivocal textual evidence for these special assumptions, Hollander and Bloomfield prefer to see the vent-for-surplus idea as being related to the widening of the market or 'productivity' theory rather than a separate theory in its own right. Hollander's conclusion is that 'in a sense, mere lip-service was paid by Smith to the vent-for-surplus doctrine' (Hollander 1973, p. 276).

Smith's analysis of foreign trade is a synthesis and integration of the better type of theorising on the subject current during his time. However, by virtue of his more systematic approach his treatment is richer and more insightful than that of his predecessors (and to some extent even of his successors). Some of the variables he considered crucial for an understanding of the basis and commodity composition of trade, such as differential factor endowments and transport costs, were neglected by several succeeding generations of economists, and the trade and growth nexus emphasised by him, though never absent, was not prominent in later classical thought. Like Hume, he did not overlook the indirect benefits of trade. Demonstration effects (changes in taste patterns induced by consumption of foreign goods), the impact of these on incentives and the transmission of technology through trade were all recognised by Smith.

On trade policy Smith is a pragmatic free-trader. The question he asks about all institutional barriers to trade is: Do they increase or diminish the benefits derived from foreign trade? Generally, he finds, they tend to diminish the benefits as compared to a regime of unrestricted trade. Trade regulations often stand in the way of self-interest based on the profit motive. Moreover, they are often unnecessary, even when they are designed to stimulate exports. Trade would take place anyway, since there is a natural 'propensity to truck, barter and exchange goods'. And Smith asserts:

> No regulation of commerce can increase the quantity of industry in any society beyond what its capital can maintain. It can only divert a part of it into a direction into which it might not otherwise have gone; and . . . the immediate effect of every such regulation is to diminish [the country's] revenue. (Smith [1776] 1976, vol. 1, pp. 453, 458)

Since free-market processes always ensure that a country's entire capital must find a profitable use, the protection of relatively inefficient industries cannot raise aggregate output. Indeed, it does the opposite; for while the output of the protected industries will be stimulated, the capital that went into such industries would have yielded more if its allocation had not been distorted by trade regulation. But, of course, the argument holds only on the assumption of full employment, at least of capital. Smith did, in fact, make this assumption, as the passage indicates. He warned against the distortions that might arise from the 'clamorous importunity of vested interests' and asserted that:

> every system which endeavours, either, by extraordinary encouragements, to draw towards a particular species of industry a greater share of the capital of the society than what would naturally go to it; or, by extraordinary restraints, to force from a particular species of industry some share of the capital which would otherwise be employed in it; is in reality subversive of the great purpose which it means to promote . . . and diminishes, instead of increasing, the real value of the annual produce of its land and labour. (Smith [1776] 1976, vol. 1, p. 687)

Departures from the free-market outcome need to be examined and justified on grounds of overriding national interest. Thus, he rejects the 'infant industry argument' for protection, but upholds the defence (national security) argument. He allows the continuation of the Navigation Acts and subsidies to defence-related industries (for example, sailcloth and gunpowder). He advocated free trade in its unilateral form (apart from the special treatment of defence), but makes reservations for the use of retaliatory tariffs as a bargaining counter in trade negotiations. He grants that moderate duties may have to be retained for revenue purposes; on this score the export duty on British wool is justified, even though it has the effect of giving a competitive edge to the domestic textile industry. He recognises, in the case of a domestic industry subject to particularly heavy excise taxation on its product, that it would be fair to levy a 'compensating duty' on competing imports so as to equalise the conditions of competition;[7] but the 'countervaling' duty should not be so high as to confer protection on competing home protection, neither should this special treatment be extended to other cases of alleged unfair treatment *vis-à-vis* foreign competitors. In other words, Smith wanted to warn against the use of this argument as a facile justification for tariffs to offset the general disabilities from which a country's industry might be said to suffer. Apart from these legitimate exceptions, all protective devices served only to promote the interests of a selfish minority at the expense of the whole community; this included the system of corn duties and bounties known as the Corn Laws.

He was too much of a practical man to be rushed into a precipitous removal of import duties which he knew would spell ruin for many merchants and manufacturers who had invested skills and capital in formerly prosperous trades. Tariffs must be reduced gradually, he cautioned, so as to give time for domestic traders to make the necessary adjustments. He urged caution in the withdrawal of protection, especially in the case of trades employing 'a great multitude of hands', but was optimistic about the prospects for the reallocation of resources resulting from tariff reform. He pointed to the relative ease with which large numbers of disbanded soldiers (100 000 of them) were redeployed after the Seven Years War and expressed the belief that it was certainly easier 'to change the direction of industry from one sort of labour to another, than to turn idleness and dissipation to any' (Smith [1776] 1976, vol. 1, p. 470). Full employment of labour could be maintained after protection was removed if the institutional barriers to free mobility were removed (namely the privileges of the great chartered companies and the statute of apprentices).

Like many thinkers of the Enlightenment, Smith believed that commercial rivalry (fostered by the false maxims of mercantilism) was at the root of the wars between England and France during the eighteenth century. He repudiated the 'malignant jealousy and envy' between nations as a foundation of international economic relations.

> France and England may each of them have some reason to dread the increase of the naval and military power of the other; but for either of them to envy the internal happiness and prosperity of the other, the cultivation of its lands, the advancement of its manufactures, the increase of its commerce, the security and number of its ports and harbours, its proficiency in all the liberal arts and sciences, is surely beneath the dignity of two such great nations. These are the real improvements of the world we live in. Mankind are benefited, human nature is ennobled by them.[8]

A reform of foreign economic policy along free-trade lines would be a step in the right direction towards a more harmonious and peaceful world. At the same time, he was not a blinkered idealist on the prospects for free trade, even in his own country. Thus he wrote: 'To expect, indeed, that the freedom of trade should ever be entirely restored in Great Britain is as absurd as to expect that an Oceana or Utopia should ever be established in it' (Smith [1776] 1976, vol. 1, p. 471).

2.2 RICARDO AND THE DEVELOPMENT OF COMPARATIVE ADVANTAGE

Smith's case for free trade was merely an application of the principle of specialization and division of labour on a global scale. It was firmly grounded on the 'eighteenth-century rule' concerning the mutual beneficiality of international exchange when each country has an absolute advantage in the production of one or more commodities. Each country gains by specialising in commodities where (with the same quantity of productive resources) a larger output than any rival can be produced.

This was a sound common-sense argument for the free movement of goods across international frontiers, but it offered no guidance for the extreme, though no less interesting and realistic case of a relatively 'backward' country having no lines of production where it is manifestly efficient relative to the rest of the world. What happens when one country is more efficient in the production of *all* commodities, that is, it can produce all goods in greater amounts with the same resources as compared with its trading partner? Is there any basis for mutually beneficial trade here? Would not trade cease under these circumstances since the backward country would take steps to insulate itself against ruinous competition from its more efficient neighbour?

Smith's analysis was incapable of dealing with the kind of situation indicated by this question. The answer was provided by his early successors in the British classical school in terms of the principle of comparative advantage. David Ricardo, James Mill and Robert Torrens extended Smith's theorising and produced a more general and precise formulation of profitable international trade by showing that a country can gain from trade even if it has no absolute real-cost advantage in the production of any commodity. The demonstration runs in terms of a world of two countries, each being capable of producing two commodities using only one factor of production, labour, which is assumed to be completely immobile between the two countries but completely mobile within each country. Thus in each country the costs (and prices or exchange ratios) of both commodities are determined by their relative labour content. The law of comparative costs can be illustrated by adopting Ricardo's example, as in Table 2.1.[9]

Table 2.1   Labour requirements per unit of output

	Cloth	Wine
England	100	120
Portugal	90	80

According to the data in Table 2.1 Portugal enjoys an absolute advantage in the production of both goods, since it can produce cloth and wine with less labour than England. Although Portugal is more efficient than England in the production of both goods the extent of Portugal's superiority is greater in wine production since 90/100>80/120. That is, the cost ratio for cloth is greater than the cost ratio for wine in Portugal compared with England. Thus the cost of producing cloth in Portugal is 90 per cent of the cost in England; but for wine production, Portugal's costs are only 67 per cent of England's. Portugal thus has a comparative advantage in producing wine and a comparative cost *disadvantage* in the production of both cloth and wine because 100>90 and 120>80. However, England's disadvantage is *smaller* in the production of cloth than in the production of wine, since 100/90<120/80. It costs England approximately 1.1 times as much to make cloth but 1.5 times as much to make wine as Portugal. Thus, it can be said, England has a *comparative advantage* in the production of cloth and a *comparative disadvantage* in the production of wine. Comparative advantage, as opposed to absolute advantage, is a *relative* term. Once one country's comparative advantage is identified, the other country's comparative advantage is logically determined. Thus the inequality used to determine England's comparative advantage, 120/80>100/90 is mathematically equivalent to the inequality 90/100>80/120, which is used to determine Portugal's comparative advantage, since England's cost ratios are simply the inverse of Portugal's cost ratios. Notice also that the inequality expressing Portugal's comparative advantage in wine can be stated either as 90/100>80/120 or equivalently 90/80>100/120, that is, it does not matter whether we compare the cost ratios of the different commodities within the same countries or the cost ratios of the same commodities in the different countries.

Such then is the basis of trade which, under these cost conditions, suggests the possibility of gains in efficiency from specialisation rather than national self-sufficiency. As long as the internal cost ratios differ between countries (that is, whenever the *relative* ability to produce goods differs between countries) specialisation by each country in the commodity in which it has a comparative advantage can increase aggregate world output from the same quantum of labour resources. Thus if England devotes her entire labour supply to the production of cloth and Portugal puts her labour wholly into wine production, the world output of cloth increases from 2 to 2.2 units and that of wine from 2 to 2.125. A real goods gain thus materialises from international division of labour which through international exchange can ultimately (or potentially) result in more consumption for both England and Portugal. The efficiency gain (that is, the higher productivity) in world production arising from specialisation and the re-arrangement of production under free trade creates the extra outputs to be shared out as consumption gains between the two countries. The extent of the increase in consumption each country obtains after trade depends on the terms of trade or international exchange ratio between the two goods. It is obvious that both countries benefit if each can trade at the pre-trade price ratio prevailing in the other country. Ignoring transport costs, the equilibrium terms of trade must lie somewhere between the two countries' comparative cost ratios, 90/80 and 100/120. Suppose, like Ricardo, an equilibrium terms of trade of 1:1. Given the opportunity to trade at this international price ratio, each country (using the same amount of labour) can increase its consumption of at least one commodity without decreasing its consumption of the other commodity through specialisation and exchange. Thus, if out of her specialised output of 2.125 units of wine Portugal should export 1.125 units to England in exchange for 1.125 units of cloth, the Portuguese would end up with the same amount of wine but a larger amount of cloth compared to the no-trade situation. England is equally better off from trade since upon specialisation trade with Portugal allows her to consume 1.075 units of cloth and 1.125 units of wine – in this case larger amounts of both commodities compared to autarky. The world consumption gains described above are summarised in Table 2.2 below.

Table 2.2   Per unit consumption gain from free trade

	in wine	in cloth
In Portugal	0	1.125
In England	1.125	1.075

This is a statement of the principle of comparative advantage – the core of the classical theory of international trade. It has a clear hortatory or persuasive message: free trade, like honesty, is the best policy. With international specialisation, free trade (a) allows each country to consume at least as much of each good as before specialisation or (b) minimises the real cost (in terms of labour time) of obtaining a given real income or quantum of consumption for the world as a whole; or what amounts to the same thing, maximises the aggregate level of real income (in terms of a given price ratio) obtainable from a given (full employment) utilisation of labour resources.

Ricardo believed in the general validity of the principle of comparative costs: the division of labour applies as much to individuals as to nations:

> Two men can both make shoes and hats, and one is superior to the other in both employments; but in making hats, he can only exceed his competitor by 1/5 (or 20%), and in making shoes he can excel him by 1/3 (or $33\frac{1}{3}$%). Will it not be for the interest of both that the superior man should employ himself exclusively in making shoes, and the inferior man in making hats? (Ricardo, *Works*, 1951, vol. 1, p. 136)

In both cases the results of specialisation and exchange are the same: a saving of labour to both parties. Thus Portugal might find it advantageous to exchange her wine for English cloth, although she may be able to produce those cloths cheaper herself. The principle, moreover, rationalises the mutual beneficiality of free international trade regardless of country sizes, degrees of affluence, absolute levels of economic efficiency or stages of economic development. The only thing that matters is a difference in the relative costs of production in the absence of trade. The hard-headed Ricardo was even moved to echo the sentiments of the eighteenth-century thinkers that were to be repeated later by Cobden and Bright when he declared that international economic relations based on the observance of the law of comparative costs

> binds together, by one common tie of interest and intercourse, the universal society of nations throughout the civilised world. It is this principle which determines that wine shall be made in France and Portugal, that corn shall be grown in America and Poland, and that hardware and other goods shall be manufactured in England. (Ricardo, *Works*, 1951, vol. 1, p. 145)

The welfare or 'normative' orientation of the early statement of the principle of comparative advantage is well-known – Viner emphasised this often enough. The principle was not meant to explain the forces determining the actual pattern of international specialisation, but rather to demonstrate how countries could gain from such specialisation and exchange. Implicit in the early accounts there were, of course, vague suggestions concerning the sources of comparative advantage: for example, in Ricardo it was 'climatic' differences and factors connected with location and 'other natural and artificial advantages'. But the arithmetical model which contained these hints was merely an ingenious vehicle for conveying the free trade policy recommendation. Indeed, the very implausibility of the particular example chosen to illustrate the principle – Portugal (*circa* 1817) portrayed as technologically more advanced and efficient than England – only served to highlight the economic logic of the argument. The idea of comparative cost was precisely to point out that even the least efficient, highest-cost country in the world could benefit from trade. That every country has, by definition, a comparative advantage is an important point in the argument.

The effect of this principle was to forestall protectionist arguments based on the fear that a more efficient trading rival would be in a position to undersell the producers of one's country in every line of production; or, conversely, from the standpoint of the producers and workers in the rich, advanced country, the fear that they would be unable to withstand competition from 'cheap foreign labour' without suffering business bankruptcies and a reduction of wage levels. Unlike some other classical propositions (for example, the wages fund doctrine) the law of comparative cost has stood the test of time remarkably well. It is, in fact, one of the few propositions in economics (perhaps the only one) that is both true and non-trivial – in the formal-logic sense. It has been hailed as one of the truly great discoveries of economic analysis – a triumph of economic logic perhaps even more significant than the famous law of diminishing returns. For whereas diminishing returns are a phenomenon observable in the physical world and intuitively fairly obvious, comparative cost is not. The latter requires not only reflection, but some economic sophistication as well.

Perhaps it is true today, as some experts ruefully complain, that it cannot be assumed that the principle is fully understood by businessmen or even, for that matter, by all those charged with the conduct of international trade negotiations. To most people, that is, 'industries that have a comparative advantage' usually signify 'industries whose cost compare favourably with the cost of imports', namely, industries that can produce goods that are cheaper than the equivalent imports. However, 'competitive advantage' is not the same thing as comparative advantage.

Before proceeding to an examination of the development of the classical trade model, it is of some interest to consider briefly the question of the origins of the law of comparative advantage. To whom do we owe the discovery of this principle? – David Ricardo, Robert Torrens or James Mill? It is less common now than it used to be to credit Ricardo with the first precise statement of the principle. From Jacob Viner's writings, students of international economics became aware of Torrens' contribution to trade theory generally and his anticipation of the law of comparative advantage in particular. Torrens' priority was, in fact, first acknowledged by Seligman in 1903 and ever since the matter has remained unsettled and disputed with writers finding grounds to press the claims to priority of one or the other classical names.

Torrens' claim to priority rests on his two publications *The Economists Refuted* (1808) and the first edition of *An Essay on the External Corn Trade* (1815). In the earlier work, however, Torrens merely enunciated the eighteenth-century rule on the gains from trade in terms of absolute advantage. So while Torrens succeeded in providing a perfectly satisfactory argument for the gains from trade, the argument was not based on comparative advantage since Torrens' example was a comparison of the domestic cost ratio (in one country) with the international price ratio. He did not compare the cost ratios between two countries. In *An Essay on the External Corn Trade* (1815) Torrens did succeed, after twice repeating the eighteenth-century rule, in expressing the essence of the law of comparative advantage in a passage which suggested that England would find it advantageous to specialise in and export manufactures in exchange for corn even though England might have an absolute advantage in agriculture.

> If England should have acquired such a degree of skill in manufactures, that, with any given portion of her capital, she could prepare a quantity of cloth, for which the Polish cultivator would give a greater quantity of corn, than she England could, with the same portion of capital, raise from her own soil, then, tracts of her territory, though they should be equal, nay, even though they should be superior, to the lands in Poland, will be neglected; and a part of her supply of corn will be imported from that country. (Torrens 1815, pp. 263–4)

'But', says Lord Robbins, 'as pure analysis it still lacks the final emphasis upon the comparison of ratios which is the ultimate essence of this principle' (Robbins 1958, pp. 22–3).

Ricardo's contribution appeared in 1817 when his *Principles* was published, but this was after Torrens had enunciated the 'essence' of the doctrine. Ricardo's first major work, *The Essay on Profits*, appeared coincidentally on the very day that Torrens' book came out – 24 February 1815.[10] Yet there was no hint of the new doctrine, even though his conclusion pointed to the advantage of free trade in corn. In point of time, therefore, Torrens was 'first in the field' (Robbins 1958, p. 23). But two years later Ricardo achieved what Samuelson called his 'greatest tour de force' with the famous three-paragraph demonstration of comparative advantage in chapter 7 of the *Principles*, complete with the 'four magic numbers that constitute the core of the doctrine'[11] namely, the cost ratios representing the amounts of labour required to produce the two commodities in each country.

The matter did not rest there. In 1976, William O. Thweatt in a fresh attempt to unravel the mystery of the origins of comparative advantage traced the doctrine to James Mill (Thweatt 1976, pp. 207–34). Mill's involvement with the concept began about the same time as that of Torrens. Both writers independently developed that idea as part of their general attack on a certain conception of Britain's economic destiny advocated by publicists like William Spence and William Cobbett. The physiocratic and underconsumptionist views represented by Spence and Cobbett – and to some extent Malthus – entertained visions of a self-sufficient, agrarian England. This provoked replies from Mill (*Commerce Defended*, 1808) and Torrens (*The Economists Refuted*). Both writers invoked the eighteenth-century rule regarding the gains from trade, but thereafter Mill's role was crucial for the development of the comparative cost doctrine. In Thweatt's view Mill took the lead; the others followed. Mill influenced Ricardo and was responsible for the insertion of the comparative-cost example in the latter's *Principles*. Shortly afterwards Mill published articles containing the comparison of cost ratios long before Torrens came out with his own, extended version of the doctrine in the fourth edition of his *Essay*. There is no doubt that Mill wanted to establish an economic orthodoxy based on what he considered 'sound principles' of political economy. He saw himself as its ideological guardian, and sought canonical status for the 'approved' doctrines of the new social science. In his role of 'taskmaster and press agent' for Ricardo he placed his full weight behind the Ricardian version of political economy. It is therefore understandable why Mill should have been eager to see incorporated in the book bearing the 'true message' (Ricardo's *Principles*) the important doctrine of comparative advantage which, for him, revealed a great truth. Peter Sai-wing Ho believes the reason why Ricardo's Portugal–England version has been given pride of place in the mainstream trade literature is 'probably because that model can be interpreted as a special case of the two-party exchange model, the latter of which is so fundamental to neoclassical economics' (Ho 1996, p. 2); and, by implication, an endorsement of the Millian version of classical economics.

In the opinion of the present author (metaphorically speaking) the three contestants in the race for the discovery of comparative advantage all breasted the tape at the same time. That is to say, what we have here is simply a case of multiple discovery, evidently fairly common in science. Like the other famous multiple discovery made about this time – diminishing returns – it emerged simultaneously in the minds of different thinkers under the pressure of relentless debate over urgent policy matters. Thus Mill, Torrens and Ricardo, in contact with each other, their minds exercised over the Corn Law issue and having before them the eighteenth-century rule, came up with essentially the same concept which they each articulated and deployed in their own fashion and for their own purposes (for example, polemical, ideological or theoretical).

2.3   THE LABOUR THEORY OF VALUE AND RICARDO'S TRADE MODEL

Whether at the instigation of James Mill or not, the insertion of the comparative advantage principle in Ricardo's chapter on foreign trade meant that it was through Ricardo and not Torrens that the principle came to be recognised as one of the sound and original doctrines of the early classical school. 'As so often happens in the history of thought', writes Samuelson, referring to the rival claims of Ricardo and Torrens, 'the greater name drives out the lesser one'.[12] Torrens' writings on economics never amounted to a systematic, consistent whole. Perhaps the reason why Torrens was neglected by the mainstream was that he sometimes reverted to absolute advantage examples in his discussions of trade policy which were often tinged with mercantilist notions and appeals to nationalism and imperial grandeur.

If James Mill had a hand in it, the choice of Ricardo as a vehicle for conveying the doctrine was therefore eminently well-judged. In another sense the choice was justified, for when later much of Ricardo's system was abandoned the comparative cost principle was retained. James Mill himself enhanced the orthodox status of the principle in his *Elements of Political Economy*, 'the first textbook in economics',[13] which contained 'a marvellously lucid and succinct early statement of the distinction between absolute and comparative advantage'.[14]

Yet it was from John Stuart Mill with his 'theory of international values' that later economists came to a full understanding and appreciation of the centrality of comparative cost in international trade theory. But because the younger Mill, out of 'filial respect' as Schumpeter (1954, p. 337, n.6) put it, played down his own achievement and praised Ricardo for his 'more accurate analysis of the nature of the advantage which nations derive from a mutual interchange of their productions' (Mill 1844, p. 1), Ricardo's name became closely associated with comparative costs. Today, beginning students in international economics come to an understanding of comparative advantage through Ricardo's example as we have just done and the first empirical test ever done on the pure theory of trade was explicitly designed to verify the Ricardian theory of the pattern of trade.

Returning now to the classical trade model, developments after Ricardo were mainly concerned with the elaboration and refinement of its logical structure. Gaps were filled in the original argument and the assumptions underlying the model were explicitly stated. Some of these assumptions were dropped and others generalised without substantially altering the logic or conclusions of the pioneers.

Let us briefly list Ricardo's assumptions:

1. Two commodities, two countries. Each commodity can be produced in both countries.
2. The labour theory of value applies.
3. Production takes place under constant cost conditions.
4. Transport costs are zero both internally and internationally.
5. Labour is perfectly mobile within each country and completely immobile internationally. Perfect competition prevails in all markets.
6. Multilateral convertibility prevails and a price–specie flow mechanism exists which ensures that the value of imports is equal to the value of exports for each country. Thus trade takes place effectively on a barter basis.

7.   Maximisation of aggregate world real income is the desired objective;
     national gains are determined by the terms of trade.

In his demonstration of the comparative-cost principle, an exercise which
is essentially one of comparative statics, Ricardo assumed, additionally, no
change in the distribution of incomes and no technical change and economic development in the two countries. But he relaxed these extra
assumptions when dealing with matters arising from trade and growth. In
fact, Ricardo used two trade models which he never managed to integrate:
the static comparative-cost theory and a dynamic long-run model. The
former model (which Ricardo only ever used once) was concerned with the
immediate static gains from a more efficient international allocation of
resources, while the latter was concerned with the more extensively discussed dynamic gains from trade and, in particular, was applied in the
analysis of the effects on the British economy of the repeal of the Corn
Laws. Ricardo's trade-growth model will be discussed later.
    The late Joan Robinson, a long-time critic of the neoclassical theory of
trade, observed two decades ago that 'the development of the theory [of
international trade], to this day, runs in the narrow channel that was appropriate to Ricardo's demonstration of the principle of comparative advantage' (Robinson 1979, p. 130) – something she deplored. What she was
referring to was the wide gap that existed between orthodox theory and
actual problems of the world economy which she traced to the restrictive
and often unrealistic assumptions inherited from the classical past. At the
time when the classical theory was formulated, however, it was a significant
breakthrough in the analysis of foreign trade simply because it was
grounded in a serviceable theory of value. From the classical and neoclassical perspective, the shortcomings of the mercantilist conception of
foreign trade stemmed from their (that is, the mercantilists') failure to artic-
ulate an adequate theory of value or of price. That is, the earliest economists had no clearly worked out idea of a price system's role in the
allocation of resources. And since trade theory is merely one aspect of
general allocation theory – the efficient deployment and use of resources on
a global scale that is, – this explains why the microeconomics of trade
proved elusive for the mercantilists. Thus Stigler, in his Nobel Lecture,
asserted: 'Without a theory of value the economist can have no theory of
international trade' (Stigler 1982, p. 534). W.R. Allen said exactly the same
thing: 'Without price theory, there can be no theory of international trade'
(Allen 1968, p. 75). But the contention still remains to be substantiated that
mercantilist thought was devoid of valid insights into allocative mechanisms – witness the writings of Petty, Cantillon and before them the
Salamanca jurists. Their value theory was rudimentary (often 'macro' in

nature), but they certainly had one which they applied to problem areas that concerned them – foreign exchange, money and interest. Few of the seventeenth-century writers 'after all, were directly concerned to formulate a *theory* of economic activity' (Meek 1965, p. 21).

A regulated foreign trade marked by the absence of competition between foreign and domestic sources of supply was a facet of economic activity that did not encourage speculation about the role of allocative mechanisms. Only later, when free trade became an issue – when economic reality was transformed by dramatic technological and social changes – did the question of how resources should be allocated and valued at the international level (that is, what should be produced and in what quantities) present itself as one requiring economic analysis for an answer.

Adam Smith had a common-sense theory of the role of the relative prices of commodities – the cost of production or 'adding-up' theory. He also understood the workings of the price mechanism and its role in the allocation of resource – insights which led him to provide an answer to the above question and the advocacy of free trade. Yet he failed to advance trade theory beyond the concept of absolute advantage. Ricardo developed his own version of the labour theory of value in connection with the Corn Law controversy and more precisely in response to what he regarded as the unsatisfactory (mistaken) views of Adam Smith on that subject; Ricardo also grounded his trade model in his labour theory of value. It is interesting to note that 'the only place where Ricardo addressed himself specifically to the allocation problem was in the chapter on foreign trade' and that 'here . . . he saw further and deeper than Adam Smith' (Blaug 1968, p. 140). Is this, then, confirmation of the assertion: no price theory, no trade theory? If so, was it further the case that both price theory and trade theory originated in and were motivated by the same cluster of circumstances, intellectual challenges and ideological preconceptions that mark the evolution of social thought? It is as easy to share Mark Blaug's doubt 'whether Ricardo would have developed his theory of international trade without a strong animus against the landed classes' as it is to agree with the sequel to the sentence 'but this theory survives the removal of his prejudices' (Blaug 1968, p. 6).

The role of the ideological element cannot be denied; and if we are convinced of the Millian influence upon Ricardo then the critic who declares that 'the international division of labour associated with the law of comparative advantage has never been "natural" but was manufactured by the very British industrial interests and their overseas allies who then enshrined this division as a supposed natural law' (Frank 1979, pp. 94–5) cannot be lightly dismissed as a prejudiced rhetorician. The attitude to foreign trade encapsulated in the principle of comparative costs sprang not only from developments in economic theory but reflected a 'shared vision' among political economists of Britain's economic future. It so happened that this coincided with the interests of the new and rising industrial bourgeoisie. As one writer puts it: 'Ricardo's economics were affected by and eminently suited to an analysis of the issues and problems of the early nineteenth-century British economy', and Ricardo's advocacy of a free-trade policy 'clearly represents a fusion of the interests of the commercial and industrial bourgeoisie' (Ballance, Ansari and Singer 1982, pp. 14, 15).

Joan Robinson puts it bluntly: 'When Ricardo set out the case against protection, he was supporting British economic interests'.[15] Fernand Braudel (1984) the eminent French historian, confesses that simple-minded tautologies such as 'growth breeds more growth' or 'a poor country is poor because it is poor' make more sense to him than 'the so-called "irrefutable" pseudo-theorem of David Ricardo'. He finds the picture too reassuring, since 'there is an unasked question here: when did the division of tasks (which Ricardo assumed in 1817 to be part of the natural order) begin and why?' (Braudel 1984, p. 48). Braudel goes on to argue, drawing on historical examples, that the nineteenth-century distribution of tasks among nations was not the result of natural and spontaneous tendencies or the operation of a set of supra-historical laws, but was the outcome of mercantilist and colonial policies based on the unequal distribution of power among nations. The world division of labour was not arrived at through agreement among equal partners and subject to review, but rather was determined by power politics and other long-standing realities which developed in an irreversible direction. Some countries ended up as primary producers, others continued and advanced further in secondary and tertiary sectors.

According to Ricardo, the ratio in which commodities are exchanged for each other depends on the relative amounts of labour they embody, that is, prices of goods are determined by their labour content. Actually, Ricardo conceived of production as taking place with inputs of capital and labour combined in fixed proportions, the units of which are qualitatively homogeneous. Changes in either the profit rate or wage rate can cause changes in relative prices which diverge over time from the corresponding changes in ratios of embodied labour. Ricardo believed, however, that the magnitude of these divergences was small; and, because of this, Ricardo has been credited with belief in a '93 per cent labour theory of value' (Stigler 1958, pp. 357–67).[16] There are, of course, well-known difficulties with the labour theory as a theory of relative prices. Taken together, the assumptions under which the theory is valid amount to a radical oversimplification of reality. Thus labour is not the only factor of production; neither is it homogeneous. In addition there are problems with the time phasing of production and questions about durability and turnover of capital as well as rates of return. For instance, with a positive rate of interest, the average cost of a commodity (and hence its price) would be influenced not merely by the amount of labour involved, but also by the length of time involved in its production. The theory can survive these complications only if, among other things, it can be further assumed (a) that the proportions in which labour is combined with other factors is the same in all industries, or what Marx referred to as 'equal organic composition of capital', and (b) fixed capital is of equal durability in all lines of production and production processes are such that all commodities require the same time to be brought to market.

Ricardo was fully aware of these complications, and clearly recognised the assumptions under which the theory was valid. For Ricardo the labour theory was primarily an explanation of *changes* in relative prices over time and the consequences of these for the distribution of income. This led him into the search for an 'invariable measure of value' (absolute value). For want of a better alternative, he settled on embodied labour and concluded (as we have already indicated) that changes in long-run exchange values corresponded closely with changes in the labour content of commodities.

At any rate, with fixed labour requirements per unit of output, production takes place at constant costs – in modern parlance, the production-possibility curve between two commodities is a downward-sloping straight line indicating a constant rate of transformation. Given the fixed co-efficients of production, relative prices are technologically determined by the invariant labour productivities. Under these conditions it follows that the supply curves for both commodities are horizontal at the given real-wage level; hence, demand has no role in the determination of relative prices in the closed economy.

This proportionality relationship between prices and labour values in each country ceases to hold once the economies are opened to trade. Ricardo writes: 'The same rule which regulates the relative value of commodities in one country does not regulate the relative value of the commodities exchanged between two or more countries' (Ricardo, *Works*, vol. 1, p. 128). Thus, while according to the law of value the labour of 100 Englishmen cannot be exchanged for the labour of 80 Englishmen, through international trade England would gladly give up the produce of the labour of 100 men for the produce of 80 foreign labourers (Ricardo, *Works*, 1951, vol. 1, p. 135). Some Marxian writers have seized on Ricardo's statement (that the labour-embodied value of 20 men is thereby transferred from England to Portugal) to underpin a theory of 'unequal exchange' in trade, that is, a pervasive tendency for labour-embodied value to be transferred from poor countries to high-wage, developed countries.

The need for a separate theory of international trade therefore arises because the theory of value appropriate to a closed economy is inadequate to explain values in international trade. This separate treatment of domestic and international trade did not cause Ricardo (as it did later economists) to question the general validity of the labour theory of value. He attributed the difference to the international immobility of capital and labour: 'The difference in this respect, between a single country and many, is easily accounted for, by considering the difficulty with which capital moves from one country to another, to seek a more profitable employment, and the activity with which it invariably passes from one province to another in the same country' (Ricardo, *Works*, 1951, vol. 1, pp. 135–6).[17] This assumption implied that the rate of profit, although uniform throughout a given country, could vary between countries. In addition, because of barriers to international migration, wage differentials caused by productivity differences could persist indefinitely. Even assuming uniform capital–labour ratios in each country, commodities would no longer exchange in proportion to relative labour inputs. The sharing of comparative advantages is thus, for Ricardo, a means of overcoming the segmentation of national markets caused by factor immobilities. Trade in commodities becomes a substitute for the international mobility of labour and capital. It increases 'the mass of commodities, and therefore the sum of enjoyment' in each of the trading countries (Ricardo, *Works*, 1951, vol. 1, p. 128).

In Ricardo's trade model international prices or the terms of trade are left largely unexplained. He admits that the general rule of cost-price based on the labour theory of value breaks down in the context of foreign trade. This led others to conclude that, however useful the labour theory of value might be as an explanation of domestic price ratios, it could not offer an explanation for international values. A 'subjective' theory of value was therefore necessary to determine relative prices between the two countries' embodied labour ratios. What is recognised here is that value in exchange in international trade is determined not only by production costs (whether limited to labour or not), but also by *demand*.

The labour theory of value focused attention on supply or the cost side of trade and neglected the role of demand. This did not matter in the analysis of domestic trade, for by the constant-cost and single-factor assumption, domestic prices are determined solely by supply. But if trade is to be generated and neither country is sufficiently 'small' to have its terms of trade determined by the cost ratio of the other, then conditions of demand have to be brought in to fix the ratio of international exchange. The fact is that (a) the actual pattern of specialisation and (b) the division of the gains from trade depend on the equilibrium terms of trade. For instance, the Ricardian model implies complete specialisation by each country in consequence of the assumption of constant-cost conditions. In this case the division of the benefit between them depends solely on the conditions of demand and relative prices are no longer governed by costs of production.

This point is illustrated in modern textbooks through the construction of a world production-possibilities frontier for the constant-costs case. See Figure 2.1.

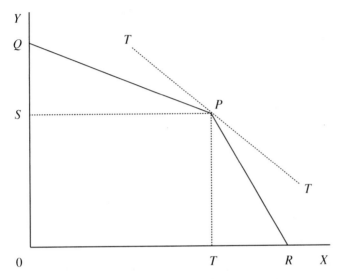

Figure 2.1   A world production-possibilities frontier

The production-possibilities frontiers of two countries, A and B, are joined together in one diagram. Except for the case of equal opportunity costs the world frontier so derived, *QPR*, is not a straight line but consists of two straight-line (linear) segments, kinked at a point, *P*. At this point, each country specialises completely in producing the commodity in which it has a comparative advantage and world production (that is total outputs of *X* and *Y*) is also indicated at this vertex point. But at this 'Ricardian point', *P*, the slope of the world production-possibilities frontier, shown by the dotted line *TPT* (the absolute value of which indicates the international price of *X* in terms of *Y* or the equilibrium terms of trade) is indeterminate. The slope at this point can range from the slope of the first country's production-possibility curve to that of the second country's production frontier as world prices vary parametrically, while remaining common to both countries. The pattern of world demand for the two commodities – usually represented by a world indifference curve (not shown in the above figure) – is then needed to determine the equilibrium terms of trade within the range spanned by the production-possibility curves (that is, cost ratios) of the two countries.

But what the theory demonstrates is that as long as the dotted line passing through the Ricardian point does not intersect curve QPR both countries gain from free trade. Conditions of world demand can be such that the terms of trade settle at the cost ratio of one of the countries. In such a case partial specialisation results, with that country producing both commodities and the other country completely specialised. Thus, in the Ricardian example, if England consumes more wine than Portugal can supply to the English market then world prices will have to reflect English costs so that some English wine production would also take place. Portugal then gains on the terms of trade in respect of all her imports. The pattern of specialisation and trade is reversed if Portugal becomes the country producing both commodities.

The Ricardian result is easily generalised for the case of many countries and two commodities, say X and Y. In this case, we have a 'chain of comparative advantage' determined by inter-country differences in labour-cost ratios (technological differences). The role of demand here is to break the chain and separate the X-exporters from the Y-exporters.

It is obvious, then, that both supply and demand differences contribute to the relationship between pre-trade commodity price ratios and the equilibrium terms of trade – hence to the pattern of trade. The recognition of the role of demand led to the first break with the labour theory of value. Although he was not the first to take demand conditions into account, John Stuart Mill provides an explicit demonstration of international equilibrium incorporating demand in his account of how 'the inclinations and circumstances of the consumers on both sides' would determine where between the two internal cost ratios the equilibrium terms of trade would lie (Mill [1848] 1920, p. 587). Mill's analysis was later developed and given geometric refinement in the offer curves of Edgeworth and Marshall. The development of marginal utility analysis in the 1870s made it an anachronism to work with two theories of value (one for internal and another for external trade) since, as Marshall observed, both blades of the scissors (costs or supply and demand) must cut to determine market-clearing prices whether in domestic or international trade.

Gottfried Haberler later went on to reinterpret the doctrine of comparative costs in opportunity-cost terms. The shift from a labour theory of value to an opportunity-cost theory provided a simpler and more general definition of comparative advantage – more general since it could (unlike the labour theory) handle cases of increasing costs and thereby explain the real-world phenomenon of partial specialisation. But some of the leading trade theorists in the classical tradition (for example, Taussig and Viner) were reluctant to abandon a 'real cost' approach to international trade related to, but not identical with the classical labour theory – an approach explored earlier by Bastable and Marshall. Viner strenuously defended the classical theory against the charge that it was somehow unsatisfactory because it was cast in terms of an outmoded theory of value. He claims that 'the association of the comparative-cost doctrine with the labour-cost theory of value is a historical accident'. And further, he observes, only Ricardo and James Mill among classical writers on comparative costs were exponents of the labour theory in its strict form (Viner [1937] 1955, p. 490).

Despite the shortcomings of the labour theory of value, it served the purpose of bringing out sharply the nature of the international division of labour and the gains from trade. Modern economists employ other definitions of costs to prove exactly what Ricardo did. In Haberler's view the sole purpose of the labour theory of value was to determine the pre-trade price ratios in the two countries. He too claims that Ricardian trade theory is not wedded to a labour theory. The restrictive assumptions of the latter could easily be dispensed with in favour of a more general theory of production 'without having to discard the results obtained from it: these will remain, just as a building remains after the scaffolding, having served its purpose, is removed' (Haberler 1936, p. 126).[18]

But this dismantling of the classical gantry of trade theory did not appeal to Viner, mainly on the ground that a real-cost approach was essential for making welfare comparisons. The merit of the classical approach resided in the fact that welfare conclusions followed *directly* from the analysis of price determination. In this approach imports and exports possess 'real value significance'; for Viner accepts, despite the difficulties involved, the proportionality relationship between real costs and money costs (or market prices). The classical theory then furnishes a simple welfare criterion according to which alternative trade policies (or the gains and losses from free trade) can be assessed. Specifically, it shows how under free trade conditions a given amount of real income (a given bundle of goods) can potentially be secured by a country at lower real costs.

The labour theory of value was, of course, of fundamental importance in the work of Karl Marx, and writers in the classical Marxian tradition, and the newer Sraffa or neo-Ricardian theorists continue to use the labour theory in one form or another in their analyses of international trade. Marx, unfortunately, never wrote his projected book on international trade; hence we have no definite statement of his trade theory. The latter has to be pieced together from various comments scattered in his published works. From what he wrote about international value or how the law of value operates in the world market, one gets the impression that his theoretical framework was not very different from the Ricardian theory as modified by Nassau Senior. He did not explicitly reject the concept of comparative advantage. Indeed, he pointed out that, in principle, specialisation according to comparative advantage could be advantageous for backward countries, since such countries 'thereby receive commodities cheaper than they could produce them'.[19] He nevertheless regarded advanced manufacturing countries as 'exploiters' in their trading relations with less-developed countries even when such trade allows both parties to gain. His contention was that poor countries (that is, countries with low average productivity) gave up more labour in exchange for less of the developed countries' labour – the terms of trade tended to move adversely against poor agricultural countries. Thus Marx wrote:

> Say, in his notes to Ricardo's book . . . makes only one correct remark about foreign trade. Profit can also be made by cheating, one person gaining what the other loses. Loss and gain within a single country cancel each other out. But not so with trade between different countries. And even according to Ricardo's theory, three days of labour of one country can be exchanged against one of another country . . . Here the law of value undergoes essential modification. The relationship between labour days of different countries may be similar to that existing between skilled, complex labour and unskilled, simple labour within a country. In this case, the richer country exploits the poorer one, even where the latter gains by the exchange, as John Stuart Mill explains in his *Some Unsettled Questions*.[20]

Marx postulated that whereas in the domestic market the law of value was based on 'socially necessary labour time' rules, in the international market this was not the case. The different quantities of commodities of the same kind, produced in different countries in the same working-time, have, therefore, unequal international values, which are expressed in different prices, that is, in sums of money varying according to international values.[21]

Marx explained this by the use of the concept of the 'average unit of universal labour' as a unit of measurement of a country's average productivity. The average 'intensity of labour' (that is, labour productivity) varies from country to country. With trade the value of labour is directly related to levels of productivity. But the value of labour (as expressed in monetary terms) in a developed country is higher than its value in a backward, poor country. Thus the transformation of international *values* into international *prices* implies the transfer of value (expended or embodied labour) from some countries to others. Ricardo would have agreed that inequalities in basic production conditions were the essence of foreign trade; for the source of the gains lay in the discrepancy between local and foreign prices which ultimately reflected international differences in relative labour productivity. But he could not have agreed that this was the source of asymmetric relationships.

In general terms, then, Marx's notion of international value based on some sort of average of national values is not incompatible with the Ricardian principle of comparative advantage. Indeed, the Marxian procedure of ranking countries according to the average productivity of labour in the production of different commodities implies the notion of comparative advantage differences. But the Marxian idea that some countries (underdeveloped countries characterised by low capital intensity and labour productivity) suffer permanent exploitation in their dealings with manufacturing capitalist countries does not correspond with Ricardian reasoning. The underdeveloped country – in fact, every country – gets the equivalent of the labour embodied in its exports, according to the Ricardian principle of comparative advantage. The total gains from trade need not be equally shared, but a net gain still remains for each country. The Marxian notion that a country can simultaneously gain and lose in trade, and also the assumption of exploitation whenever imports do not bring in the equivalent of exported labour certainly challenges the Ricardian hypothesis. Marx's sketchy and unsystematic treatment of foreign trade left scope for the development of widely differing approaches by his followers. One approach which describes exploitation derives from the analysis of capitalist accumulation on a global scale, and stresses the transfer of surplus value from the less-developed countries to the capitalist metropoles. Another approach, which makes use of classical Marxist schemas, further develops the idea of 'unequal exchange'. In the latter type of work exploitation results through a non-equalisation of wages across countries and unchanged patterns of specialised trade, even though profits are equalised internationally. But this is a twentieth-century development, and we must return to Ricardo.

2.4   THE GAINS FROM TRADE

Turning now to the results Ricardo derives from his static trade model, these are: (1) foreign trade increases 'the mass of commodities, and therefore the sum of enjoyments' (Ricardo, *Works*, 1951, vol. 1, p. 128), (2) the opening of trade or its extension does not increase the rate of profit except where the imported commodities enter the real wage. Foreign trade does not alter the 'value' of the national product.

The first proposition, as we have already indicated, is related to the sharing of comparative advantages and therefore has to do with the welfare consequences or gains from trade. What is involved here is the argument familiar from modern gains-from-trade analysis of the enlargement of consumption possibilities for the same input of labour. Through specialisation

and trade a country can consume beyond its production-possibility frontier. The real-income effect produced is the same as if there had been an
outward shift in the country's production frontier. Thus, by exploiting
gainful trade opportunities England can enjoy more wine with no less cloth
than before from its given level of employment. Here, the optimality of free
trade is assessed in terms of the maximisation of real income (a given
bundle of goods) – each good being weighted by the given world price ratio
– from a given input of labour. Equally, we can talk in terms of the minimisation of the real cost of obtaining a given amount of real income. The
two concepts of optimality are really equivalent ways of looking at the
same thing – at any rate, as long as we are concerned with marginal changes
in income or output levels.

There was a rather confusing debate between Ricardo and Malthus on
this matter. As we have seen, Ricardo adopted the increase-in-income
approach which suggests that the opportunity to trade at relative prices that
differ from those in isolation at home (autarky) must improve domestic real
incomes available for domestic consumption – the 'mass of commodities'
benefit.

In Malthus' view, the gain from trade consisted of 'the increased value
which results from exchanging what is valued less for what is valued more'
(Malthus 1820, pp. 460–1). Now, this a perfectly legitimate and satisfactory
statement of trade benefits, and one that is compatible with Ricardo's
approach. But in an attempt to rebut Ricardo's second proposition mentioned above – foreign trade does not increase domestic value – Malthus
misrepresented (or misunderstood) Ricardo's position. He attributed to
Ricardo a narrow version of the saving-in-cost approach: 'Mr Ricardo
always views foreign trade in the light of means of obtaining cheaper commodities' (Malthus 1820, p. 462).

Later, in *Notes on Malthus* Ricardo repeated his increase-in-income criterion: 'The advantage . . . to both places is not [that] they have an increase
of value, but with the same amount of value they are both able to consume
and enjoy an increased quantity of commodities.'[22] Malthus's reformulation of the Ricardian position as the alternative saving-in-cost method
posed the interesting question: in what sense are the two welfare criteria
equivalent? The issue was raised for the first time in the Ricardo–Malthus
debate and was only finally resolved with the invention of the techniques of
modern welfare analysis which added greater precision to the concept of
the gains from trade. Malthus objected to the saving-in-cost measure – the
reduced cost of obtaining imported goods through trade instead of by
domestic production – on the ground that this overestimated the gains from
trade, for example, when imported goods (a) could not be produced at
home (silk, cotton, indigo) or (b) could be produced only at extremely high

cost. In such cases the relevant goods would simply not be imported. More generally the gains from the opportunity to trade cannot be counted as being equivalent to the necessary expansion of labour input if the free trade bundle of goods is produced domestically.

Malthus' point is that the opening of trade would change relative prices. The country would have more of the imported goods but less of the native commodities. How, then, do we compare the increase with a decrease? Consumers may in fact prefer more of the potential export good if the free-trade equilibrium bundle was produced domestically by an increase in labour input. Since the closed-economy equilibrium combination of goods resulting from an expansion of labour input is preferable in terms of consumer welfare to that produced by free trade, the cost-saving approach would overstate the gains from trade. The correct procedure, therefore, to meet Malthus' criticism is to reckon the saving in cost in terms of the amount of labour needed to produce a closed-economy bundle that is equivalent to the free-trade combination in so far as consumer welfare is concerned.

Having done that there still remains the problem of how to decide whether a given bundle of goods is equivalent or superior to another bundle. A comparison of the quantity index numbers of the two situations will presumably help, as would the use of the modern technique of community indifference curves. But in a community not made up of identical individuals some people would be hurt (and others gain) by the opening up of trade. Again, modern welfare analysis suggests ways of dealing with this problem. The classical economists were aware of the welfare question – indeed, it was the paramount issue at stake during the Corn Laws debate. But in a strict sense, since labour is the only factor of production in the classical model trade cannot possibly hurt anyone; the gains from trade are certain to translate into increased real wages for workers in both countries. (In the later Heckscher–Ohlin multi-factor model things would be different.) Yet the constraints of the one-factor model did not blind the classicals to the reality of the income distribution struggle.

This brings us to Ricardo's distributional result. Ricardo writes:

> As the value of all foreign goods is measured by the quantity of the produce of our land and labour, which is given in exchange for them, we should have no greater value, if by the discovery of new markets, we obtained double the quantity of foreign goods in exchange for a given quantity of ours. (Ricardo, *Works*, 1951, vol. 1, p. 128)

And again: 'foreign trade, then . . . has no tendency to raise the profits of stock, unless the commodities imported be of that description on which the wages of labour are expended' (Ricardo, *Works*, 1951, vol. 1, pp. 132–3).

These propositions follow logically from Ricardo's theory of value and
his 'fundamental theorem', that is, the inverse profit–wage relationship. By
value, Ricardo meant the total input of labour in a country and his distributional theorem was that 'profits can be increased only by a fall in
wages'. Thus, through international trade, a country may get more use-
value but no more labour-value than another. And since the rate of profit
depends on the labour cost of producing the necessary real wage, trade
tends to raise the general rate of return only when imports consist of wage
goods (especially foodstuffs).

Ricardo thus challenges Smith's suggestion that the diversion of capital
from domestic industry consequent upon the opening up of profitable
trading opportunities tends to raise the general return on capital. The rate
of profit cannot rise, Ricardo holds, because what occurs is merely a change
in the composition of final consumer demand. Smith overlooked the shift
in demand to foreign goods which accompanies the deflection of capital
from the domestic market, says Ricardo. He argues that since demand for
domestic goods is now less, prices at home will not rise; hence higher profits
cannot be earned. 'I am of opinion', writes Ricardo, 'that the profits of the
favoured trade will speedily subside to the general level' (Ricardo, *Works*,
1951, p. 129). The implication here is that domestic prices will alter
sufficiently to restore equality of the marginal products of capital in all
trades and the reallocation of capital will go on until this is accomplished.
Ricardo also points out that an expanded money supply is a *sine qua non*
for any general price rise and profit-rate increase arising from any source,
including the discovery of new markets. It cannot be assumed that the necessary monetary means would automatically be forthcoming. Here, as elsewhere, Ricardo relied on what came to be known later as Say's Law in
opposition to Smith's 'competition of capitals' theory.

In an instructive commentary on the Smith–Ricardo differences on
foreign trade and the profit rate, E.G. West points out that Smith's anticipation of a rise in the profit rate was based on the presumption that capital
would be shifted to a controlled foreign trade where capital enjoyed monopoly profits. The reduction in the number of domestic traders would tend to
bring about a monopolistic market situation at home which raises the profit
rate through a squeeze on the real purchasing power of consumers.[23]

Ricardo considers next the effect on the savings ratio of cheaper
imported luxury goods (for example, wine, silks and velvet). The profit rate
will not be directly affected; but to the extent that the importation of such
goods increases the purchasing power of profit incomes, it raises the savings
capacity of the capitalists. The rate of profit on capital may then be altered
through the stimulus to capital accumulation provided by increased
savings. He likens the introduction of machines to extensions of foreign

trade in so far as the effects on the profit rate and capital accumulation are concerned. Mechanisation which reduces the value of wage-goods tends to raise the rate of profit, saving and the rate of capital accumulation. Similarly, the importation of wage-goods at prices lower than the internal prices has the same effect. On the other hand, the introduction of machines, which lowers the value of luxury goods and the importation of relatively cheap luxury goods, has no direct impact on the rate of profit; but it tends to increase saving and the rate of capital accumulation through enhancement of the purchasing power of capitalists (Ricardo, *Works*, 1951, vol. 1, pp. 1–20).[24]

Commenting on Ricardo's analysis of the benefit of trade in terms of his England–Portugal example, E.K. Hunt suspects that, despite his labour theory of value, Ricardo's conclusion that free trade would increase the 'sum of enjoyments' of each country implies some sort of utility theory of exchange value, that is, the theory which tends to equate price and utility; hence, the higher the price the greater the utility or satisfaction to the consumer (Hunt 1979, p. 107). Otherwise, Ricardo's conclusion would not follow from his premises. Samuel Hollander seems to lend support to this interpretation when he asserts that 'the "mutual determination" of exchange value by demand and cost considerations was a thoroughly central aspect of Ricardian doctrine' (Hollander 1982, p. 591, n. 7). Logically, then (consistent with utility reasoning), Ricardo had to assume that the import of the relatively more expensive commodity (wine) would increase the 'sum of enjoyments' – landlords and capitalists would prefer to spend their surplus on both cloth and wine. A labour-theory perspective would have suggested that the importation of wine be prohibited until every worker had adequate clothing (the domestically produced good) – workers would prefer to have more clothing and less wine. This would increase 'social welfare' more than the importation of wine which merely pandered to the tastes and monetary demands of capitalists and landlords. Hunt ascribes this contradiction in Ricardo's thought to the fact that although he fully recognised the reality of class conflict, Ricardo was blind to the possibilities of social change and took property relationships, the distribution of wealth and power and class relationships as given, natural and unchanging. Certainly, Ricardo did not consider increasing the 'sum of enjoyments' by changing the distribution of power, wealth and privilege – a reflection, no doubt, of Ricardo's class bias. But surely his conclusion on the gains from trade does follow from his labour theory-based model and nothing else. As far as economic analysis is concerned this was achievement enough.

2.5   ELABORATION OF THE CLASSICAL MODEL

In the Ricardian model the purpose of the comparative-cost example in terms of barter (that is, using *relative* prices) was to lay bare the principles on which trade is based – principles which showed how to allocate resources for the good of each country (that is, the world). However, trade actually takes place on the basis of money prices, not on the barter ratios used to illustrate the principle. Is mutually advantageous trade still possible when money is brought into the picture?

Ricardo was able to show, on the basis of assumptions about money wages and the rate of exchange, that the introduction of an international medium of exchange made no difference to barter relations. The natural distribution of specie ensures that the movement of goods across national frontiers corresponds with the trade flow under conditions of barter.

Starting from the obvious fact that traders buy a foreign good only when its price is lower than at home, Ricardo shows how comparative differences in costs can be converted into absolute differences in money prices. The country which has an absolute advantage in every commodity must have a higher money wage-rate. Thus trade is possible between England and Portugal because money-wage and price levels are higher in Portugal than they are in England. If money wage-rates were the same in both countries English cloth would not sell in Portugal and gold would flow from England to Portugal to pay for English imports of Portuguese wine. Eventually, money-wage levels and prices would rise in Portugal and fall in England until absolute differences in money prices are restored which allow profitable two-way commodity traffic. Gold inflows and outflows, therefore, cause adjustments in relative wage and price levels that not only maintain balanced trade, but also ensure that trade takes place according to comparative advantage. With competitive markets, therefore, money prices will guide merchants to an efficient international division of labour.

Notice the contrast between the presentation of comparative cost in terms of relative prices and the analysis in terms of nominal labour-cost differences. The former assumes balanced trade – indeed, it is a one-period (static) model in which trade must be balanced. By contrast, the latter analysis describes the path of adjustment (in value terms) towards the pattern of international specialisation. Here, if the exchange rate is fixed (as under the Gold Standard) the full weight of adjustment falls on wages (that is, labour).

It was, however, William Nassau Senior, writing ten years after Ricardo's work appeared, who first stated the classical theory of international prices in a fairly satisfactory manner. Senior ([1830] 1931) focuses on money-wage differences between countries and shows how these reflect productivity differentials – more precisely, productivity differences in export sectors. Money wage-rates are linked both to commodity prices and to physical productivities. Senior relates these tendencies to the process whereby silver and/or gold is distributed throughout the world – a process which forges the international linkage of domestic price levels. The explanation for higher wages in England compared with India is due to the fact that 'the diligence and skill with which English labour is applied enables the English labourer to produce in a year exportable commodities equal in value to those produced in a year by eight Hindoos' (Senior [1830] 1931, p. 11).[25] Thus, if labour in Portugal is twice as efficient as English labour in wine production, then Portuguese wages at their maximum would be double those in England. The minimum limit to Portuguese wages is then determined by a comparison between Portuguese and English labour productivities in cloth. The relative wage ratio (for example, the value of the wage rate in Portugal divided by the value of the wage rate in England measured in gold prices) sets the limits to Portuguese wages. Wages in the export sector, according to Senior, determine the general level of wages and money incomes generally in the economy and hence the level of prices. This relationship is due to the higher value-productivity of labour and capital in the export industries which enables all domestic residents to increase their command over foreign commodities. The upshot of Senior's discussion, then, is that higher wages compensate for higher productivity; hence the more efficient country has no cause to fear competition from low-wage countries, since the low wages merely reflect a low level of productivity. So long as wages are related to productivity, high-wage countries retain their comparative advantage. Every country necessarily has a comparative advantage.

As we noted previously, the theory of comparative cost as fashioned by Ricardo was incomplete; without introducing demand the theory could not explain precisely on what terms trade would take place. The role of demand and its relevance in the determination of the terms of trade was appreciated by writers such as Torrens, Longfield and Pennington; but it was John Stuart Mill who first explicitly demonstrated how the gain from trade is determined by conditions of demand both at home and abroad, and thereby proved the existence of equilibrium.

The mechanisms which determine the world price ratio (or terms of trade) are (a) 'reciprocal demand', that is, 'the amount and extensibility of demand' in each country for the other country's product, and (b) the productive resources available in each country to produce for the foreign market after meeting its own consumption needs when trade opens up. This ratio will be stable when 'the equation of international demand' is satisfied, that is, when the value of each country's exports is just sufficient to pay for its imports. Mill outlined his solution to the problem left unanswered by Ricardo in his 1844 essay 'On the Laws of Interchange between Nations'. The argument was developed in chapter 18 'Of International Values', Book III of his *Principles* (Mill [1848] 1920). Edgeworth referred to the latter as Mill's 'great' and 'stupendous' chapter (Edgeworth 1894, p. 610) and Chipman has more recently praised Mill's Law of International Value in these terms: 'In its astonishing simplicity, it must stand as one of the great achievements of the human intellect.' (Chipman 1965a, p. 484). Denis O'Brien (1975, p. 183) calls it one of the greatest performances in the history of economics. Without the benefit of marginal utility analysis and relying mainly on verbal reasoning Mill was able to develop a rigorous general equilibrium model. Within this analytical framework (two-country, two-commodity, constant cost and unitary price elasticity of demand in both countries) he is able to derive a unique equilibrium exchange ratio (the terms of trade, or the ratio of export to import prices) – lying between the limits set by the pre-trade (or autarkic) price ratios of the two countries.

Mill's analysis at one stage suggests a paradox: small countries (in productivities and/or populations) have the most to gain from trade. They affect world prices the least and therefore can trade at world prices that are different from domestic prices – a situation which nicely illustrates the 'importance of being *unimportant*'! Indeed, in the case of trade between a big country and a small one, the large country will very likely continue to produce its comparative *disadvantage* good since the small country will not be able to supply the large country with all of its desired consumptions; the latter will thus have to revert to autarky's production methods and lower real income. Here, the small country gets *all* the gains from trade.

Mill was bothered, however, by the problem of multiple equilibria (crisscrossing of offer curves) which arises when either country has an inelastic demand for the other's product and the conditions prescribed in the equations of international demand are satisfied. To deal with the indeterminacy represented by this possibility, Mill added supplementary sections (6–8) to the chapter in the third edition of the *Principles*.

Mill attempts in these sections to show that the range of indeterminancy can be removed by taking into account the shifting of resources in each country towards their areas of comparative advantage on the opening of trade and the consequent equalisation of commodity prices. He considers several numerical examples which lead him to derive an algebraic formula for the equilibrium terms of trade with respect to a hypothetical trade in cloth and linen between England and Germany: $t = \dfrac{pm}{n}$ where t stands for the terms of trade (expressed as units of linen per unit of cloth), pm stands for Germany's exports of linen and n stands for England's exports of cloth.

Mill's result can be generalised in the following form: the international price ratio, p_w, lies in the range spanned by the pre-trade price ratios of the two trading countries, that is, $\frac{a_2}{a_1} \geq p_w \geq \frac{a_2^*}{a_1^*}$, with strict inequality holding if the countries are not too dissimilar. After this extended analysis, however, Mill admits that the new variable identified as the one likely to remove the indeterminacy, that is, the shifting of resources in each country towards their areas of comparative advantage on the opening of trade and the consequent equalisation of commodity prices in the two countries is, in fact, reducible to the original and fundamental determinant of the terms of trade, namely reciprocal demand. Hence, Mill ruefully concedes that the lengthy elaboration 'does not seem to make any very material difference in the practical result' (Mill [1848] 1920, pp. 603–4). Andrea Maneschi has recently clarified Mill's derivation of the law of international values and analysed its relationship to William Whewell's more general formulation (Maneschi 2001).

The status of these added sections has, however, been the subject of some debate and controversy. Unlike the earlier sections, the new 'superstructure' met with a generally unfavourable response from a succession of economists, including Edgeworth, Marshall, Bastable, Viner and, in more recent times, Appleyard and Ingram. The new sections, the latter authors say, make no new contribution to the matter of multiple equilibria since in the earlier sections Mill had already established the existence of a unique exchange ratio for the case of unitary demand. Mill therefore 'did not come to grips with the problem of multiple equilibria that he sets out to solve' (Appleyard and Ingram 1979, p. 475). Chipman, however, formed a different opinion of the new sections as a result of applying the modern mathematical technique of non-linear programming to Mill's problem. Chipman discovered that Mill did, in fact, succeed in finding a *proof* of the existence of a unique equilibrium price ratio. He interprets Mill's verbal description of his demand conditions as specifying a particular aggregate world utility function which Chipman maximises using the non-linear programming method. Mill's problem is then easily solved. But Mill did not actually specify the magnitudes of the parameters inserted by Chipman in his utility function (except for unitary elasticity of demand).

Despite some confusion in Mill's argument in the new sections, Takashi Negishi (1989) recently praised his performance: 'Mill proved the existence of a trade equilibrium by determining the unknown value of endogenous variables from the given value of exogenous variables' (Negishi 1989, p. 180). The point here is that Mill used the given pre-trade values of the exogenous variables such as the domestic price ratio, the quantities of the commodities consumed and the product of such variables to derive the equilibrium values of the endogenous variables such as the terms of trade, exports and imports.

Whatever view one takes of this reassessment of Mill's mature work there is no denying that it was a remarkable achievement. Later neoclassical economists added little of substance to Mill's general law of international values. The offer curve analysis of Marshall and Edgeworth is no more than an exposition and elaboration of Mill's analysis in diagrammatic form. Mill also explored the effects of technological change on the terms of trade and analysed the terms of trade argument for protection. These aspects of Mill's work will be considered later.

How the gains from trade are shared out among countries features prominently in the polemics between free traders and protectionists. By his laborious analysis showing how trading gains are determined on world markets (including situations where some countries are made better off at the expense of others) Mill provided grist for the mill to later polemicists; but for him it was a piece of positive ('scientific') analysis designed to fill a gap in Ricardo's basic model. Later generations of economists sharpened and refined Mill's gains-from-trade index so that we now have at least four different concepts of the terms of trade; but the one most frequently used in policy discussion and empirical work is still the commodity or net barter terms of trade – Mill's original welfare index.

NOTES

1. Typical of the complaints against Smith are: 'we cannot say that there is any special contribution to the theory of foreign trade in the *Wealth of Nations*' (Bastable); 'all the important elements in Smith's free-trade doctrine had been presented prior to the *Wealth of Nations*' (Viner); and Robbins's remark that Smith's foreign-trade doctrines have 'very little analytical edge'. See C.F. Bastable, *The Theory of International Trade* (London, 1903), pp. 168–9; Viner [1937] (1955), pp. 108–9. L. Robbins, *Money, Trade and International Relations* (London: Macmillan, 1971), p. 191.
2. Arthur I. Bloomfield, 'Adam Smith and the Theory of International Trade', in A. Skinner and T. Wilson (eds), *Essays on Adam Smith* (Oxford University Press, 1975), p. 481.
3. Smith summarises the widening of the market through foreign trade as follows: 'By opening a more extensive market for whatever part of the produce of their labour may exceed the home consumption, it encourages them to improve its productive powers, and to augment its annual produce to the utmost, and thereby to increase the real revenue and wealth of the society.' *Wealth of Nations*, Book IV, i, p. 31.
4. H. Myint, 'The "Classical Theory" of International Trade and the Underdeveloped Countries', *Economic Journal*, 68 (June 1958) pp. 317–37; 'Adam Smith's Theory of International Trade in the Perspective of Economic Development', *Economica*, 44 (Sep. 1977), pp. 231–48.
5. See J.S. Mill, *Principles of Political Economy*, ed. W.J. Ashley (London: Longman, 1923), p. 581. Ricardo, *Works* (1951–5), vol. 1, pp. 291 n., 294–5.
6. See Gottfried Haberler, 'International Trade and Economic Development', The Cairo

Lectures, 1959, reprinted in R.S. Weckstein (ed.), *Expansion of World Trade and the Growth of National Economies* (New York: Harper & Row, 1968), pp. 103–4 n. 6. Haberler writes: 'This distinction I find unconvincing. The "vent-of-surplus" (if it is not part and parcel of the productivity theory) seems to me simply an extreme case of differences in comparative cost – a country exporting things for which it has no use.' Bloomfield, op. cit., p. 472. Samuel Hollander, *The Economics of Adam Smith* (London: Heinemann, 1973), pp. 268–76. For a brief, useful survey of the various interpretations of Smith on this issue, see E.G. West, 'Scotland's Resurgent Economist: A Survey of the New Literature on Adam Smith', *Southern Economic Journal*, 45, no. 2 (Oct. 1978), pp. 359–61. West suggests that what Myint is really saying is that the subsequent development of trade theory represented 'a degenerating problem shift' in terms of Lakatos' discourse on methodology. Ricardian and neoclassical models of trade shifted the emphasis from development and disequilibrium states (the focus of Smith's thought) to one concerned with the analysis of static general equilibrium situations. For this reason later neoclassical writers were bound to find fault with Smith's trade analysis – West, p. 361. Another good discussion is C.E. Staley, 'A Note on Adam Smith's Version of the Vent for Surplus Model', *History of Political Economy* (Fall 1973), pp. 438–48. For an analysis of general 'surplus' models of trade and growth, see Richard E. Caves, 'Vent for Surplus Models of Trade and Growth', in Robert E. Baldwin et al., *Trade, Growth and the Balance of Payments: Essays in Honor of Gottfried Haberler* (Amsterdam: North-Holland, 1965), pp. 95–115.

7. This exception to the general optimality of a free-trade policy was accepted by later classical and neoclassical economists. Harry Johnson noted a few years ago, however, that recent theorising has shown this exception to be problematical, that is, the compensating duty restores efficiency in production, but introduces inefficiency in consumption choices. See Harry G. Johnson, 'Commercial Policy and Industrialization', *Economica*, 39 (Aug. 1972), p. 265.

8. Adam Smith, *The Theory of Moral Sentiments* (New York: Kelley, 1966), pp. 266–7.

9. All the leading intermediate texts on international economics discuss Ricardo's theory. The model is analysed well in Akira Takayama, *International Trade* (New York: Holt, Rinehart & Winston, 1972), chapter 4; R.E. Caves and R.W. Jones, *World Trade and Payments* (New York: Little Brown & Co., 1981), 3rd ed., chapter 5, and M. Chacholiades, *International Trade Theory and Policy* (New York: McGraw-Hill, 1978), chapter 2. Ricardo's own statement of the principle of comparative cost is contained in his *Principles of Political Economy and Taxation*, vol. 1 of P. Sraffa (ed.), *The Works and Correspondence of David Ricardo*, hereafter cited as Ricardo, *Works* (1951).

10. Ricardo, *An Essay on the Influence of a Low Price of Corn on the Profits of Stock*, in P. Sraffa (ed.), Ricardo *Works* (1951), vol. IV.

11. P.A. Samuelson, 'Economists and the History of Ideas' and 'The Way of an Economist', reprinted in *The Collected Scientific Papers of Paul A. Samuelson*, ed. R.C. Merton (Cambridge, Mass: MIT Press, 1972), vol. 2, p. 1507, and vol. 3, p. 678.

12. P.A. Samuelson, 'The Way of an Economist', in Paul Samuelson (ed.), *International Economic Relations* (London: Macmillan, 1969), p. 4.

13. Henry William Spiegel, *The Growth of Economic Thought* (Durham, N.C.: Duke University Press, 1971), p. 344.

14. Appleyard and Ingram (1979, p. 503). Thus Mill writes: 'When both countries can produce both commodities, it is not greater absolute, but greater relative facility, that induces one of them to confine itself to the production of one of the commodities, and to import the other.' James Mill, *Elements of Political Economy*, 3rd ed. (London: Baldwin, Craddock & Joy, 1826), p. 123.

15. For Robinson's comment see 'What Are the Questions?', *Journal of Economic Literature*, 15, no. 4 (Dec. 1977), p. 1366. She referred to the ruin of Portuguese industry by free trade following the ratification of the Methuen Treaty (1703).

16. Hollander (1973, p. 469) asserts: 'Ricardo's trade model is a dual-factor model'. Ricardo's analysis of the effects of the Corn Laws certainly required a multi-factor model.

17. If not in Ricardo's time, certainly by the middle of the century, this assumption was

patently untenable. The export of British capital, the peopling of North America, the gold rush to the mines of California, South Africa, Alaska and Australia belied the international immobility assumption. As early as 1817 McCulloch criticised Ricardo for denying 'the equilibrium of profit in different countries' resulting from international capital movements. See O'Brien (1975, p. 194).

18. For a survey of the various interpretations of 'real costs', as well as a trenchant critique of the use of the labour theory in the classical trade model, see Edward S. Mason, 'The Doctrine of Comparative Cost', *Quarterly Journal of Economics*, 38 (Aug. 1926), pp. 582–606.

19. Karl Marx, *Capital*, vol. III (Moscow, 1971), p. 238. In the introduction to his *Critique of Political Economy* Marx stated that he intended to deal with external economic relations, but never got round to it. It is known, however, that Marx's voluminous notes (24 volumes) – not yet fully published – contain a discourse on international trade. For an analysis of Marx's foreign trade doctrines, pieced together from his published writings, see G. Kohlmey, 'Karl Marx Theorie von den Internationalen Werten', *Jahrbuch des Instituts für Wirtschaftswissenschaften*, no. 5 (1962), pp. 18–122.

20. Marx, *Theories of Surplus Value*, part III (Moscow: Progress Publishers, 1975), pp. 105–6.

21. Marx, *Capital*, vol. I (Moscow: Foreign Languages Publishing House, 1977), p. 525.

22. Ricardo, *Notes on Malthus* (1820), p. 215. For an evaluation of the Ricardo–Malthus debate on this point see Viner [1937] (1955), chapter IX, pp. 527–32.

23. See E.G. West, 'Ricardo in Historical Perspective', *Canadian Journal of Economics*, 15, no. 2 (May 1982), pp. 314–16.

24. Ricardo's explicit assumption is that savings and capital accumulation depend on the income of capitalists expressed in terms of luxury goods – what Sraffa calls 'non-basic' commodities as distinct from 'basic' commodities. A basic commodity is one which enters directly or indirectly in the production of all other goods.

25. For an authoritative account of Senior's contribution to trade theory and policy see Marian Bowley, *Nassau Senior and Classical Economics* (London: Allen & Unwin, 1937), chapter 6, pp. 201–34.

3. Free trade and the national economists

3.1 CRITICISMS OF CLASSICAL TRADE THEORY

Seventy-three years ago John Henry Williams of Harvard University launched a devastating attack on the English classical theory of international trade (Williams [1929] 1949).[1] He criticised the static nature of the theory, the unrealism of its assumptions and its neglect of the interrelations of trade and growth. A theory which assumed fixed quantities of productive factors already existent and fully employed and rules out international factor mobility became merely an exercise in 'cross-section value analysis', that is, a demonstration of static allocative gains. As such it was singularly incapable of dealing with the relation of international trade to 'the development of new resources and productive forces' and hence could not offer an explanation for the glaring facts of persistent inequalities of income and structural imbalances among countries. 'Logically followed through', said Williams, 'the classical doctrine of international trade contradicts itself; its conclusions contradict its premises' (Williams [1929] 1949, p. 263). J.S. Mill was criticised for failure to see (a) 'the relation of international trade to national economic development spread over time' (Williams [1929] 1949, p. 265)[2] and (b) that specialisation according to comparative advantage was in conflict with the internal mobility assumption. Specialisation for foreign markets freezes the domestic industrial structure and heightens the vulnerability of the economy to external shocks. Smith and, to a lesser extent, Marshall were exempted from this criticism. Smith's theory of absolute advantage made no distinction between domestic and international mobility of factors and moreover Smith was 'a close observer of facts' (Williams [1929] 1949, p. 267). Marshall fully accepted the assumptions of classical theory, but recognised that comparative costs were liable to change under the impact of shifting reciprocal demands. Right down to the present day, essentially the same criticisms have been made of orthodox trade theory (the classical theory and its neoclassical variants) by writers with perhaps a different perspective from that of Williams – Joan Robinson, Raoul Prebisch, Gunnar Myrdal. From a radically different (namely Marxian) perspective, challenges to orthodox doctrine continue to emanate from Emmanuel, Samir Amin, André Gunder Frank, and so on. Certainly, what unites the former group of writers is the belief (a) that the equilibrium-theoretic framework of conventional trade theory is inadequate for comprehending issues of trade and development and (b) that free trade may inhibit the growth of 'productive forces' in poor, underdeveloped countries. The expression '*Produktionskräfte*' was introduced into the literature by Friedrich List ten years after the publication of Ricardo's comparative advantage theory.[3] For a time in Germany it eclipsed the bright rays of 'free trade' which were being emitted from Britain by Cobden and Bright. It became the core of the national economic policy which spurred German industrialisation in the mid-nineteenth century. List's ideas went into oblivion, and it was only after the revival of interest in the developmental problems of less-developed countries after the Second World War that they came to animate the debate on these issues. Whether they are conscious of the fact or not, development economists the world over owe a great debt to the memory of Friedrich List, for he was the champion of their cause against the ideology of free trade and the static-equilibrium theory which underpinned it. Economists concerned with the international dimensions of economic development (Prebisch, Singer Seers, and so on) stand in a long tradition which started with the so-called 'national economists' (German and American) of the early nineteenth century.

The national economists were protectionists. They denounced free trade and called into question the classical theory on which this policy was based. Britain's commitment to and advocacy of free trade they regarded as a device for maintaining British economic hegemony. The monopoly of industrial production enjoyed by Britain was due to the productive capacities of machinery. Young nations and countries which, for various reasons, had lagged behind in economic development could not hope to compete with the British colossus without a conscious state-directed policy of industrial protection. The alternative was to remain as pastoral economies condemned to a miserable future serving only to feed the British market with food and raw materials. Without a thriving industrial sector a country could not hope to maintain an adequate population, ensure its prosperity and achieve status and influence in the world. In short, they wanted to catch up with Britain and to do so as quickly as possible.

The issues involved in the national economists' concern about the role of trade in development were prefigured in a mid-eighteenth century debate between Josiah Tucker and David Hume.[4] In his essay 'Of Money' (Hume [1752] 1955), Hume expressed the opinion that the relatively low wage-rates and costs of subsistence in poor countries would attract manufacturing industry from rich countries and, as a consequence, the rich countries would ultimately lose their wealth to formerly underdeveloped countries. In other words, trade and investment would act as 'engines of growth' working to produce an equalisation of income levels throughout a free-trade ('globalised') world economy. Tucker objected to this analysis and contended that the rich country would always maintain its advantages under free trade provided the country's wealth was acquired by 'general industry'. Such a country has

> an established trade and credit, large correspondences, experienced agents and factors, commodious shops, workhouses, magazines, etc., also a great variety of the best tools and implements in the various kinds of manufactures, and engines for abridging labour. (Tucker [1774] 1973, p. 184)

as well as good transport facilities, skilled workers and a progressive agriculture. With all these advantages, an advanced manufacturing country has nothing to fear from competition with poor countries.

Although wages might be higher in the rich country, average costs (hence prices) would be relatively low because competition in the large domestic market would encourage large-scale production and specialisation (division of labour). The higher level of productivity resulting from these processes implied that the price level would not be proportional to the wage level. Generalising from this, Tucker proposed a general principle: 'it may be laid down as a general proposition which very seldom fails, that operose, or complicated manufactures are cheapest in rich countries;- and raw materials in poor ones' (Tucker [1774] 1973, 188). Hence Tucker was confident that the 'richer manufacturing Nation will maintain its Superiority over the poorer one, notwithstanding this latter may be likewise advancing towards Perfection'. Tucker used the foregoing arguments to attack the mistaken belief that 'trade and manufactures, if left at full liberty, will always descend from a richer to a poorer state; somewhat in the same manner as a stream of water falls from higher to lower grounds' (Tucker [1774] 1973, p. 178). In answer to Hume's objections, Tucker made several observations strikingly similar to the arguments of the later national economists. Hume's main point in rebuttal was that if Tucker's arguments were true, then 'one nation might engross the trade of the whole world and beggar all the rest' (Tucker [1774] 1973, pp. 192–3). To this Tucker replied that such a monopoly position would be counteracted by the poor countries taking steps by means of legislation and state intervention to promote their own industries wherever conditions of soil, climate and native skills provide such countries with special advantages. Tucker elaborated on this point in private communication to Hume through their mutual correspondent Lord Kames. Referring to the possibility that poor countries would always be undersold in the international market, Tucker says

> It is true likewise, that all of them have it in their power to load the manufactures
> of the rich country, upon entering their territories, with such high duties, as shall
> turn the scale in favour of their own manufactures; or of the manufactures of
> some other nation, whose progress in trade they have less cause to fear or envy.
> Thus it is in my poor apprehension, that the rich may be prevented from swal-
> lowing up the poor; at the same time, and by the same methods, that the poor
> are stimulated and excited to emulate the rich.[5]

The force of the Anglican dean's arguments made the great sceptical philosopher reconsider his position, as Hume's essay 'On the Jealousy of Trade'
indicates. Tucker took comfort from the fact that although Hume never
acknowledged his indebtedness to him, he 'made him [Hume] a convert to
the doctrine he now espouses' (Tucker [1774] 1973, p. 177).[6]

Tucker's message is unmistakable. Backward countries can pull themselves up by their own bootstraps; for the same long-winded process of
mutual causation which led to cumulative growth in rich countries can be
short-circuited by policy. The conditions for economic prosperity can be
duplicated wherever circumstances are favourable by state intervention in
matters of commercial and industrial policies.

3.2   AMERICAN NATIONAL ECONOMISTS AND PROTECTIONISM

There is no evidence that the national economists in Germany or the
United States were aware of this debate and therefore we can safely assume
they derived no benefit (or enlightenment) from it. But the curious blend
of mercantilist and free-trade logic underlying Tucker's arguments was
fairly common by the early nineteenth century. The equally relevant
Spence-Mill-Torrens debate which preceded the Corn Law controversy
went largely unnoticed by the national economists. Whenever they used
theoretical arguments these were primarily directed against Adam Smith's
version of classical economics, in particular their understanding of his
free-trade doctrine. But they were essentially economic pragmatists who
looked for solutions in the sphere of policy to the problem of getting
industrialisation started. One who went to some lengths to formulate an
analytical system for dealing with the problem of national economic development in an international context was Friedrich List. Before turning to
his work, let us briefly survey the views of the early American economists
and statesmen among whom the tenets of modern economic nationalism
first took root.

The origin of American protectionism can be traced to Alexander
Hamilton's state papers, in particular the *Report on Manufactures*

(Hamilton [1791] 1934). The goal was industrialisation: the rapid transformation of the newly-independent country from the status of an economic dependent to that of a first-rate world power. Indeed, the report has been called the 'charter of American industrialism'.

A programme of government assistance to native manufacturing industry through protective duties, bounties, subsidies and drawbacks was an essential element in the strategy. As the leaders of the revolution saw it, the measures envisaged for achieving the long-term objective of industrialisation were in harmony with other immediate desirable ends: raising Federal revenue from tariff duties, lessening dependence on imports and thus the avoidance of shortages in times of war, stemming the loss of coin caused by excessive non-essential imports, strengthening of national unity and regional interdependence through the processing of Southern staples in the North. Thus a sound public credit policy, national unity, abundance of national supplies and a healthy balance of payments could all be attained by the development of native manufactures.

In the *Report* submitted to Congress in December 1791 Hamilton outlined the benefits a country derived from manufacturing industry. He evoked visions of factories, mighty machines and large-scale production throughout the land, all offering greater scope for division of labour and increases in labour productivity than could ever be achieved in agriculture. The importation of foreign manufacture checked the progress of native industry and deprived the country of great benefits (or social and economic 'spillovers' and 'linkages'). An agricultural country producing only a few staples must depend upon foreign outlets for the disposal of its surplus. Such a country (bereft of processing facilities) often traded on disadvantageous terms with manufacturing countries because of the frequent occurrence of glutted markets and depressed prices. Terms-of-trade losses, specie drains and unfavourable trade balances were the common experiences of non-industrialised countries.

Hamilton then turned to the obstacles to be overcome: shortages of skilled mechanics, machinery and capital and lack of adequate transport facilities. Since a country ought to aim at possessing 'all the essentials of national supply' it was the duty of the state to help entrepreneurs cope with the difficulties by offering inducements to invest in manufacturing industry through a government programme of eleven types of aid and protection. Hamilton considered protective tariffs, bounties, patents and infrastructural projects as absolutely essential elements of the planned programme of assistance to the private sector. Agriculture was not to be neglected. It had a role to play in national economic development. George Washington had declared that he 'would not force the introduction of manufactures by extravagant encouragements . . . to the prejudice of agriculture'.[7] Hamilton concurred and pointed out that the best prospect for agriculture lay in the growth of industry which would enlarge the market for produce and raw materials. The demand so generated would be more certain, steady and profitable than reliance on foreign markets. High transport costs across the ocean which reduced farmers' net income from the proceeds of sales would be avoided (Hamilton [1791] 1934, pp. 197–8, 228–9).

Hamilton's proposals were not put into effect immediately. The early tariffs, designed primarily for the purpose of raising revenue, afforded only incidental (or marginal) protection). The one clear protectionist measure – the Tonnage Act of 1789 – did indeed provide substantial protection to US shipowners and shipbuilders. The Act established uniform tonnage duties of 50 cents a ton on every entry into a US port by foreign vessels and 6 cents a ton on US-owned vessels. Apart from the protective element, the measure was also revenue-raising and could be used as a bargaining weapon in commercial negotiations with foreign countries to secure reciprocal reductions in discriminatory trade practices. But it was not until after the Anglo-American War of 1812 that American trade policy turned massively protectionist. The Tariff Act of 1816, for example, imposed duties of $7\frac{1}{2}$ to 30 per cent *ad valorem* on a wide range of manufactured products; but still the demand grew for more protection.

The manufacturing interests of Pennsylvania, New England and New York State called for higher import duties, and in this they were supported by the early American economists who, also in their writings, reflected the nationalist aspirations of the political leaders. Daniel Raymond, a Baltimore lawyer, championed the protectionists' cause. In his two books, *Thoughts on Political Economy* (1820) and *Elements of Political Economy* (1823),[8] he disputed Adam Smith's view that the net result of the interactions of individuals pursuing their own interests was the promotion of social welfare and economic growth. The interests of individuals, Raymond asserted, were always at variance with the national interest. The cotton and tobacco planters in the South were free-traders because it was in their interest to import cheap textiles from England; but the trade was not beneficial to the country as a whole (Raymond 1823, vol. II, pp. 225–6, 231–2). National wealth was not the sum total of individual exchange values or total expenditure on consumption; rather it was the capacity to produce goods. The pace of national economic development was determined by a country's ability to increase its productive capacity. The latter could be speeded up by an active government policy of intervention, particularly in regard to external trade. What held back US entrepreneurs was the inability to compete on equal terms with the superior skills and technology of the English (Raymond 1823, pp. 245–6). It was the duty of the state to remedy this deficiency through a policy of protective tariffs to encourage investment in 'infant industries' and ensure the full employment of labour. Besides, tariffs were the cheapest way of providing such assistance. The same conclusion was reached by John Rae on the basis of his analysis of the role of capital formation in economic development.[9] Because of the social benefits ('spillovers') of investment the state must take an active interest in capital formation. The government could positively encourage the growth of industry by subsidising inventions, new technical processes and offering tariff protection to immature industries. John Stuart Mill was apparently impressed by some of Rae's arguments and explicitly mentioned Rae in connection with the 'infant-industry argument'.

Another early protectionist writer worthy of note is Willard Phillips, a Harvard-educated Boston lawyer. He started out as a defender of free trade, but by the time his book *A Manual of Political Economy* (1828) was published he was already converted to protectionism.[10] He rejected large parts of classical doctrine after careful study of the works of Smith, Malthus, Ricardo, Say and McCulloch. His criticisms of classical writers were often well substantiated, and his own positive contributions were quite significant. His discussion of international trade was fairly sophisticated for that time (for example, his analyses of the terms-of-trade argument for protection and the international demonstration effect in consumption). Free trade, he argued, was not a rational policy for a country, given the existence of national trade barriers. Countries should rather aim for 'perfect reciprocity' whereby the effects of other countries' trade regulations could be neutralised – a policy of 'fair trade', as we should say today. Besides arguing the case for protection, Phillips made noteworthy contributions to general economic theory and method in areas such as value, distribution, location and rent.

Not all early US economists were protectionists, of course; but the free-trade writers, not unnaturally, were mainly to be found in the southern states (Jacob Cardozo, George Tucker and Thomas Cooper). But even these writers, while they upheld the free-trade logic, were severe critics of imported economic doctrines.

During the 1820s – years of ardent nationalism in the United States – the protectionist movement grew steadily, and coalesced in the Pennsylvania Society for the Promotion of Manufactures and the Mechanic Arts founded in 1826 and based in Philadelphia. Leading the agitation was Henry Clay (the politician) and Matthew Carey (the publisher). Carey's son, Henry Charles Carey, later became well known as the leading theoretical defender of US protectionism.[11] He was well-read in British political economy and declared himself a follower of Adam Smith; but he rejected much of classical doctrine as being inapplicable to a large and young country like the United States. His recipe for national economic development was a combination of domestic *laissez-faire* and protectionism. He went further than Raymond and advocated protection as a permanent feature of national policy. He saw no inconsistency in this position, and for this reason Carey has been widely regarded as the mouthpiece of American business interests at that time. He denounced the British policy of free trade, claiming that its real aim was to secure for England a monopoly of machinery. The 'American system' (the protective tariff policy) sought to break down that monopoly.[12] The term 'American System' (attributed to Henry Clay, 'Harry of the West') was popularly understood to denote the scheme whereby high tariffs would protect American infant industries against English competition while bringing in revenue to pay for new roads, canals and other public works designed to bind the country together.

But Carey was not simply a propagandist for the industrial lobby. There was a strong physiocratic streak in his economic thought and it can be argued that his ultimate aim was a prosperous agriculture. Like the Physiocrats, he contended that the basis of industrial growth came from the surplus of the agricultural sector. There was a symbiotic relationship between the two sectors. If agricultural expansion was a precondition for industrial take-off, the continued prosperity of agriculture depended on steady growth of the industrial sector. But economic diversification could only come about through a policy of industrial protection. It is in this context of a vision of balanced growth that we must see Carey's protectionism. In his empirical work relating the tariff history of the United States to cyclical fluctuations in the economy during the first half of the nineteenth century Carey observed that each of the three tariff increases were associated with periods of rising prosperity. Depressions, marked by low farm prices and falling demand for industrial goods followed with a lag every time average tariff rates fell. He concluded that industrial protection stimulated the economy since it shifted the terms of trade in favour of the United States, increased domestic industrial production and raised farm prices and incomes. A virtuous circle was put into motion every time tariff levels were increased. Increased protection widened the domestic market for manufactures, offered scope for large-scale production and resulted in low prices of competitive imports taking into account transport costs. Rising levels of urban incomes and activity increased the demand for farm products (food and raw materials) and, as farm incomes and prices rose, so the demand for manufactures was further stimulated.

3.3   LIST – THE NATIONAL ECONOMIST

In June 1824, one year before the establishment of the Pennsylvania Society, Friedrich List, the German political exile, arrived in the United States.[13] It was a momentous event in the life of the man who was to be identified by both his own and succeeding generations with the creed of economic nationalism. He was not an ordinary immigrant. He accompanied General Lafayette, who was then making a triumphal return tour of the country and met several prominent Americans, including John Quincy Adams, Henry Clay, Chief Justice Marshall and Daniel Webster, some of whom became personal friends (Andrew Jackson, James Madison). He came to America at a time when the protectionist agitation was at its height. The discussions surrounding the problems and prospects of American economic growth made a strong impression on him. He saw parallels with his native country and these observations, together with his experiences from several business projects, strengthened his earlier beliefs in national unity, protection and the possibilities for accelerated industrial growth through enlightened policies. His doubts deepened concerning the relevance of classical doctrine for countries attempting to get to the threshold of industrialisation; as he noted in his diary, the American experience forcibly brought home to him the fact that countries passed through different stages of economic development and that different policies were required for each stage.[14]

As editor of the *Readinger Adler*, an influential immigrant weekly paper, List gained a national reputation as one of the foremost defenders of the 'American System'. He plunged himself into the propaganda activities of the Pennsylvania Society and wrote a series of letters to Charles Ingersoll, vice-president of the Society, calling for the imposition of high import duties to protect American manufacturers from British competition and thus ensure steady economic growth. He campaigned on behalf of the winning Democratic presidential candidate, Andrew Jackson, and when his letters to Ingersoll were subsequently published as *Outlines of American Political Economy* (List 1827) copies of his work were circulated to Congressmen. List's literary and political efforts came to fruition a year later when Congress passed the Tariff Bill of 1828. Dubbed the 'Tariff of Abominations', this Act imposed import duties averaging 45 per cent *ad valorem*. Although tariff rates declined somewhat up to the outbreak of the Civil War, they rose again sharply afterwards and remained so for the rest of the century. The United States therefore never adopted free trade in the nineteenth century (see Figure 3.1 below).

The *Outlines* was List's first attempt at a systematic presentation of his theory on national economy. Here he justified his policy of protective tariffs,

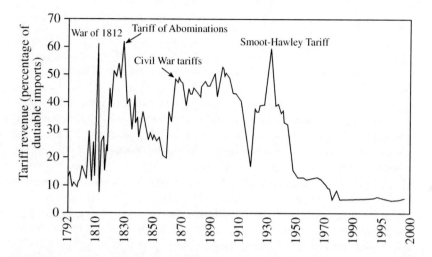

Source: S. Husted/M. Melvin, *International Economics,* 5th edition (figure 8.1 from page 221). © 2001 Addison Wesley. Reprinted by permission of Pearson Education, Inc.

Figure 3.1   US tariffs, 1792–1999

criticised the classical economists and discussed how the problems of development could be overcome. In it, all the leading ideas of his later works were foreshadowed, for example, national economics, productive powers, balanced growth and stages of economic development. These ideas were further developed and illustrated with a wealth of sociological and historical references in List's next two major works, *The Natural System of Political Economy* (1837) and *The National System of Political Economy* (List [1841] 1885).[15] List's public life, although full of dramatic and tragic turns, was all of one piece: all his activities and intellectual efforts were directed towards the realisation of the 'national idea' (*Nationalitätsprinzip*), above all its full realisation in his beloved Fatherland.

Before he left for America, as secretary of the Union of Merchants and Industrialists (*Handels und Gewerbsverein*) and editor of its journal, List mounted a campaign for the abolition of internal tolls and duties and the establishment of an all-German external tariff to protect German manufacturers from foreign (British) competition. Thenceforth he became the driving force behind the *Zollverein*. He had visions of an integrated German economy, with its national railway network and national merchant marine supporting industrialisation and the realisation of the country's full economic potential. When he returned to Germany he resumed with unflagging zeal his work on all matters concerned with the promotion of German industrialisation until he took his own life in 1846.

List set up his own system of national economics in opposition to what he regarded as the erroneous teachings of the classical economists on the subject of trade and development. He habitually refers to the classical writers as 'the School', suggesting a greater uniformity of doctrine than was in fact the case. When he mentions names, those most often cited are Adam Smith and J.B. Say. There is no indication that he was ever familiar with Ricardo's principle of comparative advantage or of the writings of Torrens and James Mill. He excluded from consideration large areas of classical thought such as the theories of value, money and distribution and concentrated his attack on the theory of trade policy, orthodox methodology and growth theory.

List considered the analytical method an appropriate procedure in understanding economic phenomena; but abstract economic doctrines have no universal validity. Changing contingent factors (sociological, political, historical and institutional) require that the axiomatic approach be complemented by inductive, empirical and historical studies; otherwise theory degenerates into vague generalisations, liable to be contradicted by divergent facts. Since theory is only as good as its assumptions allow it to be, List makes a plea not only for contextual flexibility in theory construction, but also for the realism of assumptions. Thus he criticises classical theory for its ahistorical, individualistic, cosmopolitan and natural-law concepts. In particular, he indicts the theory for its 'groundless cosmopolitanism', 'deadly materialism' and 'disorganising particularism'. The erroneous policy proposals of the classical school stem from these theoretical shortcomings. Adam Smith and his followers had discussed 'individual economics' and 'cosmopolitan economics' but had lost sight of the nation, and failed to develop a theory of national economics. They reduced all economic activity, including international trade to the free play of competitive acquisitive behaviour in the market-place (worldwide as well as domestic). But, says List, the world is divided into sovereign states. Welfare maximising individuals are also citizens, and the special interests of the individual do not necessarily coincide with the general interest of the nation. Moreover, the market is not merely a meeting-place for the exchange of commodities into money-equivalents, but is also an outlet for human relationships, that is, social interchange. The division of labour fostered by the free-market economy certainly promotes efficiency, but it only works because it is a social, co-operative system in the production process. The nation is the link between the individual and mankind. An economic theory which ignores the social and economic significance of this link is bound to be trivial and inconsequential. A relevant political economy, for List, must be one which seriously analyses the infrangible nexus between market economics and politics (List [1841] 1885, pp. 124–6).

Adam Smith had, quite properly, defined political economy as a branch of statecraft, the principal aim of which was to discover the causes of the wealth of nations; but Smith deviated from his purpose and his quest ended in a blind-alley. His analysis offered little guidance to backward countries which nevertheless possessed all the potentialities for economic growth. List conceives his national economics as an inquiry into the *real* causes of wealth in such countries. Uppermost in his mind, of course, is the case of Germany. The key concepts in List's reconstruction of trade and development theory are 'productive forces' and 'economic stages'. These are essentially dynamic constructs (in contrast to much of classical reasoning), and List handles them skilfully to show the relativity of economic doctrines and the organic nature of development.

For List, the wealth of a nation consists, not as Adam Smith would have it, in the sum total of its exchange-values, but in the full use of its productive powers. These powers of production are not the same as actual production or current income. They are the means whereby further wealth can be created in the future. By productive forces, List means not only a country's private capital equipment, natural and human resources, but also its social overhead capital (especially transport facilities), advances in science and technology, educational facilities, administrative and managerial skills, progressive political and social institutions, and so on (List [1841] 1885, pp. 138–9). In short, all the attributes of a developed country. A nation achieves the optimum utilisation of its resources when it has fully developed all the productive powers of manufacturing, commerce and agriculture in an evenly balanced fashion. It was the duty of the state to act as a catalyst in the release of productive forces that generate the industrialisation process. Once the modernisation process is under way, private enterprise and the market mechanism can be relied upon to continue the momentum. He agrees with J.B. Say that 'laws cannot create wealth', but asserts that laws can 'create productive power, which is more important than riches, i.e. than the actual possession of values in exchange' (List [1841] 1885, p. 139 n.). One of the most potent and readily available devices for activating dormant productive forces is a protective tariff. The full power of manufacturing can only be developed behind a tariff wall which creates the conditions (a secure home market, adequate return on investment, and so on) for thriving industries. In conditions of economic backwardness, a protective tariff is not only a sure means of bringing unused resources into production, it also 'imparts industrial instruction' (education) to the nation: entrepreneurs gain industrial, business and organisational experience, a workforce is trained and equipped with industrial skills – in short, all the economic success associated with 'learning by doing'. The development of industry is vital, for without it there can be no viable, prosperous agriculture and commerce. The *Normalnation* is one in which there is a harmonious balance between agriculture, manufacturing and commerce – in the absence of this harmony, a nation is never powerful and wealthy. Hence it is absolutely essential that domestic manufacturers be protected against foreign competition, for what is good for manufacturing is good for all other sectors.

List buttresses his developmental programme with a theory of the stages of economic growth. The object of this excursion into historical sociology is to make the point that different economic policies are required for each stage in a nation's development. Indeed, wise policy should aim by all possible means to ease the transition from one stage to another. At least for nations in the temperate zone the ultimate goal of economic maturity will be industrialisation. In the early stages of growth, when the economy is predominantly agricultural, the country should pursue a liberal (that is, free trade) commercial policy. As capital accumulates and craft industries make their appearance a protectionist policy must be introduced, but only moderate rates of duty should be imposed since the country will need to import machinery, tools, and so on, from the more advanced countries in order to acquire the skills and learn the techniques of manufacturing production. At the second stage of industrial development when the industrial structure of the country is being built up but domestic industries are still unable to withstand competition from more advanced countries, tariff policy should become severely restrictive and additional help provided by way of subsidies to manufacturers. The aim of policy here is to nourish and support the development of home industries, since at this stage the only available market is the national one. Only when the country has successfully surmounted all the obstacles to industrial growth and has a complement of well-established industries should commercial policy gradually revert to one of free trade 'to stop farmers, manufacturers and merchants from falling into idle habits and to encourage them to maintain the supremacy that they have achieved' (List [1841] 1885, p. 158).

Protection and Industrialisation

List the patriot and nationalist wanted to hasten German unity and industrialisation. All his economic theorising was motivated by this ambition. He wished Germany to 'strive to attain to the same degree of commercial and industrial development to which other nations have attained by means of their commercial policy' (List [1841] 1885, p. x). The biggest obstacle to the realisation of this aim was the ideology of free trade that was spreading to Germany. Free trade might be good for England, but it spelt disaster for countries like Germany and the United States. A few German industries managed to get off the ground and even thrived for a brief period under the shelter of Napoleon's 'Continental System'. But when peace came and the ports of Europe were thrown open cheap manufactured goods from British factories flooded the German market and those industries were ruined. The slump that ensued resulted in widespread unemployment, pauperism, vagabondage and drove thousands of destitute Germans to the United States and Canada. List was deeply distressed by this experience and saw it as a British attempt to stifle the birth of German industry. When later, in the United States, he heard that a similar throttling of industry occurred there owing to ruinous British competition, List's reaction was hostile and bitter:

> English national economy has for its object to manufacture for the whole world, to monopolise all manufacturing power, even at the expense of the lives of her citizens, to keep the world, and especially her own colonies, in a state of infancy and vassalage by political management as well as by the superiority of her capital, her skill, and her navy. (List 1827, Letter II)

This outburst against British economic dominance cannot be lightly dismissed as the emotional outpourings of a frustrated patriot and nationalist, devoid of substance. List's grievances were not fanciful or exaggerated. He knew from his American friends that Henry Brougham (an influential Liberal MP who later became Lord Chancellor) had called for a policy of dumping British goods on the US market so as 'to stifle in the cradles those rising manufactures in the United States which the war had forced into existence contrary to the natural course of things'.[16] List's denunciation of British economic hegemony was based on a thorough study of British commercial policy. British political economists and publicists now called for free trade because it chimed well with British national interests. But it was not always so. The British Industrial Revolution was born and nurtured not on free trade but on protection. But alas, says List: 'It was one of the vulgar tricks of history that when one nation reaches the pinnacle of its development it should attempt to remove the ladder by which it had mounted in order to prevent others from following.'[17] He praised English mercantilist policy, for whatever else might be said of it the policy certainly fostered British commercial and industrial supremacy. Whenever and wherever sufficient political pressure could be exerted, English ministers sought to wrest trade advantages for their merchants and manufacturers. He gave examples: the 1703 Methuen Treaty with Portugal; the suppression of the Indian textile industry in order to safeguard the Lancashire cotton industry; the 1713 Asiento Treaty with Spain and the Eden Treaty, which gave British manufacturers a foothold in South America and France; the prohibition of certain lines of manufacturing in the American colonies which forced on the colonists British imports that they were perfectly capable of making for themselves. All this suggested, said List, that

> England's ministers obeyed the theory of productive power when they deter-
> mined upon their industrial policy . . . by the power which she pursued,
> [England] acquired power, and by her political power gained productive power,
> and by her productive power gained wealth. (List [1841] 1885, p. 46)

The fault with the classical theory of trade, List asserted, was that it ignored the possibility of commercial manipulation through the exercise of politi-cal/diplomatic influence. It evaded the whole real-world issue of dominance and dependency and sought to elevate free trade to the status of an un-assailable principle of universal validity. The failing lay in the premises of orthodox theory, that is, the assumption that trade takes place between countries of equal economic strength and at the same level of economic development and hence, equality of bargaining power. Remove these un-realistic assumptions and the way is cleared for a theory that can relate more meaningfully in terms of both analysis and policy to conditions of economic backwardness, unequal development and the universal desire for industrialisation. For List, free trade in industrial goods can only be a distant goal to be attained when all suitably endowed countries reach the same level of industrial development, and so are in a position to engage in genuine international competition. Until that time, countries cannot dis-pense with tariff protection for they must themselves pass gradually through all the stages which Britain had undergone. Even at the time he was writing, List noted, Britain had not fully departed from protection. The Corn Laws remained in force and although Huskisson had lowered some industrial duties the average tariff level was still high enough to provide ad-equate shelter to British manufacturers. List's observation that Britain, then preaching free trade to the Americans, became rich on the basis of protectionism and subsidies was echoed in 1986 by the Canadian econo-mist Mel Watkins in a critical speech on the Canada–United States Free Trade arrangement: 'Britain moved to the practice of free trade only after it was politically and economically dominant. It did not do it to shake up its industrialists and thereby to render itself strong; rather, being already the workshop of the world, it did it the better to impose its manufactures on the weak' (Watkins 1986, p. 8).

List was a hasty writer who sometimes exaggerated to strengthen his arguments. He was also dogmatic, yet he was often correct in his general assessment of the motivations and consequences of British mercantilist policy, as modern research indicates. List's discussion of the Methuen Treaty of 1703 is a case in point. He disputed Adam Smith's claim that the treaty was not particularly beneficial to England and that Portugal got the

better of the bargain. Smith was alone in this opinion, said List, for 'all the
merchants and political economists, as well as the statesmen of England
have ever since eulogised this treaty as the masterpiece of British commercial policy' (List [1841] 1885, p. 61). Under the terms of the treaty, in return
for British naval support, the Portuguese government accepted conditions
of trade which wiped out the Portuguese textile industry, arrested economic
development and made Portugal more dependent than ever on Britain.
Portuguese trade was henceforth carried on by British merchants and
German and Dutch exports were virtually excluded from Portuguese and
Brazilian markets – 'Portugal was deluged with British manufactures and
the first result of this inundation was the sudden and complete ruin of the
Portuguese manufactories.' (List [1841] 1885, p. 61). In this instance, List
did not exaggerate. According to careful modern research the result of the
treaty was

> a strong dependence of Portugal on England . . . The large and chronic deficit
> created by the type of international division of labour in the Portuguese balance
> of payments caused Brazilian gold to outflow entirely from Portugal and to be
> directed mainly to England, where given the different conditions it contributed
> to the industrialisation of that country much more than it had done in Portugal
> whose manufacturing sector had been sacrificed to the production of wine.
> (Sideri 1970, p. 13)

India suffered a similar fate in the nineteenth century – the ruin of its
textile industry. This time, not because of unequal treaties, but by the 'imperialism of free trade'. When the commercial monopoly of the East India
Company ended in 1913 India was flooded with cheap mill-made cotton
goods from Lancashire which devasted India's old-established hand-
weaving textile industry: 'The misery hardly finds parallel in the history of
commerce,' wrote Lord William Bentinck, governor-general of India
(1828–35). 'The bones of the cotton weavers are bleaching the plains of
India.'[18] The country's foreign rulers refused it adequate protection by
tariffs. From 1814 until 1859 imported cotton piece goods in India attracted
a modest 5 per cent and cotton twist and yarns carried a 3–5 per cent duty,
while raw cotton was permitted to leave India at a purely nominal duty
(Harnetty 1972, p. 7). Meanwhile high British tariffs put Indian cotton
manufactures at a considerable disadvantage in the British market. The
import of cotton goods into India went up from £8m in 1859 and doubled
within a decade. When new, and often Indian-owned mills, started up in
Bombay they were handicapped by imperial policy which insisted on free
trade and denied them adequate trade protection. Under pressure from
Lancashire mill owners the Indian cotton duties were abolished in 1882.
Millions of weavers sank to the level of agricultural labourers: 'All the old

industries for which India had been noted since ancient times had declined under an invidious commercial policy of the British. India was left with agriculture as the only national industry of the people.' (Agarwala 1985, p. 121).

List is generally regarded as an arch-protectionist, a neo-mercantilist; others, a minority (for example, Charles Gide, Eduard Heiman, Rudolph Hilferding), see him as essentially an economic liberal whose ultimate goal was free trade.[19] One can obviously assess List's thought from different perspectives and each would give a different answer to this question. List specifically excluded agriculture from protection. He believed that the growth of industry was a sufficient guarantee of agricultural expansion. The inevitable spread of industrial technology to agriculture would increase its productivity; together with the growth of urban demand this would ensure the prosperity of domestic agriculture. Protection was not central to List's argument; hence his justification of 'educational tariffs' was not simply an 'exception' to the free-trade principle, as some neoclassical writers make out in order to emasculate List's case by subsuming it under the rubric of mainstream economic theorising. List was concerned with the development of productive powers and its role in propelling economic growth. What mattered for him was whether free trade was an inhibiting or liberating force in the release of productive potential. The adoption of a free trade policy was a matter of choice conditioned by particular historical circumstances. When free trade was a liberating factor in economic growth it could be adopted; when it was a hindrance it was folly to continue with it.

List gave no indication that he was aware of the principle of comparative cost. He understood Smith's absolute advantage theory, but his application of it was selective, to say the least. Thus, he said, if Smith's doctrine was followed, the United States would buy all its cloth from England, but this would ruin the manufacture of cloth in the United States; and although US consumers would benefit from cheap clothing there is no guarantee that they would not have to pay higher prices later when British manufacturers felt they had a monopoly position in the US market. Americans would suffer a double loss: high prices and no domestic industry. On the other hand, List thought that the principle applied with particular relevance to trade between the tropics and the temperate countries of Europe and North America.

Those who see List as a champion of industrialisation in underdeveloped countries forget that he saw no future for many of these countries along that road. Thus he did not recommend the use of educational tariffs by countries not destined to participate in the historic march towards industrialisation because of their limited, specialised resources (that is, primary producers):

> A country of the torrid zone would make a very fatal mistake, should it try to become a manufacturing country. Having received no invitation to that vocation from nature, it will progress more rapidly in riches and civilization if it continues to exchange its agricultural productions for the manufactured products of the temperate zone. (List [1841] 1885, p. 75)

List envisaged that the future pattern of world trade would be marked by a complementary relationship between the tropics on the one side and industrial Europe and America on the other. List must have realised, although he did not mention it, that the industrial countries would experience a more rapid rate of growth than the tropics since manufacturing took place at decreasing costs. However, List felt the dependency (exploitative) element in this otherwise unequal relationship would be reduced to the extent that many developed countries (not just one) would be competing for primary products. List's hopes on both these counts have not been fulfilled. The bulk of world trade in the modern age takes place among the industrial countries themselves, not between them and the tropics, and dependency is a real complaint often made by Third World representatives. Industrial countries account for more than 60 per cent of total world exports. Much of their trade is with each other. Fifty per cent of the volume of merchandise trade flows among developed countries. North–South trade (that is, trade between developed and developing countries) represents only about one-third of total trade (World Trade Organization, 1995).

In other respects List showed some analytical insights still worthy of note. Thus he clearly saw that one of the main advantages of manufacturing was that it afforded opportunities for obtaining increasing returns through enlargement of the scale of production. Long before Marshall, List recognised in 'external economies' an important source of the benefits of industrialisation. These dynamic gains fostered by high growth of demand through protection outweighed, in List's view, the inefficiencies of protection. He was not ignorant of the static allocative-efficiency losses from protection, but maintained they were a small price to pay for the long-run economic, social, cultural and political blessings of industrialisation.

The development of productive forces under protective cover means that the interests of particular individuals would be thwarted, some current income would have to be sacrificed and consumers at large would face increased prices. Unprofitable industries or branches of manufacturing would have to be set up where productivity is lower than abroad at the initial stage. They are unprofitable in terms of the cost of current output valued at world prices or the private return on capital. The nation would therefore lose a part of its exchange values, but gain immensely in the long run when the social benefits are reaped. Lord Robbins saw much evidence of 'misrepresentation and exaggeration' in List's work, but gave him credit for the early analysis of external economies and the growth of productive force, an analysis which justified the fostering of certain industries in particular historical contexts (Robbins 1968, p. 116).

List was a prominent critic of free trade and an advocate of state intervention to promote economic development, but he firmly believed that the capitalist entrepreneur had a vital role to play in the process of industrialisation. He agrees with Adam Smith that free competition within a country leads to an optimum allocation of resources. But the maximum stimulation of a nation's productive powers (industrialisation potential) requires the guiding hand of the state in the absence of an entrepreneurial bourgeois class. The policies he called for were designed to provide the essential economic structure to make a market economy work more effectively. Thus under protection, he believed that competition would prevent monopoly and ensure that prices are kept down – he did not realise that a protected market and increasing returns were ideal conditions for the emergence of monopoly and cartelisation. But his insistence on the active role of the state as a stimulator and an organiser of productive activity led E.H. Carr to say 'on the theoretical side, [the title] the father of economic planning belongs rather to Friedrich List than to Karl Marx.'[20]

It is remarkable how similar were John Henry Williams's criticisms of classical trade theory to those made by List a hundred years earlier; and, for that matter, there is a close resemblance between List's arguments and those of Joan Robinson, Gunnar Myrdal and others. The fact of the matter is, however, that although the classical model is static the theory is dynamic. This anomaly, often overlooked, was noticed by Joan Robinson in respect of Ricardo's theory of profits and his foreign trade model (Robinson 1979a, vol. 5, p. 134). It is this dynamic interpretation of Ricardo that explains his opposition to the Corn Laws, as we have previously indicated. Hla Myint has pointed to dynamic elements in Smith's trade theory and shows how closely interwoven Smith's trade analysis was with his theory of economic development (Myint 1977, pp. 231–48). Mill and Marshall retained the static model, but argued for free trade as an 'engine of growth' in a framework of reasoning which emphasised technical progress and the worldwide diffusion of knowledge. The neoclassical, however, remained stuck in the static mould which emphasised allocative efficiency. Some attempts have been made to deal with the sort of questions raised by Williams and List, but the main effort has been put, not in the direction of a modification of the assumptions, but in testing the implications of the assumptions. For List, this would have been a wasteful effort. Like Keynes, he believed that a theory was useless unless it offered sensible advice on urgent policy problems – in List's case, how to get industrialisation going in a backward but potentially powerful nation.

List had no use for a theory which by its very assumptions ruled out the most important matters that cried out for investigation. He would have heartily endorsed Joan Robinson's verdict: 'the classical model for the analysis of international trade is reduced to wreckage . . . and, for better or worse, international trade must be directed by conscious policy' (Robinson 1979b, vol. 1, p. 205).

It is a valid point, however, that List misunderstood and misrepresented Adam Smith. He failed to see the dynamic elements in Smith's theory and concentrated on Smith's espousal of free trade which he rejected. List attacked Smith's 'cosmopolitan economics', but did not appreciate that the classical economists (Smith in particular) were patriots first and foremost, as Lord Robbins remarked (Robbins 1952, p. 10). List did, in fact, appreciate this; but he felt that others (for example, the bourgeois class in Germany) did not sufficiently realise it. He saw clearly that the classical economists merely provided a theoretical underpinning for a British 'imperialism of free trade' and he wanted to warn his German readers about the dangers of that.

He agreed with the reservations Smith applied to the free-trade case on the grounds of national interests; in some cases he felt Smith went too far, in others not far enough. Thus List favoured bilateral commercial treaties whereas Smith was pessimistic, had a poor opinion of them and considered that they were all based on groundless fears and served the interests of a selfish minority. List saw national safeguards in bilateral (or multilateral) treaties and thought they were 'the most effective means of gradually diminishing the respective restrictions on trade, and of leading the nations of the world gradually to freedom of international intercourse (List [1841] 1885, p. 323). (How right he was! and how wrong Smith proved to be!) List was more prophetic, in that he saw that they were the means whereby 'the reciprocal exchange of manufactured products is promoted' (List [1841] 1885, p. 324). Since the end of the Second World War progress in dismantling tariff barriers has come from hard-bargaining multilateral trade negotiations and not from mere exhortations to national leaders about the cosmopolitan benefits of generalised free trade.

Smith had recognised in a discussion on the external corn trade that in a 'second best' world of trade barriers it might be undesirable for some countries to follow a free-trade policy: 'The very bad policy of one country may thus render it in some measure dangerous and imprudent to establish what would otherwise be the best policy in another' (Smith [1776] 1976, p. 539). List agreed, pointing out that it was precisely because Britain had not adopted a free-trade policy after the Napoleonic Wars ended that agrarian countries were forced to develop their own industries. Because of the restrictive British Corn Laws they could not sell enough of their agricultural products to pay for the British manufactured goods which swamped their markets after 1815. Smith did not believe that tariffs would help to increase the amount of employment available in the country as a whole or the level of its economic activity. The extent of industry was determined by the size of its capital stock; consequently trade controls would merely push some of this capital into socially less advantageous channels where it would not go of its own accord. Yet Smith would allow the imposition of 'countervailing duties' to equalise the conditions of competition between home and foreign products in cases where the foreign products were taxed at a lower rate than domestic products. Why not then, asked List, extend this logic to cover other disabling factors (apart from differential taxation) which discriminate against domestic production?

> if the burden of taxation to which our productions are subjected, affords a just ground for imposing protective duties on the less taxed products of foreign countries, why should not also the other disadvantages to which our manufacturing industry is subjected in comparison with that of the foreigner afford just grounds for protecting our native industry against the overwhelming competition of foreign industry. (List [1841] 1885, p. 319)

Smith's categorical denial that tariffs could increase aggregate employment or output rested on the implicit assumption of full employment of all resources as the normal state of affairs. But if this condition was not fulfilled, as in the German states after 1815, then might not tariffs contribute to the activation of idle productive capacity, asked List?

For List, Smith was at his most vulnerable when he turned from the purely national interest to a cosmopolitan perspective. How splendid it would be, said Smith, if all the countries of Europe were to adopt 'the liberal system of free exportation and free importation' and the world came to 'resemble the different provinces of a great empire'. This was indeed a grand vision, one shared by List. But, first of all, the industrially backward countries must develop their productive forces and reach the same level of development as Britain. Before that time came – an event welcomed by List – those countries must safeguard and advance their industries. The adoption of a free-trade policy would merely confirm the 'insular supremacy of Great Britain'. It is true Smith referred to this vision in connection with agricultural trade, but if extended to trade in industrial goods (as the followers of Smith were advocating) then that was the result List foresaw. List's basic objection to Smith's mode of reasoning was that Smith saw everything from 'a shopkeeper's point of view' (List [1841] 1885, p. 350). He was fond of illustrating economic phenomena by taking examples from the behaviour of individual families. He simply lost sight of the global dimension of economic decision-making, of the independent existence of group, social and national actions. He was so obsessed with the shortsighted policies of the interfering mercantilist state and so enamoured of his own system of 'natural liberty' that the release of productive potential through the organising and supportive role of the state receded from his ken. His preference was for the minimal, *laissez-faire*, 'nightwatchman' state; but such a state, however admirably suited to early-nineteenth-century British conditions, was thoroughly ill-designed and ill-equipped for the task of lifting backward peoples to nationhood and industrial status.

Writing in 1929, the year of Williams' article, Viner declared that List's arguments were 'really a plea for urbanisation' and that he reinforced his infant-industry argument with 'most of the protectionist fallacies current in his time in both America and Europe'. And further, that List's references to the doctrines of the free-traders, especially Adam Smith, were 'so unfair as to be caricatures' not deserving of serious consideration 'as objective scientific analysis'. Viner felt, however, that List was 'entitled to praise as a pioneer of the historical point of view in economics' [21] It is true List was no great analyst of abstract economic phenomena, neither was he a Karl Marx who probed into the inner dynamics of capitalist production. Yet the founders of Marxism (Marx and Engels) nevertheless regarded him as the most outstanding German economist of his day 'despite the bourgeois apologetic nature of his teachings'.[22]

List used Adam Smith as a whipping-boy in his attack on the ideology of free trade, but he missed some of the subtleties of Smith's arguments. He was concerned with a narrow field of inquiry, albeit an important one: how can economic relations between nations be fruitfully analysed to throw light on economic backwardness and international income inequalities? The policies suggested for dealing with this problem were associated with protectionism and nationalism; and for this reason List's concerns were chiefly seen as a reaction to the negative aspects of foreign trade liberalism and not as a 'research programme' in their own right.

Not unnaturally, List's ideas were not well received in the home of classical political economy. British popularisers of political economy and publicists of free trade were hostile towards him and all he stood for (including the *Zollverein*). *The Times*, as well as the two great current affairs periodicals – the *Edinburgh Review* and the *Westminster Review* – carried deprecatory articles on him. The denigration of List ran in terms very similar to those echoed later by Viner: List's views were unworthy of notice; he had departed from the 'true' principles of political economy; he was an unscrupulous propagandist; he misrepresented and distorted both the teachings of political economy and the policies of Great Britain to serve unworthy nationalist ends. Thus in 1842 John Austin, a Benthamite and friend of James Mill, wrote in the *Edinburgh Review* that List's treatise *The National*

System was unworthy of notice 'considered as a system of international trade' and that it was obviously 'the work of a zealous and unscrupulous advocate striving to establish a given practical conclusion, and not the production of a dispassionate enquirer, seeking to promote the improvement of a science'.[23] *The Times* in 1847 considered List's doctrines as 'extravagant fictions' and rebuked him for spreading 'the most erroneous and absurd notion of the policy of this country'.[24] Sir Travers Twiss, a successor to Senior in the Drummond Chair of Political Economy at Oxford, dismissed List's work as being 'too extravagant to require any serious discussion, motivated as it was by the narrowest and most shortsighted of selfishness'. This was also the opinion of J.R. McCulloch.[25]

J.S. Mill's qualified endorsement of the infant-industry thesis redeemed somewhat List's reputation among British economists, but it also served to obscure List's central message. Now that List's arguments were interpreted as constituting nothing more than mere 'exceptions' to conventional doctrine – exceptions adequately accommodated within the confines of established theory – his call for a radically new approach to the problems of economic development could be studiously ignored.

Perhaps the greatest tribute to List came late in the century (1890) from an unlikely source. 'The brilliant genius and national enthusiasm of List', wrote Alfred Marshall, 'stands in contrast to the insular narrowness and self-confidence of the Ricardian school . . . he showed that in Germany and still more in America, many of its indirect effects [free trade] were evils . . . Many of his arguments were invalid, but many were not'.[26] Schumpeter said List had 'vision' – a characteristic he shared with Keynes. It is the gift for asking the right economic questions in any given historical age, or in other words, ideological perspective. 'As a scientific economist', said Schumpeter, 'List had one of the elements of greatness, namely, the grand vision of a national situation . . . Nor was List deficient in the specifically scientific requisites that must come in to implement vision if it is to bear scientific fruits' (Schumpeter 1954, p. 504).

In Germany, of course, List enjoyed an enormous reputation; not during his lifetime, but after, and especially during Bismarck's Second Reich when Germany emerged as the industrial giant which List had wanted. Joseph Dorfman noted that not long after List's death 'he was worshipped in Germany as the greatest German economist, the source of the new and supposedly unique German political economy of national power' (Dorfman 1946, p. 584). He was called 'a great German without Germany', 'Germany's *verhinderten* [handicapped] Colbert', 'an economic genius' who made 'the first real advance' in economics since Adam Smith. List also had an influence on other European protagonists of industrial protection, including Eugen Dühring, the Austrian trade theorist Richard Schüller and the twentieth-century Romanian economist Mihail Manoilescu. Dühring combined List's national economics with elements from Carey's system in his courses at the University of Berlin. Schüller (one of the critics of classical trade theory mentioned by Williams ([1929] 1949) interpreted List's concept of productive forces as an 'employment argument' for protection. According to Schüller, List's use of the concept implied the existence of unused national resources (particularly labour) which could be brought into production through the use of protective tariffs. Manoilescu was deeply impressed with List's remark that a country which engaged in agriculture only was like a man with one arm, and developed an argument for industrial protection based on the notion that industry was superior in 'productive power' to agriculture. Tariff protection for industry was necessary to shift workers out of agriculture into manufacturing. Manoilescu's protectionism differed in important respects from both Carey's and List's. For the latter, agriculture was necessary for the maintenance of balanced growth; and List desired industrialization not primarily or only for its economic benefits (that is, higher productivity), but also for the cultural and social ethos associated with it. The protectionist arguments of Schüller and Manoilescu are reviewed in more detail in Chapter 4 of the present work. There was a less acceptable, even menacing side to List's nationalist vision. In Hans Kohn's words, List was not only the father of German economic nationalism, but also 'one of the most extreme of Pan-German imperialists'.[27] List claimed that overpopulated Germany needed *Ergänzungsgebiete* (additional territories) to give it breathing-space – shades of Hitler's *Lebensraum*! His plans for Greater Germany included the acquisition of overseas colonies, a powerful navy, control of the seaports from the mouths of the Rhine to the Elbe, and the domination of *Mitteleuropa*. In his last year List personally tried unsuccessfully to bring about an Anglo-German alliance which would allow Germany to colonise the Balkans, dominate the Near East, allow England to preserve her global hegemony and act as a bulwark against the rising power of Russia and the United States. Recently List has been hailed as a precursor of the European Union (EU) and of a politically united Europe; but as Louis Snyder reminds us 'as a zealous German patriot List looked forward to European economic unification eventually under German auspices'.[28]

   Classical trade theory failed to provide adequate explanations for (a) the asymmetries in the world trading system and (b) the observed fact that specialisation among countries was largely a result of historical accident. The national economists perceived that and started a debate that was bound to occur sooner or later. List, the visionary and prophet, articulated their intellectual response with a cogency and relevance that today continues to inspire many concerned with these matters. That the message of List and the other national economists should have this perennial appeal was well expressed by Gustav Schmoller:

> All protective movements are closely connected with national sentiments, strivings after international authority, efforts towards the balance of power, and therefore will continue to exist so long as amongst the fully developed states there are others striving after economic development, and so long as the people for economic purposes have need of every weapon that stands ready for their use.[29]

NOTES

1. Williams referred to Friedrich List as one of the writers among others (Cournot, Nogaro and Schüller) who refused to accept either the premises or the conclusions of classical theory. Williams later became a senior executive of the Federal Reserve Bank of New York.
2. Gottfried Haberler admitted that the classical theory was static, but pointed out that Mill was 'not oblivious of the indirect, dynamic benefits which less developed countries in particular can derive from international trade'. See Gottfried Haberler, 'International Trade and Economic Development' – The Cairo Lectures, reprinted in Richard S. Weckstein (ed.), *Expansion of World Trade and the Growth of National Economies* (New York: Harper & Row, 1968), p. 103.
3. The expression 'productive powers' was used by Alexander Hamilton as well as by later French writers such as Jean-Antoine Chaptal, Charles Dupin and Louis Say. List adapted the concept from these French economists and acknowledged his indebtedness, but List's application of the idea was wider than theirs.
4. The debate is discussed in Bernard Semmel (1970, pp. 14–18), who first pointed out its relevance to the national economists' claims: 'Tucker anticipated the program put forward by economists of less-developed countries who sought to challenge British industrial predominance, men such as Hamilton, List and Carey', p. 18. See also George Shelton (1981, pp. 126–32); J.M. Low (1952); Maneschi (1998, pp. 31–33) and Elmslie (1995, pp. 207–16).
5. See Scottish Record Office, Kames Collection – Tucker to Kames, 6 July 1758.
6. See also British Library Add. MS. 4319, Tucker to Dr Birch, 19 May 1760.
7. See George C. Fitzpatrick (ed.), *The Writings of George Washington* (Washington, DC: 1931–44), vol. 30, p. 186.
8. The *Thoughts on Political Economy* was the first systematic treatise on economics by an American writer. The *Elements* was an enlarged second edition of this work.
9. John Rae (1796–1872) was born in Scotland, but lived most of his adult life in Canada and the United States. Rae's protectionism stemmed from his original theory of capital and interest which was outlined in his rambling but remarkably perceptive book, *Statement of Some New Principles on the Subject of Political Economy: Exposing the Fallacies of the System of Free Trade, and of Some Other Doctrines Maintained in the 'Wealth of Nations'* (1834). Besides J.S. Mill, Irving Fisher was also impressed with Rae's work and dedicated his *Rate of Interest* (1907) to the memory of Rae. For Rae's writings see the reprint in R. Warren James, *John Rae, Political Economist*, 2 vols (Toronto: University of Toronto Press, 1965).
10. For an appreciative reassessment of Phillips's work see James H. Thompson, 'Willard Phillips: A Neglected American Economist', *History of Political Economy*, 16, no. 3 (Fall 1984), pp. 405–21. In Thompson's judgement Phillips was 'one of the best economists to appear in the United States prior to the Civil War' (p. 420).
11. Henry Carey (1793–1879) wrote extensively on economics. His major work (in 3 vols)

was *Principles of Social Science (*Philadelphia, 1858–9). His protectionist ideas were first developed in *Past, Present and Future* (1848) and further elaborated in *The Harmony of Interests, Agricultural, Manufacturing and Commercial* (Philadelphia, 1851).

12. Carey, *Harmony of Interests*, p. 72.
13. Friedrich List (1789–1846) was born in the town of Reutlingen in Württemberg (south Germany) just a few days before the French Revolution broke out. He worked as a civil servant for twelve years in his native state of Württemberg until he was appointed at the age of 28 to a newly-created Chair in Public Administration at the University of Tübingen. He was forced to resign his professorship on account of his political activities and involvement with the *Handels und Gewerbsverein*. In 1819 he was elected to the lower chamber of the Württemberg Diet as a representative of Reutlingen. But again, his liberal reforming agitation antagonised the reactionary ruling authorities and List was expelled from the Assembly and sentenced to ten months' hard labour. This led to his voluntary exile, first in Paris and later in the United States until his return to Germany in 1830 and the continuation of his work on behalf of economic unity.
14. To what extent was List influenced by American protectionist writers? The answer to this question has given rise to a long-running debate among Listian scholars. In 1897 C.P. Neill made a detailed textual comparison of Raymond's *Elements* with List's *National System*. He found remarkable similarities, and concluded that although List must have read Raymond's work, the coincidences were 'not sufficient to warrant the conclusion that List took his ideas bodily from Raymond'. See Charles Patrick Neill, *Daniel Raymond, An Early Chapter in the History of Economic Theory in the United States* (Baltimore: Johns Hopkins University Press, 1897), p. 57. Margaret Hirst found equally striking similarities between Hamilton's *Report* and List's writings and suggested that List was undoubtedly influenced by Hamilton. Margaret E. Hirst, *Life of Friedrich List* (New York, 1909), pp. 114–15. An early denial of any US intellectual influence on List was made by K.T. Eheberg in his Introduction to *Friedrich List: Das Nationale System der Politischen Oekonomie* (Stuttgart, 1853): 'The beneficial influence exerted on List by his stay in America arose from practical circumstances and not from printed books' (p. 149). List's latest biographer, W.O. Henderson, points out that List was already a critic of classical economics before he arrived in the United States, and that he was not therefore 'converted to protectionism by studying the works of American writers' (W.O. Henderson, *Friedrich List: Economist and Visionary 1789–1846* (London: Frank Cass, 1983), p. 155. But Henderson also believes that List's involvement in the US tariff controversy broadened his views, and that when he wrote his letters to Ingersoll he was influenced by the writings of US protectionists such as Hamilton and Matthew Carey. William Notz, in his study 'List in America' came to essentially the same conclusion. See William Notz, 'Friedrich List in America', *American Economic Review*, 16, no. 2 (June 1926), pp. 248–65.
15. The three titles cited in the text are included in List's collected works published in 10 vols under the auspices of the Friedrich List Gesellschaft: *Friedrich List: Schriften, Reden, Briefe,* ed. Erwin von Beckerath, Edgar Salin, et al. (Berlin: Hobbing, 1927–36). References to List's basic work, *The National System of Political Economy* (cited in the text as List [1841] 1885) are taken from the English translation by Sampson S. Lloyd.
16. Quoted in K.W. Rowe, *Matthew Carey: A Study in American Economic Development* (Baltimore: Johns Hopkins University Press, 1933), p. 48.
17. See *Friedrich List: Schriften, Reden, Briefe*, vol. 6, p. 366 cited in note 15 above. List's discussion at this point and elsewhere suggests the hypothesis that dominant countries would always support an open, liberal world trading system, while laggards would prefer a controlled system. The evidence indicates that this is indeed the case.
18. Quoted by Mike Marqusee, 'Whitewashing the Past', *The Guardian*, 24 May, 2002. In their writings, Indian historians do not fail to mention the tripling of the land tax and other British agricultural 'reforms' which led to the dreadful Bengal famine of 1770: 'Ten million people, which was more than a third of the population of Bengal, died and a third of the land turned into jungle.' See M.P. Prabhakaran, *The Historical Origin of*

India's Underdevelopment: A World-System Perspective (Langham, MD and London: University Press of America, 1990), p. 151.

19. See Charles Gide, *Cours d'économie politique* (Paris: Sirey, 1931), part II, p. 47; Eduard Heiman, *History of Economic Doctrines* (London: Oxford University Press, 1945), p. 132; Rudolf Hilferding, *The Economic Policy of Finance Capital*, edited with an Introduction by Tom Bottomore (London: Routledge & Kegan Paul, 1981), p. 304.

20. E.H. Carr, *The Soviet Impact on the Western World* (London, 1946), p. 23.

21. Viner's review of vol. 4 of List's collected works in *Journal of Political Economy* (June 1929), reprinted in J. Viner, *The Long View and the Short, Studies in Economic Theory and Policy* (Glencoe, Ill.: The Free Press of Glencoe, 1958), pp. 389–91.

22. A. Anikin, *A Science in its Youth (Pre-Marxian Political Economy)* (Moscow: Progress Publishers, 1975), p. 334.

23. 'List on the Principles of the German Customs Union. Dangers to British Industry and Commerce', *Edinburgh Review*, no. 152 (July 1842), pp. 521–2.

24. *The Times* (16 January 1847), p. 4.

25. Travers Twiss, *View of the Progress of Political Economy since the 16th Century* (London, 1847), p. 248. McCulloch's opinion is in his *Literature of Political Economy* (London, 1846).

26. Marshall, *Principles*, 8th ed. (London, 1936), p. 727. Marshall did, in fact, make a special trip to the United States to study the practical effects of the theories of Carey and the other American protectionists.

27. Kohn was one of the pioneer investigators of nationalism. The remark is contained in his book *The Idea of Nationalism* (New York, 1944), p. 322.

28. Louis L. Snyder, *Roots of German Nationalism* (Bloomington, Indiana University Press, 1978), pp. 1–34.

29. Gustav Schmoller, in 'Verhandlungen des Vereins für Sozialpolitik', *Schriften des Vereins für Sozialpolitik* (Berlin, 1902), p. 270.

4. The economics of trade and protection in the age of Marshall

In this chapter we review some new arguments for protection and other statements of the free trade case that surfaced during the transition period from the classical age to the early development of neoclassical economics – a period that might, with a certain amount of chronological latitude, be called the 'Age of Marshall'. During this period there ensued in general economics a gradual but continuous shift from the Ricardian one-factor labour theory of value to a subjective theory of value, namely, supply and demand (utility). Costs of production came to be treated not in absolute but in relative terms, that is, as alternatives foregone. However, despite this shift of direction in general economics, some notion of 'real' costs determining production was retained in trade theory well into the 1930s. The classical trade model survived the 'marginal' revolution' of the 1870s for three reasons: (1) Mill's incorporation of the demand side in his analysis of international values. (2) The transformation of Ricardo's labour theory of value into Marshallian 'real cost' theory. Even when the labour theory was retained, this was tolerated since it was simply illustrative of the gains from trade and did not clash with ideology and substantive matters – for example, over the contentious issue of income distribution among social classes. (3) The concerns of trade theory with efficient allocations of given resources and the rational behaviour of economic agents who exchange commodities on world markets, fitted in nicely with the 'exchange paradigm' ('catallactics') which came into vogue with the 'marginalists'.[1]

In dealing with these early neoclassical contributions to trade theory we start with Cournot, the forerunner. Augustin Cournot (1801–77) was a major figure in the shaping of the basic structure of twentieth-century economics. He was among the first to model the actions of economic agents in terms of optimising behaviour which was therefore amenable to analysis as solutions to maximisation and minimisation problems. Cournot pioneered the treatment of economic concepts such as 'demand' and 'cost' as being in essence functional relationships (mutual interdependence) that could be expressed by behavioural equations between variables, for example, a change in quantity demanded with respect to a change in price or of cost as a function of price. Those functions could be expressed as equations and

curves and were assumed to be continuous, even differentiable, and independent of time.

In trade theory, Cournot's signal contribution was the analysis of interspatial price equilibrium in the form of the 'back-to-back' diagram – the
type of analysis used by Cunynghame, Pigou, Schüller, Barone and subsequently by many others to this day. Cournot's explorations in trade theory
were in three areas: (1) the theory of interspatial price equilibrium, that is,
the effects of trade on markets previously isolated; (2) a welfare analysis of
the effects of trade on real national income (including an argument for protection); and (3) the theory of foreign exchange.

For our present purposes we focus on item (2), his analysis of the gains
from trade and protection.

4.1 EFFECTS OF TRADE ON INCOME

In chapter 12 of *Recherches* (Cournot [1838] 1897) Cournot presents an
argument designed to show that the removal of trade restrictions leaves a
country worse off than under protection. He investigates the effects of a
move to free trade – that is, the effects of the removal of a tariff on a single
commodity – and got peculiar results. For Cournot, according to the principle of 'compensation of demand', only the impact effect matters, which
is consistent with his treatment of price changes in a closed economy.
Cournot shows that there will be a 'decrease in real income' of the importing country, because imports reduce a country's real income. He does not
adequately take into account the effect of trade on the income of consumers but only the direct effects on the income of producers – so no reallocation of resources. He finds that in the exporting country the change in
real income is always positive, but in the case of the importing country there
is a 'decrease in real income'. Cournot concludes: imports diminish a
country's real income (Cournot [1838] 1897, p. 157). He specifies several
assumptions and qualifications to his peculiar procedure. Thus he does not
include in his calculation of the 'real changes in social income' the advantages accruing to consumers in the importing country who are able to
dispose of their income in a more satisfactory manner as a consequence of
the price reduction on the imported good, that is, the cash equivalent of the
utility that consumers derive from their purchases of the imported good in
preference to other domestically produced goods. He cannot do this, he
says, because 'this advantage is incapable of valuation . . . and does not
directly affect the national wealth in the commercial and mathematical
sense of this term' (Cournot [1838] 1897, p. 156). What Cournot excludes
from the calculation of the net benefits of trade is, of course, the increase

in consumer surplus (the utility gain) – an omission which later economists reckoned a major weakness of his approach. Cournot recognises that in the case of non-competitive imports, what he calls 'exotic' commodities, the national income of the importing country does not experience any change – the import of exotic commodities does not displace domestic production; hence no effect on the incomes of producers. He explicitly states that his analysis is confined to the instance of only one commodity, M, being imported into the home country (the importing country), and that this must of necessity have as counterpart the export of a commodity of equal value from the home country; but he says that 'we have shown that this increase in exports from the home country . . . was more than offset by the impoverishment of the home producers of commodity M in consequence of importation. We have therefore accounted for all the data of the problem' (Cournot [1838] 1897, pp. 162–3).

Cournot's results, much at variance with those derived by the use of comparative-cost reasoning, provoked a barrage of criticism from writers as early as 1844 down to Samuelson, including such acknowledged authorities as Edgeworth and Viner;[2] but as a piece of technical analysis it was path-breaking. Criticism was directed at several points of Cournot's premises, arguments and conclusion: (1) his single-commodity model was inadequate for the purpose in hand, in that it resulted in an unrealistic, static short-run view of the effects of trade on real income. (2) Because of this, the final effects of the removal of a restriction on imports were obscured, since Cournot assumed that the prices of other goods (apart from the import commodity) and other incomes remained unchanged. This prevented him from dealing with the full reallocative effects on production and consumption. Thus, in the importing country, the lifting of trade restrictions and the consequent increase in imports would be matched by a corresponding increase in exports of equal value (given mobility of resources and the maintenance of full employment). Price changes affecting import and export commodities would induce changes in income and output such that export production expands as import-competing production contracts. Corresponding changes in income and output, but in the opposite direction, would take place in the exporting country. Since the movements in the composition of output, income and consumption are symmetrical (both countries considered) there is no reason to expect that one country would end up worse than the other in terms of real income; or, what amounts to the same thing, no reason why there should not be an equal sharing of the benefits of trade. (3) Cournot fails to deal satisfactorily with the consumption effects because of his excessive concentration on the income-effect of production changes. The lack of a 'utility' or welfare criterion led Cournot to underestimate the consumption gains in the importing country. Later critics who adopted the idea of consumer surplus made this point, for example, Edgeworth, Bertrand and Landry. There were also some minor points of criticism, such as Cournot's use of money prices or values to estimate changes in real national income, and related to this, the inappropriateness of Cournot's calculation in terms of gross revenue or income instead of net income (gross income *less* costs).

Cournot's analysis and results were savagely attacked by Viner in 1937. Viner declares that Cournot's argument 'scarcely deserves attention on its own account' but cannot be wholly ignored since it is often appealed to by protectionists as a refutation of the doctrine of comparative costs (Viner [1937] 1955, p. 586).[3] Viner summarises the criticisms made by previous writers of this piece of Cournot's work, and makes an additional critical comment on Cournot's claim that his procedure of dealing with trade changes wholly in terms of money values is unobjectionable, since J.S. Mill had explicitly stated that the introduction of money would make no difference to the results obtained by barter analysis. Viner's comment is that this is an invalid inference from Mill's dictum which provides no warrant for an analysis wholly in money prices unsupported by comparative real costs. Viner implied that Cournot would have come to more sensible (orthodox) results if (a) he had started with comparative cost differences and had then translated these into money prices and (b) if he had included a satisfactory measure of consumer surplus. But Viner concludes, Cournot's analysis 'fails to deal intelligibly even with the pecuniary aspects of the problem' (Viner [1937] 1955, p. 589).

J.W. Angell – 'the only writer who finds sense and significance in Cournot's thesis', according to Viner ([1937] 1955, p. 587, n. 7) – finds the clue to Cournot's peculiar results in an 'unstated premise as to the probable loss from a displacement of domestic industry' (Angell 1926, p. 244), that is, lack of mobility of productive resources which remain unemployed when the import-competing industry contracts upon the removal of tariff protection. But in reply to an earlier critic, Carl Heinrich Hagen, who made essentially the same observation, Cournot maintained that on the contrary he had assumed a transfer of resources and had fully taken into account the generation of income caused by such transfer to more profitable employment. However, Cournot was unable to persuade anyone that he had really done so, since it is nowhere to be found in his calculations.

The confusion surrounding the reception of Cournot's analysis of this topic stems largely from the fact that no one was quite clear what Cournot's purpose really was in undertaking this analysis. Was he engaging in a purely positive exercise, the examination of 'a concrete economic phenomenon', namely the measurement of trade-related changes in income? Or was he outlining a technique for measuring the gains from trade? Many of

Cournot's critics understood him to have been quite resolved on the second question, despite the declaration that his objective was to study the 'variations in the Social Income resulting from the communication of markets'. The majority of critics wedded to comparative-cost reasoning (and this includes notably Edgeworth, Bastable and Viner) interpreted Cournot as really having been involved in finding an argument for tariff protection through a dubious exercise in national-income accounting based on an obscure notion of 'the principle of compensation of demands'. In support of this understanding of Cournot's purpose they might have referred to his declaration that his analysis of the effects of trade on social income

> when considered in its theoretical aspect, can be reduced to very simple terms of which the mere statement, by overthrowing false systems, opens the way to the practical knowledge which essentially concerns the destiny of nations. It is on this account that the considerations which we are here examining appear to us something more than mere intellectual exercises or chimerical abstractions. (Cournot [1838] 1897, p. 151)

By 'false systems' does Cournot mean the classical theory of comparative costs and its corollaries? A balanced reappraisal of Cournot's contribution has recently been presented by Theocaris. He refers to the confusion among writers about the meaning and significance of Cournot's analysis. He traces the diversity of critical opinions, and the muddle, to Cournot's use of the term 'real changes in income'. For Cournot, he says, a 'real change in income' means a change in the quantity of goods that a given change in money income commands – it 'is therefore an index of changes in quantities over which one has command and has nothing to do with measuring benefits, which is an entirely different thing' (Theocaris 1983, p. 198). Thus, in the importing country the fall in the income of producers, consequent upon the reduction of the price of the single commodity, all other prices and incomes remaining the same, means that command over goods is less compared with autarky. That was all Cournot wanted to prove – to arrive at conclusions about the effects of trade upon income within his restrictive assumptions. Theocaris therefore feels that it is unfair to charge Cournot with putting forward a flawed procedure for measuring the gains from trade. That was not his intention. Nevertheless, Cournot did suggest that his analysis could offer guidance on important policy decisions, presumably protection versus free trade. On this score, though, there are certainly serious weaknesses with Cournot's procedure. His technique was unequal to the task, which was essentially one of estimating the effects on economic welfare of a change in trade policy. As Theocaris indicates, the source of the misunderstanding created in other writers' minds lay in Cournot's attempt to deduce these basically general-equilibrium effects from a partial equilibrium model of income changes where all other prices and incomes are held constant (Theocaris 1983, p. 199).

The classical and early neoclassical economists tackled Cournot's problem with a different technique – the simple general-equilibrium model of comparative cost. They looked at changes in prices, outputs and national product throughout an economy and compared these with changes in another country, and could not therefore understand Cournot's procedure of looking at a single market and deducing from this estimates of changes in national or social income. Cournot's failure to incorporate the two-way flow of commodities involved in trade, and the tracing of this back to systematic differences in structures of costs and prices, accounted for his ambiguous reasoning and spurious results. One gets the distinct impression that it was less Cournot's faulty computations and more his general protectionist conclusion which provoked the neoclassical writers' ire, as Viner's remarks suggest. The irony of it all, though, is that Cournot's method did not die a natural death. It was revived by economists at the turn of the century, and an amended version of it has been used ever since to show how changes in trade flows in a single commodity affect production and consumption in the domestic market. It can also be used to quantify the gains from trade and show the effects of a tariff in a single market, as all modern introductory texts do.

Cournot on Protection

Cournot was, of course, a protectionist, apparently much influenced by Friedrich List;[4] although judging from his 1838 analysis of the profitability of import duties he was persuaded by the protectionist case at the level of pure theory before he encountered List's critique of free trade. Cournot's protectionist position is set out fully in the last section of his *Principes* written twenty-five years later, after the *Recherches*, where he deals with questions of economic policy. He starts from the general classical position that consumption is the end of all economic activity, but adopts a wider perspective on consumption benefits, in that besides individual consumption he includes public (or collective) consumption and considers the intergenerational streams of consumption benefits. A *laissez-faire* policy aimed at 'wealth now' is contrasted with an optimal policy which maximises the power to create 'wealth in the future'. The provision of the flows of current and future consumption benefits cannot be left entirely to the free market. State intervention, apart from all the customary functions, is necessary for the creation of productive force; for it is only through the development of the full productive potential of the economy that future consumption benefits can be satisfactorily ensured. On this premise, Cournot, like List,

supports the infant-industry argument for the protection and encouragement of selected industries:

> When a new industry has just been born (even that which is destined to have the
> most vigorous growth) must it not at first be sheltered and get acclimatized and
> all those employed by it, must they not make their apprenticeships? (Cournot
> 1863, p. 456)

Presumably recalling John Stuart Mill's endorsement of the argument, he
says that 'nobody doubts anymore, in principle, the utility of a temporary
encouragement' (Cournot 1863, p. 456). No hard-and-fast rules can be laid
down concerning the level and duration of the protective tariff; it depends
on the circumstances. Cournot presents his case in cool, moderate language, in contrast to List's aggressive and polemical style, relying on the
skilful use of rhetorical appeals for persuasive effect. Government intervention is necessary to stimulate the growth of productive forces – by reducing
uncertainty over investment projects, undertaking infrastructural and
other projects that are socially beneficial but privately unprofitable, encouraging savings, and so on. But without restrictions on international trade
such measures cannot realise their full potential; the nation will inevitably
lag behind others more fully equipped with industrial capacity and skill. In
addition, international commerce needs the protection of the state.
Business interests 'need a flag to cover them, which will make them
respected in the world; and this flag can only be that of a great nation'
(Cournot 1863, p. 493). Industry needs the guiding hand of the state primarily to ensure that private and social interests converge towards the virtuous path of growth and development. He had no time for '*laissez-faire*
dogmas' and was critical of what he called 'the dubious notion of the
natural harmony of economic interests' espoused by native writers like
Bastiat and Dunoyer. *Laissez-faire* free-trade propagandists had not shown
to everyone's satisfaction that private and social interests would necessarily and always coincide under the influence of free market forces. Why, then,
asks Cournot, 'should government encouragement not be that additional
force which might make the resultant of individual interests coincide in
direction with that of the general interest?' (Cournot 1863, p. 458).

Despite his general protectionist stance Cournot indicated that he was
aware of the dangers of promiscuous protectionism. Protection once
granted to a few deserving branches of industry tends in practice to be
extended in an indiscriminate manner to all and sundry under the pressure
of vested interests: 'The more the protective system becomes completed the
more difficult it becomes to appreciate its consequences and measure its
effect.' If the intended orderly protectionist policy threatens to become a
jungle of trade barriers, and this is envisaged, then 'the maxim *laissez-faire*,

even if it does not have (as some would like it) the value of an axiom or a theorem, must definitely be preferred in many cases as an adage of practical wisdom' (Cournot 1863, pp. 461, 462).[5] Cournot's assault on orthodox opinion was therefore less an attack on the desirability of free trade and more in the nature of an indictment of domestic *laissez-faire*. However, Cournot hastens to add that his judgement derives solely from theoretical investigations, that he does not write in support of any social system, and that there is an immense gulf in passing from theory to governmental applications.

4.2   MARSHALL

Marshall systematically developed and refined by means of geometrical and analytical methods the classical theory of international trade, in particular the ideas originally expounded by John Stuart Mill. He combined Mill's analysis of demand (in terms of reciprocal demand) with the older emphasis on supply. Marshall argues that the international exchange ratio (terms of trade) is influenced not only by demand, but also by the ability of a country to adjust supplies of its own products to the demands of foreign markets; although in practice the influence of cost factors is pushed into the background by the analytical assumption that each country specialises in one product. In addition to the presentation of Mill's reciprocal demand method in diagrammatic form, Marshall tries to improve upon labour time as a measure of costs (that is, he includes capital and other production costs along with labour costs) and to deal with the problem of aggregation over commodities. This he does by means of the concept of a 'representative bale' of a country's factors of production. In the classical spirit, he wants to express the costs of production and gains from trade in real terms (effort, abstinence, and so on). Ricardo had measured the value of commodities in labour time; but, says Marshall, 'it seems better to suppose either country to make up her exports into representative "bales"; that is, bales each of which represents uniform aggregate investments of her labour (of various qualities) and of her capital' (Marshall [1923] 1965, p. 157). Each 'bale' corresponds to a fixed input of labour and capital (or factors of production in general). An increase in the efficiency of the factors or a reduction in costs will cause the size of the bale, reckoned in exportable goods, to increase. So although the costs of production were expressed in real terms, the value of commodities was not reckoned simply in terms of labour time. With the classical labour theory there was no means of comparing the costs of commodities produced with different capital structures or different qualities of labour – particularly when applied to more than two countries and two commodities. The representative bale was an effort to deal with the problem of aggregation and it appeared more realistic than the traditional two-good (linen and cloth) model. These aggregates were then treated as the units in which national demand was expressed in world markets. But these aggregates were not clearly related to consumer tastes, for example, the preferences of individuals; because of this limitation the bale concept was not widely used by other writers.

Marshall represents reciprocal demand schedules as curves. The curves are complex; they attempt to represent general equilibrium in trade. Each point on the curve is a point of potential equilibrium, and a movement along it presupposes that the economy has rearranged its internal trade to conform to the new equilibrium conditions. Marshall uses these curves to examine the stability of world markets, the influence of elasticity on trade flows and effects on the terms of trade of shifts in the curve, for example, in relation to import duties. We select for review here his treatment of the gains from trade, the net benefit from foreign trade, the analysis of tariffs, protection and economic development.

Gains from Trade and the Terms of Trade

Mill had claimed that rich countries gain less from trade than poor countries (Mill [1848] 1920, p. 163). There are two aspects to this: (1) a general increase in productivity or neutral technological change may lead to a worsening of the rich country's terms of trade since the increased output could only be sold on world markets on less favourable terms (that is, at reduced prices), and (2), because the demand for foreign commodities is greater, the terms of trade are turned against the rich country.

Marshall referred to the role of supply factors in modifying this conclusion. He agreed that small countries tend to gain more from trade; but Marshall nevertheless pointed out that the rich country can develop (invent) new products, has extensive and highly organised transport and commercial relations with many markets and 'need not push any one variety of any product on a market which shows signs of being glutted with that variety' and 'has better opportunities for adapting her output to the receptivity of various markets than the poor one is likely to have' (Marshall [1923] 1965, p. 169). The relevance of supply conditions to the terms of trade in the case of an advanced industrial country was also emphasised in another passage; Marshall's reasoning was: 'the elasticity of her effective demand for foreign goods is governed not only by her wealth and the elasticity of the desires of her population for them; but also by her ability to adjust the supplies of her own goods of various kinds to the demands of foreign markets' (Marshall [1923] 1965, p. 167). He was convinced that the demand for imports by an industrial country was generally elastic and that the world's demand for its goods was also relatively elastic; but there were exceptions – for example, the British demand for foreign wheat was probably inelastic and the foreign demand for British coal was also inelastic.

The Net Benefit from Foreign Trade

In *Money, Credit and Commerce* Marshall suggested as a measure of a country's 'net benefit' from its foreign trade the excess of the number of 'representative bales' that it would be willing to give up for the quantity of bales it imports, over the amount it actually trades at the equilibrium 'rate of interchange' or terms of trade (Marshall [1923] 1965, pp. 161–3). The gain is therefore the amount of the export commodity of which the country could be deprived, and still be as well off as in a 'no-trade' situation. It was an application of his concept of 'consumer surplus' to the problem – the maximum amount of money a consumer would be willing to pay for a commodity and the amount she actually pays, the gain being conceived as the area between the two prices bounded by the demand curve. Applied to the gains from trade expressed in terms of specific product prices, the 'net benefit' measure is simply the sum of the excesses of the unit prices at which a country would have purchased successive amounts of imports over the equilibrium terms of trade. Marshall developed an ingenious graphical construction incorporating the country's offer curve to show the total surplus or net benefit, reckoned in terms of representative bales of export goods, as a triangular area (under the import demand curve) representing the sum of the series of unit surpluses.[6] Viner finds fault with Marshall's procedure; in fact, he says, the results are 'invalid' (Viner [1937] 1955, p. 571). Marshall's measure exaggerates the country's net benefit from trade because he implicitly assumed that the importing country's offer curve remained the same whether the country paid the equilibrium price or the maximum price it was willing to pay for the intra-marginal units of imports – that is, Marshall assumed constancy of the marginal utility of exportables. This is an unwarranted assumption, argues Viner, for since a given number of imported bales costs more if the maximum price was paid, the marginal utility of exportables must be greater. This being the case, the country will offer fewer export bales in return for a marginal import bale if previous bales were paid for at the maximum price rather than the equilibrium price. Hence Marshall's measure produces an overestimate of the gain.

Marshall's measure was an attempt to find an objective counterpart to the idea of total utility which could be applied to the gains from trade; but he mistakenly believed that the offer curve could be identified with a total utility curve, and this was responsible for his dubious results, as Viner showed (Viner [1937] 1955, pp. 571–5).

Consequently, few economists followed Marshall's attempt to apply consumer surplus analysis when working in a general-equilibrium framework. However, in partial-equilibrium work (e.g. to show the economic effects of the imposition of a tariff on the product of a single industry), Marshallian surplus analysis found a place and is now a standard tool of analysis in such partial-equilibrium treatments.

In Marshall's time, a more promising search for some index of the net benefit from the total trade of a country was undertaken by Edgeworth. He derived a 'no gain from trade' curve (indifference curve) based on a general utility function and related it to the country's offer curve. The gain from trade he measured as the distance between this curve and the indifference curve (Edgeworth 1925, pp. 31–47). Edgeworth's device, however, was not a quantitative indicator; it showed only the direction of the change in the amount of gain. Subsequent developments in demand theory led to the abandonment of measurable utility in favour of ratios of marginal utilities, and this factor reinforced the neglect of Marshallian surplus analysis. It was only after Hicks' rehabilitation of consumer surplus theory in 1941 that the concept came to be seen as a theoretically valid one. Bhagwati and Johnson [1960](1972) discussed the various ways in which this could be done in the light of Hicks' reconstruction.[7] They identified six alternative measures for a single country (Marshallian surplus, compensating variation or equivalent variation, each measured in terms of either exportables or importables) and illustrated the cases with the aid of 'no trade' indifference curves in a general-equilibrium framework. What Bhagwati and Johnson did was to show precisely how theoretically meaningful measures of a country's gain from trade could be devised. However, as Currie, Murphy and Schmitz rightly note, 'any attempt to estimate the actual gain of a country from foreign trade would lead to highly dubious results'.[8] Marshall's vision of a simple, objective (quantifiable) measure of a country's trading gains proved elusive, and the quest taken up by later neoclassical economists ran into a dead-end. Ironically, Marshall's concept of economic surplus – a concept originally due to the French engineer-economist, Jules Dupuit – retained its place in international trade theory not in the form he proposed, but as he used it in his analysis of domestic trade problems, that is, partial-equilibrium welfare analysis.

The idea of consumer surplus figures prominently in modern debates about protection vs. free trade. For the free trader, national economic welfare is measured by command over goods and services; and since all citizens, capitalists and workers alike, are necessarily consumers, everyone is better off when given the opportunity to buy from the cheapest source. Free trade, which provides that opportunity, therefore maximises the sum of consumer surplus from trade. Interfere with the free international flow of goods and services, and you reduce the total of national income that can be spent on the consumption of various goods and services, that is, you diminish the nation's consumer surplus from international trade.

The Analysis of Tariffs

Marshall used his curves to analyse the effects of the imposition of duties, and dealt with cases of both elastic and inelastic reciprocal demand (or offer) curves. His results were in line with classical economists like Mill, Torrens and Senior – but shown graphically within an analytical framework. The imposition of a tariff can improve the terms of trade of a country large enough to influence world prices. The size of the improvement may be large if the government spends the tariff proceeds on the country's export good. Such gains are, however, likely to be offset by losses from resource misallocation and the distortion of consumer choice. Moreover, in practice, Marshall thought that the possibility of rigging the terms of trade was extremely limited. The reciprocal demand of the foreign country must have a low elasticity and the country's own reciprocal demand a high elasticity. Retaliation by the foreign country can nullify the gain; and furthermore, the foreign country can divert its exports to third-country free trade markets (in the realistic multi-country case). Marshall's position was therefore quite classical – the belief that in the long run the scope for nationally profitable gains at the expense of trading partners was severely restricted.

Marshall discusses the case where tariffs are imposed across-the-board, that is, the effects of general tariffs. Having done the analysis in real terms, that is, in terms of 'representative bales', he shows that the conclusion can be stated in terms of gold prices. Gold flows and consequent changes in price levels (including money-wage levels) will adjust to the new terms of trade in equilibrium. The purchasing power of money in the tariff-imposing country will be affected (that is, lowered) by its tariff policy – tariffs will alter the general level of prices. Hence the real increase in price consequent upon the tariff may be less when redistribution of gold is considered: 'the real value that her people give in return for the foreign goods . . . are a little lower than is suggested by the high prices which they pay' (Marshall [1923] 1965, p. 212, n. 1). Mill had previously discussed this in the context of the monetary adjustment process, and said that the tariff-imposing country would obtain imports relatively cheaper consequent upon the reduction in the relative price of its import good in the outside world. The domestic price of imports would exceed what it previously was by less than the full amount of the duty, while consumers' means of purchasing them would be increased by the rise in their money incomes. Thus, in real terms, the foreigner pays a part of the duty. In general, however, Marshall shows the real effects are independent of money in the long run. The shift in the terms of trade will cause welfare changes. In the case of an adverse movement in the terms of trade, it means an increase in the quantity of the produce of her labour and capital that the country has to give in return for a given quantity of the other. Both the terms of trade and the incidence of the duties would be determined by the relative elasticities of reciprocal demands in the two countries.

Marshall on Free Trade, Tariffs and Protection

In this section we briefly summarise Marshall's views on these issues:

1. 'Taxing the Foreigner'
Concerning the possibility of taxing the foreigner through a favourable terms-of-trade shift induced by tariffs Marshall's writings contain many variations, summarised in this passage:

> There has, indeed, never been a country, the whole of whose exports were in such urgent demand, that she could compel foreigners to pay any large part of any taxes she imposed on her exports. (Marshall [1923] 1965, p. 192)

A country is not likely to be able to throw the burden of its import duties upon foreign countries 'unless, either all the exports consist of things of which she has at least a partial monopoly; or she is the only important consumer of most of the commodities which she imports from those countries' (Marshall [1923] 1965, p. 198).

Britain was able to tax the foreigner in the first half of the nineteenth century, he says, but not now: because (1) British technology has become the common property of all countries in the West, and some countries have even surpassed Britain, and (2) the growth of population in Britain has made her demand more urgent for some of her imports. However, in his early writings on trade, he felt that Britain could 'throw upon her neighbours some of the burden of an export duty on coal', and he produced current statistical evidence to show the possibility of so doing. He also suggested that the Americans could do the same with their cotton exports. 'England in selling her coal to foreign nations, is in some measure selling to strangers the birthright of her children that are to come' (Marshall, in Whitaker 1975, pp. 67, 70). There was therefore a strong case for the imposition of a duty on the export of steam coal from Britain, despite the fact that such a duty would appear niggardly and illiberal. Several years later, when the British government introduced an export duty on coal payable from 1901, Marshall strongly objected to the measure in a letter to *The Times*. The tax presented many technical difficulties, he wrote; it was not worth the disturbance it was bound to cause, and moreover, it was 'a breach of international comity . . . while we are in a specially defenceless position against some export duties that certain other countries might conceivably levy'.[9]

2. The infant industry argument

Marshall recognised the validity of the infant-industry argument for protection, and criticised the older British economists for ignoring the fact that 'protection to immature industries is a national good' and that 'it would have been foolish for nations with immature industries to adopt England's system pure and simple'. However, his American experience convinced him that the infant-industry argument could be misapplied, since it afforded excessive protection to 'industries which were already strong enough to do without it' in the United States (Marshall [1923] 1965, pp. 217, 219). Marshall criticises British economists for not taking the infant-industry argument seriously, remarking, their 'treatment of this question generally has been timid and weak'; but he credits J.S. Mill for giving a clear statement of the case.[10] Marshall writes, 'when John Stuart Mill ventured to tell the English people that some arguments for Protection in new countries were scientifically valid, his friends spoke of it in anger . . . as his one sad departure from the sound principles of economic rectitude' (Pigou 1925, p. 259). Marshall was against the imposition of retaliatory tariffs against countries which levied discriminatory duties on British goods as (a) a method of forcing them to reduce their tariffs, and (b) as a cure for unemployment. Experience did not afford any ground for believing it would achieve either of those ends, and, moreover, 'It is easier to begin than to end a war of hostile tariffs' (Marshall in Whitaker 1975, p. 87). Earlier, before the lurch to general protectionism in Europe, he thought an additional argument against the British use of such taxes was that other countries might delay going over to Free Trade if they saw that Great Britain could easily be persuaded to levy discriminatory duties.

3. On protection

Marshall had been a strong supporter of free trade policies ever since 1875 when he visited the United States to study protection on the spot. As a result of that experience, he came away quite settled in his mind that, 'if an American, I should unhesitatingly vote for Free Trade', mainly on account of the political corruption involved in tariff lobbying in a democratic society and consideration of the interests of the agricultural classes (Pigou

1925, p. 263). He contested the arguments of the American protectionists that high wages meant they could not compete with European manufacturers except with the aid of protective tariffs, and also disputed the claim that protection tended to diminish fluctuations in prices, wages and employment. Marshall's role in the British tariff controversy of 1903 will be discussed in Chapter 7.

Some writers notice a curious disjunction between theory and practice in Marshall's thought on the subject of protection. He disapproves of protectionism when he sees it in operation, yet as Jha notes, 'his theoretical writings had a contrary effect' (Jha 1973, p. 31). After all, Marshall was the first neoclassical economist to treat external economies and increasing returns in a fairly rigorous manner.[11] Adam Smith had pointed out the benefits to be derived from large-scale production, and Marshall himself observed that in the century following Smith's work, 'England's export trade has exerted a quiet but constant influence in developing broad inventions and economies of manufacture' and that 'such economies when they have once been obtained are not readily lost' (Whitaker 1975, pp. 145, 164). It appeared to Jha, therefore, that 'Marshall's concept of external economies and his emphasis on the desirability of promoting increasing returns in industries reinforced the case for the protection of manufactures in the underdeveloped countries, brought forward by Hamilton and List' (Jha 1973, p. 31). Why, then, did Marshall believe that for a country like Britain, 'a Protective policy ... would be an unmixed and grievous evil' (Pigou 1925, p. 263) and disapprove of American protectionism? It is clear that what bothered Marshall was the *practice* of protectionism, even when a theoretically valid case could be made out for it in special circumstances. He did not credit politicians with having the skill, judgement and integrity in the degree necessary for the implementation of a rational protective policy. A protective system, like any measure of government intervention in a democracy, was open to political abuse under the clamour of vested interests. The great virtue of free trade (and its irresistible attraction) for Marshall is that 'it is not a device, but the absence of any device'. As such it is immune to political mismanagement and therefore the advantage of free trade 'may continue to outweigh the series of small gains which could be obtained by any manipulation of tariffs, however scientific and astute' (Marshall [1923] 1965, p. 220). The remark about free trade being the absence of a device or policy was good rhetoric, but a trifle disingenuous; of course, for nineteenth-century Britain free trade was itself a policy, and some historians write about 'the imperialism of free trade'. Elsewhere, Marshall himself wrote that 'because it was clearly to the interests of England that her manufactures should be admitted free by other countries', any Englishman who questioned such a policy was denounced as unpatriotic. (Pigou 1925, pp. 258–9).

Marshall's attitude to protection and free trade was thus classical in spirit, close to the 'rent-seeking' view of Adam Smith, in fact. He himself believed that free trade could not be justified solely on 'absolute a priori reasoning'; that changing circumstances might, after careful consideration, signal new departures from established commercial policies – in particular, limited protection may be necessary at certain stages of development; and perhaps such intervention could not do much harm in the case of certain countries. Thus, he claimed, on account of its vast natural resources and large domestic market, 'foreign trade is not necessary to the United States'; consequently protection 'could not do her very much harm' (Marshall [1923] 1965, p. 222) and the expansion of the protected industries compensated for the economic loss. He praised the *Zollverein* as 'one of the most important movements towards free trade that the world has ever seen' (Marshall [1923] 1965, p. 222) – presumably on the ground that its trade-creating gains outweighed the trade-diverting effects. The *Zollverein* was in the forefront in the negotiation of commercial treaties incorporating the 'most-favoured-nation' (MFN) clause during 1860–70. Much of the impetus and momentum came from Rudolf von Delbrück.

Trade, Technology and Economic Development

In his classic history of production and distribution theories, George Stigler commented on an important characteristic of Marshall's work – that 'Marshall was so concerned with historical economic development that he had relatively small patience with the theoretical economics of a stationary state' (Stigler 1941, p. 62). Everyone knows the famous baffling quotation from Marshall, that 'the causes which determine the economic progress of nations belong to the study of international trade.'[12]

In his theory of international trade and even more so in his trade-policy analyses (for example, in *Memorandum on the Fiscal Policy of International Trade*, 1926) Marshall placed much emphasis upon the roles of increasing returns to scale, technological innovation and the transfer of technology in determining the pattern of trade and changes in that pattern over time. He sees the pattern of trade in manufactures as being determined by a continuing process of innovation and technology transfer. Technical progress leads to monopoly gains which are soon wiped out by a rapid international diffusion of knowledge. As a matter of practical policy, therefore, his defence of free trade is couched ultimately not so much in terms of the conventional mode of reasoning based on static allocative efficiency as on the need to keep an industrial country abreast of 'progress in the arts and resources of manufacture', that is, changes in the 'state of the arts' or technological advances abroad.

Like Mill, Marshall therefore has some interesting things to say about trade, technology and economic development. Foreign competition through trade (1) increases the efficiency of domestic industry; (2) provides opportunities for the migration of capital and labour; (3) exerts an influence on the steadiness of employment; and (4) assists in the development of large-scale industry. The chief benefit of foreign trade for Britain was that it enabled the country to obtain ample supplies of raw materials and foodstuffs at stable prices; another benefit was, through the finance of foreign trade, the development of the British money market.

On technology, Marshall feared that Britain's superiority in the production and export of manufactures would be weakened in the course of time, owing to the international diffusion of technology:

> Every improvement in the manufacturing arts increased England's power of meeting the various wants of backward countries . . . the progress of invention opened a wider field for the sale of her special products . . . But this good fortune has been short-lived. Her improvements have been followed, and latterly anticipated, by America and Germany and other countries; and her special products have lost nearly all their monopoly value. (Marshall 1920, p. 674)[13]

But Marshall realised that a technological leader could keep ahead of imitations abroad by developing new products. In 1903, he referred to the example of France:

> New Parisian goods are sold at high prices in London and Berlin for a short time, and then imitations of them are made in large quantities and sold at relatively low prices. But by that time, Paris . . . is already at work on other things which will soon be imitated in like way. (Marshall [1903] 1926, p. 404)

Marshall was quite certain that the international diffusion process had accelerated in the new environment of intense international competition

> broad ideas and knowledge, which when once acquired pass speedily into common ownership; and become part of the collective wealth, in the first instance of the countries to which the industries specially affected belong, and ultimately to the whole world. (Marshall 1919, pp. 174–5)

Germany, Marshall says, now enjoys a competitive advantage 'in industries in which academic training and laboratory work can be turned to good account'; but this was the culmination of a prior process of successful imitation and absorption of foreign technology:

> In the early stages of modern manufacture, scientific training was of relatively small importance. The Germans accordingly, recognising their own weakness in practical instinct and organising faculty, took the part of pupils, whose purpose

it was to outrun their teachers. They began by the direct copying of English machinery and methods . . . And all the while Germany has been quick to grasp the practical significance of any master discovery that is made in other countries and to turn it to account. (Marshall 1919, pp. 132–3)

Finally, Marshall noted that improvements in international transport expanded the volume of trade; they reduced the costs of imported foodstuffs and raw materials, enlarged markets for finished exports and steadied demand.

4.3   EDGEWORTH

Marshall's reciprocal demand or offer curves summarised the ultimate data for the analysis of exchange between two countries in terms of demand and supply. What was not clear, however, was: how were these curves related to the underlying utilities? An answer that suggested itself was to treat each country as a single individual. Demand functions for each country could then be derived from its preferences or 'tastes' as described by indifference curves. Modern expositions of neoclassical trade theory do likewise, that is, it is assumed that consumer preferences over the consumption of various bundles of goods can be aggregated, so that community indifference curves are radial expansions of individual indifference curves. But this is a very strong assumption, and textbook writers usually describe what it takes to ensure the assumption. It depends, for one thing, on whether the implicit social welfare function refers to the welfare *level* of the society or is used merely to describe the *behaviour* of the society – the latter use being less contentious. The offer curve is defined as the locus of points of tangency of different price lines (parametrically given for each country considered in isolation) and the country's community welfare indifference curves.

This important development of Marshall's construction was initiated by Edgeworth long before Marshall's diagrams were published. In *Mathematical Psychics* (1881) – 'presumably interpreting the subject (economics) as the personal and social analogue to mathematical physics' – Edgeworth derived the offer curve from indifference curves in the context of individual exchange or barter in a manner analogous to that now used in contemporary trade theory. Thus Edgeworth defines the offer curve as 'the locus of the point where lines from the origin touch curves of indifference' (Edgeworth 1881, p. 113). The lines from the origin being different price ratios, the offer curve thus summarises the conditions for constrained utility maximisation; for at all points on the offer curve, the price ratio equals the ratio of marginal utilities of the two individuals. Applied to international equilibrium, the offer curve analysis can then be used to show (as Marshall did) how the terms of trade are determined by the interplay of demand and supply.

Edgeworth also introduced into economics another important theoretical (geometrical) construct, the contract curve. As used in trade theory, the contract curve is the locus of points at which one country's indifference curve is tangent to the other country's indifference curve. In other words, it is the locus of points at which one country cannot increase its welfare without decreasing the welfare of the other, given the total world output of both goods. By bringing together the two countries' offer curves it can be shown how international equilibrium occurs at the intersection of the offer curves. But, moreover, this point of intersection lies on the contract curve; and by virtue of this, welfare significance can be read into the equilibrium terms of trade.

Edgeworth first illustrated this result again in the context of individual competitive barter. He showed that the competitive solution must lie on the contract curve on the assumption that individuals maximise their utilities in terms of their own consumption; and this competitive equilibrium coincides precisely at the point of intersection of the two traders' offer curves (Edgeworth 1881, pp. 20–28). Edgeworth – 'the toolmaker', as Pigou called him – added quite significantly to the common toolbox of neoclassical economists. Edgeworth's analysis was, however, conveyed in mathematical language, and when he extended it to trade problems the geometrical counterparts were not fully explained or developed. Edgeworth's techniques were subsequently refashioned for use in trade analysis by Leontief, Lerner and Meade, among others.

Edgeworth on Optimum Tariff and Protection

Edgeworth had a hand in formulating the terms of trade argument for protection and orthodox optimal tariff theory – the analysis of which goes back to Torrens and Mill and was revived by Charles Bickerdike. The welfare optimum tariff is one where the gain due to improved terms of trade exceeds the loss from reduced volume of trade by the greatest possible margin. A 'large' country concerned solely (that is, myopically) with its national economic interest can take advantage of a less than infinitely elastic foreign reciprocal demand curve and thereby exploit its potential monopoly or monopsony power by restricting trade to its advantage.

Edgeworth used his apparatus of offer curves and 'trade indifference curve' to show the geometrical basis of the optimum tariff argument. The geometrical basis was present in the work of Auspitz and Lieben who used the total demand curves similar to Marshallian reciprocal demand curves combined with 'curves of constant satisfaction' or indifference curves.

Edgeworth acknowledged that his treatment of the matter was similar to that of 'Auspitz and Lieben's beautiful and original reasoning' (Edgeworth 1925, p. 295). Edgeworth showed the optimum tariff to be one which shifts the domestic offer curve to a point located on the elastic portion of the foreign country's offer curve, where the latter curve is tangent to the highest indifference curve attainable by the home country. More formal treatments of the matter were provided by Bickerdike and Pigou, and again in the 1940s by Kaldor, Scitovsky, Kahn, de Villiers Graff and so on.

Edgeworth was a free-trader, and whilst he accepted in principle the few exceptions to the free trade argument, his position was similar to that of Marshall on the severe limitations of their practical application. In his view, any departure from a free trade policy, however nicely calculated and valid the restrictive measure might be, would open the way for illicit protection and abuse. Thus when Bickerdike came out with his own precise formulation of the optimum tariff argument (Bickerdike 1906), Edgeworth applauded the effort but warned of the practical danger involved in its use:

> Mr Bickerdike has accomplished a wonderful feat. He has said something new about protection . . . the direct use of the theory is likely to be small. But it is to be feared that its abuse will be considerable. It affords to unscrupulous advocates of vulgar Protection a peculiarly specious pretext for introducing the thin edge of the fiscal wedge. Mr Bickerdike may be compared to a scientist who, by a new analysis, has discovered that strychnine may be administered in small doses with prospect of advantage . . . Let us admire the skill of the analyst, but label the subject of his investigation POISON. (Edgeworth 1908, pp. 555–6)

Edgeworth, like Mill and Sidgwick, was steeped in the utilitarian ethic. He could not countenance the deliberate manipulation of trade taxes to exploit selfish national advantages, and particularly recoiled at the prospect of tariff wars (that is, retaliation and counter-retaliation) that would be unleashed by such selfish international behaviour: 'For one nation to benefit itself at the expense of . . . others is contrary to the highest morality . . . But in an abstract study upon the motion of projectiles *in vacuo*, I do not think it necessary to enlarge upon the horrors of war' (Edgeworth 1925, p. 17, n. 5).

Edgeworth's moral position, like that of most Victorians, was a blend of utilitarianism and evangelicalism, and this carried over to his economics. Some writers on doctrinal history (mainly those of a liberal bent), hold the position that it is irrelevant to enquire into the motives and moral/political allegiances of past economists when appraising their contributions to economic analysis and policy. But on the question of free trade versus protection, at any rate, we cannot ignore the motives or biases of writers – for the simple reason that their views may reinforce a dominant ideology. So, although they may explore disputed theoretical points and arrive at 'scientific truths', these can later be exploited by ideologists and propagandists to further their own agendas. Thus, an ideological position builds up a bank of so-called 'scientific truths'. In the present context of Edgeworth's remarks on the optimum tariff, one can reasonably reply that since the whole free-market (capitalist) ethic is based on individuals pursuing their own selfish interests, why is it wrong for a country to do so?

According to Joan Robinson, the way the serious breach in the free trade case reprsented by Bickerdike's 1906 analysis was dealt with illustrated a general point. Bickerdike's work was 'simply lost to view. Bickerdike's article . . . now well known . . . was dug out of oblivion when Abba Lerner rediscovered the same point in the Thirties . . . [B]ut till then it was effectively hushed up.' (Robinson, 1962, p. 64).

Edgeworth on Effects of Free Trade

Edgeworth was involved in an exchange with Bastable and Loria on the theoretical and practical implications of a suggestion by Henry Sidgwick that the removal of protection on manufactures could cause some workers either to emigrate or remain permanently unemployed – a proposition accepted by Edgeworth.[14] Sidgwick's hypothetical example was based on the operation of diminishing returns and increasing costs in agriculture. Under such circumstances, agriculture would be unable to absorb workers thrown out of employment by cheaper imports of manufactures, and therefore it was undesirable to adopt free trade. Both Edgeworth and Nicholson concurred with this conclusion which challenged the classical view that no large, freely mobile factor (such as labour) could suffer from tariff removal. Nicholson noted that although Sidgwick's proposition was contrary to the 'popular view of English political economy', it was nevertheless true that the removal of trade restrictions could force manufacturing workers into agriculture with disastrous results' (Nicholson 1897, pp. 317–18).

It was Edgeworth's support for the Sidgwick–Nicholson proposition, together with his suggestion that if a country's export industry was subject to increasing cost, its comparative cost ratio would become equal to that of its trading partner (at which point the value of mutual trade would stabilise), that invited objections from Loria and Bastable. Loria disputed Edgeworth's two propositions on the ground that if the countries' comparative cost ratios did indeed coincide, then all trade would cease, and consequently there need not be unemployment under the conditions envisaged by Edgeworth. Bastable agreed with Loria, stating that:

> As trade arises out of differences in the comparative cost, it would seem to be a necessary inference that should these differences cease to exist, the trade which

results from them would also come to an end. This doctrine which has been, I cannot but think, the accepted doctrine of Ricardo and his followers, is impugned by Professor Edgeworth. (Bastable 1901, pp. 227–8)

There was therefore no danger of unemployment from trade expansion following tariff reduction. On the contrary, Bastable asserted, free trade would

permit of greater efficiency in production, and therefore under a state of freedom will assign to the labourer a greater amount of wages, whatever be his comparative gains when measured against those of other classes. (Bastable 1903, p. 102)

Edgeworth's reply clarified the issues and apparently achieved a reconciliation of views. The clarification was on two points: (1) Diminishing returns to labour in agriculture, combined with a low elasticity of factor substitution due to the existence of a specific factor or a 'non-competing' labour group, imply that injury was likely to befall such a specific factor from tariff removal. (2) Trade would not cease when comparative cost ratios became equal; at that point, it would no longer pay to specialise any more; the expansion of trade would cease – the trade would not stop, but become steady. Perhaps what Edgeworth had in mind was that in a two-good Ricardo–Mill model, trade would cease only when the ratios of the two countries' productivity were the same in one industry as in the other and if relative real wage rates adjust accordingly in both countries.

   Bastable and Loria did not carefully distinguish between the conditions for trade and the conditions for specialisation; and this was the source of their confusion. They both seemed to believe that the condition for trade (namely a difference in comparative cost ratios) was the same as the condition for specialisation (that is, for each country to specialise in the production of the commodity in which it had a comparative advantage). In other words, they implied that comparative costs alone would uniquely determine the pattern of specialisation. The mistake stems from their neglect of the demand conditions and thus the possibility of partial specialisation under the specified production assumptions. Bastable later conceded his error and also accepted Edgeworth's view that under 'this special state of things, i.e. when free, or indeed any movement of labour and capital from manufactures to agriculture was impossible . . . the injury inflicted on manufactures by the introduction of free trade is great' (Bastable 1901, p. 229).

4.4   PIGOU AND BICKERDIKE

The early writings of Arthur Pigou and Charles Bickerdike on tariff theory were stimulated by the Tariff Reform controversy (1903). From this there emerged some notable theoretical developments, namely Pigou's treatment of trade, income distribution and factor movements and Bickerdike's derivation of the optimum tariff formula.

Pigou on Protection and Income Distribution

During this period Pigou wrote one article and two books on the theoretical issues involved in revenue and protective tariffs. In *Protective and Preferential Import Duties* (1906) he had something interesting to say about trade and income distribution. Basing his argument on the existence of 'non-competing' groups, Pigou asserted that tariff protection could increase the real income of a factor used intensively in the protected industry. To free traders who normally ignored non-competing groups, Pigou put the question:

> Is it not the better view that the great divisions of the industrial world, land, capital, brain-power, trained hand-labour, muscular labour, are non-competing in the sense that, against those who would pass from one to the other, there is a great gulf fixed? (Pigou 1906, pp. 58–9)

Pigou noted that these non-competing groups were usually combined in non-uniform proportions. A protective tariff which increases the output of industry A and reduces that of industry B can increase the proportion of the (altered) total product going to the factor used more intensively in A. Moreover, Pigou argues, even if the tariff reduces the real national dividend (income) as a whole, the absolute return to the favoured factor or non-competing group may be improved by the tariff. He says: 'The increase per cent in the share of the dividend obtained by the favoured factor might exceed the shrinkage per cent of the dividend itself' (Pigou 1906, p. 59). Pigou derived this conclusion from his assumption on factor immobility and varying factor proportions in production; but this anticipation of the Stolper–Samuelson treatment was preceded by Nicholson's 1897 analysis.

In the same work Pigou also noted the implications for international factor movements of restrictions on trade in goods. Thus he asserted (without providing a proof) that free trade equalises factor prices internationally. A tariff which raises the share of one factor in the national dividend (real income) will create incentives for the international movement of the disadvantaged factors. The factor most likely to move will be capital, for national immigration controls restrict the freedom of movement of labour. Thus if a tariff increases the share of national income going to labour, immigration of labour may not occur, but capital may leave the country and thus frustrate the redistributive effect of the tariff (Pigou 1906, pp. 59–60).

Pigou versus Bickerdike on Optimal Tariffs

In 'The Theory of Incipient Taxes' (1906) Bickerdike set out to answer the question, 'whether a country by means of taxes can get more favourable terms of exchange with foreigners in such a way as to have a net advantage after allowing for the disadvantages involved in turning production from its natural course?' (Bickerdike 1906, p. 529). His answer, which he developed in both the 1906 paper and his 1907 review of Pigou's *Protective and Preferential Import Duties*, gave birth to the famous theory of the optimal tariff. In modern formulations, the optimal tariff is defined as follows:

$$t^* = \frac{1}{\eta_B} \text{ (where } \eta_B \text{ is the foreign supply elasticity of exports)}$$
$$= \varepsilon_B - 1 \equiv \frac{-1}{1 + e_B} > 0$$

where ε_B = the elasticity of the foreign country offer curve
and e_B = the foreign demand elasticity for exports

Note that a small country maximises its welfare under free trade, since $t^* = 0$ when $\eta_B = \infty$. But also note that the optimal tariff formula does not imply that the optimum trade tax is uniquely determined; therefore there will be an infinite number of optimal tariff rates.

In his geometric and algebraic analyses Bickerdike used surplus concepts and the diagrams developed by Marshall and Edgeworth. He defined a country's net advantage from an incipient (or 'a small enough') tax on exports or imports and proved that except in one peculiar and unlikely case (that is, when supply and demand for the traded commodities were inelastic in both countries), the use of such trade taxes would always increase a country's economic welfare. National gains depend only on the condition that the country possesses some advantage in international markets, either as a buyer or seller or both; and no doubt thinking of Great Britain, Bickerdike says: 'No great country is an absolutely insignificant quantity in the eyes of those who buy from it and sell to it' (Bickerdike 1906, p. 529). The gains are likely to be larger, the greater the elasticity of demand for imports in the taxing country. Bickerdike showed that trade taxes could produce benefits for the nation as a whole, not merely for individual interests or groups. He clarified the conditions under which maximum gain was possible and observed that the exclusion of tariff revenues would not affect the result. He approved of the rise in prices attendant on tariff imposition as it caused a desirable transfer of income from the rentier class to the community'.

Pigou's approach was altogether different. At that time (namely before

Free trade: the economics

he wrote *The Economics of Welfare* which distinguished between private and social cost and benefits) Pigou conceived of the national dividend (national income) as the sum of private dividends, and felt that any restriction on free individual bargaining (for example, through protection) would lower aggregate real income. Pigou accepted the infant-industry argument, observing: 'Of the formal validity of List's argument there is no longer any dispute among economists' (Pigou 1906, p. 13).[15] But with respect to a developed industrial country, tariffs were of no avail in securing additional long-term gains. Tariffs could of course be used to raise a given amount of revenue, and it was for this purpose that Pigou considered the respective merits of protective and non-protective duties.

Bickerdike objected to this narrow concentration on the fiscal aspect of the problem and the unwillingness to accept the possibility of improved national gains owing to the divergence of individual interests from the national interest. 'Is there no general rule', queried Bickerdike,

> that each individual in making his own best bargain in international trade to some extent prejudices the position of his fellow countrymen, and that the maximum national advantage is not found in unrestricted individual freedom? If this is so, it would seem that a certain amount of revenue would be incidentally raised by a tariff designed primarily to maximise the advantage of international trade. (Bickerdike 1907, p. 99)[16]

Pigou concentrated on the direct effect of a protective duty – the effect on domestic prices, the distortion of consumers' choice and the misallocation of resources – and minimised the indirect effects, notably the possibility of securing better terms of trade by means of it. In contrast, Bickerdike thought that the terms-of-trade effect was the major influence to be considered in any reckoning of the national gains, and developed the analysis of the optimal tariff to make the point; and further (given Pigou's interest in raising a given revenue), that such a tax may be superior on efficiency grounds (that is, in static welfare terms) to either an equal-yield income tax or equal-yield domestic production tax. What Pigou failed to see was that the distortion costs of the tax contemplated by Bickerdike might be more than outweighed by real-income gains from a country's ability to influence international prices.

Pigou, in his rejoinder, challenged the theoretical basis of Bickerdike's analysis and conclusions, arguing on Marshall's authority that it was illegitimate to treat a supply curve as equivalent to 'a particular expenses curve' – a fault Pigou detected in Bickerdike's procedure of integrating a supply curve to obtain total cost. However, 'it was a charge which Bickerdike successfully met' as Jha observes (Jha 1973, p. 47). Citing the writings of Cunynghame, Edgeworth and Pigou himself, Bickerdike replied that since it was generally agreed that an increase in the scale of production could either raise or lower the 'particular expenses' curve, the assumption that the particular expenses curve was constant and therefore the same as the general supply curve was an equally valid one to make. Moreover, Bickerdike argued, there was no reason why the doctrine of consumer surplus should be accepted whilst the corresponding simple measurement of costs and producers' surplus may be rejected.

Edgeworth, as we have seen, regarded Bickerdike's analysis as a notable theoretical development, and later gave a masterful treatment of the argument applying Bickerdike's model to the stability problem: that is, he showed that Bickerdike's conclusion could be derived by the condition that the equilibrium of trade with which we are concerned is stable, that is, that the slope of the home country's reciprocal demand curve is greater in absolute value than that of the foreign country. On the basis of his 1906–7 analysis of the effects of trade taxes, Bickerdike some years later set forth the conditions for foreign exchange stability (for a regime of fluctuating exchange rates) and thereby provided the first formal framework for the 'elasticities approach' to exchange-rate devaluation (Bickerdike 1920, pp. 118–22).

4.5   BARONE AND PARETO

Enrico Barone (Compensation Principle)

The contribution of Barone (1859–1924) to the development of neoclassical theory was in many directions: the theory of the firm, marginal productivity theory and general equilibrium, the theory of the optimum allocation of resources in a socialist or centrally planned economy, welfare economics and international trade theory. His writings on welfare economics, in particular the early sketch of the 'compensation principle', stimulated efforts to derive criteria in connection with the optimality of free trade. He was, in other words, a pioneer in 'new welfare economics' – a welfare economics free from the interpersonal comparisons of utility that were revived by Nicholas Kaldor and Sir John Hicks in 1939. The new welfare economics introduced the idea of compensation so that community indifference curves could be used. Given that some people will gain and others lose by free trade, the compensation principle attempts to find a criterion by means of which one can say that one situation is 'better' than another.

Barone first considered this problem in connection with the question: What would be the welfare effects of policy changes in a collectivist (noncompetitive) regime? He wrote:

Some individuals will be benefited, others will suffer loss; the loss to the latter will be decidedly greater than the advantage to the former, in the sense that even taking all their gain from those who have gained in the change (which takes them back to their former condition) and giving it to those who have lost by it, the latter, even with such an addition, remain in a worse situation than originally: or, indeed, what comes to the same thing, some of the latter with such an addition might be brought back to their former situation, but all of them certainly could not. (Barone [1908] 1935)

In other words, such a situation leads to a 'destruction of wealth', an aggregate income loss (valued at the competitive-equilibrium prices) and results from the departure from the welfare maximum implied by such a competitive equilibrium.

Without making value judgements, but if the possibility of compensation exists, one can compare two situations and conclude that one is better than the other, for example, a move from autarky to free trade. Can the gainers 'bribe' the losers and still be better off? Barone was doubtful that this could be achieved in a non-competitive system (as the above quote indicates – a belief similar to that of Pareto).

Barone developed a partial-equilibrium analytical framework (the now familiar back-to-back diagram) which he applied to international trade in order to establish welfare results. The rigorous analysis of partial-equilibrium relations goes back to Cournot (as noted previously). Marshall used partial-equilibrium demand and supply diagrams for the analysis of some problems of domestic trade. But it was Marshall's pupil, Henry Cunynghame, who first applied (1904) such diagrams to trade between two countries (Cunynghame 1904, p. 98, figure 51). The prices prevailing in each country were expressed in a common currency unit and the two diagrams placed back-to-back to share a common price axis. Cunynghame used the diagrams to illustrate the theory of international trade and in particular to integrate costs of transporting commodities between countries into the traditional analysis.

Four years later (1908) Barone used similar diagrams, not only to illustrate international equilibrium but also to say something about the welfare implications (that is, the gains from trade).[17] He indicates how both countries gain when trade is opened up as compared with autarky. If in two countries, A and B, the pre-trade price of a particular commodity in A exceeds the price in B plus transport costs, country B will export that commodity to A upon the freeing of trade. Equilibrium will be established when country A's imports are equal to country B's exports and prices are equalised except for transport costs. By identifying areas under the demand and supply curves bounded by the pre-trade prices, Barone concludes that in country A the gain to consumers exceeds the loss to producers, and in B the gain to producers is greater than the loss to consumers. There is thus a net gain to each country which Barone locates as the triangles enclosed by the demand and supply curves in A and B. Barone's use of surplus analysis is different from that of Marshall, but he arrives at very nearly the same result as that produced by modern theorists using the same construction. Barone's technique explicitly allows for any change in the terms of trade, either in the movement from protection to free trade or vice versa. The Cournot–Cunynghame–Barone diagram was also used by Schüller and Haberler and is now frequently displayed in textbook treatments of trade and tariffs. Equally widely used is a variant of the diagram designed to show the economic effects on one country if it imposes a tariff on one of its imports, on the assumption that the terms of trade are unaffected. Max Corden was perhaps the first to use such a model.

Barone made an even more remarkable contribution to modern international trade theory: the diagrammatic representation of an economy's free-trade equilibrium and the gains from trade – a prototype of the diagram that now features in all elementary trade texts. Barone accomplished this in a long footnote accompanying the text in his 1908 treatise *Principi di economia politica*. Two diagrams were used to represent what he called, in one example, 'a curve of production indifference' and, in the other, 'a taste indifference curve' – transformation and indifference curves, in modern parlance. These two curves were then combined in a third diagram to illustrate an economy's trading equilibrium and gains from trade according to the theory of comparative costs.

Barone feels, however, that the static picture conveyed by this diagram does not tell the whole story about a country's involvement in the world trading system. He therefore duly takes into account dynamic factors (that is, sources of instability stemming from fluctuations in the terms of trade) in addition to the static effects in the evaluation of the relative merits of free trade and protection. Sudden swings in the terms of trade can alter the relative profitability of export- and import-competing industries and lead to a costly shifting of resources between the sectors – capital and other sunk costs may have to be written off and the willingness to invest new savings might be adversely affected due to extra risks, and so on. Such negative dynamic effects resulting from free trade can lead to 'a destruction of wealth' considerably greater than any possible losses caused by protection. For Barone, the consideration of such adverse dynamic effects 'temper[s] greatly the free trade thesis and explains[s] how . . . one cannot erect free trade to an absolute dogma, without taking into account the special conditions in which a *given* country finds itself at a *given* time' (Barone 1908, p. 96).[18]

This neoclassical method of modelling an economy's equilibrium under autarky and with trade only came into vogue in the 1940s through the works of Lerner, Viner and Leontief – at least twenty-three years after Barone had first figured it out. Barone's hitherto unacknowledged role in fashioning this invaluable pedagogical device has recently been brought to light and to the notice of the profession by Andrea Maneschi and William Thweatt.[19]

Vilfredo Pareto (Optimality Criterion)

Vilfredo Pareto (1848–1923) was, of course, the great pioneer of modern welfare economics and the optimality criterion named after him, namely a situation in which it is impossible to increase the welfare of one individual without decreasing that of another. Although not universally accepted, the criterion has exercised an enormous influence on contemporary welfare analysis, including the normative side of international trade theory. Indeed, much of the extensive literature on welfare criteria has been concerned with matters arising in trade theory. The optimality criterion relates to the simultaneous achievement of optimum efficiency in production and exchange when certain well-known marginal conditions are satisfied.

Pareto-optimality describes the essential welfare properties of a general equilibrium system of competitive markets and thus relates to the traditional concerns of writers on the gains from trade. The argument for free trade has always been that, with appropriate compensation, free trade results in an improvement in economic welfare. It puts the world out on the global production-possibility frontier. The theoretical underpinning for this belief is provided by the Pareto-optimality criterion; for it is easily shown that free trade equilibrium achieves a Pareto optimum or, conversely, that a Pareto optimum implies or denotes a free trade equilibrium.

For neoclassical economics in general, consumer theory and the theory of general competitive equilibrium are fundamental. They deal, in Pareto's words, with 'the opposition between men's tastes and the obstacles to satisfying them'; and it was Pareto who first synthesised it all by drawing together the theoretical threads spun by Cournot, Walras, Edgeworth, Auspitz, Lieben, and so on. His personal input into the synthesis, the woven fabric, is impressive enough: the perception that the theory of general competitive equilibrium can dispense with the notion of measurable utility (in contrast to Edgeworth's view that interpersonal comparisons of utility could be made on a more or less firm objective basis), and that provided certain conditions are fulfilled, such an equilibrium yields a maximum of 'ophelimity' (the power to give satisfaction) or welfare.

Pareto's problem

Pareto occupies a prominent niche in the pantheon of neoclassical economists and it is therefore of interest to hear what he has to say on some points in trade theory. Pareto had a problem with Ricardo's famous analogy between the benefits of international trade and the gains from individual barter where two persons specialise and exchange hats and shoes. Pareto took this to mean that Ricardo's illustration of the mutual beneficiality of free trade was premised on complete specialisation in production by each country. In that case, argues Pareto, it can be shown that Ricardo's conclusion (that free trade increases the world's welfare) is not generally true. Only if the total output of each good is increased after specialisation will Ricardo's conclusion hold good; otherwise, for example if specialisation leads to a reduction in the world's output of one of the goods, even though the output of the other good has increased, it is impossible to say whether specialisation has increased or decreased world welfare without taking tastes into account, that is, demand, as specified in a utility function. Pareto constructed hypothetical arithmetical examples to show that specialisation could indeed lead to such a result and thus Ricardo's presumption must therefore be false (Pareto [1906] 1972, pp. 369–73).

Pareto's observations have merit as a rebuttal of the proposition that complete specialisation is necessarily mutually beneficial as compared to no specialisation or partial specialisation; but as Viner points out, quoting textual extracts, Ricardo never placed any emphasis on complete specialisation in his model of comparative cost. Moreover, Pareto's counter-example of unprofitable specialisation would not be observed in practice since it was not a competitive equilibrium; that is, specialisation would not be carried to the point where the reduction in the value of one country's output was uncompensated through free trade – that is, citizens will normally obtain their desired level of the other good through imports, thus raising utility.

Pareto had obviously not read Mill on this point. If he had, he would have noticed that Mill provided (admittedly with the help of a special demand assumption) conditions for full specialisation in both countries and also for cases where one country would not be fully specialised.

Pareto's problem is nowadays resolved by way of the concept of an efficient point in activity analysis. Such analysis proves that the value of world output is maximised only if every country maximises the value of its own output, as indicated above. Indeed, a free-trade equilibrium in the classical model corresponds to the model of competitive equilibrium that is Pareto-optimal!

Pareto on protection

In his analysis of tariffs, Pareto does not use surplus analysis or the partial-equilibrium diagrammatics of Barone but arrives at the same conclusion as Marshall and Barone. A tariff causes consumers' loss to be greater than producers' gain and therefore 'we can *grosso-modo*, and as a first approximation, conclude that every protective tariff is the cause of the destruction of wealth within the country which levies this duty on a good' (Pareto [1906] 1972, p. 374). Conversely, the removal of a tariff by causing a transfer of resources from the import-competing to the more efficient export industry augments wealth, since under free trade the same or a greater consumption bundle can be obtained at lower factor cost. The gains are even greater if the contracting import-competing industry is subject to increasing production costs and the export industry enjoys decreasing costs.

Pareto is critical of the infant-industry argument for protection. He admits that an *a priori* case can be made out for temporary protection, but in his usual terse, crisp style says, 'there is no known example of it'. 'All the industries born under a system of protection have always sought more and more protection, and the day has never come when they declared they could do without it' (Pareto [1906] 1972, p. 375). He thus accepts the argument in principle but condemns it in practice – a position not dissimilar to that of his English counterparts.

When he considers the social effects of protection his attitude is less hostile, but this serves to reveal how confused he was on the issue. Here we have an example of the confusions and ambiguities characteristic of his writings. Consider the following passages:

> Industrial protection in agricultural countries, and free trade in an industrial country, both have the effect of developing industry . . .

> From all the preceding it can be seen how complex is the practical and synthetic problem of knowing whether protection is preferable to free trade, or vice versa. . . .

> [I]n every era and for every country, protection is detrimental and free trade advantageous. (Pareto [1906] 1972, pp. 376–7)

With remarkable frankness, Pareto confessed his own confusion. In a footnote he revealed that he had declared in 1887: 'the social effects and their economic consequences . . . are the primary issues involved and, in my opinion, the only one which could sometimes raise serious doubts about the more or less considerable usefulness of free trade, in certain cases' (Pareto [1906] 1972, p. 377, n 43). It is possible to rationalise Pareto's confusion over the issue of free trade versus protection at the time he wrote (1906) in terms of the evolution of his own personal political opinions. Terence Hutchison provides the clue: 'Pareto started as an ardent economic liberal, campaigning for free trade . . . and propagating the kind of ardent Cobdenite sentiments which he would later have treated with the deepest contempt'.[20]

In his later writings Pareto adopted a much more balanced, pragmatic attitude to the free trade versus protection issue and retracted some of his earlier dogmatic assertions about the benefits of free trade. He recognised that the choice of trade regime depends very much upon all the economic and social conditions facing a particular country at a given time. In one of his last major works, the *Trattato di sociologia generale*, he expressly withdrew his earlier blanket condemnation of protection with the new statement recognising that the increase in production due to protection

> may be great enough to exceed the destruction of wealth caused by protection; so that, sum total, protection may yield a profit and not a loss in wealth; it may therefore prove (though not necessarily so) that the economic prosperity of a country has been enhanced by industrial protection. (Pareto 1935, pp. 549–50)

However, there was one positive result of political experiences and frustrations working on a mind as acutely sociological as Pareto's: a thoroughly modern-looking socio-political theory of tariff formation – the general notion that in a democracy tariffs are shaped by the rent-seeking behaviour of interested parties (lobbyists and politicians). The concerns of this study go back to Adam Smith's comments on mercantilism as a rent-seeking society; but Pareto was exceptional among the early neoclassical economists in taking an interest in it (Pareto [1906] 1972, pp. 377–83). Pareto also had something to say about the income-distribution effects of protection a few years after Bastable's famous chapter on 'International Trade and Income Distribution' (Bastable 1903, chapter 6).

4.6   FOUR ARGUMENTS FOR PROTECTION

Schüller and the Idle Resource Effect

In 1905 the Austrian academic economist, Richard Schüller, published an argument for protection based on the normal existence of idle resources in all countries (Schüller 1905).[21] Years later, Gottfried Haberler provided a trenchant refutation of it, but commented that Schüller's argument 'ranks with justice as one of the most profound arguments for tariffs' (Haberler 1936, p. 253).

Schüller discussed the disruptive effects of free trade, particularly the adverse effects on employment. Manufacturing industry could be ruined by competitive imports and that could occur even though foreign producers were only slightly more efficient than domestic manufacturers. Human misery and economic waste (idle factories, redundant capital, and so on) may be involved before unemployed workers find acceptable jobs in new

Free trade: the economics

industries, if indeed they ever find such jobs. A low tariff may be required to protect jobs in domestic manufacturing industry.

Schüller adopts a partial-equilibrium approach, and shows, given the elasticities of home and foreign demand and supply curves, that only small tariff-induced changes in prices are necessary. He considers the loss of consumer surplus involved in tariff imposition, but judges that the increase in the production of the protected output will more than compensate for such loss. Thus:

> The smaller is, firstly, the spread between the highest and the lowest cost with which the home demand for the good can be satisfied by home production, and the smaller is, secondly, the comparative advantage of foreign producers in the case of goods which under free trade would not be produced at all in the home country . . . the greater is the increase in output due to a tariff relative to the loss on the side of consumption caused thereby, and the more favourable, therefore, are the effects of the tariff upon the total income. (Schüller 1905, p. 136)

He reckons the increase in domestic production as an increase in total national income and takes note of the objection that if more of the protected output is produced, less production must necessarily take place in other industries – hence, there will be no net effect on national income, only a shift in the composition of total output; but Schuller asserts that this objection is not generally valid.

At this point, he makes an interesting observation: in all countries, factors of production, particularly natural resources, are never fully utilised; hence, a suitably small tariff can result in the employment of destitute workers and idle natural resources. 'In no country', says Schüller, 'are natural economic forces – fertile soil, deposits of coal, ore and minerals, water power – fully made use of; rather, they are in all countries available for an expansion of branches of production for which they are needed' (Schüller 1905, p. 78). Free traders cannot therefore appeal to some general principle which suggests that all existing productive factors must find employment, since the existence of unemployed resources violates the conditions for economic optimum; also, free traders are wrong when they maintain that tariffs must result only in a change in the output mix but never an increase in total output. On the contrary, says Schüller, moderate tariffs can help to bring about a better use of existing productive resources and so increase national output (income) and welfare. In addition, moderate protection may induce the import of capital (foreign direct investment) or the immigration of skilled labour – all tending to increase total national production.

Schüller believed he had found a new, theoretically valid argument for protection; but later writers spotted the flaw in it. Schüller failed to take into account the cost of utilising the so-called 'idle resources' in terms of the foregone use of other factors. The opportunity cost of activating the idle factors may be greater than the value of output created, so that on balance it may be better to leave the resources idle. A certain amount of unutilised resources is inevitable in a dynamic, growing economy. Market adjustments will leave some 'specific' factors temporarily idle; and while such transitional adjustments may result in private losses to the owners of specific factors, the community as a whole gains from the more efficient deployment of available resources. Haberler concludes: 'the existence of unutilised means of production is no argument whatever for tariffs' (Haberler 1936, p. 187). Bickerdike reviewed Schüller's book in 1905 and commented: 'This book is an ambitious attempt to find a theoretical basis for genuine Protection' (Bickerdike 1905, p. 413). Bickerdike was, however, dissatisfied with Schüller's treatment. It did not provide a satisfactory basis for a general theory of permanent protection and would not convince the English free traders, particularly Schüller's claim that competitive imports cause greater loss to producers than gain to consumers. Jha (1973, pp. 44–5) notes that Bickerdike was 'keenly exercised' by the book and suggests that it was Schüller's 'half-finished task that Bickerdike attempted to complete in his "Theory of Incipient Taxes"'.

Manoilescu and Wage Differentials

In 1929, the Romanian economist and Minister of Trade and Industry in his country's prewar government, Mihail Manoilescu (1891–1950), made a case for protection of industry in poor countries which attracted considerable interest (Manoilescu [1929] 1931). His case for industrial tariff protection rested on imperfections in the labour market of an underdeveloped country that disfavoured industry, that is, the existence of permanent differences in money wages between industry and agriculture due to differences in marginal productivity – 'the productivity of capital and labour'. Ricardo's comparative-cost principle loses its universal validity when, as so often happens in underdeveloped economies, a country's comparative advantage in terms of labour costs is in sectors of relatively low value productivity per unit of labour. The advantage of free international trade exists only for industrial countries (that is, rich countries), not for poor countries whose exports consist of agricultural products.

Manoilescu produces a variety of statistical evidence supporting the view that capital and labour are always more productive in industry than in agriculture and consequently average incomes tend to be higher in industry. However, because the structure of internal costs and prices is distorted between industry and agriculture in a way that handicaps industry, poor countries find themselves 'over-importing' industrial products in exchange for agricultural exports. Industry has to pay a wage-rate in excess of the opportunity cost of labour in the economy, that is, in excess of the marginal product of labour in agriculture. There is too little labour at too high a price in industry – factors are inefficiently allocated between the sectors – so not enough will be produced in manufacturing and too much will be produced in agriculture. This results in inappropriate specialisation and trade under the Ricardian assumption of constant costs. On this reasoning, Manoilescu argues that agricultural countries can benefit by imposing tariffs on industrial imports to offset the inappropriate market encouragement to imports. The rise in the price of imported goods which protection entails will allow domestic industrialists to expand production and thereby facilitate the movement of workers from low-productivity agriculture to high-productivity industry. Protection to industry will enable the country to get manufactured goods at lower labour-time costs by domestic production than via imports.

Do intersectoral differences in wages provide a valid argument for protection? Critics at the time wanted to know more about the reasons for the existence of wage differentials, but felt in any case that numerous qualifications must severely limit the validity of the new doctrine. Viner pointed out that the wage differential might be due to what he called, following Taussig, 'equalising differences in wages', that is, differences in money wages which merely equalise the 'net advantages' of different occupations. Thus the higher industrial wage might reflect the 'disutility' of greater economic costs incurred by labour in the industrial sector. In this case, there is no justification for protection, since specialisation according to money costs will then be in accordance with comparative real costs (measured in terms of 'disutilities') although not in accordance with labour-time costs, that is, with wages and value of marginal products in agriculture.[22]

However, if the wage differential is due to trade union activity, social legislation, custom or political and humanitarian considerations on the part of employers which prevent complete occupational mobility, then there may be a case for government intervention in trade. These impediments to labour movement may cause a genuine distortion – as Haberler notes, 'the price ratio is not the same as the substitution ratio' (Haberler 1936, p. 197). Here, Viner finds 'the one grain of truth which is embedded – but not displayed' in Manoilescu's exhaustive argument (Viner 1951, p. 122). The free-trade solution will not provide a welfare maximum. Real income can be increased by a redistribution of the factors so as to bring private costs in line with social costs. The correction may be brought about through tariffs on industrial imports. But this is only a 'second-best' remedy, since although the production distortion is eliminated it appears on the consumption side. The ideal policy will be one which directly removes the distortion or imperfection in factor-market pricing. The 'first-best' policy means therefore free trade combined with a subsidy to the employment of labour in the manufacturing sector, that is, a subsidy per unit of labour used in industry equal to the difference between the higher unit labour cost in industry and the lower labour cost in agriculture. Viner concludes that Manoilescu's attempt to defend protection 'has not been carried forward by this attempt' and that it confirms the conventional view that 'the existence of differences in wages does not suffice to overturn the doctrine of comparative costs' (Viner 1951, p. 122).

Ohlin discussed the argument in terms of Cairnes' idea of 'non-competing groups' (imperfect mobility) and conceded that free trade might lead to a lower national income than protection, but observed: 'It does not follow that the existence of artificial non-competing groups is a sufficient argument for protection. The more natural remedy is, of course, to increase the labour mobility.'[23] Haberler agreed with Viner and Ohlin, but in addition noted that Manoilescu's analysis could be extended in a dynamic fashion so that it 'approaches the infant-industry argument' (Haberler 1936, p. 198, n. 1, and p. 284); although it should be noted Manoilescu himself distinguished his plea from that of the infant-industry or 'educational tariff' case. This is the case where (in the development of a manufacturing sector) a higher industrial wage is necessary to attract and retain skilled workers, an adequate supply of whom may not be forthcoming because of market failure. But here again, the theory of domestic distortions provides no support for intervention in trade to remedy the situation – the optimal policy is a subsidy to labour training.

Manoilescu's case for protection was revived in the early postwar period in the context of the economic development of poor countries. It was restated in modern form by Gunnar Myrdal and W. Arthur Lewis; and Everett Hagen subjected it to rigorous analysis using a two-commodity, two-factor model with a constant wage differential. Bhagwati and Ramaswami discussed the argument in light of the modern theory of domestic distortions and arrived at conclusions essentially the same as those of Viner, Ohlin and Haberler.

The Graham Protection Controversy

During the interwar years, a prominent critic of the Ricardo–Mill–Marshall model of trade was Frank Graham, a former student of Frank Taussig. His complaint concerned the question of dimensionality in the basic classical model – the assumption that many interesting issues about international trade could be adequately handled by means of an analysis based on two countries trading in two commodities. Graham rejected this reductionist procedure and believed that classical and neoclassical economists were led astray on substantive matters by generalising from the 2x2 case. Several of the propositions propagated by these writers as being relevant to complex trading relationships in the real world of many countries and many commodities, were in fact true only of simple bilateral trade of the England–Germany, cloth and linen variety considered by Mill. Graham called for a more realistic theory of international values incorporating many commodities and many countries; and in fact (using numerical examples) he did attempt such a generalisation, and showed how the results could be applied to a number of practical problems. He also disputed Marshall's position on demand shifts and the terms of trade. Graham also had some interesting things to say about the theory of tariffs and argued that decreasing costs could justify protection – a contention which stirred controversy. We select this topic for review here.

Graham argues that decreasing costs could justify protection. A country with a comparative advantage in an industry subject to decreasing returns to scale and a comparative disadvantage in an increasing returns to scale industry, may lose from free trade when trade leads to a reallocation of resources (labour) from the increasing-returns industry to the decreasing-returns industry. Gross domestic product evaluated at constant commodity prices falls (that is, output per man falls in both industries), indicating a welfare loss. Consequently, the country may be worse off with free trade than under autarky, and may be able to improve on its free trade welfare by means of tariff protection (Graham 1923, pp. 199–227). Moreover, since increasing returns are irreversible, tariff protection needs to be kept permanently in place.

Although Graham's contention was not a new one, it provoked extensive criticisms, most notably from Frank Knight, but also from Haberler and Viner. The controversy is reviewed in Caves (1960, pp. 169–74) and more recently in Irwin (1996, pp. 138–52). The criticisms, many of which were not really relevant to Graham's basic contention, were about the empirical relevance of external economies, failure to note the distinction between internal and external economies, the incompatibility of internal economies with standard notions of competitive equilibrium, the irreversibility of returns to scale, the confusion between average and marginal costs in Graham's pricing rules and whether scale economies were to be associated with industry generally or with specific products, and so on. For instance, Knight's position was that competitive conditions were incompatible with internally decreasing costs (internal economies of scale) – a proof of which was given by Piero Sraffa in 1926. Hence, Graham's conjecture about possible losses from free trade could only apply where the economies of scale were external to the firm and internal to the industry. Knight, however, objected to the concept (and even the reality) of external economies, saying, 'I have never succeeded in picturing them in my mind' (Knight 1925, p. 332); and that external economies in one business unit are internal economies in some other one within the industry. Upon these grounds Graham's case was summarily dismissed in judgements typified by the following: 'the basis for the kind of protection defended by Graham is all but completely destroyed'; 'little or nothing remains of it'; '[Graham's] thesis reduces to little more than a theoretical curiosity'.[24]

Nevertheless, from these criticisms there emerged two clarifications which proved useful in subsequent discussions about the role of economies of scale in international trade: (1) external economies may depend on world output rather than national output, that is, 'international' returns to scale resulting from an increased international division of labour – this was suggested by Viner ([1937] 1955): a national firm derives cost savings from the expansion of world output of its product; in Viner's words, 'if the external economies are a function of the size of the world industry, and not of the national portion of it'; and (2) market structure and the equilibrium allocation of resources depend on the precise nature of the economies of scale, that is, assumptions about the behaviour of firms depend on what forms the economies of scale take.

It must be noted here that Graham was not a protectionist; nor was he a doctrinaire free-trader. In *Protective Tariffs* (Graham 1934) he accepted various well-known neoclassical exceptions to the case for free trade – the traditional infant-industry argument, the terms of trade argument, the temporary adoption of a tariff as a bargaining counter in tariff negotiations; but stressed the benefits of specialisation according to comparative advantage. He added: 'The presumption is always in favour of free trade . . . This presumption is rebuttable but it is ever present; and, in this sense, the classical economists were right in insisting that free trade is a ubiquitous and timeless principle' (Graham 1934, p. 59). Graham, however, retained the argument for permanent protection of decreasing-cost industries – despite the sharp criticisms of it – and included a chapter on 'Rational Protection'.

Graham presented his case using a two-country model incorporating one factor of production (labour) producing two commodities (wheat and watches) whose costs are expressed in terms of output per unit of labour time. The argument as it stood failed to convince his contemporaries – Caves notes that Graham's arguments and numerical examples were 'grossly insufficient for establishing' his case (Caves 1960, p. 169). But the question about the logical consistency of Graham's case was not seriously addressed until many years later when Jan Tinbergen gave a geometrical proof of it, utilising for that purpose the comparatively new technique of the production-possibilities frontier combined with indifference curves – an analysis which improved on Graham's exposition in respect of the evaluation of real national income. Tinbergen's reformulation (validation) of Graham's case seems to have clinched the matter – Caves (1960, p. 169) observed: 'Trade theorists now generally concede [Graham's] point' – and the controversy subsided.

Recent developments in international trade theory – specifically, the increased attention now given to the effects of increasing returns to scale and non-competitive behaviour in international competition – have led to renewed interest in the 'Graham protection controversy'. Several papers have addressed the issue either explicitly or briefly in more general contexts, resulting finally in a more thorough analysis than this classic externalities model has hitherto received. What new interpretations emerge from recent theoretical innovations?

It turns out that Tinbergen's reconstruction of Graham's case is not the definitive answer. It is now seen to be incorrect. Murray Kemp (1976, p. 111) points out: 'Tinbergen's treatment is wrong in essentials.' This has been supported by Wilfred Ethier (1982, pp. 1243–68) and Arvind Panagariya (1981, pp. 221–30). Tinbergen's error pertains to the shape of the production-possibility frontier, especially near the axes. He draws the production-possibility frontier concave to the origin near the decreasing-returns industry axis and convex to the origin near the increasing-returns industry axis. But as Herberg and Kemp (1969), also Panagariya (1981) show, if the technology is such that production functions are homothetic or homogeneous then the production-possibility frontier is convex near the decreasing-returns industry axis, concave near the increasing-returns industry axis and has a single inflection point.[25] This slip misled Tinbergen into drawing the inference that temporary protection would reverse the free-trade equilibrium and lead to complete specialisation in the increasing-returns industry. Ethier (1982, p. 1262) points out that in the realistic small-country/large-country case, 'the small country would never, as a result of the tariff, export manufactures' – the increasing-returns commodities; hence it is not an infant-industry argument. Compare this with Haberler's suggestion that if external economies could be ascertained, Graham's 'argument for a tariff is clearly an exact parallel to the infant-industry argument' (Haberler 1936, p. 207). Panagariya also mentions that Tinbergen fails to recognise the divergence between social and private marginal products (the externality distortion) at the competitive equilibrium.

In the modern treatments, external scale economies are output generated, that is, each firm's output depends on the industry output. This implies that the firm perceives its production to be subject to constant returns to scale. Price therefore equals average cost. Even when economies of scale occur at the firm level (scale economies internal to the firm), average-cost pricing may still prevail if markets are contestable (entry to the industry is free). Competitive equilibrium then requires a single firm earning zero profit – free entry or threat of entry enforces average-cost pricing.

Turning to the substance of the case, we find that there are a variety of possible types of equilibria. Assuming tastes are represented by a Mill–Graham utility function identical in both countries (a constant fraction of income is spent on each commodity), the most likely outcome in a two-country world will be for the larger country to export the good subject to industry-level increasing returns. The small country is likely to specialise in the decreasing-returns industry as a result of the opening of trade. This is Graham's case, the country with a comparative advantage in wheat.

Before trade, the small country will be underproducing the increasing-returns commodity (since firms cannot internalise all the benefits from increased production). If free trade causes output in the increasing-returns sector to fall, this will increase the distortion caused by underproduction, and drive the economy further away from the Pareto-optimal allocation, that is, the economy suffers a welfare loss. This also results in a decline in the economy's average productivity. Yet a loss is not inevitable, since the economy gains from trade, that is, the gains from importing the increasing-returns commodity at an even lower cost, and securing for the commodity it exports (the decreasing-returns commodity) a higher price than under autarky. The smaller the 'small' country is, relative to the larger country, the greater the likelihood that it will gain.

But the impression one gains from reading Graham is that he is discussing the case of two countries of nearly equal size. Ethier characterises the Graham case as 'the case of two approximately equally matched countries confronting each other in a situation where one must gain and one must lose' (Ethier 1982, p. 1262). Nevertheless, gains from trade are possible as long as the world output of the industry with scale economies exceeds the national output under autarky.

On the other hand, if we apply the Graham conjecture to the case of an open economy facing a given world price, we see that his argument is considerably strengthened. Here, if the country specialises in the decreasing-returns industry, welfare maximisation would seem to require a permanent tax-cum-subsidy measure to encourage expansion of the increasing-returns industry and contraction of the decreasing-returns industry. Graham argued for tariff protection; but modern economists tend to favour production and/or consumption subsidies to deal with country-specific externalities, as in the present case. However, given the existence of multiple equilibria in the presence of increasing returns to scale, some circumstances may in fact call for tariff protection as the optimal policy.

Granted that Graham's argument has intrinsic merit (that is, with respect to sector and country-specific economies of scale), is it relevant to international competition in the modern world? Should a government seek to promote domestic production of goods that yield positive externalities? Does it matter in an integrated world economy which country succeeds in becoming the producer of externality-generating goods? A significant strand of the modern literature gives a negative answer to each question. In many instances of industrial/financial services competition, external economies are not country-specific – they are international in scope; hence, some say, the relevant concept is 'internationally decreasing costs'. The appropriate way to think about industries linked with external economies is in terms of externality-generating industries at the *international* level. These industries, it is alleged, are the major sources of economies of scale which are diffused to individual firms throughout the world by multi-stage production and trade in intermediate inputs (Ethier 1979, pp. 1–24). Making the point that it is in everyone's interest that industries be concentrated so as to reap the gains from scale economies, Krugman says 'it is important that the industries be concentrated, not where they are concentrated' (Krugman 1987, p. 226). Essentially the same suggestion was made by Viner over fifty years ago in connection with the Graham controversy. If the theory of international trade and increasing returns is conceived in this manner, 'it would, incidentally, invalidate Graham's argument for protection', according to Ethier (1982, p. 1263, n. 27). There, for the time being at any rate, rests the Graham protection controversy; but before we leave this section it may be of interest to mention one related issue where Graham's view clashed again with orthodox opinion.

Graham's emphasis on the supply side, his attack on the idea of reciprocal demand, and the importance he attached to the possibility that international prices might reflect the actual cost ratios in some country (in a multilateral trading system), brought him into conflict with another classical bit of conventional wisdom, that is, to the effect that a country might improve its terms of trade by levying a tariff – except in the singular case of a small country unable to exercise any influence over world prices. Contrary to Torrens and Mill, Graham maintains that the opportunities for rigging the terms of trade are extremely limited, if not non-existent:

> In the world as it is, with many countries producing commodities in common, and with most or all commodities *somewhere* on the margin of producers' indifference as regards various other commodities, the chance of shifting the normal international ratio of exchange through the imposition of protective duties is always small. (Graham 1948, p. 178)

There is therefore little or no scope for securing national gains at the expense of others. Foreign producers discriminated against by the home country's tariff policy may become competitors with the country's export producers. What Graham fails to recognise is that for many products with inelastic demand (typically products that figure in trade between less developed and industrialised countries) the theory of reciprocal demand is indispensable. One only has to recall the massive increase in oil prices engineered by OPEC in the 1970s which dramatically altered the terms of trade between oil-producing and non-oil countries.

The Australian Case for Protection

Reference was made earlier to the late 1920s Australian tariff controversy. This was sparked off by the findings of the semi-official 1929 Brigden Report (the work of a committee of four eminent Australian economists and the Commonwealth Statistician, C.H. Wickens, set up by Prime Minister Stanley Bruce to examine the workings of the protective tariff – Brigden et al. 1929).[26]

The debate centred on the economic rationale for the committee's unorthodox ('heretical') conclusion that the tariff operated in Australia's national interest since, without it, the Australian population could not have enjoyed its current high level of real income – as the Report puts it: 'The evidence available does not support the contention that Australia could have maintained its present population at a higher standard of living under free trade' (Brigden et al. 1929, p. 1, also p. 140). This statement encapsulates what is known as the 'Australian Case for Protection', the reasoning behind which was challenged by orthodox free trade stalwarts such as Viner, Haberler, Anderson and Benham.

The authors of the Report derived their conclusion from nothing more sophisticated than the Ricardian theory of trade and growth, without terms of trade effects. In response to criticisms of the Report by the free trade theorists just mentioned, Marion Crawford Samuelson in 1939 (M.C. Samuelson 1939) showed that the Australian economists' findings were analytically consistent with a form of the Heckscher–Ohlin theory incorporating certain classical assumptions – a model that Paul Samuelson has also described as 'precisely the Ricardian model that David Ricardo used in his arguments with Malthus on the Corn Laws' (Samuelson 1981, p. 153). Two years later a fully fledged neoclassical model appeared – the Stolper–Samuelson theorem (1941) which thenceforth became the standard treatment of changes in trade and factor shares.

The episode is noteworthy both for the interesting analytical issues raised in the debate (such as the income-distribution implications of the classical theory, the relationships among factor intensities, factor prices and commodity prices, terms of trade effects, and so on), as well as for the explicit recognition of the relevance of political and social factors in the debate on free trade and protection. Even when protection ceased to be a live issue in Australia and the Stolper–Samuelson theorem found its place in the textbooks, echoes of the earlier debate rumbled on in the academic literature right up to the early 1980s. The debate took place in a specific historical context and so it may be useful to look briefly at that context before moving on to the debate itself.

During the nineteenth century the six Australian colonies had different levels of customs duties. Victoria (the most populous) adopted high tariffs in 1866 to raise revenue but also for protectionist purposes (that is, to protect local production against competing products of other colonies in order to relieve the unemployment among ex-'diggers' caused by the running down of gold production after 1856), while New South Wales derived the bulk of its revenue from land sales and pursued liberal trade policies. This divergence in colonial trade practices led to conflicting views between free traders and protectionists which continued in the Federal parliament (established in 1901) over the level of the Commonwealth's common external tariff. The protectionists won that battle by 1908 when a protective tariff for the whole Commonwealth incorporating an element of imperial preference was adopted. The new federal tariff provided for a doubling of import duties on most categories of goods. Fear of socialism and the growing popularity of Labour drew protectionists and free-traders together and the next year they formed an anti-Labour coalition, the Liberal Party. The new political grouping endorsed the prevailing high tariffs. Business joined farmers in supporting that policy. The rural interests (wool, wheat), for instance, supported protection for industry in return for subsidies or protection for the less efficient rural industries (sugar, dairy, fruit, tobacco, and so on). That historic compromise became national policy and settled the Australian tariff issue. Thereafter, there was no significant support for freer trade from any quarter. Australia remained committed to protectionism well into the 1970s and only undertook substantial trade liberalisation after 1983.

Thus by the early twentieth century Australia was pursuing protectionist trade policies designed to promote industrial development (that is, import-substituting industrialisation), population growth and the maintenance of high living standards.

The disruption of normal supplies during the Great War (1914–18) forced the pace of industrialisation and led to a policy of 'Protection all round' during the 1920s. By 1925 Australia's average tariff was 25 per cent. Between 1928 and 1930 the number of items subject to tariffs of over 50 per cent more then quadrupled. In the eyes of many Australians the national policy was a hugely successful one, since at that time Australia possibly had the highest per capita income in the world. An optimistic, expansive mood swept the country – the popular phrase was 'Australia Unlimited', signifying an untapped continent needing only capital and labour to unlock its riches. Stanley Bruce summed up the policy in 1923 with a memorable alliterative jingle: 'Men, money and markets' (Macintyre 1999, p. 168).[27]

The tariff was the linchpin that kept the 'Australian system' going. That system was one which sought to reconcile the twin objectives of (a) the maintenance of a high standard of living (that is, high real wages) and (b) an increasing population through natural increase plus immigration. These objectives were, in turn, predicated on the continued prosperity of the staples export sector (wool, wheat, meat) which in the 1920s still accounted for fully 95 per cent of the country's exports (Macintyre 1999, p. 174). The system was in effect a 'wages standard' or an automatic wage-protection mechanism, and the administrative machinery which ran it comprised (a) the Australian Tariff Board and (b) wage-fixing Arbitration Courts. The two parts of the machinery worked in tandem: when domestic prices increased through tariff increases allowed by the Tariff Board, workers' wages were raised by the Arbitration Courts. In this way, the higher profits resulting from protection were partly redistributed to workers in city factories which helped maintain their real wages and living standards (Manger 1981a, pp. 200–1). The significance of the Brigden Report was that it provided the intellectual argument for this tariff-protection system. Calculations contained in the Report indicated that free trade would have resulted in a level of national income as great as under protection, but the population would have been at least 230 000 less. That is to say, the expansion of export volume in the less labour-intensive primary exporting sector (at given world prices) required to keep real national income constant would have been unable to absorb the 230 000 people (workers and their dependants) released by the import-competing industries. But, as Neville Cain remarks: 'Presumably, however, if the real wage were reduced, these persons would be absorbed' (Cain 1973, p. 9). At any rate, the committee's calculations came up with a figure of 750 000 workers being made redundant upon the abolition of the tariff. Given that the tariff had raised costs for the export industry by 9 to 10 per cent, it followed that the removal of protection would have allowed the export industries to reduce their prices by around 10 per cent. But the committee estimated that even that reduction in export prices would not expand export sales sufficiently to warrant the employment of all the workers thrown on to the labour market. In fact, only 520 000 could be re-employed – leaving a net figure of 230 000 unemployed (Brigden et al. 1929, pp. 8, 82, 95).

Returning now to the debate on the 'Australian Case', we propose to discuss this under two headings: (1) how relevant and cogent were the contemporary criticisms of the Brigden Report's findings and conclusions? (2) How did the Report's authors justify their conclusion in the light of recent commentaries, analyses and post-mortems on the controversy?

The defenders of orthodoxy (Viner, Anderson and Haberler) questioned the committee's belief that real wages would rise with tariff protection. They were prepared to admit only that the relative share of labour (out of a reduced total national income) might be increased by protection in a labour-scarce, land-abundant country such as Australia. But, in their opinion, there was no way that the *absolute* income or real wage could be augmented by protection above the free trade level. These critics were locked into a theoretical straitjacket wherein the presumption was that what was good for the whole community was correspondingly so for all sectors or groups in the community. Hence, for example, Anderson's claim that the equality of marginal products of a factor in all employments suffices to maximise its absolute return; then it must be true that since free trade maximises total national income, it must also maximise each and every factor's absolute income.

Since they could not work out the economic reasoning behind what they regarded as the committee's heretical assertions, they assumed it must be heavily value-laden, if not non-economic in status. Thus, they claimed the Report focused on the income of the working class and ignored the effect on total income. Provided labour's share was increased, that was sufficient to establish that the standard of living of all Australians had been augmented by the tariff. Hence, Viner's jibe: 'I cannot go far in support of a policy of reducing Jones' income by six shillings in order to increase Smith's income by five, even if Jones is a landowner or capitalist, and Smith a worker' (Viner 1929, p. 308).

These orthodox criticisms, particularly an article by Anderson, were demolished by Marion Crawford Samuelson, as described earlier. She showed how in the case of an economy such as Australia protection of manufactures would call forth an increased demand for labour-intensive manufactures. This would shift labour out of agriculture, lower real land rents and hence, total landowners' incomes. In the opposite direction, it would raise workers' real incomes both relatively and absolutely – all as later on envisaged in the standard two-commodity, two-country Stolper–Samuelson theorem including favourable terms-of-trade effects of the tariff. In addition to the terms-of-trade effects, the mobility of the two (presumably homogeneous) factors, land and capital, is crucial to M.C. Samuelson's conclusions (M.C. Samuelson 1939, pp. 144–9).

But was that the argument of the authors of the Brigden Report? Did they justify the Australian case for protection along these lines? No, they did not, says Manger in a 1981 paper on the controversy (Manger 1981a). Manger provided chapter and verse to show how: (1) The report played down the favourable terms of trade effect of the tariff; (2) its authors cannot be regarded as 'forerunners or progenitors' of the Stolper–Samuelson theorem. Indeed, he claimed the authors of the report used a Ricardian growth/distribution model combined with an official wage-protection mechanism such as operated in Australia at the time (as mentioned above). If anyone can be said to be the author of the Australian case for protection it must be Marion Crawford Samuelson with her 1939 rebuttal of the free-traders' criticism of the report.

Manger gives two reasons why the authors of the Brigden Report became associated with the terms-of-trade and Stolper–Samuelson type redistribution argument for protection – key features of the 'Australian case' as traditionally defined:

1. The fact that Anderson's (1939) summary of the report (which many others accepted) contained the terms-of-trade effect as one of three arguments he believed the Australian authors had used to justify protection.
2. It was Marion Crawford Samuelson who, by justifying the conclusion of the Report's authors as against Anderson, gave the impression that the authors of the Report used a prototype of the Ohlin model (Manger 1981a, pp. 193–204).

Yet, whatever label one chooses to describe the work of the authors of the Brigden Report, they did present an authentic case (or justification) for the peculiar Australian system of protection with the Report's emphasis on the redistribution or 'pooling' effect of the tariff. The Report was meant to come to some judgement on the protective system, hence its 'empirical' slant and low-key theoretical argumentation. Yet the Committee members evidently had deeper, relevant insights into their subject-matter than were to be found in the pages of their Report.[28] For instance, they saw a symmetry between the British Corn Laws debate and Australia's circumstances as a labour-scarce agricultural exporter, namely that for Australia, protection of labour-intensive manufactures might be theoretically justifiable. On this point, Sir Douglas Copland noted in 1931:

> Australian conditions are almost exactly the converse of those which gave point to the free-trade argument in Great Britain . . . and it is rather remarkable that economic literature contains so little reference to the possibility of protection being economically sound under such conditions. (Copland 1931, p. 290)

Copland also knew, and indeed referred to Henry Sidgwick's 1883 hypo-thetical analysis of what is entailed in a move from industrial protection to free trade for a country faced with diminishing returns in the primary sector and exporting agricultural products. Suppose that on the adoption of free trade, manufactures can be obtained at half the price from trading partners. What impact will this have on the country? Sidgwick painted a dismal pros-pect for such a country. Import-competing manufacturing production would contract and manufacturing jobs would be lost. It would be neces-sary then to expand production elsewhere to compensate for the loss of pro-tected manufacturing output. That means expansion of output in the primary or agricultural sector. But since agricultural production is subject to diminishing returns, extra output will only be obtained at increasing cost. Devoting more resources to agricultural production would lower output per capita. The less labour-intensive agricultural sector would be unable to absorb all the redundant manufacturing workers, even at reduced real wages taking into account the lower consumer prices made possible without the tariff. Unemployed workers would then face a stark choice: either accept a reduction in their standard of living or emigrate. The logic of the situation implied an end result which Sidgwick expressed as 'that the natural result of Free Trade may be that [the country] will only support a smaller, though wealthier, population'; but that the resulting per capita income gain would be one which 'would require violent government interference to distribute so as to retain the labourers thrown out of work' (Sidgwick [1883] (1901), pp. 494–5). Copland no doubt drew his own conclusions from that example. The remaining population might be so small that only agriculture would be viable. The appeal of industrial protectionism was then obvious. It was the only way to retain the existing population at a stipulated real wage.

Earlier, in 1925, Brigden presented a case for Australian protection which was the genesis of the subsequent debate (Brigden, 1925). Brigden's argu-ment was that whether under free trade or protection, the exploitation of Australia's national resources could not have supported an increasing pop-ulation at a constant high standard of living. In particular, free trade would have pushed the increasing population into agricultural production and the dead-end of diminishing returns. In addition, Australia would have suffered deteriorating terms of trade for its increased output of primary commodities. On balance, Brigden judged that the gain from improved terms of trade more than offset the increased cost of imports in the Australian market. Brigden fully recognized that the maintenance of the standard of living of the Australian worker, despite massive immigration, was bought at the expense of landowners who, under free trade, would have enjoyed higher real incomes. That was essentially the gist and tenor of the Brigden Report.

On terms-of-trade effects, we know that these must have been at the back of the economists' minds, even though such effects did not feature prominently in the Report. During the period 1925–9 a debate on the terms of trade gains from protection was carried on in the Australian economics journals, with Brigden and Giblin arguing that Australia had market power with respect to wool and probably wheat in international markets which could be exploited by imposition of a sufficiently small general tariff – Australia accounted for over a third of world wool exports in 1929. By reducing agricultural production, the tariff induces improved terms of trade, increases the Australian real national income and redistributes (or 'pools') the enhanced total income to achieve the national standard of living objective. In fact, as we have noted, this mechanism was the main theme of the Report: the use of the tariff as a tax on the rent from rural exports to increase employment in the manufacturing sector without reducing real wages. The income to support a greater number of workers was therefore extracted from landlords and capitalists.

It must be mentioned that the Brigden economists are not to be labelled as inveterate protectionists. In several places in the Report they referred to the protective/redistributive policy as having reached 'the economic limits' and, indeed, one of their conclusions was that further tariff increases would not be justified since the costs might outweigh benefits. However, it is true they did not recommend any reduction in the amount of protection afforded to Australian industry. The Australian economists knew that a successful tariff policy depended critically on the performance of the export sector in world markets, that is, its ability to profit from increased relative prices. The assumption that Australia had monopoly power in world markets for its principal export, wool, was widely held and, perhaps, accounted for the fact that the Report's authors failed to consider less favourable terms-of-trade effects that might have resulted from the vagaries of supply and demand conditions in the world market.

As a concluding remark on the work of the Australian economists (faced with the confusion and muddled thinking of leading British economists) Samuelson's summing up is worth quoting:

> Perhaps this Marshall–Pigou confusion gave them the courage to buck the tide of the then current dogmatic orthodoxy, and in that sense served a useful purpose after all. (Samuelson 1981, p. 154)

What the Australian episode illustrates, however, is the remarkable adaptability of Ricardian-type models for dealing fairly rigorously with a wide range of trade-related issues such as the effects of technological progress on patterns of specialisation, the income distribution consequences of trade and the distribution of gains from trade. Nicholas Kaldor, a noted British economist and economic adviser to Labour governments in the mid-1960s and 1970s, used to criticise classical and neoclassical trade theory for its claim that all types of trade are equally beneficial to all of the trading countries (Kaldor 1978; 1980). Kaldor maintained that this proposition was only true under the specific abstract assumptions of perfect competition and constant returns to scale (linearly homogeneous production functions) for all processes of production. Under the more realistic assumption of diminishing returns to transferable factors of production and/or increasing returns to scale, we immediately recognise that agricultural production is subject to diminishing returns and manufacturing industry typically enjoys increasing returns to scale, both of a static and of a dynamic kind. Kaldor claimed that under these conditions 'the presumption derived from Ricardo's doctrine of comparative costs . . . no longer holds. For under these conditions it can be demonstrated that free trade may lead to stunted growth, or even impoverishment of some regions (or countries) to the greater benefit of others' (Kaldor 1978, p. 237) – depending on the pattern of trade of the trading countries. Kaldor referred to Ricardo's corn model of trade and distribution as a powerful argument against the protection of agriculture in Great Britain, but remarked: 'For completion he [Ricardo] should have added that free trade may not be *equally* advantageous to foreign countries who, whilst exporting more foodstuffs and raw materials to Britain, may suffer a loss of income through the shrinkage of their *own* manufacturing activities' (Kaldor 1978, p. 238). Without referring to the Australian case or to Sidgwick's hypothetical example, Kaldor analysed a case where, under diminishing returns in primary production, a competitive free trade equilibrium might be unfavourable to the primary producer in trade with a manufacturing country where export industries enjoy increasing returns. Trade between a manufacturing country and a primary producer would destroy the manufacturing sector of the primary producer and drive a substantial part of the labour force into unemployment. Because of the land constraint not all the available labour would be able to find employment – the excess labour would remain unemployed. The argument, Kaldor stated, depended on the absence of constant costs in agriculture in terms of transferable factors of production and also on the Ricardian assumption that labour had a minimum supply price whether or not the demand and supply of labour were equalised (Kaldor 1980, p. 95). Because of this, both the capital stock and the amount of labour employed could be smaller under free trade than under protection.

In his 1996 history of free trade, Douglas Irwin comments on the Australian case, noting that 'it never constituted a direct indictment of free trade, but showed that not all groups in an economy are necessarily positioned to benefit from free trade' (Irwin 1996, p. 179). Although categorised as an interesting non-economic argument for protection, Irwin further observed that the Australian debate revived theoretical analysis of trade-related distributional effects neglected since Ricardo's attack on the Corn Laws and prompted 1930s discussions into the welfare economics of free trade. Part of Viner's (1929) criticism of the Report was that tariff protection was a grossly inefficient means of redistribution, and more recently Anderson and Garnaut (1987) argued that the imposition of high import duties on manufactures was certainly not the best tax policy for Australia in the 1930s. Were more efficient ways of income redistribution available to the authorities? What was the first-best policy for redistribution of income towards labour? Various suggestions have been made: for instance, a tax on land rents could have been used to create jobs in manufacturing, or an export tax on wool which could have generated additional revenue for redistributive purposes. Brigden et al. (1929) must have considered these alternatives but clearly felt that the current system (the 'Australian system') was the only feasible one, given the constraint of a national policy hitched to the objective of a larger population at a given standard of living. At one point in the Report, the authors seem to argue that since the channel (that is, the tariff) through which redistribution came about was largely 'hidden' from taxpayers, that tended to make the redistributive effect greater than would have been possible by income taxation (Brigden et al. 1929, pp. 5 and 95). What we have here is clearly a case where economists endorsed a policy aimed at goals other than the free trade one of maximising per capita incomes; in this instance, one aimed at redistribution designed to minimise income inequality.

In 1996 Mahinda Siriwardana (1996) reported the results of an empirical investigation into the impact of the Australian tariff by simulating a computable general equilibrium (CGE) model of the 1930s Australian economy consisting of nine sectors. The Brigden Report conclusions are supported by the simulation on the supposition that the terms-of-trade effects were favourable. Siriwardana's estimates indicate that the export demand elasticity for Australian wool was within the range 0.5 and 3.2 during the 1930s. For wheat the export demand elasticity ranged from 1.5 to 8.0. The model was simulated under various assumptions to arrive at the counterfactual effects resulting from a 20 per cent increase in all Australian tariffs in the late 1920s. Three different scenarios relating to these values of the export demand elasticities were analysed. In the case of a 'low' elasticity, an increase in tariffs would expand national income via the terms-of-trade effect. The projected macroeconomic effects of the simulations were: under the 'low' export demand elasticity assumption, the Australian terms of trade would have increased by 17.9 per cent resulting in a rise in real national income by 3.5 per cent. Real growth in the economy (6.2 per cent) would have increased the demand for labour by 6.2

per cent. By contrast, if Australia was unable to exploit any terms-of-trade advantages owing to a 'high' elasticity of demand for its exports, then increased protection would merely have resulted in inflation accompanied by a decline in real income and employment by 2.4 per cent and 4.3 per respectively (Siriwardana 1996, pp. 377–9).

Export demand elasticity for Australia's principal exports during the time period under consideration is not available, but since it is generally believed that the relevant elasticity for Australian wool was low at that time, Siriwardana's results seemingly support the conclusion of the Brigden Report. Of course, shortly after the publication of the Report, Australia was hit by the world slump and the collapse of commodity prices which resulted in adverse terms of trade and a substantial loss of real incomes for the population. Eventually, too, Australia's monopoly power in world wool markets declined as synthetic fibres became popular and new sources of wool supplies came on stream.

In a 1958 article asking whether there is still an Australian case, A.J. Reitsma concluded that the case for protection should have been based on dynamic grounds, that is to say, that the Australian tariff stimulated economic growth along the lines of the infant-industry argument. Instead, the protagonists confused the argument by focusing on essentially static income distribution effects and claimed that more could be gained by regarding the Australian policy of protection in the past as an instrument for stimulating economic growth. 'This, I believe, the tariff has done.' (Reitsma, 1958, p. 188).

NOTES

1. The origin and development of neoclassical international economics is surveyed in Gomes (1990).
2. The 1844 criticism was by Carl Heinrich Hagen in his book *Die Nothwendigkeit der Handelsfreiheit für das Nationaleinkommen, mathematisch nachgewiesen* (Königsberg, 1844), pp. 30–1. Samuelson praises Cournot's treatment of interspatial price equilibrium as being 'marvellously modern and fruitful', but adds, 'his analysis of tariff protection appears to be ambiguous and of doubtful validity'. P.A. Samuelson, 'The Way of An Economist', in Samuelson (1969, p. 5).
3. Reghinos Theocaris writes that Viner 'appears to have misunderstood Cournot's reasoning' in regard to income changes resulting from free trade in the importing country. See Theocaris (1983, p. 229). What most critics failed to realise was that Cournot used a 'first order approximation' rather than a full equilibrium system in his study of the benefits of the opening-up of trade.
4. Citing a passage from Cournot stressing the need for the development of productive powers, Theocaris notes: 'The influence of List is obvious' (Theocaris 1983, p. 234, n. 36). According to Cournot, an extensive industrial sector and a skilled labour force were the objectives of a programme geared to the development of 'productive powers'. A country so equipped would be an exporter of manufactured goods and an importer of agricultural products and raw materials.

5. Cournot judged free trade a desirable objective in the long run when productive forces have been built up – again a position similar to that of List. Thus 'new products can indefinitely be exchanged one against another, provided that a suitable direction is given to the various branches of production' (Cournot 1863, p. 287). Towards the end of his life Cournot became conservative-minded on account of his fear of socialism. Thus in the book published in the year of his death, *Revue sommaire des doctrines économiques* (1877) Cournot departed from his early interventionist views and espoused the tenets of economic liberalism.

6. The graphical technique is set out and described in Marshall [1923], 1965, appendix J, sec. 3, pp. 338–40.

7. Hicks' article is 'The Rehabilitation of Consumer's Surplus', *Review of Economic Studies*, 8 (1941), pp. 108–16.

8. J.M. Currie, J.A. Murphy and A. Schmitz, 'The Concept of Economic Surplus and Its Use in Economic Analysis', *Economic Journal*, 81 (December 1971), p. 779.

9. Marshall, 'An Export Duty on Coal', letter to *The Times* (19 April 1901), reprinted in *Economic Journal*, 11 (June 1901), p. 265; also Pigou (1925), p. 322.

10. See Marshall in Whitaker (1975), p. 56. For Marshall's further views on this matter, see Pigou (1925), pp. 258–60.

11. The concepts of internal and external economies of scale are extensively discussed in Marshall's *Principles* (Marshall, 1920, Book IV, chapters 9–11). In his trade theory he discussed the relationship between economies of scale and the terms of trade. If Germany imports cloth from England in exchange for linen, and cloth is produced under conditions of increasing returns to scale, then by expanding her demand for English cloth Germany can improve her barter terms of trade: 'an increase in Germany's demand for English cloth may cause each yard of linen to be sold here on such terms as to give command over a larger amount of cloth than before; it is possible that the increase in Germany's demand for English cloth may cause her to obtain an import of English cloth increased *in a greater ratio* than is her export of linen to England'. Marshall, 'The Pure Theory of Foreign Trade', in Whitaker (1975), p. 145.

12. Quoted by Ronald Findlay in R.W. Jones and P.B. Kenen (eds), *Handbook of International Economics*, vol. I (Amsterdam: North-Holland, 1984), p. 186.

13. As early as 1903 (two years before the Battle of Tsushima Strait, May 1905, when the Japanese sunk the Russian Baltic Fleet) Marshall wrote about the industrial potential of the Japanese and was prophetic about their industrial and technological challenge to the Western industrialized countries. He noted that Britain was losing its trading advantage to 'people like the Japanese, who can assimilate every part of the work of an advanced factory'; and 'they [the Japanese] are so alert, so closely in touch with western thought, and so full of independent enterprise, that her manufactures for export are growing rapidly' (Marshall [1903] 1926, p. 404, and Marshall [1923] 1965, p. 173).

14. For a useful summary of the arguments in this controversy, see Jha (1973, pp. 39–41).

15. In an introductory text published many years later, Pigou again supported List's infant-industry argument in these words: 'by putting obstacles in the way of foreign trade, a country, though it would sacrifice income-getting power at the moment, would gain on the whole, because it would be building up income-getting power in the future.' A.C. Pigou, *Income: An Introduction to Economics* (1946) (London: Macmillan, 1966), p. 42.

16. A seventeenth-century mercantilist could not have put the question any better. The justification for chartered trading companies (as distinct from the competition between individual merchants) was that they enabled such national gains to be secured.

17. E. Barone, *Grundzüge der Theoretischen Nationalökonomie*, trans. by Hans Staehle (Bonn: K. Schroeder Verlag, 1927), fig. 30, p. 102, and fig. 32, p. 105. This German translation of the 1913 edition of Barone's 1908 work, *Principi di Economia Politica* (Rome: Tipografia Nazionale di G. Bertero) is the source almost exclusively relied upon by English-language writers.

18. The translation is due to Andrea Maneschi. See Maneschi (1998, pp. 147–50) for a clear, informative analysis of Barone's contribution.

19. Andrea Maneschi and William O. Thweatt, 'Barone's 1908 Representation of an

Economy's Trade Equilibrium and the Gains from Trade', *Journal of International Economics*, 22 (1987), pp. 375–82. A translation of Barone's footnote is here provided by Andrea Maneschi.

20. T.W. Hutchison, *A Review of Economic Doctrines 1870–1929* (Oxford: Clarendon Press, 1953).
21. A summary translation of Schüller's work is in F.W. Taussig (ed.), *Selected Readings in International Trade and Tariff Problems* (Boston: Ginn & Co., 1921), pp. 371–91.
22. See Jacob Viner, 'Mihail Manoilescu on the Theory of Protection', *Journal of Political Economy*, 40 (1), pp. 121–5, reprinted in Viner (1951).
23. B. Ohlin, 'Protection and Non-Competing Groups', *Weltwirtschaftliches Archiv*, 33, Heft 1 (1931), p. 44.
24. The first remark was made by K.L. Anderson, the second by Haberler and the third by Viner. The references are: K.L. Anderson, 'Tariff Protection and Increasing Returns', in *Explorations in Economics: Notes and Essays Contributed in Honor of F.W. Taussig* (New York: McGraw-Hill, 1936), p. 167; Haberler (1936, p. 201); Viner ([1937] 1955, p. 481).
25. H. Herberg and M.C. Kemp, 'Some Implications of Variable Returns to Scale', *Canadian Journal of Economics*, 2 (1969), pp. 403–15; Panagariya (1981, p. 222). Apparently, Herberg and Kemp were the first to sort out and correct the common misunderstanding about the shape of the production-possibility frontier for the case under discussion.
26. The economists were J.B. Brigden, D.B. Copland, E.C. Dyason and L.F. Giblin.
27. Prime Minister Bruce used the phrase at an Imperial Conference in 1923. Stuart Macintyre explains the elements of the policy as: 'Men from Britain were needed, along with women and children to fill up the empty spaces, but most of all men to make the land productive . . . Money was required from British investors . . . Markets had to be found for the increased primary production' (Macintyre 1999, p. 168).
28. Cain (1973, p. 7, n. 8): 'With the exception of the real-wage argument (which may have owed something to Sidgwick) the ingredients of Brigden's case [that is, his writings of 1925–8] had been plainly Marshallian. His contribution, however, was to bring them together in the "special circumstances" of Australia in the 1920s.'

5.   Trade and general equilibrium

5.1   THE APPROACH TO GENERAL EQUILIBRIUM

The 1930s Watershed

The transformation curve (or concave production-possibility frontier) was introduced into trade theory by Enrico Barone in 1908, but for various reasons his contribution went unnoticed (as previously mentioned). Twenty-two years later, Haberler reintroduced the construction under the label of 'production substitution curve'. It was a diagrammatic representation of a country's maximum attainable set of outputs for two commodities from a given supply of productive factors, and described the rate at which commodities could be substituted for each other not only under constant opportunity-cost conditions, but also under increasing and decreasing costs as well. Under increasing costs (the assumption frequently made) the production-possibility frontier is drawn strictly concave to the origin, that is, the production-possibility set is convex, reflecting the law of diminishing marginal productivity.

For Haberler, the great advantage of the approach was that it dispensed with the need for a labour theory of value, or a real cost theory or indeed for any other specific theory of costs. It enabled relative commodity prices to be analysed under conditions of variable factor proportions in a more straightforward manner than was possible with the real cost approach espoused by Taussig and Viner. It restored simplicity to the original Ricardian doctrine of comparative costs by making obsolete the use of ill-defined concepts like 'bales' and 'units of productive power' introduced by Marshall, Edgeworth and others to deal with the analytical problems posed by a multiplicity of productive factors.

Although others had utilised the concept of opportunity costs before him, Haberler, with his training in the Austrian School, was the first to see its potential as a simple but versatile tool for modelling production in trade theory. With the transformation curve device, costs are measured subjectively, not by the absolute amount of labour and other factors required to produce a given output, but by the alternative output foregone – that is, the cost of a commodity is the amount of another commodity which might have been produced with the same resources. Under increasing costs the

exchange ratio, or the ratio of internal relative prices, of two commodities
will vary with the relative demand for the commodities, that is, the ratio at
which the two commodities exchange against one another in the market will
equal the ratio of their marginal costs.

Haberler's brilliant display of the production-possibility frontier triggered a remarkable outburst of seminal papers by Lerner, Leontief and
Viner which not only revived the lacklustre image of trade theory, but also
lifted it to a new plateau from which it was able to advance with speed and
assurance.

In 1931 Viner presented a paper (at the London School of Economics)
in which he combined the transformation curve and 'consumption
indifference curves' (community indifference curves) to represent free trade
equilibrium and the gains from trade, in a diagram that is now all-too-
familiar to beginning students in international economics – 'the sacred
diagram of the international trade economist', as some call it.[1] This was followed by four equally fundamental papers – three in quick succession by
Lerner, and one by Leontief. Haberler had suggested that the gains from
trade could be indicated, if not measured, by means of his production-
possibility curve. In a classic 1933 paper which did much to establish the
concept of community indifference curves for analytical purposes, Wassily
Leontief combined Haberler's curve with a system of indifference curves to
make the idea more precise. Leontief makes the important assumption that
community indifference curves do not intersect; but he does not consider
the question of how they may be obtained from individual preferences.

During these years, too, Lerner published another famous paper, 'The
Symmetry between Import and Export Taxes', which fully clarified and
resolved a disputed point in the theory of trade policy between Edgeworth
and Bastable. The question was, were taxes on imports and exports symmetrical, in the sense that they had identical real effects? Marshall,
Bastable, Pigou and the classical economists, stressing as they did the *barter*
nature of all trade, took it for granted that the two taxes were symmetrical.
Edgeworth alone evidently held the contrary view and criticised Bastable
for failing to see the difference between the two taxes. Edgeworth, however,
later retracted his criticism of Bastable, but maintained that the difference
between the imposts was true only of 'taxes in kind'. Edgeworth's error was
due to the fact that he failed to see that the difference was not about how
the taxes were levied, but how the proceeds were spent. Edgeworth mistakenly interpreted the result of his method of shifting the duty-imposing
country's offer curve as indicating a real difference between the two types
of taxes.[2]

Lerner established the correct results by means of the ingenious device
of a geometrical pencil formed by the two different price radiants to the

offer curves – a difference created by the tax, whether on imports or exports. Only the commodities on which the tax proceeds are spent create a difference – for example, the more spent on imports, the less favourable the impact on the terms of trade.[3] With balanced trade, the revenues collected by the two taxes are the same. An export tax on one good has a real effect similar to an import tax on the other good. Similarly, equilibrium remains unaltered if an import tariff is substituted in place of an export tax. In effect, Lerner's result shows that the import-competing sector as a whole can be protected as easily by an export tax as by an import duty. Would the symmetry proposition continue to hold in a monetary economy? Mundell has recently argued that the result must be qualified when the central bank's assets and relative changes in home and foreign price levels are taken into consideration, and concludes that his analysis 'suggests that the symmetry theorem Lerner proved applies strictly to the barter world of two commodities on which his proof rests'.[4]

Haberler's Contribution

Haberler's prominent role in the formulation and development of the modern theory of international trade was widely recognised when an English translation of his 1933 treatise on trade theory and policy appeared in 1936. Even as late as the 1960s his book continued to be widely read and quoted.

In his book, Haberler introduced the useful concept of 'specific' factors of production which he attributed to Wieser. This idea provided the basis for 'specific-factors' models of trade (which focus on asymmetry in the degree of factor mobility between sectors) developed by Jones and Samuelson forty years later. This was used to deduce the curvature of the 'substitution curve' (production-possibility curve) – an explanation similar to that commonly used today to account for the shape of the curve in terms of factor-intensity differences: that is, products can be classified in terms of their relative K-intensity or L-intensity in production. Haberler revealed that the distinction between specific and non-specific – the latter being capable of employment in a number of different uses – was first mentioned by Friedrich von Wieser, his teacher at the University of Vienna. Some factors of production are, at least to some extent and especially in the short run, 'specific': either they can be used only for one particular purpose – that is, they are completely immobile among industries – or they would yield so much less if transferred to another use (machinery, for example, being used as scrap-iron) that in fact they are not transferred. At the international level, specificity may arise because of obstacles to movement (for example, national immigration controls or prohibitive transport costs, and so on).

Haberler's exposition of the theory of comparative costs was a masterful achievement, as was his clear and comprehensive evaluation of the
various arguments for protection. Observing that 'economists are nearly
as unanimous in favour of a liberal trade policy as are Governments in
favour of the contrary' (Haberler 1936, Preface to the German edition, p.
viii), he set out in true scientific earnest to discover what was valid and
what was nonsense in the protectionists' perennial pleas. Haberler's celebrated 1950 paper on 'Some Problems in the Pure Theory of International
Trade' (1950, pp. 213–29) initiated a line of enquiry concerned with
optimal trade policy in the presence of domestic distortions (divergences
between private and social marginal costs) caused by external economies,
factor immobility or factor-price rigidity, which was later more fully developed by Bhagwati and Ramaswami and Johnson. Haberler's purpose was
to show that free trade did not necessarily imply *laissez-faire*. The case for
free trade still holds (excepting the optimal tariff argument) even when the
various simplifying assumptions associated with it are removed, although
domestic *laissez-faire* may have to give way to policy interventions.
Meade's 1955 work on trade and welfare, as well as that of Hagen, were
also pioneering pieces in the development of this literature on policy intervention in open economies.

Haberler called for further efforts to develop the pure theory of international trade; in particular, he said, the theory of imperfect competition
'must be applied to the problems of international trade', and referring to
the progress made in that field by Chamberlain and Joan Robinson felt that
'it will soon be possible to do this in a systematic way'.[5] But the hoped-for
development was long delayed and is only now being tackled. Together
with Viner's classic *Studies*, Haberler's book did much to enhance the intellectual status of international economics in the 1930s. The other book published around this time which had a powerful, indeed revolutionary, impact
was of course Bertil Ohlin's *Interregional and International Trade*.

The Heckscher–Ohlin–Samuelson Model

Since the spring of 1922 Ohlin had formulated his factor endowment
theory of trade based on a mutual interdependence (or multiple-market)
theory of pricing. For the first time, the analysis of factor markets became
integrated into trade theory. Ohlin's new approach was much influenced by
the work of two of his teachers, Eli Heckscher and Gustav Cassel. From
Cassel he acquired a version of the Walrasian system of general equilibrium, and from Heckscher the view that international trade flows could be
explained in terms of the relative scarcity or abundance of different factors
of production, if both countries had access to the same technology; and the

further idea that factor returns would be equalised by free trade in goods alone if there was a difference in the factor-input combinations for different goods. Heckscher in turn acknowledged his indebtedness to Knut Wicksell for the analysis in terms of factor endowments.

Ohlin built on this Swedish approach and combined elements of his own. He felt that the theories of international trade, interregional trade and location shared enough common characteristics that made them amenable to unified treatment under the rubric of a general locational analysis of spatial pricing, migration and capital movements. In fact, Ohlin declared: 'The theory of international trade is nothing but *internationale Standortslehre*' (Ohlin 1933, p. 589). The hoped-for integration of international trade theory into locational analysis has, however, not occurred. Regrettably, in the view of location theorists, the space factor and costs of transporting commodities between countries (or transfer costs, in general) have never been satisfactorily integrated into the competitive general-equilibrium theory of international trade – in 1960 Richard Caves omitted the economics of location from his survey of trade theory on the ground that 'trade and location theory have not been successfully juxtaposed' (Caves 1960, p. 3). The scant regard, until recently, for the role of non-traded goods was partly connected with the usual assumption of 'no transport costs' – although in the case of non-tradeable services, transport cost is infinite. Yet it is pretty obvious that differential transfer cost between individual trading countries is not a negligible factor, despite recent developments in containerisation and jet transport facilities.

Ohlin emphasised the role of increasing returns to scale as a cause of international specialisation and trade. Such economies of scale, he pointed out, can supplement the incentives created by cross-country differences in factor endowments and, even in the absence of such differences (including tastes and technology), can give rise to lasting and mutually beneficial trade. Analytical convenience was decisive, however, in the retention of the assumption of constant returns in much of trade theory, at any rate until very recently – witness Samuelson's comment: 'The phenomenon of increasing returns negates the nice convexity properties that are so beloved by us lazy mathematical economists hell-bent for elegance of formulation' (Samuelson 1986, p. 152). Relaxing the assumption of a constant-returns technology means, of course, confronting the issue of market structure; in particular, the analysis of imperfect competition. For, as is well known, except under special circumstances (for example, where total demand is large relative to the potential economies of large-scale production), perfectly competitive markets cannot prevail where returns to scale are non-constant. Nevertheless, Ohlin joined Haberler in calling for a useful theory of imperfect competition in international trade; but as Samuelson notes, 'that call has thus far not evoked a very exciting response' (Samuelson 1986, p. 152). The signs are, however, that things may be changing, as evidenced by the recent spate of important and useful writings on imperfect competition, increasing returns and international trade.

Ohlin's model is a multi-factor one; he recognises not only three basic factors of production considered in neoclassical writings – land (or natural resources), labour and capital – but also varying *qualities* of the first two of these factors. Labour, for example, is divided into three groups: unskilled labour, skilled labour and technical labour. He also recognises that there are international differences in the qualities of labour in all three classes. Ohlin explains the reasons for differences in prices and comparative advantage between countries and adopts two simplifying assumptions (for the two-factor case): (1) that the technology of production is the same in both countries, and (2) that 'the productive factors enter into the production of different commodities in very different proportions' (Ohlin 1933, p. 30). Like Haberler, he considers the possibility that endogenous changes in relative factor returns (brought about, for example, by international trade) will eventually alter the available supplies of some of these factors, that is, capital and the various types of labour. Ohlin observes that asymmetrical taste patterns will generate mutually profitable trade; for each country will then find it advantageous to import the commodity for which its demand is more intense. Similarly, he shows that differences in factor endowments or the occurrence of increasing returns are sufficient to generate viable trade among countries. Of all the factors liable to cause differences in autarky price ratios Ohlin considers differential factor endowments as the most important. Countries tend to export those commodities requiring more of their relatively abundant factors (that is, low-priced factors) and import commodities intensive in the use of their scarce, hence high-priced, factors. Free trade in goods thus compensates for (or relieves) factor scarcities in the trading countries (that is, the uneven geographic distribution of productive resources) since traded commodities are really 'bundles' of factors.

In a discussion of the effects of trade on factor supplies, factor returns and the structure of demand and taste patterns, Ohlin takes up Heckscher's proposition about the absolute equalisation of factor returns under free trade. Ohlin finds, however, that there will only be a partial equalisation; and he mentions factors which prevent complete equalisation – that is, when some factor of production is found only in one country, the positivity of transport costs, and if specialisation leaves one country with an unproduced good. Free trade in goods is thus a partial substitute for the free migration of factors.

Ohlin regarded his new theory as the first decisive break with Ricardo's law of comparative costs. In his keenness to emphasise the novelty of his factor-endowment approach, he even refused to use the phrase 'comparative advantage'. His strong criticism of the classical theory is partly explained by his dislike of the labour theory of value. Of course, his theory was not a rejection of comparative advantage, but merely a restatement of it along neoclassical lines as part of a more general theory of the causes of trade.

The Heckscher–Ohlin theory made its appearance at an opportune time. The time was ripe for the reception of such a theory by the new enthusiasts for general equilibrium theory. In particular, it was quickly seized upon by Samuelson, who re-shaped and refined it in a series of articles in the late 1940s and early 1950s to produce what now appears in the textbooks as the standard 2x2x2 H-O model of trade – the most popular model of production relationships in an open economy. Indeed, Samuelson's imprint on it is so marked that it is often referred to as the Heckscher–Ohlin–Samuelson model. Samuelson achieved that much because, as a leading practitioner of general-equilibrium theorising, he was uniquely equipped to appreciate the potential it afforded for giving substance (or structure) to the notion of general equilibrium – an area he discerned as being ripe for development.

The 1930s was a watershed between the old and the new (or modern) neoclassical economics. In the 1930s there was growing dissatisfaction with the Marshallian tradition which led to Hicks' *Value and Capital* (1939) and Samuelson's *Foundations* (1947) and the consequent reconstruction of economic theory in a general-equilibrium framework. A 'research programme' was initiated concerned with the existence, uniqueness, stability and Pareto-optimality properties of a competitive economy in general equilibrium.

In the field of international trade, the general theories of Heckscher and Ohlin offered a splendid opportunity for Samuelson to display the analytical techniques and propositions he had fashioned. The two-factor H-O theory (in contrast to the classical one-factor model) enabled the analyst to deal with the functional distribution of income within countries and the allocation of factors between industries. It also suggested new questions, such as the effects of capital accumulation and international factor movements on trade. Moreover, the two-factor H-O model was intrinsically more revealing than the Ricardian model about production relationships and the structural characteristics of an exchange economy, since it fully recognised 'mutual interdependence' and 'simultaneous determination' in commodity exchanges among economic agents – that is, the simultaneous interaction of all goods markets and factor markets. Trade and economic structure were tightly knit together, and this went well with the new vogue (initiated by theorists like Lerner, Haberler and Leontief in the 1930s). In short, the factor-endowment theory considerably widened the scope for the application of the full techniques of marginal analysis (comparative statics) to trade theory. The core ingredients of the simple Heckscher–Ohlin theory were assembled from the basic relations of the general equilibrium of a two-sector economy upon which special assumptions were imposed so as to obtain sharp conclusions or unambiguous qualitative results.

Thus, in a perfectly competitive economy in which two commodities are produced with two factors utilising production functions characterised by constant returns to scale and diminishing marginal rates of substitution between factors, minimum unit cost depends only on factor prices, not on the level of output. Assuming perfect mobility of factors and adopting the marginal productivity theory, it follows that the price of each factor will be equated to the value of its marginal product and that the price of each factor will be the same in both industries. Then if a positive amount of each commodity is produced, competitive output-market assumptions guarantee that the price of each will equal its cost of production. It then follows that there is a one-to-one relation between the commodity price ratio and the factor price ratio. Further, if the factor endowment ratio is fixed and an assumption is made about the invariance of relative factor intensity, then the ratios in which the commodities are produced will be fixed, since their aggregate factor requirements must just absorb all of the available factor supplies. Using this framework, extended to a free-trade world of two countries each producing both goods, Samuelson provided meaningful sufficient conditions to prove two theorems – the Stolper–Samuelson theorem and the celebrated factor-price equalisation theorem. Just before Samuelson's article on prices of factors and goods in general equilibrium appeared, the third principal pillar in the H-O structure was put into place – the Rybczynski theorem. Tadeusz (Tad) Rybczynski (then at the LSE), using a simple diagrammatic technique, proved the following theorem: if the supply of one factor increases with the supply of the other factor constant, the absolute output of the good which uses the increased factor less intensively must diminish so as to keep the relative price of the goods constant (Rybczynski 1955, pp. 336–41).

Given the focus of this book, our interest naturally turns at this point to the first of these results, the Stolper-Samuelson theorem.

In a 1941 article with Wolfgang Stolper, Samuelson re-examined an old problem in the theory of trade policy: can a tariff effectively raise the real return to a large factor such as labour? In the first clear resolution of the problem expounded with the aid of a simple diagrammatic and algebraic analysis of the Heckscher–Ohlin model, Stolper and Samuelson indicated that protection will unambiguously increase the real wage if labour is the scarce factor of production, and concluded: 'We have shown that there is a grain of truth in the pauper labour type of argument for protection' (Stolper and Samuelson [1941] 1994, p. 60) – in terms of effects on the real wage, protection makes workers unambiguously better off or, alternatively, workers are hurt by free trade. The statement of the theorem was prompted by the US trade unions' traditional concern about competition from cheap foreign labour, and was possibly also related to the prewar Australian debate on protection.

At the time it was published, the Stolper–Samuelson result must have appeared pretty obvious to politicians and the public at large. Intuition suggests that protection of labour-intensive industries in a labour-scarce country such as the United States is very likely to tilt the distribution of income in favour of workers since it makes American labour compete with foreign labour that may be paid a fraction of the American wage. Economists at the time, however, would have been doubtful. Their reasoning would have been: yes, protection may in the short run benefit labour, but it is certain to lower overall income and, hence, will hurt workers too. What the Stolper–Samuelson result did was to show in an impeccably rigorous manner that the doubting economists' reasoning was flatly wrong and that the obvious was really true after all.

The analysis clarified the logical structure of the Heckscher–Ohlin theory and paved the way for the factor-price equalisation theorem and numerous other results in simple general-equilibrium models of trade. In effect, it launched the 'Ohlin–Samuelson research programme'.

A crucial assumption made by Stolper and Samuelson was that a tariff would raise the relative domestic price of importables: that is, the terms of trade do not change – an assumption later challenged by Lloyd Metzler (1949, pp. 1–29). The rise in this relative price brings about a rise in the price of the 'scarce' factor relative to all commodity prices. Thus, in a relatively labour-scarce country that imports the labour-intensive good, the real wage of its workers will be increased in terms of the price of capital or the price of any good by the imposition of an import duty.

Stolper and Samuelson eliminated the index-number problem that previously bedevilled attempts to arrive at a clear-cut answer: do you evaluate income at the free trade or post-tariff prices? – given that protection will change all prices and money incomes. They also resolved the apparent paradox contained in the result that factor proportions (for example, the ratio of capital to labour) in both industries respond in the same direction, despite the fixity in the overall factor-endowment ratio. The solution is found in the fact that the overall endowment (capital/labour) ratio is a weighted average of the two industries. As the relative outputs of the two industries change, so do the 'weights' – the expansion of the protected industry must give it a heavier weight. A crucial assumption here is that labour and capital are mobile between industries and therefore are paid a common factor price wherever they are employed. The effect of a change in relative commodity prices on a particular factor depends not on the sector in which the factor is located, but what it implies for its national factor-market equilibrium. Stolper and Samuelson used the production box (the counterpart of the Edgeworth–Bowley consumption box) to derive their proof – the first published account of its construction; although Lerner had used it earlier in 1933. With the aid of the Edgeworth–Bowley box diagram (for a single country) they showed how the production-possibilities curve could be derived, and how factor proportions varied along the curve.

The Stolper–Samuelson conclusion depends only on the direction of change of the commodity price ratio after tariff imposition. It does not depend on the validity of the Heckscher–Ohlin theory; for instance, it does not depend on the assumption that countries share the same technologies. Nor does it depend on factor prices being completely equalised through commodity trade. What can affect the cogency of the proof, however, is the possibility mentioned by Metzler that when demand effects and foreign repercussions are included (that is, the effects of the tariff on the terms of trade), the relative domestic price of importables may perversely fall – contrary to the Stolper–Samuelson assumption. Metzler's paradox occurs when foreign demand for the country's export good is extremely inelastic and, either, all or most of the tariff revenue is spent on exports, or is redistributed to consumers whose marginal propensity to spend on the export good is very high – with the result that the relative price of the export good rises significantly on the world market so that the domestic price actually rises rather than falls.

Today, however, the theorem is commonly interpreted as a standard result independent of the tariff context in which it was first formulated. The theorem suggests that there is a unique relation between the commodity price ratio, the factor-price ratio, the real returns of factors and the structure of production (if no joint production prevails). Thus the relationship holds for any change in the domestic price ratio; this changes the real return to the factor used intensively in producing the commodity affected by the price change. In this more general context, the essence of the Stolper–Samuelson theorem is immune to the Metzler effect.

The Stolper–Samuelson theorem can be illustrated with the aid of the Lerner–Pearce diagram where the factor prices consistent with producing two goods are inferred from the unit isocost line that is tangent to both of two unit-value isoquants. As long as both goods are produced, there is a one-to-one relationship between goods prices and factor prices. A change in goods prices causes the curves to shift in a determinate way that indicates the resulting change in factor prices. In Figure 5.1, two unit value isoquants are shown for goods A and B (at initial prices) in the space of factors capital

(K) and labour (L). A is a labour-intensive good and B is a capital-intensive good. If both goods are produced under perfect competition, they must also cost one unit and therefore the unit isocost line must be a straight line GH that is tangent to both of these isoquants indicating the factor prices consistent with the production of both goods (that is, incomplete specialisation). Point Q shows the capital and labour required to produce one dollar's worth of A and point R the requirements for one dollar's worth of B. The wage is $1/OH$ and the rental on capital is $1/OG$. Now suppose that the price of A (the labour-intensive good) increases through the imposition of a tariff on good A with the price of B unchanged. The unit value isoquant for A shifts proportionately towards the origin to the ray from the origin through S; the quantity SQ/OQ reflecting the proportionate rise in the price of A. The unit isocost line shown by $G'R'Q'H'$ rotates to maintain tangency with the two isoquants having intercepts G' and H'. The increased slope of the new isocost line immediately indicates that the ratio of labour's wage to the rental on capital has increased. Since $1/OG' < 1/OG$, the rental on capital has fallen, and since $1/OH' > 1/OH$ the wage has risen. These changes in wages and rental are nominal changes. For the Stolper–Samuelson theorem, however, we also need to know that the wage has risen more than the price of A. This is confirmed since $H'H/OH$ (the proportionate rise in the wage) exceeds SQ/OQ (the proportionate rise in the price of A, the labour-intensive good). The wage has increased more than the price of the labour-intensive good and we get the Stolper–Samuelson result.

How does dimensionality (that is, allowing for more than two factors and two commodities, and so on) affect the Stolper–Samuelson result? The theorem is not materially altered by an increase in the number of goods but only when there are many factors, and then the following statement applies: a rise in the price of one good must raise the real return of at least one factor and lower the real return of at least one other. Thus, every good is both a 'friend' and an 'enemy' to certain factors, to use the terminology of Jones and Scheinkman (1977, pp. 909–35).

An obvious trade-policy implication of the Stolper–Samuelson result is that scarce factors will lobby their government for protection whilst abundant factors will tend to lobby for free trade. In other words, coalitions will be based solely on factor ownership, not industrial affiliation. Is this prediction true about the way a country's lobbying activities are organised? Apparently not, according to the well-known 1978 empirical study by Stephen Magee (1978, pp. 138–52). He showed (using evidence from US Congressional hearings on the US Trade Reform Act, 1974) that contrary to the prediction of the Stolper–Samuelson theorem, labour and capital agree overwhelmingly on trade policy (that is, in nineteen of twenty-one cases). Trade unions and manufacturers in a given industry often take the

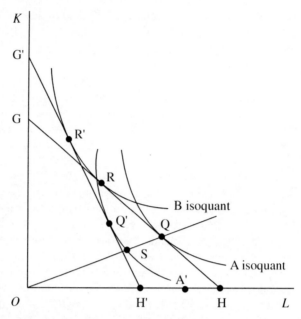

Figure 5.1   The Stolper–Samuelson theorem

same side on the trade question – not ranged one against the other, as theory suggests. It is the industry of employment that determines whether both factors lobby for trade liberalisation or against it. Both capital and labour in import-competing industries favoured protection while capital and labour in the export industries preferred freer trade. The clash of class interests is noticeably absent. The phenomenon of pressure groups organised by industry rather than by factors of production was noticed long ago by J.E. Cairnes (1823–75); and his name is joined to that of Ricardo and Viner in the so-called Ricardo–Viner–Cairnes model – another label for the specific factors model.

One explanation of Magee's findings is that in the short run capital and some types of labour are immobile between sectors – implying effects on domestic factor prices different from those suggested by Stolper–Samuelson. Magee's findings are exactly what one would expect from some version of the specific factors model and that therefore the suggestion that that model provides a better explanation for short-run tariff lobbying behaviour. Stephen Magee (1994) recently admitted (arising from his further work on endogenous protection) that a 'specific-factor model explains lobbying over trade policy in the short run . . . while the Stolper–Samuelson approach works better in explaining why countries protect their scarce factor in the long run'; and also, that when it comes to explaining the level of a country's tariffs, a politicised version of the Heckscher–Ohlin–Samuelson model of international trade is more insightful than the Ricardo–Viner–Cairnes model for predicting long-term behavior on trade policy' (Magee 1994, pp. 279, 288).

Recent developments concerning trade, wages and jobs in the United States lend support to the predictions of the Stolper–Samuelson theorem, for example, protection received by an industry tends to be higher when it is a labour-intensive, low-skill, low-wage industry – reflecting no doubt the common perception that the blue-collar worker (unskilled worker) is a scarce factor in the United States. This result is consistent with the Stolper–Samuelson theorem. If the USA is well endowed with highly-skilled labour, then the movement to free trade would tend to increase the incomes of skilled labour, leaving a significant widening in the gap between wages paid to high-skilled workers and low-skilled workers. But of course it is not easy to evaluate the degree to which international trade has contributed to this trend. Many other factors than trade are relevant, notably, rapid technological change, de-unionisation and an eroding real minimum wage. Yet it is a fact that blue-collar workers are politically aligned with the protectionist Democrats in the US Congress while the managerial and highly-skilled workers in the 'new economy' (through their trade associations) are allied with the freer-trade lobby. The reason may be, as Scheve and Slaughter (2001a and 2001b) suggest in a recent study, that those with relatively less education and skill expect the labour-market results stemming from further international trade flows to be harmful.

The Specific Factors Model

One development has been the revival of interest in the specific factors model which has its roots in the writings of Cairnes and Bastable. This model of production was developed by Haberler in the interwar years; but its recent vogue stems from the formal mathematical treatment of it by Jones (1971) and Samuelson (1971).[6] Samuelson referred to it as the Ricardian–Viner model, since it combines the Ricardian analysis of rent (diminishing returns in agriculture, extended to all sectors) with the analysis of variable costs of production contained in Viner's classic article on cost and supply curves.

The properties of the specific factors model contrast with the basic 2x2 H-O model, in that one of the factors (for example, capital) is immobile between industries, so that its specific use in the two sectors means that it is a three-factor model (although each good is produced by only two factors). Clearly, in this model (where effectively the number of factors exceeds the number of produced commodities) factor-price equalisation is unlikely; trade will bring factor prices closer together, but not to the point of equality. The effects on domestic factor prices are also different from that suggested by the Stolper–Samuelson theorem. The Stolper–Samuelson theorem describes the effect of trade on a country's factor prices (the functional distribution of income): free trade will raise the relative price of labour as well as the real wage in a labour-abundant country, and decrease the real rental value of capital. This result follows from the assumption that factor prices are determined in national markets. The effect of a change in relative commodity prices on a particular factor depends not on the sector in which the factor is located, but what it implies for its national factor-market equilibrium. A productive factor, say, capital, may suffer a loss in real earnings even though there is a rise in the price of the product it helps to produce. This is liable to occur when the relative commodity price change causes the capital market to become depressed on account of the more intensive use of other units of capital in another industry.

In the specific factors model, the earnings of mobile (or all-purpose) factors are determined by national factor-market equilibrium; but the real return to the mobile factor in each industry is equal to its marginal product in that industry. Changes in relative commodity prices always raise the reward of the mobile factor in terms of one good and lower it in terms of the other – for example, the real earnings of the mobile factor fall in terms of the commodity whose price has risen and rise in terms of the commodity whose price has fallen. That is, the mobile factor, for example, labour, will move towards the sector favoured by the price rise, thereby lowering the value of labour's marginal product in terms of that sector's good; while the reduction of labour supply in the other sector raises the value of labour's marginal product in terms of that other sector's good. Thus, changes in the real return to the mobile factor cannot be predicted without a knowledge of taste patterns, and we again encounter the 'neoclassical ambiguity' on this issue that was supposed to have been eliminated by the Stolper–Samuelson theorem.

Returns to specific factors move in the same direction (and to a magnified extent) as the prices of the goods they help to produce, that is, returns change more than in proportion to the price changes. This theoretical result corresponds very well with observed reality. Owners of capital trapped in a depressed industry earn less than the economy-wide average rate of return on capital invested. Mayer, Mussa and Neary treated the specific factors model as a short-run version of the standard H-O-S model. Given enough time and allowing for the processes of depreciation and replacement to exert their effects, all factors are perfectly mobile. Therefore, the short-run behaviour of the economy can be described by the specific factors model, but we still need the H-O-S model to determine its long-run equilibrium. The model has also been proposed as a more realistic framework for analysing the trade of developing countries.

The specific factors approach exhibits many of the features of a fully specified general-equilibrium model, but the production structure of the former makes it a convenient mode for partial-equilibrium analysis of a particular sector. This and other properties of the specific factors model make it a useful vehicle for suggesting empirical hypotheses, and to that extent it enhances the theory's relevance for practical policymaking. Thus, it provides a theoretical model for dealing with adjustment costs and other short-run problems when particular domestic sectors are forced to contract under the pressure of international competition and changing patterns of specialisation. The problem that economists call 'the Dutch Disease' – the case where the discovery of an exhaustible resource, for example, oil, distorts a country's comparative advantage away from traditional manufactures in a manner which may be irreversible when the resource runs out (initially one sector depressed while others boom) – can readily be handled by the model, by virtue of the fact that a sector's 'profitability' is identified with the return to its specific factor.

In general, the specific factors approach captures features of the real world that escape the H-O-S model, and by showing how many of the strong theorems of the latter need to be modified, it helps to break the rigid mould of standard trade theory. Trade theory now has at its disposal a greater variety of models each of which can yield useful insights when applied to limited but appropriate problem areas.

5.2 THE NEW TRADE THEORY

Increasing Returns, Imperfect Competition, and so on

A recent major development has been the incorporation into trade theory of new work in industrial organisation theory. We now have an ongoing research programme concerned with the analysis of trade and trade policy in a world characterised by imperfect competition, differentiated products and economies of scale. It took trade theorists half a century to respond to the call by Haberler, Ohlin, Lord Robbins and others for a more realistic theory of imperfect competition and increasing returns in international trade. The new analytical approach has implications for such issues as the volume and direction of trade and also the gains from trade that alter perceptions about what trade theory can convey. In addition, the new tools of analysis have already proved serviceable in dealing with salient features of today's trading environment and policies; and to that extent, they have remedied the deficiencies of the conventional model. In this section, some of the common features and conclusions of these new ideas are summarised before we turn to the trade policy implications of the new work.

The Heckscher–Ohlin–Samuelson model which dominated trade theory for over twenty-five years, besides its empirical failings, could not properly explain (a) multinational corporations, intra-firm trade and foreign direct investment in general; (b) intra-industry trade; (c) the consequences of trade liberalization;[7] and (d) why a government should believe that through trade intervention it could appropriate for its country a larger share of monopoly profits or rent of the rent-yielding industries.

The new thinking in trade theory offers explanations in terms of imperfectly competitive market structures. What is at issue concerns the answer to the question: is trade caused by differences or similarities between countries? The dissimilarities have traditionally been thought of in terms of differences in endowments, technology or tastes. These differences (or characteristics of countries) suggest that countries will export a different group of goods from those which they import. But the fact is that a large and growing share of world trade takes place among relatively similar countries (in terms of size and factor endowments) – a noticeable trend in manufactured goods trade since the end of the Second World War. In this intra-industry trade (even when measured with a high degree of disaggregation), countries export and import relatively similar products. Commodities embodying similar factor proportions (similar input coefficients in production) feature in two-way trade in horizontally differentiated products, that is, products belonging to the same industrial category. Intra-industry trade is particularly high in some sectors. For instance, in pharmaceuticals intra-industry trade accounted for 98 per cent of trade in finished products in the United States, 70 per cent in France and 32 per cent in Japan in 1991.[8] Basic endowments and technological differences no doubt still shape the pattern of trade where there are cross-country differences in technology, income, skills and natural resources, as in North–South trade. But the intra-industry trade of the industrialised countries is not well explained by the factor-endowments model. However, attempts have been made to explain North–North trade, that is, trade among the developed countries as traditional, comparative advantage trade based on technology and endowments, that is, the Heckscher–Ohlin approach. One example, by Davis (1997, pp. 1051–60) assumes homogeneous products to explain the huge volumes of North–North trade, without any need for product differentiation. Davis concludes that 'the volume of N-N trade cannot be used as evidence to prefer theories based on increasing returns rather than comparative advantage' (Davis 1997, p. 1060). Helpman (1999, pp. 121–44) is not convinced by these traditional Heckscher–Ohlin type explanations of trade flows based on homogeneous goods on the ground that such explanations require 'too much fine tuning of the technology to be convincing. The broad structure of world trade is more naturally explained with the aid of product differentiation than without it' (Helpman 1999, p. 139).

Increasing Returns

At least since the time of Adam Smith it has been recognised that by participating in international trade a country could reap significant economies of scale, and scale economies have long been associated with the infant-industry argument for tariff protection. A trade theory which assumed that all markets were perfectly competitive could recognise that potential technological externalities provide a case for trade intervention, and yet preserve its integrity. Firms could still be regarded as perfectly competitive, but could not perform optimally because of the technological externality represented by increasing returns. To fully admit the phenomenon of increasing returns into neoclassical trade theory generally would have meant facing the problem of complete specialisation, multiple equilibria, indeterminacy of production and the loss of the idealised world of perfect competition; hence the topic remained on the periphery of the theoretical field.

Analysts have recently redirected their attention to economies of scale in the form in which they had been traditionally treated, that is, allowing increasing returns to scale to exist in industries, countries or the world, but external to individual firms; also, more boldly, they have tackled head-on the matter arising from increasing returns that are internal to the firm. The latter enquiry inaugurated, of course, the long awaited integration of imperfect competition into the main body of trade theory.

Economies of scale linked to national levels of output can provide a basis for trade as an alternative to differences in factor endowments. That is, such economies alone can create a comparative advantage for a large country in a commodity which is produced under increasing returns to scale. Thus, if increasing returns exist at the national level, Markusen and Melvin show that country size can determine trade patterns.[9] The large country will tend to export the good which is produced under economies of scale even if relative factor endowments are the same in two countries.

What about increasing returns linked to the scale of world output? In this case, a firm's effectiveness in production (or the cost savings enjoyed) may depend on the scale of world demand for, and output of, its product. The expansion of world output of a particular commodity allows greater degrees of specialisation (division of labour) which give rise to cost savings by the firm through intra-industry trade in intermediate inputs. Thus, for example, the productivity of the British computer industry depends not only on the size of Britain's semiconductor industry, but also on the size of the US (or Japan's) computer industry. If external economies arise from the possibility of trade in intermediate goods subject to scale economies, then the pattern of trade is determined by relative factor endowments. If, however, increasing returns attach to the firm, such favoured firms will expand output, dominate the market, and we end up with imperfect competition – that is, we face the issues of market power, monopoly rents and strategic behaviour.

A variety of models, borrowed from the industrial organisation literature, have been pressed into service to aid the analysis: the Chamberlinian model of monopolistic competition, the contestable market hypothesis of Baumol, Panzer and Willig (according to which incumbent firms are forced to keep prices low to avoid entry), and the Cournot model of industry structure. The resulting work has done much to incorporate into general-equilibrium theory features of differentiated products and monopolistic/oligopolistic competition.

The specification of consumer preferences (the demand for differentiated products) includes two forms of the utility function: one, the 'love-of-variety' approach, and the other, the Hotelling–Lancaster model. the first assumes that consumers are identical, and they like to consume a large number of varieties; they are better off, the wider the variety of products on the market. The second, the 'ideal-variety' approach, assumes that consumers themselves are differentiated in terms of their preferences, that is, every consumer has an ideal product, perceived as being one which embodies the consumer's most desired combination of characteristics.

Despite their different specifications of demand, these monopolistic competition models are essentially similar, and they all tell the same story: in the presence of economies of scale and imperfect competition, intra-industry trade takes place, even between countries with identical factor endowments. Such countries can be expected to engage in considerable two-way trade, exchanging different varieties of the same basic product. The gross trade in manufactures is apparently driven by economies of scale and non-competitive market structures, while net trade is related to differences in factor composition.

Increasing Returns, Imperfect Competition and Gains from Trade

What are the implications of the new wave of analysis for the gains from trade and commercial policy? Rather surprisingly, it adds to the list of trading gains and widens the scope for trade intervention policies. In addition to the exploitation of comparative advantage benefits (a more efficient allocation of resources), the following gains from trade are likely in the presence of increasing returns and imperfect competition:

1. Trade increases product variety and raises consumer welfare. The opening of trade results in a decrease in the number of domestically produced varieties, but this is more than compensated for by the availability on the market of a wider range of both imported and domestic varieties.
2. With each country producing only a limited subset of the products in each industry subject to scale economies, this increases efficiency in those industries (through longer production runs) and results in lower prices for all consumers.
3. Trade may encourage rationalisation in firms where output per firm determines the extent to which economies of scale are realised. Trade that increases output per firm lowers average cost: that is, individual firms move down their average cost curves.
4. Trade has a pro-competitive effect. Trade can reduce the degree of monopoly power in the economy: that is, it forces oligopolistic industries to become more competitive, thereby increasing the potential gains from trade.

With imperfect competition, market prices do not equal marginal social valuations and it is possible for trade to reduce welfare in a Pareto-optimal sense. Expansion of market size through trade, in a situation where markets are not contestable (that is, where monopoly profits persist), may in fact serve to buttress monopoly power, leave consumers with a variety of products less suited to their needs and reduce welfare.

Trade Policy in Imperfectly Competitive Markets

The theories discussed above suggest new arguments for the use of commercial policy. The changing character of trade and the new theoretical models of imperfectly competitive markets widen the scope for the active use of trade policy to promote the interests of domestic firms against their foreign competitors. Three incentives for trade intervention have been identified:

1. A government can change the variety of products available in the domestic economy through tariff policy. At the same time, tariffs can be used to increase welfare through the inducement they provide for the expansion of domestic firms which set prices above marginal costs.
2. A country which consumes a good supplied by a foreign monopolist

can improve its terms of trade through an optimal tariff. The domestic government can use the tariff to extract a portion of the rent (monopoly profits) from the foreign exporter. If there is a rival domestic firm, then the tariff policy can be used to shift profits from the foreign to the domestic firm; this is particularly attractive if the domestic firm can export and earn foreign monopoly rents, as in the example used by James Brander and Barbara Spencer (1981, pp. 371–89). Besides tariffs, export subsidies may help a country's firms to capture a larger share of global monopoly profits and thereby raise national income at other countries' expense – a conclusion derived from a model where the foreign and domestic firms interact as a Cournot duopoly (each firm chooses its output level, taking the other firm's level of output as given).

3. Trade policy can be used to achieve strategic advantages for the national economy. Thus, a case can be made for the promotion, through protection and export subsidies, of certain domestic sectors which generate valuable 'spillovers' (R&D and experience) to the rest of society by way of technological innovation and external economies. Such trade intervention on behalf of certain key sectors may raise national income, since the producers in such sectors may not, in fact, be paid the full social value of their production.

Many economists, while welcoming the new analytical perspective, remain unmoved by the associated arguments for trade intervention. Critics detect a neo-mercantilist ('beggar-my-neighbour') slant in the policy implications of the new models. The arguments are exploitative – one country benefits at the expense of the rest of the world. We could face the Prisoners' Dilemma: if all countries simultaneously pursue selfish trade policies, all are likely to lose.

The ideas behind profit-seeking intervention in imperfectly competitive and strategic environments, it is claimed, are merely disguised optimal-tariff and second-best arguments for trade intervention, as commonly understood. The results of the partial-equilibrium models of monopoly and oligopoly in international markets are sensitive to changes in assumptions: for example, if firms compete in terms of price rather than quantity, if entry barriers are low, and if multinational firms are brought into the picture, then the interests of firms and nations diverge. The gains from government intervention may accordingly be rather limited and narrowly diffused. The allocation of resources still matters, critics say; and they point out that sectors promoted by interventionist policies must compete with all others for scarce resources. Free traders are fond of quoting the following declaration in favour of a free trade multilateral system by Brander and

Spencer, prominent among the architects of the new trade theory (three years after their famous 1981 paper):

> it should be emphasised that our arguments should not be taken as support for using tariffs. The highly tariff-ridden world that would result from each country maximising domestic welfare taking the policies of other countries as given would be a poor outcome. Our analysis is meant to contribute to an understanding of the motives that might underlie tariff policy and provides support for the multilateral approach to trade liberalisation. (Brander and Spencer 1984, p. 204)

This is very reminiscent of Edgeworth's warning about poison in daring theoretical innovations, while admiring the ingenuity that goes into developing them.

In a 1987 review of current issues in trade policy, Deardorff and Stern conclude that they do not regard the new interventionist arguments as affording 'sufficient grounds for seriously compromising or rejecting outright the principles of free trade as the basis for trade policy'. This, no doubt, sums up the opinion of the majority of neoclassical economists. Paul Krugman, having done so much to push increasing returns and imperfect competition models as alternative explanations of trade, has argued that free trade remains a good rule of thumb even if not the optimal policy in an imperfectly competitive world (Krugman 1987, p. 143). However, one fact must be applauded: trade theory has taken a leap into the concerns of the real world. It is now dealing with issues that are relevant to those actually engaged in and directly affected by new trends in trade policy. In this sense, the rethinking of the analytical bases of trade policy is a useful step forward – not a walk on the wild side!

Multinational Corporations, Endogenous Tariff Theory

Finally, two additional developments are worth mentioning briefly – multinational corporations and endogenous tariff theory.

Until recently, trade theory had little to offer by way of a convincing explanation of the multinational firm. The field was cultivated by business school economists who emphasised imperfect market structures, ownership-specific advantages (for example, a patent, superior or secret technology, marketing skills, and so on) and transaction costs lower than would be the case in open, arm's-length markets. These factors, highlighted as being relevant to an understanding of the existence and activities of multinational firms (referred to by John Dunning as the 'eclectic theory'), cannot be analysed adequately with the traditional trade model that assumes perfect competition and free access to the most efficient method of production.

Equipped with their new models of trade in imperfectly competitive markets, trade theorists have returned to the subject of multinationals and have made useful contributions to the literature concerning the activities of such firms and their impact on patterns of trade. Helpman and Krugman (1985) show how monopolistic competition and firm-specific economies of scale can explain the presence of multinationals. The firm requires a head-quarters service to coordinate its production activities in several overseas plants. The 'head office' activity is a fixed cost of production that generates scale economies internal to the firm and simultaneously available to separate plants in different countries – that is, the multinational firm enjoys multi-plant scale economies which are internalised. Ethier (1986, pp. 805–33) uses a general-equilibrium model for the purpose of endogenising the internationalisation decision (the exchange of information between agents) – a matter not explored in previous studies. Ethier shows how the results can be incorporated into general trade theory.

Public choice theory and estimates of nominal and effective rates of protection have provided economists with an entrée into a field long dominated by political scientists – the political economy of protectionism. The rapidly expanding literature is concerned with theoretical and empirical analyses of how, in a democracy, tariffs and other trade measures are endogenously determined by a lobbying process in which opposing economic interests compete.

Findlay and Wellisz (1982) were the first to devise a general-equilibrium model of endogenous tariff formation using a 'specific factors' framework. Magee and Young (1987) explain the history of tariffs in the United States during the twentieth century with a formal two-good, two-factor general-equilibrium H-O model incorporating two lobbies and two political parties.[10] However, many alternative hypotheses besides those suggested by the authors are possible. It is doubtful whether models like these can explain the average level of protection – a view recently expressed by J. Peter Neary.[11] Mayer and Riezman (1985)[12] argue that the literature on lobbying theory is deficient, in that it does not explain why a rational lobby would prefer tariffs to other forms of protection (for example, domestic subsidies), since the political process will favour subsidies to achieve a given degree of protection. Targeted subsidies can be obtained at cheaper cost.

If what the models of lobbying and endogenous tariff formation are saying is true (namely that there is an active political market for protection), is there any use for a normative theory of trade? Normative trade theory assumes the existence of a benign, omniscient government (or an 'efficiency-minded dictator') that guides trade policy in a manner calculated to ensure maximum national welfare. If that is not the way things are done in the real world, what is the point of policy-orientated normative theory or welfare-theoretic analysis? Max Corden answers this question and concludes that normative theory provides 'one reference point for judging institutional arrangements'.[13] What the new literature on endogenous protection does is to crack the apolitical mould of the theory of trade policy; but the impact is likely to be rather minimal. Endogenous protection theory is founded on a narrow conception of the concerns of political economy. Although conflict is recognised, the role of the state, relations of power and authority, social classes and disruptive change within historical settings, are excluded. The determinants of the level of protection are related to domestic factors without explicit reference to considerations of international political economy and global institutional arrangements – for example, the use of trade policy to achieve foreign policy and national defence objectives, the constraints imposed by foreign retaliation and strategies of reciprocity, and so on.

A wider perspective than that offered by public choice theory is required to deal with these issues. In the case of tariff history, for instance, Charles Kindleberger documents the inadequacies of hypotheses derived from public choice and orthodox trade theory in dealing with actual events and outcomes – for example, the response of various European countries to the fall in world wheat prices after 1880 – and remarks that what they offer by way of explanation is 'not a great deal'.[14] Economic history has a role here: it can check the tendency for theorists to get carried away by a single model.

NOTES

1. Viner later summarised his paper in Viner [1937] (1955), p. 521.
2. Lerner gives a good summary of the dispute between Edgeworth and Bastable in his article 'The Symmetry between Import and Export Taxes', *Economica*, n.s. 3 (August), 306–13.
3. In the classical discussion of this question by Marshall (and Edgeworth also), two limiting examples were considered: the customs revenues were assumed to be spent either entirely upon export goods or entirely upon imports. Lerner's geometrical technique was able to handle the realistic intermediate cases as well, namely the case where preferences are not aggregable and the government has preferences that differ from the public.
4. Robert A. Mundell, 'Abba Lerner on the Theory of Foreign Trade', in H.I. Greenfield, A.M. Levenson, W. Hamovitch and E. Rotwein (eds), *Theory for Economic Efficiency: Essays in Honor of Abba P. Lerner* (Cambridge, Mass.: MIT Press, 1980), p. 144.
5. Haberler (1936), Preface to the English edition, p. v. Long ago Haberler called attention to the phenomenon of intra-industry trade and described some of its manifestations: product heterogeneity within aggregates, seasonal fluctuations, border trade (for example, wheat imported into West Germany and exported from East Germany). Ibid. p. 34, n. 2.
6. See Ronald W. Jones, 'A Three-Factor Model in Theory, Trade and History', in J.N. Bhagwati, R.W. Jones, R.A. Mundell and J. Vanek (eds), *Trade, Balance of Payments and Growth: Essays in Honor of Charles P. Kindleberger* (Amsterdam: North-Holland, 1971); Paul A. Samuelson, 'Ohlin Was Right', in *Collected Scientific Papers*, vol. 4, part VI, no. 254.

7. For example, the Stolper–Samuelson approach suggests that economic interests organ-
    ise across industries along factor lines. Some gain and others lose from trade liberalisa-
    tion. In fact, such effects have not been detected in cases such as the formation of the EC
    (European Community) and the US–Canada Autopact. As a result of rationalisation
    within firms, there have been gains to all factors of production.
8. See OECD, *Globalization of Industry* (Paris, 1996).
9. James R. Markusen and James R. Melvin, 'Trade, Factor Prices and Gains from Trade
    with Increasing Returns to Scale', *Canadian Journal of Economics*, 14 (1981), pp. 450–69.
10. Stephen P. Magee and Leslie Young, 'Endogenous Protection in the United States,
    1900–1984', in Robert M. Stern (ed.), *US Trade Policies in a Changing World Economy*
    (1987), pp. 145–95.
11. See J. Peter Neary, 'Comment on 'Endogenous Protection in the United States,
    1900–1984', in Stern (1987), op. cit,. p. 205.
12. Wolfgang Mayer and Raymond Riezman, 'Endogenous Choice of Trade Policy
    Instruments', Working Paper No. 85–8, January 1985, University of Iowa.
13. Max W. Corden (1984), 'The Normative Theory of International Trade', in Jones and
    Kenen (eds), *Handbook of International Economics*, vol. 1, p. 112, Amsterdam: North
    Holland.
14. Charles P. Kindleberger, 'A Further Comment', in William N. Parker (ed.), *Economic
    History and the Modern Economist* (Oxford: Blackwell, 1986), p. 85.

PART II

FREE TRADE: RHETORIC, EVENTS,
POLICIES AND IDEOLOGY

6.   The economists, the Corn Laws and commercial policy

6.1   THE ECONOMISTS AND THE CORN-LAW DEBATE

The repeal of the English Corn Laws on 26 June 1846 was an epoch-making event in the history of international economic policy. The decision was significant, perhaps more because of its symbolic value than for any dramatic impact on international economic relationships.

It was, however, preceded by a momentous and controversial debate in which most of the best minds in classical political economy participated. Nothing comparable to it was seen until a century and a half later, that is, the protracted debate on Britain's membership of the EEC (European Economic Community) – except, perhaps, for the British Tariff Reform Debate, 1903. As in another famous economic debate – the early seventeenth-century controversy on the foreign exchanges and the balance of payments – which engaged the attention of leading economic thinkers, the nineteenth-century discussion was accompanied by a great outpouring of economic writings. The shift in policy leading up to the rescinding of agricultural protection has been hailed as one of the greatest triumphs of enlightened economic reasoning, in particular, the law of comparative cost. But this is pure invention, a caricature of the facts as far as they can be ascertained. The myth does not stand up to scrutiny. Thweatt writes 'it is misleading to say the doctrine of comparative costs was influential in the discussion leading to the repeal of the Corn Laws in 1846' (Thweatt 1976, p. 208). Surveying public opinion at one of the crucial moments (1820) when the first decision was made in favour of free trade, William D. Grampp could find no trace of comparative advantage in the economic opinion of 1820, that is, what was said in Parliament, the press and in petitions. 'The arguments for free trade were not drawn from the economic theory of the day' (Grampp 1982, p. 508), he noted. As one observer remarked at the time, the issues of 'cash and corn' touched on many technical points which were 'intricate and foreign to the taste of country gentlemen'.

Apparently, a taste for the finer points of economic analysis has not changed since then. According to Stigler, tariffs are still with us 'because the theory of comparative cost is beyond the comprehension of ordinary citizens. A recital of Ricardo's three-paragraph statement to a tired factory hand or physician is liable to cause the layman to embrace not the English theory of free trade, but a bottle of Portuguese wine' (Stigler 1976, pp. 374–8). Corn and currency were not the only economic and social subjects of the debate: the Poor Laws, emigration, unemployment and the machinery question were all on the agenda. Food riots were frequent (1795, 1799, 1804). The political rows were fierce, the pamphleteering wars unrelenting, the clamour of vested interests noisy and divisive. In the background, behind the drawn battle-lines, the political economists carried on their 'highly technical discussions', in Briggs' phrase (Briggs 1959, p. 201). These discussions on the Corn Laws and commercial policy in general are the subject of this chapter. First, a few words on the factual and intellectual background.

At the heart of the controversy lay the population problem. During the wars of the period 1790–1815 food prices rose. The inflationary situation was further aggravated by heavy wartime expenditures which forced Britain off the gold standard. With an inconvertible pound, the money supply expanded rapidly and overall prices increased by some 93 per cent over the period 1792–1814. Farmers were well-off during the 1790s; their production costs also rose, but the enclosure movement accelerated, and new ploughland was opened up. To many radicals the obvious answer to rapid population growth and rising food prices was a programme of assisted emigration and the abolition or reform of the Corn Laws. The Rev. Thomas Malthus, whose *Essay on Population* came out at this time, refused to countenance these solutions. But contrary to Adam Smith's optimistic vision of high wages, steady increases in industrial productivity and future economic and social progress, Malthus' prospect hinted at conflict between landowners and the rest of society: 'It threatened to undermine whatever remained of the "moral economy"', as one writer puts it.[1] Agricultural protection and export bounties on grain exports were required to encourage domestic production, advised Malthus. Smith's doctrine of free trade came under fire; so too did his reliance on a manufacturing economy for creating wealth and improving the standard of living of the poor. Physiocratic notions resurfaced, proclaiming agriculture as the sure foundation of Britain's prosperity. Inevitably the landed interest got its way and agricultural protection was increased in 1791 and 1815. The increases were approved in order to protect the interests of British farmers who had invested heavily in agricultural production during the Napoleonic Wars. The Corn Law of the latter year, for instance, fixed the price level of wheat above which imports became free at 80 shillings per quarter (a quarter of wheat was 217.7 kg);

and barley and oats when the home price reached 40 shillings and 27 shillings, respectively. But this meant that the price of food and therefore the wages that manufacturers were forced to pay were levered up ever further.

The issue became truly contentious between the contending interests at the end of the war when the fall of food prices led to renewed demand for greater agricultural protection. Even before the final end of hostilities a serious economic crisis developed (1810–11), resulting in large-scale unemployment in the manufacturing districts. At this juncture the law of diminishing returns and its corollary, the theory of rent, was discovered jointly by Malthus, West, Torrens and Ricardo. Integrated into the rest of classical theory this discovery suggested that a country with a growing population would face ever-increasing food prices and money wages. Unrelieved by the free importation of foodstuffs, this situation implied reduced profits, decreased exports of manufactured goods and ruin for British industry. At least this was the dreadful scenario as envisaged by merchants and manufacturers. The landowners and spokesmen for the squirearchy retorted that a prosperous agriculture was necessary for England's national defence as well as for the preservation of traditional ways of life. Agriculture then accounted for one-third of national income and about the same proportion of total employment. Manufacturing labour was 'unproductive' compared with agricultural labour, and far from contributing to the increase of the 'necessaries and conveniences of life', the expansion of manufacturing by draining workers off the land would actually diminish the available food supply. The great issue at stake then was: should the country try to maintain its agrarian economy or turn itself into a giant manufactory? The debate resolved itself into a consideration of the following: (1) the place of agriculture in society; (2) the relationship between consumers and producers; and (3) the competing claims and ideologies of the squirearchy and the industrialists.

The point at which Ricardo and the other economists besides Malthus entered the debate on the Corn Laws is usually marked by the appearance of William Spence's *Britain Independent of Commerce* (1807) and the replies it provoked. In 1806 Napoleon launched his Continental System of economic warfare against Britain by the Berlin Decrees which ordered the closure of all continental ports to British trade. At a time of serious food shortage at home, the propaganda value of this action was enormous for Spence and the British Physiocrats. Agriculture, not commerce, said Spence, was the basis of England's strength; thus the Napoleonic blockade could have no serious consequence for Great Britain. The expansion of commerce and manufacturing created economic instability and insecurity; only the agricultural sector promoted economic growth, stability, and security, as it always had done. Therefore, if the agricultural sector was starved of investment funds because of the diversion of capital to trade and industry, then that vital sector would decline; it would be unable to employ the resources (including new technology) to provide the economic surplus required to sustain a growing population at improved standards of living. Spence emphasised the danger of reduced purchasing power (and the threat to continued prosperity) which stemmed from excessive savings by the niggardly capitalist class. All that was necessary for survival and prosperity was for landlords to spend the social surplus and generate incomes in the rest of the economy. Spence's pamphlet was highly praised by Cobbett in his series of 'Perish Commerce' articles in the *Political Register*.[2] Two critical replies appeared, however, which as we have already indicated were crucially important for the emerging orthodoxy, that is, James Mill's *Commerce Defended* and Torrens' *The Economists Refuted*.

Mill rejected Spence's allegation that foreign trade was a mere swapping of commodities of equal value which benefits no one but the profiteering merchant. A country can benefit from 'the trade of export and import' because it involves the exchange of less valuable commodities for more valuable ones. Trade, no less than agriculture, increased Britain's wealth, since imports were purchased 'with a quantity of British goods of less value'. Mill also attacked the 'dangerous doctrine' according to which landlords must spend all their incomes to avoid gluts, invoking for this purpose an early version of Say's 'law of markets' – production equals purchasing power, that is, a level of income sufficient to purchase all that is produced: 'Whatever be the additional quantity of goods therefore which is at any time created in any country, an additional power of purchasing, exactly equivalent, is at the same instant created.' Therefore there was no possibility of inadequate demand for all goods in an economy, either because of underinvestment or underconsumption. The new industrial system was a harmonious, self-sustaining order which did not entail reliance on foreign trade as an outlet for surplus produce:

> Foreign commerce . . . is in all cases a matter of expediency rather than of necessity. The intention of it is not to furnish a vent for the produce of the industry of the country, because that industry always furnishes a vent for itself.[3]

Trade was rather a means of procuring cheap and abundant supplies of commodities which enhanced the British standard of living. Tacitly, Mill's reply to Spence was also a critique of Smith's 'vent-for-surplus' idea of foreign trade. The assertion that a nation could never be without a market was, moreover, a supremely confident belief in the existence of a competitive equilibrium – that the free-market mechanism was self-regulating, both with and without the benefit of foreign trade.

Malthus's Caution

Torrens's reply, while distinctly anti-physiocratic, was a curious mixture of mercantilist reasoning and elements of the new political economy. He attacked Spence's 'idea of agriculture being the only source of wealth' and used the eighteenth-century rule to illustrate the gains from trade. However, his general views on trade and colonies were less enlightened than those of Mill. For instance, he (1) accepted Smith's vent-for-surplus theory; (2) believed that a country's gain from trade was greater when it exchanged perishables (wine, fruit) and necessaries (food, woollen cloth) for durables (hardware) and luxuries (silks, lace); (3) felt that domestic trade was, in some sense, more permanent and beneficial than foreign trade; and (4) favoured restrictions on colonial trade along the lines of the 'old colonial system' (Torrens [1808] 1857, pp. 15–26, 30–1, 50–1). From the side of the new orthodoxy Mill's critique of Spence was the more telling, but combined with that of Torrens it laid the physiocratic ghost to rest. Shortly after this controversy, first James Mill and then Torrens became acquainted with Ricardo – the three who were to provide the intellectual argument against the Corn Laws.

When the debate on the Laws resumed at the end of the war Malthus came out with two Corn Law pamphlets which greatly disappointed his Whig friends for his 'heresy' in urging restrictions on the importation of grain. The remedy for the stagnation of the British economy, said Malthus, was a continuation of the policy of limited protection of the landed interest from the competition of imported foodstuffs which would sustain agricultural income and investment. He recognised that falling food prices (hence wages) would favour the expansion of British manufactured exports, but felt that it was more necessary to maintain demand at home through a high level of domestic spending. He boldly asserted that a high money-price of corn would benefit workers in the purchase of other commodities. The Corn Laws, he believed, made real wages higher than they would otherwise have been. The assumption was that money-wages moved proportionately with the corn price, but other prices which entered the wage basket either did not move (for example, prices of imported goods) or moved proportionately *less* than the price of bread. On the added assumption that workers regularly spent two-fifths of their income on bread and flour and the rest on other commodities (meat, milk, butter, cheese, potatoes, house-rent, linen, soap, and so on). Malthus reasoned that the Corn Laws, by keeping up or increasing the price of corn, thereby advanced workers' real income more than the rise in the cost of living. In addition, of course, dearer food meant fewer children and hence, a higher standard of living for the labouring poor. Francis Horner wrote to a friend on 30

January 1815: 'The most important convert the landlords have got is Malthus, who has now declared himself in favour of their Bill'[4] to increase protection. Two years later Malthus repeated his objection to dependence on imported food and raw materials. He disagreed with those who wanted to expand foreign trade so as to lower food costs and thereby the wages of labour. If that was the way to capture and hold markets, it was patently not worth the effort; for although extra exports might be secured through low wages, the benefit might be more than counterbalanced by a decline in demand at home. He stressed the need for agricultural self-sufficiency, the balanced development of agriculture, industry and commercial services and the maintenance of a high level of effective demand in the domestic market:

> If food and raw materials were denied to a nation merely manufacturing, it is obvious that it could no longer exist . . . its progress in wealth must be almost entirely measured by the progress and demand of the countries which deal with it. (Malthus 1826, pp. 408–9)

He warned that even if Britain became the workshop of the world and common carrier, such an international division of labour could not be relied upon to continue indefinitely – it would be merely 'accidental and temporary, not natural and permanent'. Technological leadership and other competitive advantages must inevitably be eroded as other countries industrialised. On the other hand:

> A country with resources in land . . . if its industry, ingenuity and economy increase, its wealth and population will increase, whatever may be the situation and conduct of the nations with which it trades. When its manufacturing capital becomes redundant, and manufactured commodities are too cheap, it will have no occasion to wait for the increasing raw products of its neighbours. The transfer of its own redundant capital to its own land will raise fresh products, against which its manufactures may be exchanged, and by the double operation of diminishing comparatively the supply, and increasing the demand, enhance their price . . . A country, in which in this manner agriculture, manufactures, and commerce . . . act and react upon each other in turn, might evidently go on increasing in riches and strength, although surrounded by Bishop Berkeley's wall of brass. (Malthus 1826, pp. 426–7)

But this could only be achieved if Britain continued to tax imported corn and maintained the system of bounties upon its exportation so that farmers should not be discouraged by low selling prices at home in years of good harvests. Malthus seemed to believe that the ultimate check to population growth was set by the growth of *domestic* food supply. A policy of supporting domestic agriculture would therefore ensure that there would always be sufficient 'funds for the maintenance of labour' which alone could ensure full employment. A predominantly manufacturing nation – without the aid of high-consuming landlords – could not avoid the problem of overproduction ('gluts') and falling prices and profits. Nevertheless, for a country with a sufficiency of home-grown foodstuffs the export of manufactured goods could play an important role in sustaining effective demand:

> It is obvious then that a fall in the value of the precious metals, commencing with a rise in the price of corn, has a strong tendency . . . to encourage the cultivation of fresh land and the formation of increased rents.
> A similar effect would be produced in a country which continued to feed its own people, by a great and increasing demand for its manufactures. These manufactures, if from such a demand the money value of their amount in foreign countries was greatly to increase, would bring back a great increase of money value in return, which increase could not fail to increase the money price of labour and raw produce. The demand for agricultural as well as manufactured produce would thus be augmented. (Malthus 1826, p. 166)

And Malthus professed his adherence to the theoretical ideal of universal free trade, but with an important caveat in regard to its practical application – some restriction was desirable to safeguard the staple food of the people:

> According to the general principles of political economy, it cannot be doubted that it is for the interest of the civilised world that each nation should purchase its commodities wherever they can be had the cheapest . . . It is evident, however, that local interests and political relations may modify the application of these general principles; and in a country with a territory fit for the production of corn, an independent, and at the same time a more equable supply of this necessary of life, may be an object of such importance as to warrant a deviation from them. (Malthus 1826, p. 237)

Malthus took issue with Smith in the 1798 edition of the *Essay on Population* on the welfare significance of increases in national wealth as conventionally measured. In particular, Malthus maintained that it could not be assumed that every increase of wealth necessarily benefited the labouring poor. A more abundant supply of 'silks, laces, trinkets and expensive furniture' (consequent upon freer importation or expanded domestic manufacture) certainly indicated an increase in national wealth (or 'the revenue of society'), but that could not be considered of the same importance as an increase of food – the principal revenue of the great mass of the people. Investment in manufacturing might, indeed, increase national wealth and nominal wages, but if that occurred as a result of reduced investment in agriculture (accompanied by a movement of labour from agriculture to manufacturing) then the increased costs of domestically produced subsistence goods might more than swallow up all the enhanced nominal wages and leave wage-earners worse off than before.

Ricardo's Critique

But what were the consequences of the Corn Laws for the distribution of income and the rate of economic growth? In particular, what would happen to the rate of profit and the accumulation of capital? For Ricardo, this was the crucial question. Until 1813 Ricardo was preoccupied with monetary questions (that is, the bullion controversy). Thereafter he turned his attention to the Corn Law question and published his *Essay on Profits* in February 1815 as his contribution to the debate. The subtitle to the pamphlet suggests that this was the motivation for his corn model of profits, that is, the reference to Malthus' recent pamphlets on the Corn Laws. Blaug, Dobb and O'Brien state that the significance of the work can only be understood in the context of the public debate about the proposed restrictions upon the importation of corn. Hollander, however, on the basis of the Ricardo–Malthus correspondence and other evidence, traces the origin of Ricardo's profit theory to the latter's criticism of Smith's view that increases in wage rates led to general inflation – especially as contained in Smith's chapter on bounties.[5]

At any rate, whether inspired by current controversy or not, Ricardo drew immediately relevant political conclusions from his model. In the *Essay*, Ricardo demonstrated that a failure to import more corn would be exceedingly costly to the country – it would lower profits, which, in turn, would mean lower levels of investment, employment, output and income. In an imaginative synthesis Ricardo brought together the fundamental building blocks of contemporary theory and constructed a model which indicated that the profits of the farmer regulated the profits of all other trades. As early as March 1814 Ricardo stated his conclusion in a letter to his stockbroker friend, Hutches Trower:

> that in short, it is the profits of the farmer which regulate the profits of all other trades, – and as the profits of the farmer must necessarily decrease with every augmentation of Capital employed on the land, provided no improvements be at the same time made in husbandry, all other profits must diminish and therefore the rate of interest must fall. To this proposition, Mr Malthus does not agree. (Ricardo, *Works*, 1951, vol. VI, p. 104)

The feeding of a growing population necessitated the cultivation of progressively poorer parcels of land and/or the more intensive use of existing land. In either case, because of diminishing returns and the competition by farmers for the more fertile land, the cost of producing food increases over time. The only beneficiaries in income-distribution terms would be the landlords, with their swollen rent rolls. Himself a landlord by that time (the previous year he had bought Gatcombe Park, Gloucestershire, now a Royal Residence), Ricardo's analysis hinted at class conflict:

the interest of the landlord is always opposed to the interest of every other class in the community. His situation is never so prosperous, as when food is scarce and dear: whereas, all other persons are greatly benefitted [*sic*] by procuring food cheap. (Ricardo, *Works*, 1951, vol. IV, p. 21)

The losers, the farmers, would suffer a squeeze on their profits. Moreover, argued Ricardo, the rising cost of producing the subsistence wage would depress the general rate of profit in other industries. The pace of capital accumulation would inevitably slow down and thus act as a brake on economic expansion. Malthus, of course, did not accept the last part of this scenario; but it must have frightened others. As Edwin Cannan remarked a century later: 'As a basis for an argument against the Corn Laws, it would have been difficult to find anything more effective than the Ricardian theory of distribution' (Cannan 1953, p. 391). The dismal prospect ahead – diminishing returns, rising real-wage costs and falling profits – could, as a matter of logic, be relieved if additional portions of fertile land could somehow be tacked on to the British Isles. But the more realistic practical alternative was obviously to allow the free importation of grain. Since 'rent never falls without profits of stock rising' it follows that Great Britain will benefit greatly by imports of cheap grain. Wages will be lower (reflecting the falling costs of subsistence) and rents will sink as marginal land is abandoned:

> If by foreign commerce, or the discovery of machinery, the commodities consumed by the labourer should become much cheaper, wages would fall; and this, as we have before observed, would raise the profits of the farmer, and therefore all other profits. (Ricardo, *Works*, 1951, vol. IV, p. 26 n.)

Foreign trade provided the means of escape from the consequences of diminishing returns and a falling rate of profit. 'I never was more convinced of any proposition in Pol: Economy', he wrote to Malthus in June 1814, 'than that restrictions on importation of corn in an importing country have a tendency to lower profits' (Ricardo, *Works*, 1951, vol. VI, p. 109). Should the Corn Laws be repealed, Britain would be able to draw on low-cost food supplies from abroad (presumably importing such wage goods at constant terms of trade). Should this 'wise policy' be adopted (namely, exchanging manufactured goods for low-cost food and raw materials from abroad) Great Britain

> could go on for an indefinite time increasing in wealth and population, for the only obstacle to this increase would be the scarcity, and consequent high value, of food and other raw produce. Let these be supplied from abroad in exchange for manufactured goods, and it is difficult to say where the limit is at which you would cease to accumulate wealth and to derive profit from its employment. (Ricardo, *Works*, 1951, vol. IV, p. 179)

Ricardo left no doubt in his readers' minds about his anti-Corn Law position when he concluded the *Essay* with this peroration:

> I shall greatly regret that considerations for any particular class, are allowed to check the progress of the wealth and population of the country. If the interests of the landlord be of sufficient consequence, to determine us not to avail ourselves of all the benefits which would follow from importing corn at a cheap price, they should also influence us in rejecting all improvements in agriculture, and in the implements of husbandry; for it is as certain that corn is rendered cheap, rents are lowered, and the ability of the landlord to pay taxes, is for a time, at least, as much impaired by such improvements, as by the importation of corn. To be consistent then, let us by the same act arrest improvement, and prohibit importation. (Ricardo, *Works*, 1951, vol. IV, p. 41)

We shall return to Ricardo presently, but for the moment let us take note of two other critiques.

Torrens' Position

Torrens' *Essay Upon the External Corn Trade* came out the same day as Ricardo's *Essay*. It was not a pamphlet, but a book of 348 octavo pages. In it Torrens returned to the attack on those who advocated agricultural self-sufficiency. He called for free trade in corn as a means of securing power and prosperity. The cheapest means of obtaining food supplies for a growing population was to obtain it from abroad in exchange for manufactured goods. This would further extend Britain's undoubted industrial lead since it would widen the market for manufactures.

Like Ricardo, he argued that restrictions on corn imports would inhibit capital accumulation and stunt economic growth. He derived these results from a model incorporating classical postulates on rent and wages; but in a curious reversal of Ricardo's conclusion held that the rate of profit was held up under the protected system. He did not quite see the link Ricardo forged between wages and profits and, consequently at this stage, the 'fundamental theorem' eluded him, and with it, the proposition of a secular decline in the rate of profit arising from diminishing returns to land. In fact, Torrens went on to argue that, with the Corn Laws repealed, capital accumulation would pick up and result in a lower rate of profit. This was obviously a Smithian-derived theory of profit based on the 'competition of capitals'. At any rate, Torrens held that the lower rate of profit under free trade would somehow prove beneficial to industry and commerce (which he saw as the leading sectors of the economy). The contention was that lower capital costs combined with lower money wages would reduce average costs and prices generally, and thus boost the sales of British manufactured goods abroad.

Later, Torrens made use of the more orthodox Ricardian model to analyse the effect of cheap corn imports on economic growth. Thus in 1819 he wrote:

> Under any given degree of skill and economy in the application of labour, the return upon capital will be determined by the quality of land in cultivation; and as inferior soils are resorted to, the rate of profit will consistently diminish, until that stationary state is attained, in which no additional capital can be employed.[6]

Free trade in corn which allowed Britain to exchange manufactured goods for cheap foreign food would raise the rate of profit and allow the country 'indefinitely to advance in the career of improvement'. Like Ricardo, he reasoned shortly afterwards that free trade between Britain and 'the new and thinly inhabited countries' overseas would throw 'the stationary state to a greater distance' and lead to higher rates of capital accumulation and economic growth (Torrens 1821, pp. 252–60). In a perceptive passage in the third edition of the *External Corn Trade* (1826) Torrens suggested that in any event Britain would naturally tend to specialise in manufacturing since, unlike agriculture, the former was characterised by increasing returns to scale. Britain was eminently suited to manufacturing production because of its dense population and large domestic market which permitted the full exploitation of the 'effective powers of manufacturing industry' through division of labour:

> As an increasing population compels us on the one hand to resort to inferior soils, and thus to raise the productive cost of raw produce, so it leads on the other hand to more accurate divisions of employment, and to the use of improved machinery and thus lowers the productive cost of all wrought goods. (Torrens 1821, p. 119)

Torrens is here referring to the spontaneous (endogenous) factors which, under the influence of the profit motive and the possibility of industrial productivity, determine the composition of national output.

Self-sufficiency in food grains was neither feasible nor desirable for a country like Great Britain. Without participating in the international division of labour, a country could 'never make any very considerable advances in wealth and power' (Torrens 1827, p. 257). He repudiated the hope entertained by spokesmen for the agricultural interest that Britain might become a grain exporter once again. A corn-exporting Britain, he said, would be 'bankrupt and depopulated, sunk from her place in Europe, and, perhaps, deprived of her existence as an independent nation' (Torrens 1827, p. 256).

The theme that runs through Torrens' work is that of the maximisation of national power and imperial greatness. As an advocate of 'free-trade imperialism', Torrens had visions of a 'trade empire' more reminiscent of those glimpsed by Josiah Tucker as early as 1750 rather than of anything imagined by his contemporaries among the classical economists. Thus he wrote:

> The power that is derived from extended commerce is, perhaps, less unstable than that which is derived from extended territory . . . The question, as respects England, is not, whether her power would be more independent and stable if she possessed the extended territory and numerous population of France, or Austria, or Russia; but, whether, being inferior to those great continental states in natural resources, she should avail herself of the artificial, and even perhaps, less permanent advantages placed within her reach, and by the wonders of her commerce, create the means for taking an ascendancy in Europe . . . Now, we should never cease to remember, that manufactures and commerce are necessary, not only to compensate for our deficiency in extent and population, but also as the source of that justly cherished naval preponderance, without which an insular empire can take up no position among the nations of the world. (Torrens 1827, pp. 235, 331–2)

In Torrens' later writings these nationalistic sentiments became more pronounced. Thirty-seven years later, he felt compelled to rebuke the free-traders for neglecting the use of commercial policy to foster Britain's imperial power (hegemony):

> The country is undergoing a process of denationalisation. The power and glory of England find no place in the entries of the ledger. The cosmopolites of the Manchester School would not blush to see the western stars triumphantly floating over St. George's Channel. They would give Jamaica for a hogshead of sugar. They would sell Canada for a bale of cotton. For an additional million of exports they would yield up the trident without a struggle; and transfer from the hand of Victoria the sceptre of Anglo-Saxon empire. (Torrens 1852, pp. 48–9)

A more orthodox critique of the Corn Laws was made by James Mill in 1814 in reply to Malthus's first Corn Law pamphlet. As in his 1808 booklet Mill used the 'eighteenth-century rule' to demonstrate the efficiency gains of foreign trade:

> If we import, we must pay for what we import, with the produce of a portion of our labour exported. But why not employ that labour in raising the same portion at home? The answer is, because it will procure more corn by going in the shape of commodities to purchase corn abroad, than if it had been employed in raising it at home. A law, therefore, to prevent the importation of corn, can have only one effect – to make a greater portion of the labour of the community necessary for the production of its food.[7]

There were practical advantages, too, in a policy of free importation of food. Excessive price fluctuations for food grains could be avoided, and more regular supplies assured if instead of relying only on domestic resources, diversification of sources of supply was made use of through free importation of corn from several countries. The remedy for corn-price instability was to extend international trade. That would tend to smooth out cyclical fluctuations, thereby lessening the effect on prices of any one country's production. Complementary trading relationships would develop with foreign corn-exporting countries – relationships that would be costly for foreigners to disrupt because of their specialisation in primary production. He referred (as Torrens had, some months earlier) to the example of the Netherlands which had attained unparalleled opulence without reliance on domestic self-sufficiency in foodstuffs. He thus made light of Malthus' misgivings about reliance on imported foodstuffs, but ignored the argument that a nation specialising in manufactures could easily find its advantages eroded by foreign competition; and that such specialisation entailed a strong dependency on the continuous prosperity of the country's trading partners. Implicitly, that is, Mill assumed that the international division of labour so envisaged was going to be maintained permanently in Britain's favour. This, of course, followed from his static mode of reasoning which could not handle the sort of complications raised by Malthus.

Ricardo's Dynamic Arguments

What about Ricardo's advocacy of repeal? Did he not, as is commonly believed, base his arguments on: (a) the law of comparative cost, and (b) a secularly falling rate of profit in the absence of repeal? The fact is, however, that Ricardo never made use of the comparative-cost idea in his attack on the Corn Laws, but relied instead on absolute cost differences between Great Britain (in manufactures) and the rest of the world (in agriculture). In an insightful analysis of the dynamic aspects of Ricardo's international trade theory, Andrea Maneschi concluded: 'Ricardo's advocacy of the repeal of the Corn Laws was not based on comparative advantage and did not require it' (Maneschi 1983, p. 79). The comparative-cost example was irrelevant for Ricardo's argument in favour of repeal of agricultural protection for a manufacturing country like Britain, since that example merely highlighted the mechanism whereby consumers' preferences were satisfied in a context where international resources were optimally allocated. As Joan Robinson observed, a lower cost of procuring wine in England did not directly affect the profit rate and did not lower the real cost of wage-goods – the whole advantage went to the drinkers of wine. But, as we have already suggested, Ricardo clearly understood that there were two distinct benefits of foreign trade – the static gains in terms of a larger consumption bundle, and the dynamic effect on the growth rates of profits and the wage fund – as the following passage indicates:

> it is quite as important to the happiness of mankind that our enjoyments should
> be increased by the better distribution of labour, by each country producing
> those commodities . . . for which it is adapted, and by their exchanging them for
> the commodities of other countries, as that they should be augmented by a rise
> in the rate of profits. (Ricardo, *Works*, 1951, vol. 1, p. 132)

In his polemical campaign against the Corn Laws it was obviously more
impressive to stress the dynamic argument based on absolute advantages.
This is what he did in numerous correspondences, parliamentary speeches,
two pamphlets and four chapters of his major work.

What, then, about the other proposed string to Ricardo's bow – the prospect of a falling rate of profit? There is a shadow over this as well. Leading
authorities on Ricardo since Cannan's time have recognised that the theory
of distribution was his most effective weapon against the protectionists –
the argument suggesting how cheap imported corn could raise the rate of
profit. Yet Hollander's detailed reading of Ricardo's writings and parliamentary speeches leads him to assert 'the case made [by Ricardo] against
agricultural protection was not based upon the secular downward trend in
the rate of return on capital' (Hollander 1979, p. 604). Professor O'Brien
(O'Brien 1981, p. 376) takes strong exception to this contentious interpretation of Ricardo, saying: 'I find this about the most difficult thing to
swallow in the entire book' [that is, Hollander's book on Ricardo]. The
point at issue turns upon the question: is Ricardo rightly to be regarded as
an optimist or as a pessimist in regard to the prospects for British growth?
The conventional view labels Ricardo as a pessimist because of his 'prediction' of a falling rate of profit and an inexorable drift towards the 'stationary state'. Blaug did much to modify this traditional opinion of
Ricardo, pointing out that the stationary state was Ricardo's 'methodological fiction': 'The alleged "pessimism" of Ricardo was entirely contingent
upon the maintenance of the tariff on raw produce . . . the notion of an
impending stationary state was at most a useful device for frightening the
friends of protection' (Blaug 1958, pp. 31–2). Hollander goes further in
painting an optimistic image of Ricardo. Ricardo was so confident of the
dynamism of the British economy, he says, that even the Corn Laws and a
protected regime could not prevail against the steadfast march of technical
progress both in agriculture and in manufacturing.

If Ricardo did not attach much empirical (as distinct from analytical)
significance to the stationary state then he also did not believe that the Corn
Laws posed serious problems for the profitability of British industry. In this
interpretation, technical change mattered as much for Ricardo as did free
trade. Even after the 80s-a-quarter Corn Law was passed on 10 March 1815
Ricardo continued to speak out against agricultural protection both in
Parliament and in his writings (including correspondence). In view of the fore-

going reconstitution of Ricardo's basic theory, what then were the grounds for his opposition? It appears he had three objections to the Corn Laws:

1. They caused the profit rate and the rate of capital accumulation to be lower than would be the case under free trade. While protection in itself was not sufficient to bring about the stationary state, the rate of economic growth was rendered lower than in its absence.
2. They caused excessive fluctuations in grain prices. Fluctuations in prices initiated by the alteration of good and bad harvests were amplified by the artificial wedge placed between domestic and foreign prices so as to maintain high-cost farming in Britain. Thus in times of good harvests (and excess supply) domestic prices had to fall dramatically to the level of world prices before increased sales could be made abroad. Greater stability in the price of corn would result from repeal since domestic prices would then be determined by the worldwide conditions of supply and demand.
3. On efficiency or static-allocative grounds the Corn Laws were condemned since they caused domestic grain output to expand at the expense of domestic manufactured goods. On the given assumption that Britain's absolute advantage lay in manufacturing, the country's welfare would therefore be increased by repeal independently of any effect on the profit rate and the growth rate.

There is some uncertainty as to the relative weight placed by Ricardo on these distinct disadvantages. Consistent with Hollander's interpretation it is suggested that Ricardo did not himself take the first disadvantage too seriously. He was more concerned with the price instability and efficiency problems. It is one thing to suspect that Ricardo in his public utterances had a motivation to exaggerate the prospect of diminished profits for its propaganda value; but it is quite another to suggest that he himself did not believe it. Again, O'Brien disagrees with Hollander's account, alleging that the latter has 'emphasised the secondary at the expense of the primary', and his comment on Hollander's restatement on this point is that 'it seems to be characterised more by rhetoric than by reasoned argument' (O'Brien 1981, p. 381).

On corn-price instability there is no doubt that Ricardo was concerned with this problem during the early 1820s – a period of general deflation, falling food prices and rural distress. The high food prices of the Napoleonic wars fell and farmers found it increasingly hard to pay their wartime debts. Price instability added to the discontent felt not only among displaced village labourers, but among both landlords and substantial tenant farmers. Ricardo's pamphlet *On Protection to Agriculture* (1822) was partly devoted to this topic and he made several speeches in Parliament attributing grain-price fluctuations to the restrictive tariff policy. But considering Ricardo's anti-Corn Law writings prior to 1822 (and incidentally a long section in *On Protection to Agriculture*) the bulk of which is concerned with profits and economic growth, it cannot be maintained that Ricardo set great store on the price-instability argument. Blaug was no doubt stating the correct position when he wrote: 'the matter of price variability was a secondary element in the Ricardian attack on the corn laws' (Blaug 1958, p. 211).

If anyone can be said to have been seriously bothered by the price-instability problem it is surely J.R. McCulloch. To a much greater extent than Ricardo, he consistently urged repeal on the assumption that it would result in greater stability of corn prices. He also felt that the abandonment of protection would stem the flow of capital abroad caused by a declining profit rate. Malthus, Torrens and Thomas Tooke also referred to price fluctuations in connection with the debate on protection. Thomas Tooke collected data on harvest cycles and presented his analysis of the associated price fluctuations to the Commons Select Committee on Agriculture in 1821. In contrast to the free-traders' expectation that free trade in corn would reduce price fluctuations, Malthus asserted that in fact only protection (regulation) could ensure a modicum of stability to an otherwise (that is, naturally) unstable business.

We may summarise Ricardo's anti-Corn Law position as follows: free trade in corn was needed to offset diminishing returns in agriculture, the consequences of which acted as a brake on a potentially dynamic economy. Free importation of 'basic' commodities which entered into workers' consumption would alter the dynamic path of the economy, pushing it onto a higher trajectory appropriate to a country with an undoubted (absolute) advantage in manufacturing. Once launched on such a blissful course, wages, profits and growth-rates could be expected to increase indefinitely. In a speech to the House of Commons on 16 May 1822 (a year before his death) his optimistic vision was reported as follows:

> Of all the evils complained of, he [Ricardo] was still disposed to think the corn laws the worst. He conceived that were the corn laws once got rid of, and our general policy in these subjects thoroughly revised, this would be the cheapest country in the world; and that, instead of our complaining that capital was withdrawn from us, we should find that capital would come hither from all corners of the civilised world . . . If the government would pursue a right course of policy as to the corn laws, England would be the cheapest country in which a man could live; and it would rise to a state of prosperity, in regard to population and riches, of which, perhaps, the imaginations of hon. gentlemen could at present form no idea. (Ricardo, *Works*, 1951, vol. V, pp. 187–8)

Ricardo did not call for immediate and total repeal of the Corn Laws. In 1822 he wrote: 'that is not, under our circumstances, the course which I should recommend' (Ricardo, *Works*, 1951, vol. IV, p. 243). Like Adam Smith, he was a pragmatic free-trader conscious of the power of vested interests. He wanted the system replaced by a 'countervailing duty' of 20s a quarter initially, reducing annually over a ten-year period to stand permanently as a flat-rate duty of 10s a quarter on all imported grain. This would be combined with a corresponding 'drawback upon exportation' (that is, an export subsidy or refund of the domestic tax) of 7s. He considered this level of protection adequate compensation for the special tax burdens which fell on agriculturists compared with industrialists (for example, land tax, contributions to the poor rates, tithes and other direct charges on land). Given the existing tax system, this arrangement would also produce the best allocation of national resources and optimum level of aggregate national output. Ricardo's proposal for moderate protection was, however, turned down by the House of Commons – only twenty-five members supported it.

On free trade in general and commercial policy, Ricardo's position was less than forthright compared with his resolute stand against the Corn Laws. Despite the comparative cost example, his thought in the direction of free trade apparently stopped short at the juncture where capital, in the form of wage-goods, needed for industrial growth could more readily be obtained at better terms from abroad. It is true, generalised free trade only became a matter of public debate from about 1820, shortly before Ricardo's untimely death; but he was in the House of Commons when the famous Merchants' Petition (1820) calling for freer trade was debated. The Petition, presented to the House by the banker Sir Alexander Baring was drafted by Thomas Tooke with members of the Political Economy Club to which Ricardo belonged. His performance on this occasion was, however, disappointing. W.D. Grampp writes: 'He supported the petition, of course, but he did not enlarge on the case for free trade and made no mention of his own ideas (which he did do on other issues)' (Grampp 1982, p. 510).

For Ricardo, the significant contribution of trade to national economic development lay in its impact on agricultural prices. When he thought of free trade it was always in terms of a manufacturing country being able to obtain cheap food and raw materials from other countries better endowed with natural resources. Thus: 'while trade is free and corn cheap, profits will not fall however great the accumulation of capital' (Ricardo, *Works*, 1951, vol. VIII, p. 208). The crucial test was thus the effect of trade on the rate of profit and hence accumulation. The importance of luxury goods (wine, silks, velvets – 'trinkets for the rich') does not matter on this criterion, since trade in such goods leaves the profit rate unaffected.

In his formal theory he clearly distinguished between national and cosmopolitan gains from trade and changes in trade policy. Thus, in his analysis of colonial trade, he agreed with Adam Smith that the colonies were disadvantaged by the regime of regulated trade and would benefit from freer trade. But he argued that 'the trade of a colony may be so regulated that it shall at the same time be less beneficial to the colony and more beneficial to the mother country than a perfectly free trade'. And, 'a measure which may be greatly hurtful to a colony may be partially beneficial to the mother country' (Ricardo, *Works*, 1951, vol. I, pp. 343, 340). It was nearly always from the perspective of the metropolitan country that he viewed matters relating to colonial trade, just as in trade policy it was always the interest of Britain which mattered. He did not extend the dynamic implications of his model to the countries that were to supply Britain with foodstuffs. He assumed that an elastic supply of food could be obtained from overseas; and although the implications of world-wide diminishing returns in primary production must have been obvious to him, he relegated that eventuality to the distant future. In the meantime, as far as Britain was concerned, free international trade on that basis could make an important contribution to Britain's economic growth. He considered the static benefits accruing to those countries, that is, the opportunity, given free trade and the reallocation of resources, of obtaining cheap British manufactures. But he failed to recognise that the pattern of product specialisation determined by free trade might be detrimental to the long-term interests of the food-producing countries and that they would take steps to alter the comparative-advantage bases of their national economies. He believed that the world economy functioned in a setting of reasonable international equilibrium and did not envisage problems associated with a balance-of-payments constraint on growth, cyclical slumps and conditions of price and income inelasticity of demand for primary products. Diminishing agricultural efficiency was the centrepiece of his growth analysis, yet he did not stop to consider that this (combined with free trade) would prove a handicap to the development of primary-producing countries in the absence of massive capital investment to counteract the forces of diminishing returns. He was right in his diagnosis that Britain's comparative advantage lay in manufacturing, and that the implied national specialisation would be further strengthened 'by the improvements in machinery, by the better division and distribution of labour, and by the increasing skill, both in science and art, of the producers' (Ricardo, *Works*, 1951, vol. 1, p. 94). The remarkable growth he predicted did occur, and free trade, when it came, did produce substantial material benefits for the nation. He supported a commercial policy which led to the intense involvement of Britain in the international economy and tied the country's growth in output and living standards to the vicissitudes of the international environment. He espoused more balanced international growth, even though it meant more 'unbalanced' domestic growth. This orientation of the economy was, as we have seen, much regretted by Malthus. His formal theory left unanswered the question: What would become of the source of comparative advantage if knowledge, skills and technology were to be diffused throughout the world economy?

To be sure, as presented in terms of the pure theory of barter, his model suggested that the distribution of tasks among nations was fixed for all time, that is, that the world distribution of comparative advantages was something static and permanent. This is the conventional view; but it neglects what Ricardo had to say later on in his trade chapter about the international distribution of specie. Here he discussed cases where comparative advantage could change under the impact of technical change, improvements in the arts and machinery or the discovery of new processes. He supposes a situation where English wine technology improves to such an extent that it becomes profitable for England to export wine in exchange for Portuguese cloth – a reversal of comparative advantages and the emergence of a new pattern of trade: 'If the improvement in making wine were of a very important description, it might become profitable for the two countries to exchange employments; for England to make all the wine, and Portugal all the cloth consumed by them' (Ricardo, *Works*, 1951, vol. I, pp. 137–8). The idea was, however, not developed; it remained embedded in the particular hypothetical context designed to show the effects of monetary movements, and it is not clear that the circumstances depicted represent a true trading equilibrium. Moreover, the example does not arise in a dynamic setting in which the efficiency of production may change over time, for example, due to increasing returns, external economies, and so on.

Like his father, John Stuart Mill was a severe critic of the Corn Laws. But when he came to write on the issue (in the late 1820s) the matter – at least in principle – was fairly well rehearsed. The parliamentary debates were still intense and lengthy, but there was general recognition of the impossibility of agricultural self-sufficiency in the face of growing population pressure. In addition, the competitive ability of British manufacturers in foreign markets seemed reasonably secure; and the Tory government was on the verge of conceding the necessity for some modification of the Corn Laws. J.S. Mill felt it unnecessary, therefore, to go over the ground covered by his father twenty years earlier in *Commerce Defended*. He was relieved to say: 'One part of the argument we may safely omit . . . the beneficial tendency of free trade in general' (Mill 1963, p. 47). He repeated Ricardo's charge that the landowners had a permanent interest in protection. But they were misguided, since the landlord 'if he has an interest opposed to that of the community, he has also an interest in common with them' (Mill 1963, p. 64). Mill then stressed the mutuality of interests: cheap foreign food would mean lower poor rates, which would lighten the burden on agriculturists. He allayed the fears of landowners and farmers by predicting that the price of corn would not fall to such levels that would cause widespread bank-ruptcies and unrelieved distress and endorsed Ricardo's plan for a compen-sating duty after the phasing out of protection.

Two years later, exasperated by the temporising attitude of the govern-ment, he castigated the 'fury of the band of enraged monopolists', namely the landlords, whose obstinacy stood in the way of national progress. Resignedly, he lamented:

> Let those be disappointed who looked for any thing better: we confess that our hopes were never very sanguine. It would argue little experience of human affairs to expect from monopolists the abandonment of a monopoly; from landlords the voluntary abatement of rent. (Mill 1963, p. 143)

But Mill did not give up. He continued to support the popular campaign against the Corn Laws, and his last recorded effort in this direction was the drafting of a petition unanimously adopted at a free-trade meeting in Kensington (London), 15 June 1841. This brings us to a consideration of the classical economists' views on commercial policy in general.

6.2   COMMERCIAL POLICY

In a book on the rise of modern protectionism, Melvyn Krauss writes: 'the conflict between the economic interests of specific groups within the com-munity and the economic interests of the community as a whole is the essence of the 'issue of free trade versus protectionism' (Krauss 1979, p. xxiii, also p. 6). The classical economists were only too well aware of this. In a speech to the House of Commons on agricultural distress, Ricardo observed that protection 'might be beneficial to a particular trade, but it must be injurious to the rest of the country'.[8] But much as it is today, the nineteenth-century controversy was wider than this. It ranged from matters relating to national security to fears over the export of machinery. Thus apart from the pleas of the lobbyists, the free-traders had to contend with the arguments that free trade would: (a) diminish national power and make the country dependent on foreigners; (b) reduce government revenue and therefore increase the national debt; (c) be a renunciation of the country's ability to improve its bargaining position *vis-à-vis* other countries (that is, the terms of trade argument); (d) lead to the transfer of technology abroad (through the export of machinery) and therefore to the erosion of national competitive advantages; and (e) leave the country without the means of fos-tering the growth of 'infant industries' against competition from abroad.

On the purely nationalistic, beggar-thy-neighbour and politically inspired arguments some of the economists felt that the fears behind them were exaggerated and minimised the force of the arguments while others supported all or some of them.

There were those among them who managed to give free trade a mercantilist twist, as clearly exemplified in the works of Torrens. Free trade was seen as a means of gaining for Britain a monopoly of trade in manufactured goods. This projected economic hegemony could be realised by persuading other countries to adopt free trade.

Even the more orthodox of the early classical economists were not extreme and uncompromising free-traders. Like Adam Smith, they qualified their advocacy of free trade in a number of ways: (1) the 'national defence' argument for protecting strategically important industries; (2) the revenue argument; and (3) the desirability of imposing a compensatory tax on imports where an excise tax on domestic production existed, so as to maintain fair competition between foreign and domestic producers.

As the debate on free trade progressed, the economists became clearer what the purely economic arguments were. As a result of this, two major exceptions to international *laissez-faire* were conceded: (1) the 'terms of trade' argument and (2) the 'infant-industry' argument. The logic of these arguments had to be admitted, for they met the economists' own criteria of (a) buying in the cheapest market and selling in the highest, and (b) long-run efficiency in the allocation of resources. Reservations relating to the practical application of these devices were made, of course, and, in addition, some cosmopolitan-minded economists (particularly later neoclassical writers like Edgeworth and Marshall) objected to the narrowly national self-interest on which the arguments rested.

We shall briefly discuss how these economically defensible arguments for protection came to be accepted, but first a comment on the income-distribution aspect. Ricardo, Torrens and Malthus recognised early in the Corn Law debate that agricultural protection tended to raise landlords' share in the national income. As noted previously, Malthus (in his two Corn Law pamphlets) explicitly discussed the question in terms of the effect of a rise in the price of corn and other commodities. He concluded that high corn prices meant high wage-rates and that therefore the Corn Laws benefited labour as well, since the purchasing power of workers' income over non-food commodities was thereby enhanced. But, as we have seen, this was not a deduction from the 'one-factor only' formal model of comparative cost – with a one-factor model, income-distribution changes simply do not arise. Neither was it derived from any generalised concept of marginal productivity. What was clear from the Torrens–Ricardo model, though, was that free trade in corn would maximise Britain's national income as a whole. From this larger total income, landlords who lost out from free trade would ultimately benefit; for they knew for sure that repeal of the Corn Laws would benefit capitalists and injure landlords. Alternatively, they implicitly assumed that the change in income distribution could be compensated for by appropriate changes in taxation. Indeed, Lord Landsdowne, the Whig spokesman on economic affairs in the Lords and later a member of the Political Economy Club, made just such a proposal in connection with a specific case: the compensation out of public funds for the losses incurred by silk workers consequent upon the freer entry of French silks into Britain. However, in the absence of an automatic mechanism for compensation, could it still be maintained that the gains from free trade constituted an unambiguous improvement in welfare? Henry Brougham was one who implicitly denied this on the ground that since obviously all individuals were not identical in every relevant respect it was impossible to make interpersonal comparisons of utility (or well-being); hence, 'the destruction of one portion of the community could not be considered a benefit because another portion gained by it. This was a proposition which no philosopher or political economist had ever attempted to deny or dispute'.[9] Finally, then, those who sought to minimise the 'adjustment costs' of free trade were forced to fall back on the factor-mobility assumption. Taking their cue from Adam Smith, and confident that resources (including labour) would be redeployed speedily, the income-distribution effect did not pose a problem for the free-trade case.

The Terms of Trade Argument

There was, however, a logical flaw in early statements of the free trade doctrine. When writers recommended free trade, they often gave the impression that it was a choice between free trade and no trade, whereas in reality it was about free (or freer) trade versus protection. Generally, these writers underestimated the adverse short-run effects likely to be caused by removal of restrictions. In particular, they implicitly might have assumed that the movement from protection to free or freer trade would not alter a country's terms of trade. Of the leading writers, Malthus first faced this issue and Torrens and John Stuart Mill and others analysed the commercial policy implications of the terms of trade. No construct in the pure theory of trade has given rise to greater public controversy and heated debate in international forums than the terms of trade; and the credit (or blame) for initiating the terms-of-trade debate goes to the early classical political economists. Torrens (1852) claimed: 'No questions in political economy are of greater importance than those which relate to the terms of international exchange' (Torrens 1852, vol. II, p. 32). One of the doubts Malthus harboured about the benefit of free trade against the enthusiastic supporters of industrial growth through unrestricted international commerce concerned the possibility of adverse repercussions on the terms of trade. If free trade stimulated the cheapening of manufactures (through productivity growth) and no significant expansion of demand took place abroad

> then the increasing ingenuity and exertions of a manufacturing and commercial state (such as Britain) would be lost in continually falling prices. It would not only be obliged, as its skill and capital increased, to give a larger quantity of manufactured produce for the raw produce which it received in return; but it might be unable, even with the temptation of reduced prices, to stimulate its customers to such purchases as would allow of an increasing importation of food and raw materials; and without such an increasing importation, it is quite obvious that the population must become stationary. (Malthus 1826, pp. 409–10)

In other words, if foreigners did not have anything with which to trade in return for all the goods that British exporters were so keen to sell them, then inevitably there would be a deterioration in Britain's commodity (or net barter) terms of trade. But even with such lower prices, British manufacturers might not be able to sell their goods because of deficient demand abroad. The result of this overproduction would be continually falling prices and profits.

Another source of stagnation might arise from foreign competition. Thus:

> When a powerful foreign competition takes place, the exportable commodities of the country in question must soon fall in prices which will essentially reduce profits; and the fall of profits will diminish both the power and the will to save. Under these circumstances the accumulation of capital will be slow, till it comes nearly to a stand. (Malthus 1826, pp. 403–4)

Malthus worried about the problem of 'effective demand', that is, the permanent and persistent tendency for the total supply of goods to outstrip demand. His fears were shared by others (Sismondi, Chalmers, Lord Lauderdale), but brushed aside by James Mill, J.B. Say, Ricardo and McCulloch on the grounds of the adjustability of production and insatiability of demand. 'I consider the wants and tastes of mankind as unlimited'; and 'if there is a glut of one commodity, produce less of that and more of another' was Ricardo's reply to Malthus (Ricardo to Malthus, 16 September 1814 in Ricardo, *Works*, 1951, vol. VI, p. 134, and Ricardo, *Works*, vol. VIII, p. 22).

Nevertheless it was Malthus' belief that specialisation in international trade was the source of both glutted markets and adverse terms of trade. The industrial economy would, no doubt, adjust to disequilibrium in the way suggested by Ricardo, that is, by the reduction in output of the over-produced and unprofitable commodities. But this would 'throw labourers out of work' and lead to general unemployment (through further reductions in spending and income). Malthus knew that Sismondi, another critic of industrial capitalism, came to the same conclusion about the effects of overproduction and glutted world markets inherent in unrestricted international competition – falling prices, redundant capital, stagnation, unemployment and crises. Sismondi had reported (1819):

> We have seen merchandise of every description, but above all that of England, the great manufacturing power, abounding in all the markets of Italy in a proportion so far exceeding demand, that the merchants, in order to realize even a part of their capital, have been obliged to dispose of them at a loss of a fourth or a third, instead of obtaining any profit.[10]

Say's answer to the problem: 'The quantity of English merchandise offered for sale in Italy and elsewhere is too great, because there is not sufficient Italian or other produce suitable to the English market' (Say 1821, p. 8) did not satisfy Sismondi and Malthus. Equilibrium would, no doubt, be established at market-clearing prices if a counter-set of commodities were produced and offered for sale in the glutted market. But that was precisely the problem! As Joan Robinson once remarked on another occasion: 'The hidden hand will always do its work, but it may work by strangulation' (Robinson 1979b, vol. I, p. 189). Given the specificity of factors, the existence of inertia, indolence, and so on, the adjustment to equilibrium can be a protracted and painful process. Chipman, in his survey article, gave credit to Torrens for his early attempt to prove the existence of competitive equilibrium (via price adjustments) in such a case, including a statement describing a 'cobweb' path to equilibrium (Chipman 1965, pp. 711 and 713). But a decade later Torrens completely reversed his position on this question when he asserted that 'in a country exporting manufactured goods, and importing raw materials, there may be a general glut of capital, and excess of production, in relation to foreign demand, which cannot be remedied by transferring capital from one branch of manufacturing to another'.[11]

Malthus reverted to the possibility of deteriorating terms of trade (resulting from increased investment in export production) in his 1820 *Principles of Political Economy*. There he outlined the argument in greater detail, hinting also at single-factor terms-of-trade losses (where one unit of labour exported bought fewer foreign goods):

> as capital continued to be accumulated and employed in large quantities on the exportable manufactures, such manufactures upon the principles of demand and supply, would in all probability fall in price. A larger portion of them must then

be exchanged for a given portion of corn . . . more work being necessary to earn the same quantity of corn. (Malthus 1820, p. 329)

Sir William G. Sleeman, an anti-Ricardian writer, noting the fall in manu-factured goods' prices caused by the efficiency of British industry, said that foreign countries 'are continuously giving less and less of the produce of their domestic industry for the same thing, or receiving more and more of our produce for the same portion of theirs' (Sleeman 1829, p. 198). In 1833 George Poulett Scrope made a case for colonisation based partly on alleged unfavourable terms of trade to Britain when it obtained its food supplies from foreign countries under free trade conditions. The efficiency of agri-cultural production in these other countries might not keep pace with Britain's own growth, and thus 'we carry on what may be called a losing trade with them; we are continually exchanging larger quantities of the produce of our industry for less quantities of theirs'. The answer to this adverse trend under generalised free trade was for Britain to develop agri-cultural resources in the colonies with British capital and labour and thus free itself from dependence 'on the slow increase of the productive capac-ities of foreigners' (Poulett Scrope 1833, pp. 378–82). In an earlier article, Poulett Scrope referred to a phenomenon now known in the literature as 'immiserising growth'. This is the case where factor accumulation and the resulting growth in output actually make an open economy worse off than under autarky. That is, if (a) the growing country is large enough to influence the international terms of trade; (b) demand is inelastic; and (c) the productivity growth is largely experienced in the export industry, then it is possible for the deterioration in the terms of trade to be so large as to outweigh the effect of the physical increase in output and therefore leave the country worse off than before. Poulett Scrope contended that deteri-orating terms of trade (initiated by faster growth in the home country than elsewhere) would cause wages and profits to fall in England, with the result that 'the general condition of that country must rather deteriorate than improve through its increasing productiveness' (Poulett Scrope 1831, p. 24). Poulett Scrope stated the problem; he did not analyse it. Although one can take his reference to lowered wages and profits as implying a reduction in aggregate national real income, it is not clear how 'immiserising growth' actually arises from his hypothetical example – as Bloomfield observed (Bloomfield 1984). Torrens frequently wrote about the adverse repercus-sions on the terms of trade of British growth. In 1837 he observed:

If in the markets of America, the demand for English goods should remain sta-tionary, while the supply of them should be increased, then, in the American markets, a given quantity of English goods would exchange for a less quantity of American produce than before. (Torrens 1837, pp. 132–3)

From these writings it was obvious that unfavourable terms-of-trade trends could be arrested or reversed by commercial policy. It was soon realised that by imposing a tariff a country could, by restricting the volume of its imports, lower the price of importables relative to its exports – thereby improving the terms of trade. Torrens was the first to see the benefit of a tariff to Britain, and became a firm advocate of 'reciprocity' as the indispensable basis of a country's commercial policy. The government should not contemplate the unilateral reduction of British tariffs, as this would adversely affect the terms of trade. The wise policy would be to use the existing tariff structure as a 'bargaining chip' in commercial negotiations to force other countries to reciprocate by reducing their tariffs against British goods. Torrens was, of course, always at his best when advocating or attacking specific policies. He had no hesitation in changing or modifying his basic theory to suit the shifts and turns in his practical opinions. He criticised Malthus for abandoning principles firmly held; but he himself was guilty of this charge, for in his early writings Torrens advocated unconditional free trade or unilateral tariff reductions – he was, after all, a co-discoverer of the comparative cost principle. As a member of the Political Economy Club he was a signatory of the Merchants' Petition (1820), which he also supported in his newspaper, *The Traveller*. A year later he was still an unequivocal free trader, as his *Essay on the Production of Wealth* attests. But by the 1830s he moved away from free trade, pure and simple. He expressed doubts about the wisdom of a unilateral reduction of import duties, By the 1840s, these fundamental reservations developed into active opposition, to the point where he came close to repudiating his own concept of 'territorial division of labour'. Initially, at any rate, Torrens' defence of 'reciprocity' seems to have rested on fear of deflation and general economic stagnation, as F.W. Fetter pointed out.[12] It was an old mercantilist argument, of course: tariffs are necessary to stem the outflow of specie (international money) which would otherwise cause deflation and unemployment. But Torrens soon after coupled this with the more orthodox terms-of-trade argument. The unilateral removal of import duties turned the terms of trade against Britain; therefore the country should not lower its tariffs unilaterally, but only if British tariff cuts were matched by equivalent tariff reductions on the part of other countries. Torrens' recommendations were challenged by, among others, Nassau Senior and J.R. McCulloch.

Like Frank Graham a century later, Senior seemed to have claimed that demand variations had no practical effect in the long run. An equilibrium price ratio determined exclusively by reciprocal demand was the exception rather than the rule. The pattern of international specialisation, influenced as it was by productivity differences, was, he held, remarkably stable. Thus, costs of production determine value in international trade. Senior habitually thought of international trade in monetary terms, and was fully conscious that in the real world trade takes place in many commodities among many countries. Given this approach, he faulted Torrens' argument on several grounds:

1. World prices are comparatively little affected by changes in supply or demand from particular countries, that is, the elasticity of supply in world trade is infinite. Substitution effects on the supply side exert a stabilising influence.
2. Tariffs interfere with optimal resource allocation by limiting the division of labour and specialisation. It forces capital and labour into branches of production where their value-productivities as measured by world-market prices were less than fully maximised.
3. Torrens was misled by his 2x2 model. In a multi-commodity, multi-country world, the diminished efficiency of capital and labour in the tariff-imposing country would lead to a deterioration of the country's international competitive position, both in the domestic market and in markets abroad. The gain from tariff restriction is therefore purely illusory, according to Senior; for whatever extra specie is obtained by this policy would rapidly be lost again because of reduced factor productivity and higher unit costs relative to those abroad.

Senior did not deny that there was a valid terms-of-trade argument on purely theoretical grounds, but he doubted that the conditions under which the argument was valid did, in fact, prevail generally in the real world. Most countries were not in a position to practise favourable manipulations of the terms of trade, and it was highly unlikely that cartel-type arrangements among groups of countries (principal suppliers) would prove viable in the long run. Special cases of inelastic demand and rigid price structures were conceivable, but it was unrealistic to assume that the supply response of the rest of the world remained the same whether or not tariffs were imposed. Foreign producers might have other outlets for their exports, or they might prefer to shift to other products or simply reduce output (Senior 1843, pp. 1–47).

Like Senior, McCulloch ruled out the practical possibility of rigging the terms of trade on the ground that the elasticity of supply in international trade is infinite (an assumption he shared with Senior). But according to Professor O'Brien, his argument was more convincing than that of Senior because McCulloch consistently held a cost-of-production theory of trade based squarely on absolute differences in such costs between countries. Costs of production, not demand, govern world prices and these were further constrained within limits set by a competitive international average rate of return. Thus, unique among the classical economists, McCulloch was able to reject Torrens' case on theoretical grounds. In addition, because of the certainty of retaliation and the loss from trade diversion, McCulloch dismissed Torrens' case as irrelevant and inconsequential.[13] Torrens was hinting at the optimum-tariff argument; but, as Peter Sai-wing Ho rightly reminds us, this should not be taken to mean that Torrens wanted Britain to exploit her monopoly power in trade to extract greater gains from trade. On the contrary, says Ho, Torrens' concern (as mentioned above) was to warn that Britain's economic stagnation and 'distress' would intensify 'if, while she would lower her duties, her trading partners would retain theirs'. He wanted the British government to adopt 'reciprocity' as the guiding principle of commercial policy. However, as far as the theoretical point about such an optimal tariff was concerned, Torrens did not analyse fully the conditions under which the argument was valid. In his reply to Senior's criticisms, he claimed that if the tariff caused wage rates in the export sector to be higher than under free trade, despite the allocative-efficiency losses from a reduced volume of trade, this showed that the country enjoyed a net gain. But aggregate wages (and profits) might fall, and therefore it was not at all clear that total national income (or welfare) would have been augmented with trade restrictions. Torrens was misled by his naive assumption that the efficiency of labour could only be measured by the terms of trade. The issues involved in this argument only became clearer with J.S. Mill's elaboration of reciprocal demand functions, which were, in principle, welfare functions representing net incomes.

Torrens's real aim was the creation of an imperial Zollverein (a free trade area protected by discriminatory tariffs against the outside world) linked to an active programme of colonisation so that

> England might become a vast industrial metropolis, and the colonies agricultural provinces of unlimited extent . . . By extending our colonial system, and opening new and expanding markets in our trans-marine dependencies, coupled with the rigid enforcement of the principle of reciprocity, we may arm ourselves with accumulating force to break down hostile tariffs, and to establish free trade throughout the world. (Torrens 1844, pp. 177 and 66)

Torrens backed up Wakefield's theory of self-financing colonisation with economic arguments based on his fears of adverse terms of trade (arising from protective tariffs in America and Europe), oversupply of capital and labour in England and the depressive effects these produced on the domestic rate of profit and wages. He evidently sincerely believed in an 'economy of high wages' and sought an escape from Malthusian pessimism (diminishing returns, falling rate of profit and excess population) in emigration. From the late 1820s, therefore, Torrens linked colonisation with British capital redundancy and commercial policy. Thus, after remarking on the tendency towards adverse terms of trade, he continued:

> On these obvious, and universally admitted principles of commerce, we can explain the process by which, in a commercial and manufacturing country, importing raw produce, the increase of commercial and manufacturing capital may lower the wages of the operative class. (Torrens 1837, p. 133)

This led him to repudiate the Mill–Say 'law of markets' which obviously did not square with observed facts. But, as Chipman reminds us, even as Torrens' thought took a different turn, analytically he did abandon his previous position on gluts. That is, Torrens always maintained that surplus capital and gluts would not occur in crisis proportions if there was 'a proportional extension of the foreign market'. By the latter he meant a proportional increase in foreign demand or a sufficient increase in the supply of foreign exportables, that is, the 'counter-commodity' argument. Torrens' diagnosis was substantially correct. There was a crisis in the export sector at that time, and Britain experienced adverse movements in her net barter terms of trade – a combined tendency which acted as a drag on Britain's growth. In these circumstances of sluggish trade in goods, he reasoned, the general economic stagnation could only be relieved by labour and capital movements to the 'empty' lands of the Empire in Canada, Australia and South Africa – a policy he summarised in a parliamentary speech (15 February 1827): 'England had a redundant population, while the colonies had redundant land. Emigration therefore was merely a method of the application of the redundant capital and population of the United Kingdom to the redundant lands of the colonies.'[14] Commenting on this imperial strategy, a modern historian approvingly observes, 'without a most unlikely restructuring of the economy and society, it does not seem possible that any large part of the resources devoted to supplying the export trade and to overseas investment could have found alternative uses' (Davis 1979, p. 75).

This consciously designed policy was, of course, a breach of strict *laissez-faire* principles – even though under Wakefield's scheme, private companies, not the state, were the principal agents; and one might have queried whether colonisation was indeed the only answer to surplus capital. The rate of return was as high (perhaps even higher) in South America and Europe as it was in the colonies. There was no particular reason why capital should be directed in a certain direction. As early as 1821, one writer pointed out: 'Should capital find no profitable employment in one country it will soon go to seek for it in another . . . capital will not lose its uses anywhere, till every corner of the world has acquired as large a share of it as can be productively employed.'[15] Huskisson (at the Board of Trade) also warned that colonisation merely shifted the problem elsewhere 'by causing a glut of population there, and thereby creating a production beyond any demand the emigrants could obtain for it in an advantageous interchange with other countries.'[16] But as far as Torrens was concerned, the case for colonisation did not rest solely on economic considerations; it was part of the plan to enhance Britain's imperial greatness. In the 1827 speech in Parliament he unfolded the grander purpose of emigration:

> In giving effect to extensive and improved plans for colonisation, we are multi-plying the British nation; we are rocking the cradles of giant empires; we are cooperating in the schemes of Providence, and are its favoured instruments in causing civilization to cover the earth, as the waters cover the sea.[17]

Such fervent nationalistic rhetoric invoking Divine blessing for England's project had not been heard in the land since the days of Oliver Cromwell who is, on certain interpretations, in the words of Sir Ernest Barker, 'the author of colonial expansion and imperial policy – the arch-founder, if not the first begetter, of the British Empire' (Barker 1948, p. 162). Besides Torrens, Wakefield's project was also endorsed by J.S. Mill, Poulett Scrope and Jeremy Bentham.

Mill on the Terms-of-Trade Argument

As far as Mill was concerned, the terms-of-trade argument arose naturally from his work on the market mechanisms in international trade. Mill revealed in the preface to the *Essays on Some Unsettled Questions of Political Economy* that they were actually written much earlier (that is, in 1829–30) and were published (1844) in response to the writings of Torrens, with whom he disagreed as to the practical application of the argument, but that 'opinions identical in principle to those promulgated by Colonel Torrens . . . have been held by the writer for more than fifteen years' (Mill 1844, pp. v–vi).

Mill's analysis showed that tariffs affect the ratio of interchange between exports and imports, that is, the reciprocal offers of the trading countries can be altered by exploiting monopolistic/monopsonistic advantages in foreign trade. Writing on British tariffs, Mill noted: if the restrictions were removed, we should have to pay rather more for some of the articles which we now import, while the articles which we are now prevented from import-ing would cost more than might be inferred from their *present* price in the foreign market' (Mill 1963, p. 258). Under certain circumstances, Mill's analysis showed, taxes on imports and exports can be paid entirely by the foreigner. Although he drew too sharp a distinction between 'revenue' and 'protective' duties, he never suffered from any misconception about the benefits which a single country could derive (at the expense of its neighbours) from imposing revenue duties. Recognising this, Mill was a strong supporter of reciprocity in commercial negotiations:

> A country cannot be expected to renounce the power of taxing foreigners, unless foreigners will in return practise towards itself the same forbearance. The only mode in which a country can save itself from being a loser by the duties imposed by other countries on its commodities, is to impose corresponding duties on theirs. (Mill 1963, p. 291)

Equally, however, Mill clearly recognised the theoretical limitations and practical drawbacks of a policy of 'taxing the foreigner'. First, it only applies if the reciprocal demand of the outside world has a low elasticity and the tariff-imposing country's own reciprocal demand has a high elasticity. Secondly, retaliation is likely; this tends to neutralise the initial advantage to the tariff-imposing country. Thirdly, it is a desirable policy strictly from the national point of view. Better terms of trade for one country necessarily implies worse terms of trade for its trading partners. The misallocation of resources (that is, the distortions in production and consumption) resulting from the pursuit of national gains is a general loss for the world as a whole. If the losses of trading partners exceed the gains of the tariff-imposing country, then such an outcome is patently unjust as well as economically undesirable.

Mill candidly discussed the difficulties which attended a policy of unilateral free trade except for imports that could be classified as 'necessaries of life' or 'materials and instruments of production'. Writing in the aftermath of the crisis of 1825 and the depression which followed, he felt a strong sympathy with the businessmen who complained about the flood of imports, and criticised the doctrinaire free-traders for their uncritical acceptance of Hume's Law, namely that increased imports necessarily and automatically generated more exports. An influx of imports, he wrote,

> is a forced increase, produced by an efflux of money and fall of prices; and this fall of prices being permanent, although it would be no evil at all in a country where credit is unknown, it may be a very serious one where large classes of persons, and the nation itself, are under engagements to pay fixed sums of money of large amount. (Mill 1963, p. 258)

Apart from the disruption caused by the rush of imports, Mill also consistently wrote about the adverse shift in the terms of trade that was bound to follow the unilateral abolition of tariffs.

The mere removal of trade restrictions was not sufficient to keep up the domestic rate of profit. Population pressure and excessive capital accumulation called for expanding markets for exports, additional sources of supplies of produce and raw materials and new investment opportunities overseas. In recognition of these needs Mill found in emigration, colonisation and foreign investment, solutions to the problems of the British economy. Consequently, at the theoretical level, Mill's position moved closer to that taken by Malthus, Sismondi and Torrens. In the second of his early essays, 'On the Influence of Consumption on Production', he mounted a trenchant refutation of Say's Law:

> Of the capital of a country there is at all times a very large proportion lying idle. The annual produce of a country is never anything approaching in magnitude to what it might be if all the resources devoted to reproduction, if all the capital, in short, of a country were in full employment. (Mill 1963, p. 55)

And again:

> This argument [Say's Law] is evidently founded on the supposition of a state of barter . . . If, however, we suppose that money is used, these propositions cease to be exactly true . . . Although he who sells, really sells only to buy, he needs not buy at the same moment when he sells; and he does not therefore necessarily add to the *immediate* demand for one commodity when he adds to the supply of the other. (Mill 1963, p. 70)

Mill returned to a more orthodox line in his *Principles* for, although bits and pieces of the earlier analysis are there, the stress in the later work is on the stability of equilibrium. Mill's position on reciprocity in trade relations also rested partly on his belief that

> the richest countries, *ceteris paribus*, gain the least by a given amount of foreign commerce: since, having a greater demand for commodities generally, they are likely to have a greater demand for foreign commodities, and thus modify the terms of interchange to their own disadvantage.[18]

The explanation for 'Mill's paradox', as Edgeworth called it, was, of course, that an expanding industrial economy such as Britain would soon run up against deteriorating terms of trade unless wider export markets for manufactures could be found, and a more rapid development of agricultural resources took place. In the short run, reciprocity would ensure a more balanced growth of trade without imposing welfare losses on Britain; but in the long run, the answer lay in the export of British capital and labour to develop the resources of the 'larger community' of the British Empire. Mill explained the matter as follows:

> It is to the emigration of English capital that we have chiefly to look for keeping a supply of cheap food and cheap materials of clothing proportional to the

increase of our population; thus enabling an increasing capital to find employment in the country, without reduction of profit, in producing manufactured
articles with which to pay for this supply of raw produce. Thus, the exportation
of capital is an agent of great efficiency in extending the field for that which
remains and it may be said truly that up to a certain point the more capital we
send away, the more we shall possess and be able to retain at home. (Mill [1848]
1920, p. 739)

But Mill did not go along with Torrens when the latter claimed that the
advantages from trade could only be realised on terms of perfect reciprocity;
and that therefore increased British duties were required to force foreign
countries to negotiate reciprocal reductions in tariffs on manufactured
goods, or as retaliation against the imposition of hostile foreign tariffs. As
early as 1829 Mill pointed out that, despite deteriorating net barter terms of
trade, Britain still gained substantially from trade:

> On the whole, England probably, of all the countries of Europe, draws to herself
> the largest share of the gains of international commerce: because her exportable
> articles are in universal demand, and are of such a kind that the demand
> increases rapidly as the price falls. (Mill 1844, p. 45)

This statement does not conflict with 'Mill's paradox', noted above. The
latter is a general proposition about the adverse effects of growth (factor
accumulation, technical progress or a general increase in productivity) on
the growing country's net barter terms of trade. The point he is now making
is that trends in the ratio of import and export prices (whether favourable
or unfavourable) do not tell the whole story about the total gains from
trade. One needs to take into account also trends in the volume of trade,
since the actual gains from trade depend on both the terms of trade and the
volume of exports and imports. The two are partly interconnected and
partly independent. A country may have highly favourable terms of trade,
but if this means that its exports are too expensive for foreigners to buy then
the country has zero trade volume and makes no gain at all from trade. Just
as a firm's success in the market is measured by the extent to which it maximises net revenue from sales (quantity sold times unit price), so a country's
total gain from foreign trade is measured by its net proceeds from foreign
sales. This is what Mill was referring to in the passage quoted. Britain's gain
from international trade was still substantial, for although export prices
were falling (for example, for cotton goods), the volume of exports was
rapidly expanding (relative to other European competitors) because of
high income and price elasticity of demand for British manufactures in
world markets.

To round off this discussion of the terms-of-trade argument, it is of some
relevance to consider the claim of a modern historian (D.N. McCloskey) in

a counterfactual comparative–static exercise that the level of British
national income might have been higher during the period 1841–81 had the
country remained under protection. The abandonment of general protection resulted in a deterioration of the British terms of trade over the period;
and in this sense, free trade imposed a welfare loss (of about 4 per cent
of national income) on the British people (McCloskey 1980, pp. 303–20).
This finding challenges the conventional view that trade was for Britain a
powerful 'engine of growth', and that the coming of free trade was a
significant factor in the explanation of the marked rise in the British growth
rate at mid-century. By implication, McCloskey attributes the 'grotesque
prominence' given to foreign trade as a causal factor in Britain's growth to
the uncritical acceptance by historians of free trade ideology and the free
trade bias of economists from Smith to Marshall whose practical motive
'was in large part the early encouragement and late defense of Britain's
policy of free trade' (McCloskey 1980, p. 305). However, the charge that the
early classical economists ignored the risks attached to greater involvement
in the international economy cannot be sustained. Malthus and Torrens
would not have been surprised by McCloskey's findings, neither would
John Stuart Mill, who developed the theoretical tools for dealing with precisely this problem. The popular enthusiasts for free trade (Perronet
Thompson, Harriet Martineau, Jane Marcet and later, the Anti-Corn Law
League) and, perhaps, Ricardo and James Mill were guilty of failure to per-
ceive that free trade would entail terms-of-trade losses for a growing
economy like Britain; but the other major economists saw the connection
and discussed it in great detail, as we have seen.

Torrens, for one, took a pessimistic view of the course of the terms of
trade as it related to Britain and other industrialised countries. He also predicted that as the less-developed countries industrialised (against a background of diminishing returns in agriculture and increasing returns in
manufacturing) the relative price of agricultural products would rise to
such an extent that the comparative-advantage basis of trade would cease
to exist. Hence trade between industrial and agrarian countries, while not
ceasing altogether, would be reduced to exchanges based on irreducible
absolute cost differences:

> As the several nations of the world advance in wealth and population, the com-
> mercial intercourse between them must gradually become less important and
> beneficial . . . Hence, in all new settlements, the increasing value of raw produce
> must gradually check its exportation, and the falling value of wrought goods
> progressively prevent their importation; until at length the commercial inter-
> course between nations shall be confined to those peculiar articles, in the pro-
> duction of which the immutable circumstances of soil and climate give one
> country a permanent advantage over another. (Torrens 1821, p. 288–9)

Torrens was thus an early exponent of the hypothesis later known as '*das Gesetz der fallenden Export Quota*' (law of falling importance of foreign trade) from the writings of Werner Sombart, the German economic historian, and others. Mill and Torrens' defence of reciprocity was partly based on the terms-of-trade argument, as was noted above. Both of them therefore had no time for the crude propaganda of the Anti-Corn Law League. Mill did concede though that Britain still enjoyed a favourable trading relationship (compared with other European countries) owing to high income and price elasticities of demand for its exports in world markets, and that improvements in agricultural technology were likely to slow down (postpone) the inevitable rise in the relative price of agricultural products. Ultimately, then, Mill's case for reciprocity rested on the belief that it was essential to ensure an adequate long-term increase in trade volume to counterbalance the stagnant or downward trend in Britain's net barter terms of trade.

Leading politicians and officials likewise were not remiss in taking seriously the terms-of-trade problem. They repeatedly took action or made threats designed to force reciprocal reductions in other countries' tariffs. In 1825 Huskisson (at the Board of Trade) announced:

> As a stimulus to other countries to adopt principles of reciprocity, I shall think it right to reserve a power of making an addition of one-fifth to the proposed duties upon the productions of those countries which may refuse, upon a tender by us of the like advantages, to place our commerce and navigation upon the footing of the most favoured nation.[19]

These efforts were largely unsuccessful, in so far as trade with Europe was concerned, for as Sir John Clapham observed, 'no amount of tariff manipulation or reciprocity would have opened very much wider the European markets' (Clapham [1939] (1967), p. 479). To summarise, then, McCloskey is no doubt correct that Britain's free trade policy arose from the declining importance of tariff revenues in government finance, as well as the triumph of free trade ideology – 'an economic truth [which] acquired . . . the dignity and vitality of a moral law' as the Victorians saw it.[20] But it is misleading to suggest that contemporary economists subscribed to this, or uncritically accepted the popular slogans of the doctrinaire free-traders.

Mill on the Infant-Industry Argument

The other exception to the classical case for free trade – the infant-industry argument – was also legitimised by John Stuart Mill. The argument in a crude form was, of course, of long standing, dating back to Elizabethan times when it was frequently invoked in pleas for the grant of monopolistic privileges; but the later mercantilists made little use of it. Adam Smith noted the possibility of gain from temporary infant-industry protection, but expressed considerable scepticism on the ground that even if the infant industry ultimately grew up, the reduction in the value of capital accumulation during the learning period was likely to outweigh the benefits in terms of future growth potential (Smith [1776] 1976, vol. 1, p. 453). As we saw in Chapter 3, 'Free Trade and the National Economists', the argument was reformulated with reference to young and developing countries by Alexander Hamilton, George Washington's Secretary of the Treasury in 1791, and later by the German national economist Friedrich List (1841).

The majority of English writers dismissed the writings of the national economists as being no more than naive reversions to a pre-scientific mercantilism; but Mill saw that the arguments of the national developmental economists did not contradict the main propositions of classical trade theory. Accordingly, says Schumpeter, J.S. Mill 'accepted the infant-industry theory, realising that it ran within the free trade logic' (Schumpeter 1954, p. 505). Indeed, Mill provided the clearest formulation of the argument and since his exposition is beautifully concise it is worth quoting in full:

> The only case in which, on mere principles of political economy, protecting duties can be defensible, is when they are imposed temporarily (especially in a young and rising nation) in hopes of naturalizing a foreign industry, in itself perfectly suitable to the circumstances of the country. The superiority of one country over another in a branch of production often arises only from having begun it sooner. There may be no inherent advantage on one part, or disadvantage on the other, but only a present superiority of acquired skill and experience. A country which has this skill and experience yet to acquire, may in other respects be better adapted to the production than those which were earlier in the field; and besides, it is a just remark of Mr. Rae, that nothing has a greater tendency to promote improvements in any branch of production, than its trial under a new set of conditions. But it cannot be expected that individuals should, at their own risk, or rather to their certain loss, introduce a new manufacture, and bear the burden of carrying it on, until the producers have been educated up to the level of those with whom the processes are traditional. A protecting duty, continued for a reasonable time, will sometimes be the least inconvenient mode in which the nation can tax itself for the support of such an experiment. But the protection should be confined to cases in which there is good ground of assurance that the industry which it fosters will after a time be able to dispense with it; nor should the domestic producers ever be allowed to expect that it will be continued to them beyond the time necessary for a fair trial of what they are capable of accomplishing.[21]

Mill thus rescued the argument from its association with special pleading and economic nationalism and gave it theoretical and practical respectability under one condition: the infant industry must eventually overcome its historical handicap and grow up, able to withstand foreign competition without benefit of further protection – the 'Mill test', as Kemp calls it (Kemp 1960, pp. 65–7). Bastable later pointed out that the 'Mill test', though necessary, was not a sufficient condition. He proposed an additional criterion: the protected industry (or firm) must eventually generate sufficient savings in costs to compensate society for the consumption losses incurred during the period of maturation. Mill was, however, disillusioned by the use of his argument at the hands of self-seeking protectionists in the United States and Australia where protection was indiscriminately and permanently extended to a wide range of industries, many without promise, and in later life regretted his endorsement of the use of import duties for the purpose and strongly qualified his statement quoted above. If protection for infant industries were needed at all, it should be in the form of subsidies rather than tariffs. An annual subsidy, being clearly visible to taxpayers, was less likely to be continued on a permanent basis than a protective duty.[22]

Modern economists generally agree with Mill on this. A tariff introduces a consumption distortion without necessarily ensuring the realisation of the social benefit claimed for the policy. The optimal (or 'first-best' policy) is to subsidise directly the acquisition of knowledge by the firm or industry. Moreover, since a domestic not a foreign distortion is involved, some sort of subsidy rather than tariffs is called for. The argument has been subjected to a good deal of analytical scrutiny involving the theory of domestic distortions, economics of knowledge and elements of human capital theory. Thus, Harry Johnson writes: 'What is involved is an investment in a process of acquisition of knowledge which is socially profitable but privately unprofitable because the private investor cannot appropriate the whole of the social return from his investment.'[23] In the contemporary world, the argument has been used by Third World countries to justify their protective duties in the interests of industrialisation. The former General Agreement on Tariffs and Trade (GATT) rules even allowed it for such countries, and the various preferential arrangements for developing countries' manufactured exports in the markets of developed countries are based on an extension of this argument.

Mill must have been familiar with the works of the national economists such as Henry Carey and Friedrich List, but he never recommended the 'infant-stage-of-development' argument favoured by these writers. There were more efficient means of promoting national economic development, not the least important of which is trade itself. Trade, in fact, he held was even more important for less-developed countries than it was for rich ones. In particular, the indirect benefits as they affect growth were of a high order. The opening of foreign trade initiates 'a sort of industrial revolution' in poor countries. More generally, every extension of the market through

trade tends to improve the processes of production: 'A country which produces for a larger market than its own, can introduce a more extended division of labour, can make greater use of machinery, and is more likely to
make inventions and improvements in the processes of production' (Mill
[1848] 1920, p. 581).

6.3   THE EXPORT OF TECHNOLOGY

An important issue in trade policy which exercised the minds of the political economists was the export of machinery and emigration of skilled artisans. Although not comparable in economic and political significance to
the Corn Laws controversy, this debate was equally wide-ranging and
aroused the same sort of intellectual passion. The protagonists in the
debate – Torrens, Senior, McCulloch, Hume, and so on – if resurrected,
would have been on familiar ground had they witnessed the US
Congressional battles in the 1970s over foreign trade and investment where
the key question was the regulation of the exportation of technology. The
arguments were essentially the same in both cases. In the 1970s, US trade
unions (AFL/CIO) blamed the export of jobs on 'runaway plants' in
Mexico, Hong Kong, Taiwan and Korea, which operated with cheap labour
and efficient, borrowed American technology. This allegedly jeopardised
the traditional living standards of American workers; and there were calls
for stringent controls on all US direct investment activities, that is, export
of skills and technology. The only difference was that the economists in the
twentieth-century debate had the advantage of sophisticated theories and
hypotheses on 'brain-drain', international product cycles, multinational
corporations and the international diffusion of technology.[24]

The nineteenth-century policy debate presented an agonising challenge
to the free-traders. It forced them to think through the practical implications of free trade and it generated new ideas in economic thought, in particular the development of concepts and models for analysing the impact
of growth and technological change on comparative advantage and trade
patterns. Did free trade apply only to commodities, or must the principle
be extended also to capital and labour? Did the restrictions on machinery
exports signify protection for one industry only – the capital goods or
machine-making industry – or were they the means whereby all industries
were protected? What were the implications for Britain's comparative
advantage in manufactures of freer transfer of technology? How did trade
patterns alter under the impact of technological change and the international transfer of technology? These were some of the questions suggested by the terms of the debate.

It was widely believed that machinery gave Britain a peculiar advantage over her trading rivals, and that whatever social disadvantages (for example, technological unemployment, de-skilling of the labour force, and so on) attended its use, nevertheless, international considerations made it imperative to take full advantage of technology embodied in machinery. Ricardo admitted in a parliamentary speech (30 May 1823) that the extensive use of machinery

> must, in some degree, operate prejudicially to the working classes. But still he would not tolerate any law to prevent the use of machinery. The question was, – if they gave up a system which enabled them to undersell in the foreign market, would other nations refrain from pursuing it? Certainly not. They were therefore bound, for their own interest, to continue it. (Ricardo, *Works*, 1951, vol V, pp. 302–3)

In the 1821 edition of his *Principles*, he reaffirmed the advantages of machinery:

> If a capital is not allowed to get the greatest net revenue that the use of machinery will afford here, it will be carried abroad, and this must be a much more serious discouragement to the demand for labour . . . By investing part of a capital in improved machinery, there will be a diminution in the progressive demand for labour; by exporting it to another country, the demand will be wholly annihilated. (Ricardo, *Works*, 1951, vol. I, pp. 396–7)

Like Adam Smith it appears that Ricardo was against the restrictions on the export of machinery. Sraffa tells us that shortly before his death Ricardo promised Joseph Hume (the leading campaigner for repeal) that he would support his proposed motion for a parliamentary committee of inquiry to look into the matter (Ricardo, *Works*, 1951, vol. V, p. xx).

In a debate on tariff reform in 1825 Sir Henry Parnell confidently proclaimed that 'in all cases where we employ machinery, and have the raw material as cheap as foreign nations have it, we have no grounds for apprehending any injury from the most open competition'.[25] On the other hand, there was a growing feeling that British superiority in machine production was only relative, in view of both continental industrialisation and the speed of diffusion of technical knowledge. Malthus, for example, pointed out 'how difficult it is to confine improvements in machinery to a single spot'. Torrens said much the same thing: 'the adoption of the latest improvements in scientific power cannot be confined to a particular country'.[26] McCulloch observed that the processes of knowledge diffusion are such that significant inventions soon become public (free) goods to the world as a whole: 'It is no longer possible to monopolize an invention. The intimate communication that now obtains amongst nations renders any important discovery, wherever it may be made, a common benefit.'[27] McCulloch exaggerated the trade consequences of rapid diffusion: invention is one thing, but innovation or development of the idea into a marketable product is another. Where innovations are the result of basic research freely available (via journals) there need be no connection between the country originating an idea and the country subsequently developing it into a marketable product. The key elements in the process are much more the innovation and marketing stages rather than that of invention. Technological leadership is much more closely associated with ability to innovate and develop – an ability outstandingly characteristic of Britain in the early nineteenth century. The example given by McCulloch – an invention (or technical improvement) spreading from China or Peru to England – would appear more plausible had he reversed the direction of the technical diffusion.

As early as 1805 William Playfair (1805) sketched the dynamic process whereby technological progress works to confer a temporary monopoly on the innovating country, but which tends to be eroded by imitative production elsewhere. He shows why it is sometimes uneconomic to apply the 'best' technology, and how the imitation of foreign technology can be advantageous (avoidance of the initial costs of acquiring new knowledge). He asserted that the only difficulties in manufacturing occur at the invention and development stages – what we would now call the research and development stages (R & D) – but since these have been overcome by the industrial leaders, the imitating countries could catch up fairly quickly. Technology was therefore easily transferred from country to country. Because of short imitation lags and the chance that the imitating country may itself begin to innovate, Playfair argued that to maintain a favourable balance of trade the leading country must continually introduce new and better products and processes. Referring to England, he warned: 'the nation the farthest advanced in invention has only to remain stationary a few years, and it will soon be overtaken, and perhaps surpassed' (Playfair 1805, pp. 212, 200, 203).

The debate on the pros and cons of lifting the restrictions on the export of technology and emigration of artisans took place between 1824 and 1841. It was conducted in the usual forums: Parliament, the London and provincial press, memorials, petitions, and in the writings of the political economists. Most of the restrictions against machinery export were imposed between 1750 and 1785, and were designed to guard against competition in manufacturing from potential foreign rivals on the Continent – legislation which Adam Smith deplored. The tools, equipment, utensils and machinery used in the cotton, woollen, silk, iron and steel industries were all banned from export. The matter was investigated by three Select Committees of the House of Commons. The ban on the emigration of skilled artisans (imposed by Acts in 1719 and 1750) was lifted in 1824, following the recommendations of the Select Committee on Combination Laws, Artisans and Machinery (mainly because it proved impossible to enforce); but the prohibitions on machinery remained in force until 1843 when they were repealed on the recommendations of the 1841 Select Committee on the Export of Machinery. In the meantime (that is, from 1825 until 1843) the Board of Trade was vested with discretionary powers to grant licence for the export of machinery. Licences were easy to obtain (although on average a quarter of applications were refused); but the textile manufacturers made sure that the machinery exported was obsolete models or those that did not threaten their current exports.

Leading the campaign for repeal was Joseph Hume, the radical free trade MP, on behalf of the machine-makers and other interested parties. When Hume (after much obstruction from Huskisson and Peel) laid his motion for repeal before Parliament in December 1826, Torrens, newly elected MP for Ipswich, true to form, voiced his opposition. Insisting that he was generally a friend of free trade, declared that *laissez-faire* was not a recipe for all seasons, that repeal would mean the surrender of a valuable and exclusive national advantage, and it would injure England to let other countries share in those advantages:

> in every science, there must necessarily be exceptions. There could be no universal principle applicable to all circumstances. Now, it was admitted on all hands, even by the hon. member for Aberdeen [Hume], that we made better machinery than our rivals . . . If such was the case, he would ask, why should we give up our exclusive advantage?[28]

In fact, Torrens later claimed, not enough was being done to forestall foreign competition; he went further and urged a duty of 50 per cent on all British coal exports to Europe, since without cheap British coal French manufacturers would be unable to operate steam-engines efficiently. To an old Marine like Torrens, comments Fetter, the free export of machinery and coal was 'as much folly, as presenting enemy troops with improved weapons' (Fetter 1962, p. 165).

This attitude, perhaps in a less extreme form, was shared by many who, on other issues (for example, the Corn Laws), were fond of using *laissez-faire* slogans and free trade rhetoric, namely Baring, Peel, Bright and, surprisingly enough, Nassau Senior.

Senior's argument was more sophisticated. Writing in 1830 he protested that it was idle to pretend that England would not suffer from the enhanced technological capability of its neighbours, for both England and Europe were competitors in the general market of the world. He dissented from the view (held by J.S. Mill) that if, through the acquisition of superior British technology, the Europeans managed to produce cheaper cottons, then Britain would benefit from cheaper cotton imports and could put its resources to other, more profitable manufactures. England, he said, 'might find it easier to obtain cottons, but we should find it more difficult to import everything else'. If England, through default, gave up its technological leadership and resigned itself to simple, less skill-intensive manufacturing, 'it is guilty of the same folly as the farmer who should plough with a race-horse'.[29] Briefly, his reasoning was: wages and living standards in Britain depended on the prosperity of foreign commerce and the country's trade rested on the efficiency of labour in manufacturing. What made British labour comparatively more productive was the combination of higher skill levels and the more intensive use of machinery than elsewhere. Senior made it clear in a footnote that his remarks bore significantly on the question of technology exports. Senior's line of reasoning was adopted by other free-traders who objected to machinery exports in public debate (for example, Lord King).

The arguments for removal of the restrictions were: (1) they were ineffective in achieving their objective; (2) they were unnecessary, since even with the free availability of British machinery foreigners were unable to rival British manufacturers; and (3) they were, on balance, beneficial to Britain since earnings from machinery exports contributed to Britain's future economic growth. Much like illegal arms traffic today, there was extensive smuggling of machinery – hidden in cotton bales, consigned via distant fishing-ports, and so on. The dealer networks were well-organised, and there was even a market for insuring and guaranteeing shipments. Industrial espionage took place, and the patent laws were such that plans, models and patent specifications could easily be acquired by visiting foreigners. The diffusion process was also helped by the rapid dissemination of scientific knowledge through journals, learned societies, and so on. Exports of machinery did not materially affect the supply on the domestic market, for when machinery was in short supply, foreign orders (for which licences were granted) were either not accepted or had to wait until domestic requirements were attended to. These facts were referred to by McCulloch and Malthus, the only two economists of note who gave evidence before the 1824 Committee. These circumstances were part of their argument for the lifting of the restrictions. Further, they pointed out, the effect of the restrictions (in so far as they were effective) tended to encourage the growth of machine-making industries on the Continent and in America by raising the price of machines abroad and thereby stimulating production there. British machine-makers lost business without any commensurate benefit to British manufacturers in the long run. Malthus' opinion was that free machinery export would not endanger Britain's trade or its technological leadership. Malthus also sounded his customary warning (caution) about the wisdom of the pursuit of further industrialisation on (a) the economic ground of insufficiency of investment funds and aggregate demand, and (b) the technical limits to the division of labour. The restrictions, McCulloch said, deprived Britain of 'an additional branch of manufacture'.[30]

The second point, that prohibition was unnecessary for the reason mentioned above, rested on several premises relating to conditions for the effective international transfer of technology, the role of skills and human capital in the process of technological innovation, and technological leadership and comparative advantage. Thus, it was argued, Britain's technological leadership rested on a complex of factors including a highly skilled and industrious workforce, efficient management and organisational techniques, better division of labour, an intellectual and social environment conducive to enterprise, the application of science to technology and responsiveness to change, and so on. These were the sources of Britain's comparative advantage in manufactures, and, since the effects were cumulative, these advantages could not easily be eroded. In the hands of foreigners, machines by themselves were insufficient if they lacked the skilled labour needed to erect, adapt and service the equipment. 'Even when the Belgians employed British machines and skilled workers, they failed to import the English spirit of enterprise and secured only disappointing results.'[31] The Select Committee on Machinery Exports listened to much evidence along these lines, as summarised in the following passage:

> Supposing, indeed, that the same Machinery which is used in England could be diffused on the Continent, it is the opinion of some of the most intelligent of the witnesses that the want of arrangement in foreign manufactories, of division of labour in their work, of skill and perseverance in their workers, and of enterprise in the masters, together with the comparatively low estimation in which the master manufacturers are held on the Continent, and with the comparative want of capital, and of many other advantageous circumstances detailed in the evidence, would prevent foreigners from interfering in any great degree by competition with our principal manufacturers.[32]

Those who held the view that skills and 'mental' capital were more important than the machines in which these were embodied suggested that, if machinery were freely exported, then there would be little emigration of mechanics and other skilled artisans. The retention of these skills was necessary if Britain was to keep ahead of foreign competitors in technological development. Against this, it was argued by others, for example, John Kennedy and the Manchester Chamber of Commerce, that there was a complementary relationship between machines and skills, so that the more machinery was exported the greater would be the demand for skilled British artisans and therefore the greater the loss to continental rivals. Kennedy put it this way:

> The exportation of machinery absolutely compels the foreign manufacturer to possess the means of becoming his own machine maker; and the more machines you send abroad, the greater the number of mechanics become necessary to keep their parts in order. Hence again arises a demand for those tools which are necessary to mechanics, the mechanics with their tools are sure to be ultimately employed, not merely in repairing the existing machines, but in the making of new ones. (Kennedy 1824, p. 17)

The third point above was made by John Stuart Mill in terms of an efficient allocation of global resources. It was, he argued, 'in the common interest of all nations that each of them should abstain from every measure by which the aggregate wealth of the commercial world would be diminished'. It was therefore in Britain's interest to promote this by every means, including the free export of machinery, since restrictions tended to be generalised to no country's advantage. Foreign countries would use British machines to produce goods in which they already possessed natural advantages. To the extent that they were successful in that, the demand for British manufactures would fall; but Britain would gain from the greater efficiency of foreign producers in the manufacture of goods sold on the British market. He disputed Senior's point that England would not benefit from cheaper imports consequent upon improvements abroad. William Ellis, a philosophical radical and friend of Mill, made a similar point in favour of free exportation, but based his remark on the observation that exports are only needed to pay for a country's imports, and it was the volume and price of the latter which really measured the benefit from trade. Like McCulloch, he regarded the restrictions as hindering the expansion of a potentially major British industry.

Mill, however, had some reservations; for he conceded that the export of machinery could be a source of disadvantage until all restrictions on trade were done away with, and concluded that until that time came 'the exportation of machinery may be a proper subject for adjustment with other nations, on the principle of reciprocity' (Mill 1844, p. 32).

The restrictions on the export of machinery were lifted three years before the repeal of the Corn Laws and, as in the greater debate on the latter, economic conditions finally dictated the change of policy. The depression of 1841–2 resulted in a slump in the demand for textile machinery following the boom conditions a few years earlier. Export markets were therefore necessary to maintain prosperity, and this added urgency to the machinery manufacturers' demands for repeal. The groups opposed to free exports were divided, and the influential Manchester Chamber of Commerce lost the will to carry on the opposition. One knowledgeable witness revealed to the Select Committee in 1841: 'the master manufacturers are almost desponding as regards the state of our trade, and the general expression of feeling is, that the legislature may do whatever they please they cannot make things worse'.[33] Commenting on the lifting of the restrictions, a modern historian wrote: 'Manchester had decided that, if it was impossible to kill off the industry of others by restrictions . . . then perhaps Corn Law repeal might do the trick instead.'[34]

NOTES

1. Gertrude Himmelfarb, *The Idea of Poverty: England in the Early Industrial Age* (London: Faber & Faber, 1984), p. 101.
2. Cobbett's *Political Register*, issues for November and December 1807.
3. See Mill's review of Spence's pamphlet in *Eclectic Review*, 3 (December 1807), p. 1056, and *Commerce Defended*, in D. Winch (ed.), *James Mill: Selected Economic Writings* (Edinburgh, 1966), pp. 23–35. The quoted passages are from *Commerce Defended*, 2nd ed., pp. 81 and 86. Earlier than Spence, John Wheatley asserted that 'an exchange of equivalents is the foundation of all commerce'. Both Huskisson (1810) and Brougham took him up on this. Huskisson asked: 'if commerce is nothing more than an exchange of *equivalents*, and, the *Balance of Trade* . . . only the measure of our foreign expenditure, in what way is a country enriched by trade?' (*The Question of the Depreciation of Our Currency Stated and Examined* (London, 1810). Huskisson went on to answer with some suggestive thoughts on the gains from trade. Chipman suggests that Huskisson's remarks must have been a great stimulus to both Torrens and Ricardo (particularly Torrens) in their development of the law of comparative advantage. See J.S. Chipman, 'Balance of Payments Theory', in J. Creedy and D.P. O'Brien (eds), *Economic Analysis in Historical Perspective* (London: Butterworths, 1984), pp. 209–10.
4. Leonard Horner (ed.), *Memoirs and Correspondence of Francis Horner, M.P.*, 2 vols (London, 1843), vol. II, p. 227. The letter was to the publisher John Murray. Malthus' first Corn Law pamphlet (1814) was entitled *Observations on the Effects of the Corn Laws, and of a Rise or Fall in the Price of Corn on the Agriculture and General Wealth of the Country* (44 pages). The second pamphlet came out on 10 February 1815 – *Grounds of an Opinion on the Policy of Restricting the Importation of Foreign Corn* (48 pages).
5. Hollander's interpretation is contained in Hollander (1979, pp. 599–642) and Hollander (1977, pp. 1–47). For the traditional view that Ricardo's profit theory originated in concern over the Corn Laws see Blaug (1958, pp. 31–2); Maurice Dobb (1973, pp. 89–90); O'Brien (1970, p. 296). O'Brien maintains: 'Secular stagnation resulting from the Corn Laws is the core, indeed the purpose, of the Ricardian model.'
6. 'Mr Owens's Plans for Relieving the National Distress', *Edinburgh Review*, 32 (Oct. 1819), p. 459. All articles in the *Edinburgh Review* were unsigned, but the work has been attributed to Torrens, although McCulloch is sometimes mentioned as being the author.
7. *Eclectic Review*, n.s. 2 (July 1814), pp. 4–5.
8. *Parliamentary Debates* (Hansard) 1: col. 673 (30 May 1820).
9. *Annual Register 1820* (London, 1822), vol. i, p. 70.
10. J.C.L. Simonde de Sismondi, *Nouveau Principes d'Economie Politique*, Paris: Calman-Levy, [1819] 1971, pp. 265–6.
11. R. Torrens, 'A letter to the Right Honourable Lord John Russell' (London: Longman, Rees, Orme, Brown & Green, 1837), p. 143.
12. F.W. Fetter, 'Robbins on Torrens', *Economica* (November 1958), p. 346.
13. O'Brien's comments are in O'Brien (1970), pp. 227–8.

14. Colonel Torrens, *Speech in the House of Commons on the Motion for the Reappointment of a Select Committee on Emigration, February 15 1827* (London: Longman, Rees, Orme, Brown & Green, 1828). Quoted in S.A. Meenai, 'Robert Torrens 1780–1864', *Economica* (February 1956), p. 55.
15. John Craig, *Remarks on Some Fundamental Doctrines of Political Economy* (Edinburgh, 1821), pp. 101–2.
16. Hansard, n.s. 18 (1828), cols 1553–5.
17. Torrens's speech of 15 February 1827, quoted in Fetter (1962, p. 163).
18. Mill, *Principles* (1852), 5th ed., vol. II, p. 163.
19. Hansard, n.s. 12 (1825), col. 1213. When the US Congress increased tariffs sharply in 1828 Huskisson called for retaliation. See Hansard, n.s. 19 (1828), cols 1768–70.
20. Lord Welby, *Cobden's Work and Opinions*, p. 18, quoted in J.A. Hobson, *Richard Cobden: The International Man* (London, 1919), p. 20.
21. Mill, *Principles*, ed. W.J. Ashley (London: Longmans Green, 1909), p. 922. The role of ideology is quite apparent here. The economics establishment would swallow the argument from Mill, but not from List! Douglas Irwin writes: 'The endorsement by an economic theorist of first rank was not so easily dismissed as similar statements coming from a Hamilton or a List' (Irwin, 1996, p. 128).
22. Cobden Club Pamphlet, *John Stuart Mill on the Protection of Infant Industries* (London, 1911), pp. 11, 13–15, 17. See also J.S. Mill, *Collected Works*, vol. 16, ed. F.E. Mineka and D.W. Lindley (Toronto: Toronto University Press, 1972), pp. 1043–4, 1150–1, 1419–20 and 1520–1.
23. Harry Johnson, 'A New View of the Infant Industry Argument', in I.A. McDougall and Richard H. Snape (eds), *Studies in International Economics: Monash Conference Papers* (Amsterdam: North-Holland, 1970), p. 60.
24. For an interesting recent discussion on the nineteenth-century debates on trade and convergence, technology exports, and so on, see Bruce Elmslie and Antoinette James Criss, 'Theories of Convergence and Growth in the Classical Period: The Role of Science, Technology and Trade', *Economica*, 66 (1999), pp. 135–49.
25. Hansard, n.s. 13 (1825), col. 1233.
26. Malthus, *Additions to the Fourth and Former Editions of Essay on Population* (London: John Murray, 1817), p. 108; Torrens, *The Budget* (1844), p. 235.
27. J.R. McCulloch, *On Commerce* (London, 1833), p. 9.
28. *Parliamentary Debates* (Hansard), Second Series, vol. xvi (6 December 1826), col. 294–5. Sir Alexander Baring (the merchant banker), who introduced Torrens to the House, congratulated him afterwards on his speech: 'It had been for so long a time the habit to look upon any man as a Goth who dissented from the modern doctrine of political economy', that it was indeed a pleasure to welcome Torrens to the House. Ibid. col. 296.
29. Nassau Senior, *Three Lectures on the Cost of Obtaining Money and Some Effects of Private and Government Paper Money* (1830), pp. 25–6, 30.
30. For McCulloch's and Malthus' testimony before the Committee see Select Committee on Combination Laws, Artisans and Machinery, *Parliamentary Papers* (1824), vol. V, cols 592, 597 and 598.
31. H.R.C. Wright, *Free Trade and Protection in the Netherlands, 1816–39: A Study of the First Benelux* (Cambridge: Cambridge University Press, 1955), p. 130.
32. Report of the Select Committee on the Laws Relating to the Export of Tools and Machinery (30 June 1825), no. 504, p. 15.
33. *Parliamentary Papers* (1841), vol. VII. Testimony of Holland Hooke, p. 52.
34. P.J. Cain, *Economic Foundations of British Overseas Expansion 1815–1914* (London: Macmillan, 1980), p. 20. For a detailed account of the restrictions and the role of Manchester manufacturers see A.E. Musson, 'The "Manchester School" and Exportation of Machinery', *Business History* (January 1972), pp. 17–50.

7. The British tariff reform debate, 1903

7.1 INTRODUCTION AND BACKGROUND

In 1852 Queen Victoria remarked to her uncle, the King of the Belgians, 'Protection is quite gone.'[1] A generation later, however, a chorus of voices rose up in Britain against the continuance of the policy of free trade. At the time Victoria wrote, the British economy entered a period lasting twenty years of unparalleled prosperity. The way Britain prospered was by manufacturing goods for sale abroad, which her customers paid for in raw materials and food. Leading economists attributed the mid-Victorian boom to the enlightened policy of free trade which justified and supported that favourable international division of labour. In 1865 John Stuart Mill referred to the 'flush of prosperity occasioned by free trade' (Mill [1865] 1961, p. 384). William Stanley Jevons, in the same year, ascribed the buoyant economic conditions to 'the unprecedented commercial reforms of the last twenty years'.[2]

The onset of the depression in agriculture (1874) and the milder general recession shattered confidence in the immutability of British industrial progress and triggered a reaction against free trade. It altered perceptions of Great Britain's situation in the world economy. The combination of domestic distress and Britain's *relative* decline as Germany and the United States rose in global economic stature produced in Britain a national malaise aptly described as 'diminished giant' syndrome – a condition that was to afflict the United States a century later as it confronted the rise of Japan and the 'Tiger economies' of East Asia. 'Fair Trade' and 'Reciprocity' became fashionable demands and slogans by many popular writers, politicians and journalists. They also became the focus of organised lobbying by industrialists who felt threatened by the changed circumstances.[3]

The challenges to free trade doctrine and the debate on the state of the British economy ranged over matters such as the growth of foreign competition, the rise of protectionism in Europe, the competitiveness and efficiency of the British economy, the prospect for living standards, imperial preference and the role of the Empire; and the implications of all these factors for Great Britain's superpower status and its industrial future. The

Conservative and Unionist Party was deeply split on the issue; in fact, from top to bottom – from the Cabinet downwards to the rank and file in the constituency associations. The views of the economists were canvassed, and many were eager to participate publicly in the debate. The national controversy erupted at a time when the economists were themselves involved in an often fierce debate over the nature and purpose of economics – a debate which was intensified by Marshall's efforts to assume a leadership role, seek a professional consensus and thereby establish the academic status of economics as a recognised, scientific discipline.

The economists found themselves in disarray when confronted with the Tariff Reform issue. Although a majority was behind the free-traders, the protectionists' case was ably represented by several academic economists, particularly the economic historians. The free-traders won the national debate; and although divisions within the ranks of the economists were exposed, international trade theory benefited in terms of a sharpening of its tools and techniques of analysis. There were two phases to the debate: (1) the Fair Trade Movement of the 1880s and (2) Joseph Chamberlain's Tariff Reform campaign of 1903. The earlier phase was a trial run, a warm-up to the more serious 1903 challenge to free trade orthodoxy and practice in which the economists on each side were ranged in front of, behind and at the side of the politicians, publicists and vested interests. We shall focus on the economists' involvement in the 1903 Tariff Reform debate, but before doing so it will be helpful to survey briefly the historical background and indicate the highlights in the controversial saga.

As indicated above, the reaction against free trade in Great Britain stemmed from the 1874 agricultural depression and the less severe general depression lasting from 1873 to 1896. Some economic historians balk at the use of the terms 'general depression' and 'Great Depression' to describe this period. They dispute the connotation, since it suggests that the period was somehow special in terms of the pronounced downturn of leading economic indicators, and that Britain and several other countries faced a uniform pattern of economic problems unlike those experienced in the preceding and subsequent decades. However, the phrase 'general depression' has stuck, and remains serviceable as a description of the opinion of contemporaries who experienced it and will do in the present context. The world decline in the price of wheat stemmed from the rapid expansion of the American rail network which substantially reduced the cost of moving wheat to the ports. Similar developments occurred in Eastern Europe where the vast Ukrainian wheat fields were connected to the Crimean ports. In addition, the iron-clad steamship reduced transatlantic freight rates. Partly in response to the depression, but also for budgetary reasons connected with the finance of defence expenditures and the belief that protection was an effective method to spur industrialisation, tariff barriers went up around the world. British farmers felt they had good grounds for complaint against the rigours of free trade, and industrialists badly hit by foreign – in particular German and American – competition claimed to have been disadvantaged by 'one-sided free trade' owing to the failure of other countries to commit themselves to free trade. The United States never adopted free trade; but up to the eve of the Civil War in 1861 the southern states had succeeded in moderating the worst excesses of American tariff policy, so that by 1857 the United States had the lowest tariff level since 1816. At the end of the Civil War, however, the urgent need for federal revenue and pressure from manufacturing interest led to an increase in customs duties culminating in the highly protectionist McKinley tariff of 1890 and Dingley tariff of 1897 (on wool, iron and steel and other manufactured items). The Morrill Act (1861) inaugurated the high tariff policy. Tariff rates were raised again in 1862 and 1864. Of the 1864 Act, Frank Taussig wrote: 'It established protective duties more extreme than had been ventured on in any previous tariff act in our country's history' (Taussig 1892, p. 167). The McKinley tariff raised average duties to 49.5 per cent, and by the Dingley tariff (which remained in force for twelve years) the average level increased to 57 per cent.

The Cobden–Chevalier commercial treaty (1860) between Great Britain and France marked the final triumph (the 'last hurrah') of British free trade diplomacy. It led over the next sixteen years to a whole series of commercial treaties embodying the MFN ('most-favoured nation') clause involving France, Belgium, the German *Zollverein*, Italy and Great Britain.

In the British Empire, the colonies with responsible governments (that is, the 'White Dominions') were at least as protectionist as Germany. Customs duties were at first imposed primarily to raise revenue, but they became increasingly protective as the manufacturing interests exerted pressure on colonial legislatures (which were, in fact, largely made up of representatives of those same interests). In 1846 an Act of the British Parliament allowed the colonies to withdraw the preferences they had hitherto been forced to accord British goods. They were conceded the right to enact their own tariff legislation and therefore free to erect barriers against imports from the mother country. In Canada, Alexander Galt's tariff of 1859 raised duties on manufactured goods to an average of around 20 per cent, designed to provide funds for railway development. Sheffield manufacturers complained, nevertheless, that the measure was blatantly protectionist. The Canadian tariff was the first in a long list of such colonial enactments – South Africa (1866–7), Victoria (1877), and so on.

At the time of the Great Exhibition of 1851 it was natural for Britons who thought about the country's role in the world economy to succumb to the comforting belief that the existing international division of labour would endure indefinitely, that is, other countries would continue to provide Britain with food and raw materials in exchange for manufactured goods. Indeed, it was the scenario envisaged by Ricardo in his attack on the Corn Laws as distinct from the predictions of his formal model of comparative advantage. But there were those (for example, Malthus, in particular) who, even in Ricardo's time, doubted this optimistic vision of Britain's role. Several writers, often on impressionistic or intuitive grounds but sometimes also on the basis of comparative-cost logic, expressed fears that Britain's industrial and trading supremacy would be eroded in the course of time by the spread of industrialisation abroad aided by the diffusion of technology, the appeal of protectionist arguments and the greater resource potential in some foreign countries. The consequences for Britain, such writers felt, would inevitably be a retardation of the rate of economic growth, falling export shares in world markets and even increasing penetration of the home market in manufactured goods. From the 1880s there were unmistakable signs that these fears were not simply pessimistic fantasies but living reality, reflecting a fundamental and irreversible shift in the pattern of international specialisation and trade. In 1860, manufactured goods comprised only 6 per cent of British imports. As other countries industrialised, British manufacturers faced competitive pressure in home markets from foreign manufactures for the first time. By 1880, manufactured goods accounted for 17 per cent of imports, rising to 25 per cent by 1900.

Great Britain lost her position as the leading manufacturing power to the United States in the 1880s, and by 1900 was also overtaken by Germany in terms of percentage shares of world industrial output. In pig-iron and steel production – regarded by contemporaries as a vital indicator not only of industrial prowess but also of military and naval might – Britain's dominance came to an end, and by 1905 slipped to third position after the United States and Germany. Germany's output of pig-iron increased more than sixfold between 1850 and 1869 – from 212 000 to 1 413 000 tonnes. Britain's output doubled from 2.25 million to 5.5 million tonnes. The British steel industry declined in competitiveness because firms lagged behind foreign rivals in the adoption of new mass-production methods (Elbaum and Lazonick 1986, pp. 52–5). The pace of technological innovation faltered after 1870. Productivity fell from 1.87 per cent per annum between 1860 and 1880 to 0.25 per cent per annum until 1914. From the 1870s there was a deceleration in the overall rate of economic growth from 3.5 per cent to 1.7 per cent per annum by the turn of the century. The commodity composition of British exports and their principal market destinations made them vulnerable to both protectionism and changing demand patterns. The staples (coal, cotton, iron and steel) still accounted for more than 70 per cent of British exports in 1880. After running at the rate of 3.3

per cent during the mid-Victorian boom years, the rate of growth of British manufactured exports fell to only 1.6 per cent per annum between 1873 and 1899, and there was a relative decline in British exports to Europe and the United States. British imports slowed slightly, but continued at a rate (4.5 per cent) much in excess of export growth.

The sluggish growth of British exports, not only to Europe (which reflected protectionism) but also to markets like Latin America, the Middle and Far East, was due to German competition. Partly as a consequence of structural and factor-endowment changes in the late nineteenth-century world economy, increased output abroad, the rise of protectionism and intensified competition, the British share of world trade in manufactures fell from 37 per cent in 1883 to 28.4 per cent in 1900; but to some extent it reflected underlying structural weaknesses of the British economy itself: a marked failure to match the levels of investment in human capital under- taken by international competitors – even before the turn of the century, both Germany and the United States were spending higher proportions of GNP on education and training. This relative failure meant that Britain remained heavily reliant on existing product ranges and techniques of pro- duction, and therefore met with relative lack of success in technologically advanced goods (chemicals, industrial equipment, electricals. cameras, optics, and so on) – the products of the so-called 'second industrial revo- lution'. From 1880 to 1913 the United States expanded its share of world trade from 2.8 per cent to 12.6 per cent and Germany increased its share from 19.3 per cent to 26.5 per cent.

From the evidence revealed in his detailed study of human capital formation in nineteenth-century Britain, Jeffrey Williamson (1981) con- cluded that 'it may well be said that the "failure" of British industry in the late 19th century can be laid at the doorstep of inadequate investment in human capital . . . compared to her main competitors in world markets' (Williamson, quoted in Crafts and Thomas 1986, p. 641). This suggestion has recently been supported by a superb econometric study of the compar- ative advantage basis of UK trade in manufactures over the period 1910–35 (including a tentative study of the earlier period 1870–80) based on the human-capital version of the Heckscher–Ohlin theory (Crafts and Thomas 1986, pp. 629–45). Ever since Leontief's pioneering study of the factor content of US trade it has been clear that a test of the H-O theory can validly be used to infer the factor-endowment characteristics of trade between two or more countries. This point was understood by Marshall (1919, p. 3), who asserted, on the basis of a modified version of classical trade theory, that 'one of the best indicators of the nature and extent of a country's leadership is found in the character of goods which she exports, and of those which she imports'.[4]

Crafts and Thomas found that the UK trade pattern over the period 1870–1935 exhibited the characteristics of 'having a comparative disadvantage in goods intensive in the use of human capital', and that 'the pattern of exporting manufactures intensive in the use of unskilled labour appears characteristic of the United Kingdom in her "pre-eminent" period right through to the 1930s'. The authors concluded that 'Britain's handicap in the latter part of the century was a scarcity of the human capital which was an essential input to the technologically progressive product-cycle industries that dominated the Second Industrial Revolution.'

Historians are far from unanimous on the interpretation of the factors behind Britain's relative economic decline from the last quarter of the nineteenth century, despite the wealth of accumulated information. Evidence is still being heard, and the final verdict is yet to come on what has been called that 'critical inquest into the state of the British economy' (Crafts and Thomas 1986, pp. 629, 637, 643).

Those involved in the political and economic debate were bereft of some of the vital data bearing on the issue and they lacked, of course, our perspective. The debate stimulated research into various aspects of the economic problem. At the turn of the century, that part of trade theory known as the theory of commercial policy was fairly well developed, and the economists therefore had a very serviceable tool of analysis; but both the theory and its empirical applications benefited from the need to provide answers to the questions thrown up by the debate. But, as in all great critical national controversies where the terms of debate tend to widen in scope from any initial specific focus, so in this debate the agenda was far wider than the usual boundaries of international trade theory and policy. It was set within the context of the growing foreign rivalries and imperialism of the 1880s (in particular, the humiliation of the Boer War – 'Joe's War') and a new popular mood in favour of strengthening the bonds of Empire. For the economists who participated in it, the debate was therefore an occasion to ventilate their prejudices, fears and ideological dispositions; in addition, it afforded them an opportunity to offer advice on technical matters within their professional competence. Before moving on to the economists' perceptions of, and answers to the question before the public, a brief account must first be given of how tariff reform became a disputed political issue.

Tariff Reform as a Political Issue

In 1879 (the year German tariff policy changed) Gustav Schmoller noted: 'The times of boom, of increasing exports, of new openings of overseas markets, are the natural free trade epochs, while the reverse is true in times of foreign slumps, of depressions, of crisis.'[5] This observation has since become part of the conventional wisdom, and it aptly applies to the anti-free trade agitation in Britain under the banner of 'Fair Trade' during the 1880s. The leading figure in the movement was Farrer Ecroyd. In an 1881 article, he claimed: 'Our manufacturers are more and more excluded from the markets of the civilised world, not by fair competition, but by oppressive tariffs.'[6] He proposed: (1) the imposition of retaliatory tariffs (10 per cent) on all foreign manufactured goods in order to secure tariff reductions on British exports and to safeguard the British share of international trade; (2) that raw materials be admitted duty-free; (3) the imposition of a 10 per cent duty on foreign foodstuffs, whilst allowing duty-free entry of Empire food products. Farrer Ecroyd claimed that his proposals were not protectionist, but were designed to enable British manufacturers to capture a larger share of the domestic market and stimulate Empire trade. He expected food and manufactured goods' prices to be increased only slightly.

In 1881 a National Fair Trade League was formed. The movement gained support from manufacturers suffering from foreign competition (for example, West Riding woollen and worsted clothing manufacturers) as well as landlords and some members of the Tory party. The Royal Commission on the Depression of Trade and Industry (1885–6) supported free trade, but a minority report recommended the 'fair trade' solution by invoking the unemployment argument. 'Safeguarding', 'Reciprocity' and 'Fair Trade' were the slogans of the movement; but the fair traders failed to win mass support for their programme. They lacked the leadership capable of focusing the issues at the political level, and, in addition, changes in national political and economic circumstances pushed the free trade issue into the background – the Home Rule for Ireland issue and the trade revival in the late 1880s. Ironically, it was Joseph Chamberlain (the advocate twenty years later of Imperial Preference and general protection) who most tellingly undermined the credibility of the fair traders' proposals by emphasising their consequences for an urban working-class population, that is, the rise of food prices. This he did in his capacity as President of the Board of Trade, 1880–85, that is, his task was to lead the counter-attack. As Julian Amery points out:

> His reply to Ritchie's motion in the House of Commons and his speeches in the country were generally regarded as masterly expositions of the Cobdenite doctrine. But his persecution of the Fair Traders proved to be the first step on his journey to Damascus. It was while preparing his speeches in defence of Free Trade that serious doubts first rose in his mind. (Amery 1969, vol. 1, pp. 209–10)

The story of Chamberlain's conversion to tariff reform and his crusading campaign to rouse national sentiment in favour of imperial preference, protection for British industry and social reform, is well known, and only the highlights need to be recounted here.

Chamberlain (then aged 67) launched his 'raging and tearing' campaign at Bingley Hall in Birmingham on 15 May 1903.[7] He called for the abandonment of Britain's longstanding adherence to the policy of general free trade in favour of a system of imperial preference designed to achieve three objectives: (1) drawing the Empire closer together through the promotion of imperial economic unity; (2) the provision of revenue to finance expenditures on social reform (for example, old-age pensions); and (3) the reduction of unemployment through the protection of British industry. The achievement of those objectives would in turn protect British living standards and prevent the country slipping into the status of a second-rate nation. After describing the altered international economic environment as 'a [new] situation that was never contemplated by any of those whom we regard as the authors of Free Trade [that is, Cobden and Bright]', he put the question to his audience: 'You want an empire. Do you think it better to cultivate the trade with your own people, or to let that go in order that you may keep the trade of those who are your competitors and rivals?' If the people's decision was to strengthen Empire trade links, then

> we should insist that we will not be bound by any purely technical definition of Free Trade; that while we seek as our chief object free interchange of trade and commerce . . . we will nevertheless recover our freedom, resume the power of negotiation, and, if necessary, retaliation whenever our own interests or our relations between our colonies and ourselves are threatened by other people. (Boyd 1914, p. 139)

Four months later (16 September) Chamberlain resigned as Colonial Secretary from·Arthur Balfour's cabinet in order to have a free hand in his battle against free trade. He and his supporters in the Tariff Reform League (formed on 21 July 1903 and chaired by Arthur Pearson, the newspaper magnate) conducted the campaign at public meetings up and down the country, in the daily press and in innumerable periodical articles and books. The defenders of the status quo did likewise. Freed from the need to observe the proprieties of office, Chamberlain heightened the fervour of his rhetoric. Speaking at the Town Hall, Greenock on 7 October 1903 on the need to adopt a policy of reciprocity, or in default, one of retaliation, he raised the awful prospect of the decimation of British industry through the loss of export markets closed by foreign tariffs and the widespread penetration of the domestic market: 'Agriculture . . . has been practically destroyed. Sugar has gone; silk has gone; iron is threatened; cotton will go! How long are you going to stand it?' The remedy was obvious, he suggested: in the absence of reciprocity of access, British tariffs must be used to neutralise foreign tariffs in a tit-for-tat strategy. 'I do not believe in a war of tariffs, but if there were to be a war of tariffs, I know we should not come out second best', he confidently declared (Boyd 1914, pp. 177–8).

The Tariff Reform League's proposals involved only a limited form of protectionism: import duties on raw materials; 2 shillings a quarter on wheat and a corresponding duty on flour (about 7 per cent of the domestic price); 5 per cent on meat and dairy produce, excluding bacon – the food of the working-class; and, with South African production in mind, an indeterminate amount of wines and fruits. To offset the increased cost of living which these food taxes would entail, an appreciable reduction (averaging 60 per cent) in the existing revenue duties on tea, sugar, cocoa and coffee was envisaged. Those reductions would produce a net fiscal deficit which would be recouped by a 'moderate duty on all manufactured goods, not exceeding 10 per cent on average, but varying according to the amount of labour' involved in their manufacture. All these tariff changes were to be incorporated into a reciprocal preferential system for the Empire.

The Tariff Reform campaign played upon the fears and frustrations of ordinary Britons, nationalists and several vocal manufacturing interests alarmed by pessimistic analyses of the state of the nation and the manifest unfairness of playing by asymmetric rules. International commerce was now perceived to be 'one-sided' and there was no longer a 'level playing field'. Manufacturing industry, the Tariff Reformers claimed, was gradually being destroyed by foreign competition with grim social consequences in the shape of growing unemployment and poverty. Foreign manufacturers enjoyed the advantage of tariffs and subsidies to protect them in their domestic markets, but the British market was wide open to all. That British handicap could be overcome by pursuing a course of economic nationalism and a strategy of 'retaliation' with the aim of forcing other countries to reduce their protectionist barriers – as outlined in Chamberlain's Greenock speech referred to above.

The Free Trade cause rested on optimism. The great export trades were doing well – indeed, the year 1905 saw a revival of British trade and industrial production: the total value of exports rose by 9.7 per cent (9.9 in value terms); the seemingly inexorable rise of the country's merchandise trade deficit had finally peaked at 181.3 million (pounds sterling) two years earlier, and the volume of GNP by 3 per cent (or 2.1 per cent per capita) – so long as this favourable trend continued it was in Britain's interests to retain a policy of free imports. Free imports were cheap imports which kept down industrial wages and costs, and above all, guaranteed cheap food for the working class. The Tariff Reformers' proposals posed the threat of 'dearer food', since small duties on food were necessary in order to give the Colonies a preference. Since the working classes spent a very high proportion of their incomes on foodstuffs, they would be the hardest hit.

The Tariff Reformers failed to convince the public; in fact, as a writer recently put it, 'the people were not interested' (Porter 1987, p. 64). Chamberlain, an accountant by training, was a Birmingham manufacturer of screws. He attracted support from the industrialists in the metal-working trades of the West Midlands and the iron and steel magnates who complained about foreign 'dumping'. Press support came from J.L. Garvin of *The Observer* and Leo Maxse, the feisty, imperialist editor and owner of the right-wing *National Review*. Against Chamberlain, there was a formidable array of interests, including the Treasury, the TUC (Trades Union Congress), cotton manufacturers, shipbuilders, shipowners, dealers in commodities. export–import merchants and international bankers (for example, Sir Ernest Cassell, Albert Beit).

Chamberlain never impressed the City of London with his programme; the merchants and financiers there saw nothing in it for them. Working-class voters were particularly influenced by the Liberal poster which showed a big 'free-trade loaf' side by side with a little 'tariff loaf'. Joseph Chamberlain's own cousin, Arthur, felt as early as January 1904 that his uncle's campaign was doomed, since 'I don't believe they will vote for Protection because I can't think they will be so silly as to ask the Government to tax the food they eat, the clothes they wear and the commodities they use, on the promise of the politician that their wages will rise' (*Daily Chronicle*, 18 January 1904). The young Winston Churchill, having switched to the Liberals, defined the 1906 election issue as: 'Dear food for the millions, cheap labour for the millionaire.' The Liberal landslide victory at the 1906 elections (377 seats out of 670) put an end to the political battle which raged from the second half of 1903, the whole of 1904 and 1905 up to the elections. But the issue remained unresolved, and the arguments continued right up to the outbreak of war in 1914. Britain's departure from free trade had to wait until the slump of the 1930s. It was Chamberlain's son, Neville, who realised his father's dream when, as Chancellor of the Exchequer in the National Government, he introduce the Import Duties Bill (1932) into Parliament – the abandonment of free trade.

How the economists responded to the national controversy, what arguments they used to justify their various positions, is the subject of the next section.

7.2   THE ECONOMISTS AND TARIFF REFORM

For the majority of mainstream economists free trade remained an unquestioned and almost unquestionable article of faith, but an active and vocal minority supported tariff reform. In 1903, it has been said, the entire country was called upon to take sides 'over an abstract not to say highly technical economic theory' (Young 1963, p. 213) – the theory of commercial policy as it was called, or more specifically, a choice between free trade and protection.

Needless to say, the outcome was not determined solely or even mainly on that simple basis. Nevertheless, arguments from international trade theory did figure prominently in the debate, as Chamberlain's dramatic political initiative did put free trade firmly 'in the dock'. As usual in such momentous national debates, economic arguments were combined with much rhetoric and play on national fears and sentiments. This ploy was particularly marked in the case of the tariff reformers who often deployed economic arguments in support of wider political and strategic objectives, for example, imperial unity and security, the maintenance of Britain's world status, social reform, and so on. The free-traders (including the majority of economists) had an easier time. Since by common consent the free trade policy was innocent unless proved guilty, the defenders of the status quo could rely on the traditional argument developed over the previous hundred years. But they were sometimes forced to deal with the broader issues raised by their critics. In facing up to this, they were stimulated into further theoretical developments which led to a much clearer definition of assumptions and conditions under which a free trade policy would achieve a particular outcome in terms of economic welfare.

In this account we are concerned only with the economic arguments as they related to international trade theory; and in this connection shall examine the contributions of Marshall, Giffen, Pigou, Bastable (free trade advocates), and Ashley, Cunningham, Hewins, Price (tariff reformers). In general, free trade found support among the theoretical economists, whilst the most ardent advocates of protection were the economic historians; but there were exceptions – for example, Clapham (historian) supported free trade, but Price (economist) dissented from his orthodox colleagues.

Throughout the summer months, almost from the start of the Tariff Reform campaign in May 1903, William Hewins, first Director of the London School of Economics, published a series of anonymously signed articles (sixteen in all) in *The Times* newspaper in support of Chamberlain's proposals. Hewins' articles appeared under the title 'The Fiscal Policy of the Empire', with the byline, 'An Economist'. Hewins collaborated with Chamberlain from the time they first met in June 1903 until the end of the year. Chamberlain asked Hewins 'to supply the economic arguments' (Hewins 1929, note 11, p. 68). Later in the year Hewins became secretary of the Tariff Commission – an unofficial body consisting of forty-nine leading businessmen set up by Chamberlain and his supporters to investigate the probable consequences of the proposals for tariff reform sponsored by the group.

Hewins became a protectionist at the time of the 'Fair Trade' agitation when he expressed deep concern about the effects of foreign competition which he felt posed a serious threat to British industrial supremacy, employment, prosperity and Britain's world-power status. He described himself as a 'constructive imperialist' and felt that tariffs were necessary to revive British industry and consolidate the Empire. Three years before the appearance of Hewins' newspaper articles, at the invitation of Schmoller, he wrote an article on 'Imperialism and its probable effect on the commercial policy of the United Kingdom' for *Schriften des Vereins für Sozialpolitik* published in 1900 (the article is published in Hewins 1929, vol. I, pp. 50–61) in which he further enlarged on the need for fiscal change and protection. Hewins circulated privately an English-language version of the article to political friends and acquaintances.

Hewins' arguments for protection were usually 'non-economic' ones, as for instance his attempt to turn the traditional infant-industry argument into a 'senile-industry' argument for protection, claiming that by protection 'in the modern sense is meant the use by the Government of special forms of regulation or restraint, particularly import duties and analogous fiscal expedients, in order to encourage or to maintain essential industries which must be determined by the requirements of public policy'.[8] Similarly, he tried to argue, contrary to traditional reasoning, that protection would increase economic welfare, on the ground that 'the protectionist policy, properly administered, will bring about a balance of economic activity, involving a higher maximum of efficiency to the community as a whole and a more equitable distribution between the economic groups'.[9] Hewins' meaning here is clear, but the statement is very unspecific in terms of economic content. Evidently, Hewins is here dwelling on the political and social benefits of protection and playing down the role of net economic welfare gains. Protection may, indeed, bring about a better 'balance of economic activity', but no economist can seriously argue that the policy brings about 'a higher maximum of economic efficiency' (under the standard assumptions of full employment, factor mobility, and so on). Trade policy, no doubt, has the capacity to change the free trade domestic income distribution, but the question of the 'equity' of the altered income distribution surely involves non-economic considerations, and therefore a matter of socio-economic judgement. Hewins' stance was thus vulnerable to criticisms on purely economic grounds.

Marshall declined an invitation to answer Hewins' criticisms of free trade policy in the columns of *The Times*. However, on 15 August 1903, *The Times* published a letter signed by fourteen leading economists rejecting Chamberlain's proposals and affirming support for free trade. The letter, which became known as the 'manifesto of the fourteen professors', was drafted by Edgeworth, and the signatories included Marshall, Cannan, Bowley and Pigou.[10] A summary of this letter is warranted, since it has been called 'a very important historical document showing the attitude of British economists to the question of commercial policy and its relation to recent theoretical developments' (Jha 1973, p. 57). It is not clear how many practising economists were asked to sign. Six of the signers were professors of political economy. There were not many professors about at the time, and a number of the signatories were very young, for example, Arthur Pigou was only 26.

The economists expressed their sympathy for Chamberlain's aims, namely imperial unity, but objected to the fiscal means (that is, preferential tariffs) for attaining that objective. Specifically, they feared that 'any system of preferential tariffs would most probably lead to the reintroduction of protection into the fiscal system of the United Kingdom'. Protection would be attended by ineradicable evils both material and moral, among the latter being 'the loss of purity in politics, the unfair advantage given to those who wield the powers of jobbery and corruption, unjust distribution of wealth, and the growth of sinister interests'. Refuting the protectionists' arguments, the economists made five observations:

1. They denied that an increase in imports meant more unemployment.
2. A tax on food imports would be unlikely to raise wages; what it would most probably do, would be to lower real wages.
3. An import tax on wheat would injure British consumers since its price would rise; the injury would be less, to the extent that 'a small proportion of the burden being thrown permanently on the foreign producer'. But they regarded this lightening of the burden as 'very improbable' under existing circumstances.
4. It was impossible, they believed, to devise any tariff regulation which could simultaneously protect British agriculture and expand colonial food production without injuring British consumers.
5. To the argument that although the public would suffer from higher food prices they would secure an equivalent benefit from the distribution of the tariff revenues collected by the government (for example, through more social expenditures), the economists countered with the observation that the argument ignored the welfare loss from the interference with the free circulation of goods, that is, the detriment caused by 'diverting industry from the course which it would otherwise have taken'. In addition, the government tariff revenue gain would be small compared with consumers' losses, since consumers would have to pay nearly the whole tax on all imported wheat, whilst the government would only collect the taxes on foreign wheat.

The economists' manifesto was an attempt to mount a solid, authoritative front against Chamberlain's proposals; but it backfired: it occasioned more ridicule than respect. It particularly enraged the tariff reformers; and far from stifling academic dissent, it actually intensified the controversy. It served to revive the old antagonisms over the role of 'facts' in economic analysis and policy which raged during the 1890s; and since Hewins had revealed that there were at least two sides to the question, the manifesto destroyed the appearance of consensus that the authors wished to convey to the public at large.[11] In some quarters of the press, the academics' intervention was dismissed as irrelevant; in others, it became the target for satirical pieces and cartoons. Eighty years later, another economists' manifesto suffered a similar fate, namely the anti-monetarist statement by 364 economists published in national newspapers on 30 March 1981. Phyllis Deane's remarks fairly sum up contemporary opinion on the economists' *faux pas* on each occasion: 'It seems that this joint declaration [1903] had as little impact on either the public at large or the policy makers as the short statement signed by 364 professional economists nearly eight decades later', and 'in 1981 as in 1903, those who practised the art of political economy were unimpressed by the collective authority of academic economists' (Deane 1990, pp. 122, 130, n. 12). Marshall's association with the manifesto is in itself interesting: having first declined to draft it, Marshall was reluctantly persuaded to sign. Marshall's behaviour was evidently the result of two motives: first, entering into public debate meant one had to 'mix up politics and economics' – an activity bound to compromise the credibility of the modern economist's claim to scientific objectivity; but secondly, and decisively as it turned out, was Marshall's desire to have a tilt at the 'historical economists' who, in the 1890s, entertaining visions of a resurgence of 'political economy' threatened to obstruct his plans for the establishment of professional orthodoxy in economics through the teaching of neoclassical (Marshallian?) economics, as represented by the projected Cambridge Economics Tripos. Coincidentally, 1903 was the year that saw the establishment of the Tripos. Marshall later regretted getting embroiled in the tariff controversy. His participation in the public debate was not only out of character, but also contrary to his frequently expressed view of the economist's public role. That was to be a rather limited and modest one requiring caution and reticence on controversial policy issues. The analytical method of modern economics required the practitioner to cultivate the habit of studious impartiality. Economic analysis was to be neutral, hence 'having done its work it retires and leaves to common sense the responsibility of the ultimate decision; not standing in the way of, or pushing out any other kind of knowledge, not hampering common sense in the use to which it is able to put any available knowledge, nor in any way hindering; helping where it could help, and for the rest keeping silence' (Pigou 1925, pp. 164–5). Elsewhere Marshall indicated how difficult it was for the economist to keep to the straight and narrow scientific path, and as his writings show, he often failed to 'keep silence'. Gerald Shove, a Cambridge don in the 1920s, referred to Marshall's 'pious asides and prim moralisings'.

The fact is that the tariff reform debate brought to the surface and right into the public arena a row that for nearly two decades had been simmering among the economists between the 'historical economists' and adherents of the rising neoclassical school – a dispute known as the 'English *Methodenstreit*', the counterpart of the 1880s methodological dispute in Germany between the younger school of historical economists and the neoclassicist, Carl Menger. Hewins, Archdeacon Cunningham and Ashley all clashed with Marshall over what they perceived as the latter's hegemonic ambitions for the emerging neoclassical brand of economics. Marshall, in turn, feared that the historical economists' influence and teaching would be detrimental to the establishment of his own analytical and theoretical teaching programme. His fervent hope was that his neoclassical brand (founded on the canons of classical economics and the new 'marginalist revolution') should prove dominant and eventually lead to the professionalisation of economics. The academic conflict had its casualties: Cunningham's resignation from his teaching post at Cambridge, Foxwell being passed over for the Cambridge chair; but there was also one institutional gain: academic economics found another home at the London School of Economics (LSE) which was established partly in conscious opposition to Marshall's imperial vision of the subject.

Langford Price, a former pupil and protégé of Marshall, was one of the few economists of non-professorial rank asked by Edgeworth to sign the manifesto. Price declined and sent his letter of refusal to *The Times*, whose editor printed it just below the manifesto. In his letter to Edgeworth (his senior colleague at Oxford), Price alleged that the manifesto was a misleading statement, since the details of tariff reform were not then known, yet the economists dwelt at length on the costs of the proposed policy without mentioning the costs of the status quo. That ill-advised declaration diminished the authority of academic economists in the eyes of the public, continued Price, since it showed them to be no better than professional politicians in an eagerness to prejudge a complex issue of public policy by hurling one-sided and ill-informed criticisms. Price called for a Royal Commission to investigate the matter.[12]

There were further attacks on the manifesto in letters to *The Times* by colleagues such as Herbert Foxwell and Robert Harry Inglis Palgrave (18 and 20 August).[13] Foxwell took exception to the assertion of the manifesto's signatories that the tariff reform proposals were contrary to the doctrines of economic science; on the contrary. he insisted: 'the vital issues are more political than scientific . . . [and] I do not think that economists have any right to attempt to prejudge these issues by a pronouncement which assumes scientific authority, though nearly every sentence is obviously and necessarily political'. Pointing to the fact that none of the academic dissenters signed the manifesto, Foxwell claimed that it 'goes far to justify the position they hold as to the importance of historical study in economics'. The implication was that the 'fourteen professors' were promoters of an ideology masquerading as impartial 'science' of universal and timeless validity which purported to settle historically contingent and inherently contentious political questions with unfounded and undeserved authority. William Ashley, the noted economic historian and occupant of the newly created chair of Commerce at Birmingham University, deplored the fact that 'a majority of British economists have signed a pronouncement intended to veto any serious reconsideration of the commercial policy of this country' (Ashley 1905, p. 137).

Langford Price had adopted a conciliatory stance in the 1890s methodological dispute; but after the economists' manifesto he became disenchanted with what he regarded as the abstract, *laissez-faire* theory of the Marshallian school and therefore felt free to voice his dissent from free trade orthodoxy in more forthright language. What current theory (as interpreted by the professors) seemed to offer was 'a mere complacent acquiescence in the *status quo*' and an unwillingness to consider other options: 'For the conclusion, to which abstract theory conducted the signers of that pronouncement on a political problem of great delicacy and vital moment, appeared to me to be but a barren negation.' (Price 1904, p. 375). In consequence, he felt even more drawn to economic history which, by contrast, suggested more positive, 'useful and abundant hints for practical reform' and therefore contributed the more credible intellectual input to the national debate. He took exception to the 'vulgar notions, expressed in the absolute form, that the general argument for Free Trade is complete, theoretically,' and that 'Free Trade is the economist's policy' (Price 1904, p. 380). He deplored the use of such ploys to stifle dissent at a time when economics was undergoing fundamental change (for example, the 'marginal revolution', recognition of monopoly, industrial trusts and cartels, and so on). Such developments in economic theory meant, he insisted, that 'the debate between Protection and Free Trade is not closed, but open' (Price 1904, p. 376).

He severely criticised Pigou's *The Riddle of the Tariff*, and in 1906 (soon after the general elections and the rejection of the Tariff Reform programme), Price had another swipe at the manifesto, declaring that at a time when serious cracks were appearing in the theoretical foundations upon which the 'free trade dogma had been, as it was thought, securely raised, an appeal was made by interested politicians to an authority to which they had not been accustomed for some while to pay much deference, and professors were invited to confirm the populace in their traditional beliefs. Free trade was presented as correct economics' (Price 1906, p. 137). As a consequence, it was easy for the public to be persuaded that a careful weighing up of the relative merits of the fiscal question could be reduced (or simplified) to a consideration of the exact consequences of a comparison 'between imaginary loaves [of bread] of less or greater magnitude' (Price 1906, p. 133). Price felt that too many issues were raised at the election which distracted voters' attention from 'the single distinct question of fiscal reform'. The issues which crowded out each other for the electorate's attention included the Boer War, the burden of increased taxation, the bitter resentment felt in some circles over the Education Act, the Taff Vale decision, concern over the introduction of Chinese labour into the mines of the South African Rand, and so on (Price 1906, p. 133). Price tersely summed up the public's attitude to Balfour's policy and Chamberlain's scheme thus: 'They could not swallow the one, and they would not be persuaded to taste the other' (Price 1906, p. 132).

The economic historians – Hewins, Ashley and Cunningham – were of course the principal critical dissenters from the free trade orthodoxy represented by Marshall and his followers, and they intensified their onslaught after the appearance of the manifesto. Referring to the economists' démarche, Cunningham voiced popular feeling when he observed: 'The professors who protested that there could be no change of circumstances which made it desirable to reconsider the trading policy of the country did much to discredit the scientific character of the doctrine they taught' (Cunningham 1916, p. 13).

The dissenters were much influenced by the German Historical School (Ashley studied with Schmoller in Berlin), Arnold Toynbee, Cliffe Leslie and, on matters of trade and protection, by Friedrich List. They were particularly impressed by List's ideas on 'productive powers' and 'stages of development' and the relation of these to tariff policy. Thus Ashley admitted that Chamberlain's proposals would increase food prices in the short run, but that was a small price to pay for the revival of British industry which would be the long-run benefit of moderate protection. List had convincingly maintained, he said, that 'the question of the productive powers of a country and their possible development is far more important than that of present values; it might be well worth while to incur a loss for a time in order to secure a more than proportionate future gain' (Ashley 1904, pp. 140–1). Ashley praised List for rejecting individualism and rebutting the cosmopolitanism of free trade ideology and the static-equilibrium theory which underpinned it, and for the assertion of national interest as the central concern of economists. For this, Ashley regarded List as the only writer to be placed for his influence on the world by the side of Adam Smith. Cunningham agreed with List's analysis of the role of free trade in the maintenance of Britain's industrial and commercial hegemony and the reasons which led other countries to defend their nascent industries through tariff protection; but Cunningham declared that circumstances had altered for England and hence free trade was 'no longer the appropriate policy for the nation to follow' (Cunningham 1912, p. 144). Ashley agreed with this position. He held that economic theories were only true relative to time and circumstances, that is, economic 'laws' and doctrines were always relative and hypothetical. Economic theories reflected economic circumstances and conditions, and what was 'sound' economic advice at one time might be totally inappropriate for another age. Conversely, old doctrines deemed to be erroneous by modern canons of economics might, in fact, have had value and relevance in their time. The policy of free trade was clearly unsuited for Britain's present stage of evolution, and hence protectionism in some form could not be ruled out as an alternative simply on the ground that Adam Smith and David Ricardo had rejected it for their time and circumstance.

One of the historical economists' anxieties about the economic future of Britain concerned the possible de-industrialisation of the country if current trends continued without a change in trade policy. Several writers recognised and deplored the steady shift from manufacturing to the tertiary sector and services which was exacerbated by the huge annual export of British capital. British investment in foreign enterprises only served to reinforce the competitors who were undermining British industry and agriculture. However, they did not quite work out how exactly this pessimistic scenario was related to Britain's standing in the world as the leading creditor country (that is, London's dual role as the leading international financial centre and the world's principal gold and produce market).

The employment argument for protection figured prominently in the writings of the dissenters, and much use was made of it by Chamberlain and his supporters both in the press and in public meetings. Protection, it was felt, would be a defence against displacement of labour caused by import penetration, as well as a device for securing regular employment of labour. In this context, the mobility of labour and full employment assumptions of orthodox theory were called into question. Ashley, for instance, contended that one of the principal benefits of a programme of protective tariffs and imperial preference would be a guarantee of regular and secure employment for the working classes. Such attempts to link tariff reform with employment conflicted, of course, with the professors' explicit denial that a rise in imports brought a corresponding fall in domestic employment. Despite Charles Booth's suggestion that 'the interests of the mass of the people, and of the poorest not the least, are found in regularity of employment more than in cheapness of food' (Booth 1904, p. 699),[14] the TUC (Trades Union Congress) was more alarmed at the prospect of an increase in the price of food, and lent its support to the free-traders.

At the height of the Tariff Reform campaign the Prime Minister, Arthur Balfour, presented a memorandum to the Cabinet (13 August 1903) entitled *Economic Notes on Insular Free Trade* which was published a month later (London: Longman Green). This was an attempt to find a *via media* between the contending factions within his own (Unionist) party; but apart from its political purpose, the memorandum raised some interesting questions in the theory of trade policy. Balfour turned out to be a 'retaliationist', that is, he wanted to use tariffs as bargaining weapons to pry open foreign markets, not for protective purposes, and summarised his position in the slogan: 'Freedom to negotiate that freedom of exchange may be increased (Balfour 1903, pp. 30–1). This amounted to a big policy shift, that is, Balfour signalled that he was willing to depart from the traditional maxim 'taxation for revenue alone'. In principle, retaliation or 'fair trade' can lead back to universal free trade. When dealing with recalcitrant commercial rivals, the only alternative to exhortation, Balfour argued, 'is to do to foreign nations what they always do to each other and instead of appealing to economic theories in which they wholly disbelieve, to use fiscal inducements which they thoroughly understand' (Balfour 1903, p. 30).

Balfour indicated that his position on the tariff issue was prompted by the question, 'whether a fiscal system suited to a free trade nation in a world of free traders remains suited in every detail to a free trade nation in a world of protectionists?' He concluded that the answer must be 'No!' and consequently affirmed that Britain should openly and avowedly announce that the country no longer considered itself debarred by economic theories from making the best commercial bargain it could with other countries. Balfour's proposals were a compromise. This would place tariffs only on manufactured goods from countries whose own tariffs kept out British products, and would continue the policy of duty-free import of foodstuffs. Balfour's compromise sought to avoid electorally unpopular food taxes while at the same time retaining the party's protectionists within the fold.

The free trade die-hards, of course, rejected the notion that reciprocity was necessary to pry open foreign markets – the power of example, rather than sanction would in the end induce other countries to follow free trade, rather in the manner of Cobden, the 'apostle of Free Trade', fifty years before. Others, more receptive to the rationale underlying the use of tariffs for reciprocity (that is, Balfour's position), felt that it could be the thin end of the protectionist wedge; the policy would wind up being captured by populists, protectionists and vested interests. Marshall added his concern by mentioning his favourite 'slippery slope' or 'inclined plane' argument against state intervention. Will not the use of even moderate trade barriers for Balfour's purpose be 'captured' by one's own protectionists for their purpose, leaving one saddled with an incubus of tariffs?

Economic theory in Marshall's time was certainly hostile to the idea of using tariffs in the manner recommended by Balfour; yet the principle and practice of doing so was endorsed by John Stuart Mill (a strong supporter of reciprocity) as early as 1829 (Mill 1963, *CW*, p. 251). Tariff bargaining was, from the 1860s onwards, a normal process in European commercial diplomacy; but in such negotiations Britain's hands were tied, since it had no reductions to offer on account of its free trade policy.[15] This was the weakness referred to on Balfour's memorandum. The modern principle of the 'second best' as applied to the economic theory of tariff bargaining does indeed provide an economic justification for Balfour's position within the strict limits of neoclassical postulates on welfare maximisation. In Balfour's obituary notice written for the *Economic Journal*, June 1930, Keynes described Balfour's *Economic Notes* as 'one of the most remarkable scientific deliverances ever made by a Prime Minister in office' and added:

> I think that economists today would treat Balfour's doubts, hesitations, vague sensing of troubles to come, polite wonder whether unqualified *laisser-faire* is quite certainly always for the best, with more respect, even if not with more sympathy than they did then. (Keynes, *CW*, X, 44).

In 1906, Langford Price referred to an earlier (1882) critical article on Cobden written by Balfour wherein Balfour drew attention to the 'yawning gaps in the Cobdenite articles of faith' and the 'limited and distorted perspective of his [Cobden's] political prophecies, and his animus against the landlords'. Price claimed that Balfour's 1903 pamphlet was similar in tone and attitude to the ideas expressed in that article (Price 1906, p. 135).

Marshall's Memorandum

Marshall was apparently 'quite excited' by Balfour's memorandum, and in the same month that the economists' manifesto appeared, he took the opportunity of addressing some of the issues when asked to do so by the pro-free trade Chancellor of the Exchequer, Charles Ritchie. Marshall's memorandum was subsequently published in revised form in 1908. In it Marshall discussed the changing international position and prospects of Great Britain, and surveyed British trade policy in light of the economic changes of the preceding sixty years. Marshall's convictions as a unilateral free-trader come across strongly in this memorandum. Marshall broaches the general issue of the historical relativity of the case for free trade – a matter raised by many in the debate, including Hewins and Balfour. He concedes that the great truths of trade theory 'which are as universal as the truths of geometry and mechanics' did not strictly hold in 'transitional circumstances', that is, under changing economic situations. He himself believed that free trade could not be defended solely on 'absolute a priori reasoning ... it is based on a study of details'; that changing circumstances might, after careful consideration, signal new departures from established commercial policies – in particular, limited protection may be necessary at certain stages of development; and perhaps such intervention could not do much harm in the case of certain (underdeveloped) countries. However, for a country like Britain, Marshall asserts, 'a Protective policy ... would be an unmixed and grievous evil' and he disapproved of American protectionism. It is clear what bothered Marshall was the *practice* of protectionism, even when a theoretically valid case could be made out for it in special circumstances. He did not credit politicians with having the skill, judgement and integrity in the degree necessary for the implementation of a rational protective policy. A protective system, like any measure of government intervention in a democracy, was open to political abuse under the clamour of vested interests and the greed of politicians. Marshall then discussed the reasons why, in his opinion, protection was not a practical option for Great Britain in 1903 in the course of which he dismissed one by one the arguments of the tariff reformers.

However, Marshall is not complacent. He identifies sources of weaknesses undermining Britain's competitiveness in world markets, but is quite sure that protectionism is not the answer. More fundamental changes are required (for example, in the attitudes of management and labour). Among the developments which had altered the international economic environment of British industry Marshall surveyed the following:

1. Intensified competition and industrial growth abroad have resulted in the relative economic decline of Britain compared with the United States and Germany.
2. Modern technology – 'the progress of the arts and resources of manufacturing' – has benefited Britain less than any other country. British industrialists have been slow in innovating and adopting new techniques.
3. Industrial processes and technology upon which British industrial ascendancy was built have been diffused abroad and some countries have even improved upon such processes and techniques.

4.   The growth of foreign trade cartels and protective tariffs have tended
     to narrow the market for British manufactures.

Despite these unfavourable developments, Marshall believed that Britain
still possessed considerable advantages over competitors, namely its abundant capital, cheap coal and favourable climate for the production of fine
cotton yarn.

Marshall felt that sales in the home market could compensate for the loss
of export markets due to tariffs in industrial countries. Some of the advantages of economies of scale would be lost, but no serious injury was likely
to be inflicted on British industry. Nor was there any danger in the immediate or near future from the tariffs of underdeveloped, including Colonial,
countries. Protection was not a feasible solution to the problems facing
Britain, and political pressure to go along the protectionist road must be
resisted. No lasting advantages could be gained from imperial preferences,
attempts 'to tax the foreigner' or retaliatory action against hostile tariffs;
nor was there any theoretical and practical justification for the so-called
'senile-industry' argument for the protection of British industry. Marshall
conceded that rejection of reciprocity in favour of free trade with all countries (that is, the argument against using tariffs as bargaining weapons, or
in retaliation against 'dumping') 'has not the strength of scientific demonstration'. But an economic analysis of the 'facts' led him to the conclusion
that

> England is not in a strong position for reprisals against hostile tariffs, because
> there are no important exports of hers, which other countries need so urgently
> as to be willing to take them from her at considerably increased cost; and because
> none of her rivals would permanently suffer serious injury through the partial
> exclusion of any products of theirs with which England can afford to dispense.
> (Marshall [1903] 1926, p. 408)

Therefore Britain could not hope to arrest and reverse its relative industrial
decline by the method of protection or tariff retaliation. At a time of rapid
technological change and intense commercial rivalry, it was absolutely
essential for Britain to keep 'her markets open to the new products of other
nations and especially those of American inventive genius and of German
systematic thought and scientific training', for that was the surest way of
'increasing the alertness of her industrial population in general, and her
manufacturers in particular' (Marshall [1903] 1926, p. 409). Marshall
emphasised in another passage the urgent need for a positive British
response to the challenge of technology and competition – a response that
a mere change in commercial policy could not hope to elicit. Britain would
not be able to 'hold her own against other nations by the mere sedulous

practice of familiar [industrial] processes'; she must strive to retain industrial leadership. She cannot be the leader, 'but she may be a leader'. Elsewhere in the document, Marshall expressed his confidence that under free trade Britain would be able to retain her place among the leaders because of the country's tradition of 'unrestricted freedom of movement', or 'viability' – an attribute essential to industrial success.

Marshall's memorandum, written in layman's language – his own preferred style – was a persuasive reaffirmation of the free trade case in the new century. There is little or no mention of any theoretical point, although it is obvious that behind his survey and recommendations lies solid analysis, for example, the estimate of the elasticities of demand for British exports and the supply of imports. Marshall himself was responsible for the development of much of the analytical techniques used by his contemporaries, and when he rewrote the memorandum was certainly aware of the contributions to the theory of trade and protection by people like Edgeworth, Cunynghame and Bickerdike. As we have seen (in Chapter 4), these writers explored the possibilities of state intervention in international trade and found theoretically plausible instances where such intervention could be beneficial. None of this appeared in Marshall's memorandum. He knew that free play was made of those economists' writings by tariff reform propagandists who often twisted and slanted them to suit the flow of their rhetoric and polemics. Marshall decided not to play that game and to stick to the 'facts', leaving the finer points of pure theory on one side as being irrelevant to the central issue of the debate. Marshall himself admitted elsewhere: 'It is very difficult to defend Free Trade on absolute a priori reasoning . . . it is based on a study of details.'[16] As we noted above, he believed that ultimately the defence of Free Trade must rest on the 'facts'. He would have agreed with what Pigou said of Balfour's *Economic Notes* – Balfour's fault was that he failed to 'bring . . . these undisputed or indisputable hypothetical reasonings into relation with the actual facts of the present circumstances of England'.[17] However, by failing to give due recognition to these 'undisputed hypothetical reasonings' (namely the possible benefit from tariffs), Marshall laid himself open to the charge that his defence of Free Trade was not an impartial one.

However, even to readers today, Balfour's discussion paper is impressive both in its sober grasp of the policy issues before the public and its lucid, open-minded exposition of general economic principles bearing on the debate. 'Against it', as Phyllis Deane remarks, 'Marshall's own memorandum seems not only stylistically inelegant, but verging on the polemical'; and further, that Balfour's discussion of the controversial issues 'was economically literate, statesmanlike, well written and above all, undogmatic' (Deane 1990, p. 127).

Shortly after the publication of Marshall's memorandum, *The Times* subjected it to a scathing leader: (1) German experience under protection belied Marshall's loyal defence of the 'traditional truths of free trade', while Marshall could only criticise American protective practices on 'moral grounds'; (2) the memorandum's assurances on the employment consequences of free trade were unsatisfactory, since the adjustment costs were not addressed; and (3) Marshall recognised that the world economic environment had altered since Britain had embraced free trade, with the result that Marshall's 'truths of geometry lead him one way, but the occasional intrusion of truths of another order give him pause and force him in the other direction'.[18] To be sure, the national controversy did nothing to stimulate Marshall to rethink the free trade question: if anything 'his ideological commitment to uncompromising free trade seems to have [been] hardened by the heat of the tariff reform debate' (Deane 1990, p. 129).

7.3   FACTUAL EVIDENCE

Marshall relied on facts; so did other free-trade writers, most notably Sir Robert Giffen,[19] the leading official statistician of the day, and immortalised in the pages of economics textbooks for the concepts in the theory of consumer behaviour ('Giffen good', 'Giffen paradox') attributed to him by Marshall. For Fair Traders, Reciprocitarians and Tariff Reformers, Giffen proved a formidable adversary through his high-level press contacts and privileged access to official trade statistics which he was able to control and interpret for polemical purposes. That gave him a tremendous advantage over his opponents, as the latter were often forced to concede their reliance on outdated, incomplete or unreliable data, whereas he came across as the national 'statistical expert'.

Giffen in particular did much to remedy the paucity of statistical information available to the public and politicians at the time of the debate. Wide margins of error were detected in the extant official data, which led to calls for more comprehensive and reliable coverage. There were, for instance, no regular balance of payments figures; only the balance of trade accounts were published and those excluded, of course, data on factors that were recognised as bearing significantly on the international economic position of the United Kingdom, the growth of 'invisible' earnings, transfer payments and overseas investment. The official publication of unemployment figures started as a result of the tariff debate; so too did the compilation of data on production. Under the Census of Production Act 1906, the first Census of Production was undertaken in 1907. The Act provided that manufacturing output and employment data were to be classified so as to be consistent with the 'Headings in the Import and Export Lists'.

Giffen undermined the case for tariff reform by his statistical work which controverted the protectionists' claim that (1) tariffs were responsible for the industrial success of the United States and Germany; (2) tariff retaliation would be an effective defence against foreign competition; and (3) Britain's export performance and rate of economic growth were being crippled by foreign competition. Giffen criticised the protectionists for attempting to show 'that the United States is prosperous'; but, he pointed out, that is not what they have to prove. 'What they have to prove is that it is more prosperous than it would have been under a free trade regime, a statement in which statistics cannot help them'. Giffen is here challenging the tariff reformers to engage in a counterfactual exercise to substantiate their contention. He continued: 'The assumption that foreign manufacturing has largely increased by means of protection', he wrote, 'is one of those wild assumptions which constantly crop up . . . but for which it is never possible to find a scintilla of evidence, and which are entirely opposed to broad facts regarding which there can be no dispute.'[20] Giffen was wrong, however, to assert that statistics could not help the protectionists and that they needed the 'proof' of a counterfactual. Had they known of its existence, empirical evidence existed which could have been cited in support of their cause. Professor Paul Bairoch in his 1989 survey of 'European Trade Policy 1815–1914' for the *Cambridge Economic History of Europe* presents facts that

> constitute real paradoxes to diehard supporters of free trade: not only did the period of reinforcement of protectionism coincide with a more rapid expansion of trade, but also, and even more paradoxically, the most highly protectionist European countries experienced the more rapid expansion of their trade. Even if this cannot be taken as proof that protectionism generates international trade, it at least proves that protectionism does not always and necessarily hinder such trade . . . Furthermore, in continental Europe the rate of economic growth reached its peak from the moment all countries strengthened their protectionism. (Bairoch 1989, pp. 88–90)

Giffen was convinced that protectionist policies were incompatible with the conditions of modern industrial production. Such policies were particularly ineffective in 'new countries' with small domestic markets. Referring to Australian experience under protection, he confidently predicted that protectionist politicians would disappear from the scene 'in a generation or so . . . the breed, I am confident, is very nearly extinct, because the modern atmosphere and conditions, not theory, are making the policy next to impossible'.[21] Giffen's prediction turned out to be wrong, of course. Australian politicians continued to urge protectionist policies.

Giffen constructed balance-of-payments figures to demonstrate that Britain's overall international economic position (including the national balance of indebtedness) gave no cause for alarm, and certainly did not justify protection. The balance of trade figures did indeed show a rising deficit, but that was more than compensated for by a large positive balance on 'invisible' trade (that is, earnings from shipping, insurance, banking, and so on). Some British industries (iron and steel, textiles, shipbuilding) suffered from a certain lack of competitiveness in overseas markets, Giffen admitted; but the remedy was for those industries to increase their efficiency and productivity. For British industry in general, the free trade recipe was best; it would spur some industries to increase their efficiency and would 'encourage those industries which have a comparative advantage' (Giffen [1887] 1970, p. 113).

Giffen's passion for free trade cooled considerably after the Liberals' return to power in 1906 when they announced plans for a wide-ranging policy of 'social reform' (old-age pensions, national insurance against sickness, and to some extent, against unemployment – later incorporated in Lloyd George's 'Peoples Budget' of April 1909) to be financed by increases in personal taxation and revenue taxes on land, with a threat of tax progressivity in its distinction between 'earned' and 'unearned' incomes, namely the 'supertax' on higher incomes. Also, the Labour Party had arrived on the political scene and steadily increased its parliamentary representation. For Giffen, these developments were distasteful; the new danger was 'creeping Socialism'. Suddenly he found himself in the camp of his ex-enemies, for the historical economists had ranged themselves against Lloyd George's budget proposals. On the eve of the general election of 1910, he announced his abandonment of free trade in a letter to *The Times* (17 January 1910). According to Roger Mason, Giffen 'wanted to halt socialism more than he had wanted to defend free trade, and to achieve this had been prepared to abandon Liberalism and to become an unconvinced apologist for tariff reform. Many of his free trade friends considered this an act of betrayal' (Mason 1996, p. 187).

Empirical work bearing on the tariff controversy was also carried out by A.L. Bowley and A.W. Flux. Bowley provided the empirical counterpart of the 'terms of trade' concept widely used in the theory of international values. His 1903 estimates of the British terms of trade revealed that 'over sixteen years, goods exported have risen about 4 per cent in price, while prices of imports have fallen 9 per cent. This looks like profitable business'.[22] Jha comments: 'Such a statement would have silenced any advocate for a change in fiscal policy' (Jha 1973, p. 66).

Bastable claimed that an Imperial Customs Union, as proposed by Chamberlain, 'would divert two-thirds of the foreign trade of the United

Kingdom into the Colonialist direction'. Britain would suffer, since 'the cheapest sources of supply for many articles of prime necessity are outside, not within the Empire'. The scheme, he declared, 'rests on the false economic idea that trade between members of the same political body is better than trade with foreigners . . . The true line of progress lies in greater freedom of commerce for and within all countries' (Bastable 1902, pp. 507–13).

Having briefly reviewed the two divergent strands of economic opinion in the tariff reform debate, with free trade under attack (by the historical economists) and defended (by the liberal or neoclassical economists), one might ask: what was the basic reason for this confrontation? We have already noted the fact that Chamberlain asked Hewins to 'supply the economic arguments' in June 1903. Were people like Hewins, Ashley, Price, Cunningham, and so on in Lenin's phrase, mere 'coolies of the pen', sophisticated hacks or propagandists brought in to lend support to the Conservative party's tariff arguments? The cynical answer is 'yes', but it is not the whole story. Certainly, the tariff-reforming Conservatives needed the intellectual firepower of academic economists – as Andrew Bonar Law wrote to Ashley: 'There is nothing which tells more against us than the idea that *scientific* authority is against us.'[23] In the propaganda war, the backing of economic 'authority' in the form of an appeal to economic 'science' was politically of crucial importance. But of course, the match of interests was perfect: since the 1890s, as we have seen, the historical economists sought to engage the political class and the wider public in a national economic debate. For the Conservatives they were thus ideal propagandists, since their critique of free trade and liberal economics predated the launch of Chamberlain's campaign, and their particular diagnosis and remedy for Britain's economic problem found a resonance among the Conservatives and imperialists. In his acclaimed (1995) study of the crisis of British Conservatism during this period, E.H.H. Green found abundant evidence for his opinion that 'the historical economists were selected as the ideologues of Edwardian Conservatism because the perspective they offered on Britain's economic problems seemed plausible and helpful to the Conservative party' (Green 1995, p. 183).

It is sometimes asserted that, at the least, what the historical economists achieved was the creation of an intellectual environment friendly to tariffs – no mean achievement, given that Protection was a taboo subject for fifty years. The role of ideas in shaping events and policy changes is too often exaggerated. In fact, what lent credibility to the historical economists' intellectual campaign was the conjunction of 'diminished giant' status, economic distress and the appropriation of their agenda by a great political party. But despite the fact that their agenda, clothed in the rhetoric of political 'knockabout', was rejected by the people, did they succeed in making gains towards their primary objective of checking the progress of neoclassical economics with its axiomatic, deductive methodology? We know, of course, that the answer is 'no'. Ashley wished to apply economics to politics, Cunningham wanted to bring in the social dimension, and Foxwell was animated by the conviction (in the paraphrase of J.M. Keynes) that 'economics is not a branch of logic or mathematics, but belongs to the art of managing public affairs by the application of sound reasoning to the whole corpus of experience.'[24] The tariff controversy afforded them a wider platform for a display of force, but they failed to breach the walls of the citadel of economic orthodoxy, as Ashley conceded in his Presidential address to Section F of the British Association in 1907: 'The criticisms of the historical school have not led, so far, to the creation of a new political economy on historical lines' (Ashley [1907] 1962, p. 237). Their real achievement and most tangible legacy was the creation of economic history as a recognised academic discipline. This Ashley ruefully acknowledged in the 1920s when he observed that the historical economists' attack had been peacefully diverted into the creation of the new and separate field of economic history, leaving the bastion of orthodox economic theory fundamentally intact' (Koot 1988, p. 192).

Final Thoughts

At the conclusion of this chapter on the British tariff controversy, one is prompted to ask the following two questions: (1) did the tariff reformers address the real issues? (2) was the free trade solution the appropriate one for Britain at that time?

Answers have, of course, been suggested by economic historians. This is not the place to debate the matter. Suffice it to say that the most frequently recurring responses say 'no' to the first question and 'yes' to the second; but the reasons are not altogether consistent. In retrospect, Marshall's judgement as set forth in his memorandum has been upheld: retaliatory tariffs, permanent tariffs on manufactures and imperial preference would not have worked to Britain's advantage, and as one writer puts it, 'protection and preference would not have done much to revive the fortunes of British industry or to ensure rapid growth in the future',[25] or, as another suggested, 'tariff reform might really have over-committed British industry to traditional markets' (Sked 1987, p. 20). What about the tariff reformers' strategy? Here, we are told that they helped to create 'new forms of conceptualizing the economy', but they failed to spell out how that conception conflicted with Britain's traditional role in the late-nineteenth-century world economy, that is, as the 'manager' of the Gold Standard and leading creditor nation, both of which were dependent on free foreign access to the

British market. Thus, it has been said, the tariff reformers neglected to attack the pillars of the free trade system – they were 'singularly reticent about pursuing the relation between free trade, the gold standard and foreign investment beyond rhetorical generalities' (Tomlinson 1981, p. 55). And again: 'What defeated Chamberlain in the last analysis was the City of London, which still dominated the British economy, and whose wealth did not derive any longer from manufacturing industry . . . The City merchant bankers not only dominated the economy; even more surely they dominated Government circles' (Brown 1970, p. 105). 'Domination' is not quite the word to describe the City's subtle influence on the policymakers; nor was manipulation needed. Government ministers were persuaded to go along broadly with the wishes of British finance, since most of the former were stockholders and shared a common culture with the financial class.

But if Britain's economic problem was really 'structural' in nature, in that 'the sources of weakness in the economy of Edward VII were still paramount in the economy of Edward VIII' (Crafts and Thomas 1986, p. 643), it is difficult to see what difference free trade made; or, for that matter, what difference tariff reform would have made.

NOTES

1. Theodore Martin, *The Life of His Royal Highness The Prince Consort*, vol. II, p. 451, quoted in Sir John Clapham [1939] (1967), p. 1.
2. W.S. Jevons, *The Coal Question: An Enquiry Concerning the Progress of the Nation and the Probable Exhaustion of Our Coal Mines* (1865), 3rd edn (London: Macmillan, 1906), p. 241.
3. J. Bhagwati and D. Irwin, 'The Return of the Reciprocitarians: US Trade Policy Today', *The World Economy*, 10 (1978), pp. 109–30, compare the two historical episodes, drawing both parallels and contrasts. See also on this topic, Jagdish Bhagwati, 'Fair Trade, Reciprocity and Harmonization: The New Challenge to the Theory and Policy of Free Trade', in A.V. Deardorff and R.M. Stern, *Analytical and Negotiating Issues in the Global Trading System* (Ann Arbor: University of Michigan Press, 1994), chapter 13, especially pp. 547–68.
4. The inference is, of course, valid only if we make the assumptions of identical homothetic preferences and international equalisation of factor prices.
5. Quoted in Hans Rosenberg, *Grosse Depression und Bismarckzeit: Wirtschaftsablauf, Gesellschaft und Politik in Mitteleuropa* (Berlin: Walter de Gruyter, 1967), p. 170. Schmoller supported Bismarck's new protectionist policy when the matter was debated before the Verein für Sozialpolitik in 1879; so did most of the other leading German political economists. The ideas of Friedrich List became popular in academic circles at that time. Ludwig Josef (Lujo) Brentano, professor of political economy at Munich University from 1892, although a prominent member of the Historical School, remained a free-trader. He was a friend and correspondent of Marshall during the tariff controversy. Brentano contributed to the British public debate with an article in the *Fortnightly Review* under the title 'The Proposed Reversal of English Commercial Policy' (vol. 74, August 1903, pp. 212–21) in which he criticised both Chamberlain and Balfour, calling them 'the docile pupils of our [German] Protectionists'. Whilst Marshall agreed with the tenor of the article, he offered some minor criticisms on points of detail.

6. W. Farrer Ecroyd, 'Fair Trade', *The Nineteenth Century*, 10 (1881), p. 589.
7. The colourful description of the speech came from the Bishop of Hereford who complained about 'this raging tearing Protectionist propaganda manufactured in Birmingham', as quoted in *Edwardian Heritage: A Study in British History 1901–1906*, William Scovell Adams (London: Frederick Muller, 1949), p. 197. Leo Amery, later a prominent Conservative cabinet minister, wrote in his memoirs: 'The Birmingham speech was a challenge to free trade as direct and provocative as the theses which Luther nailed to the church door at Wittenberg' (see Leopold S. Amery, *My Political Life*, London: Hutchinson, 1953, vol. 1, p. 236).
8. W.A.S. Hewins, 'Papers and Correspondence', in the *Hewins Papers*, Sheffield University Library, Box Mss. 160, p. 182.
9. *Hewins Papers*, Box Mss. 160, pp. 183–4. A summary of Hewins' argument was published in *Economic Journal* (September 1903), p. 445.
10. 'Professors of Economics and the Tariff Question', *The Times*, 15 August 1903, p. 4. Those who signed the letter were: Bastable, Bowley, Cannan, Courtney, Edgeworth, Gonner, Marshall, Nicholson, Phelps, Pigou, Sanger, Scott, Smart, Armitage Smith. The manifesto was later reprinted in *Economic Journal*, 13 (September 1903), pp. 446–8. All the critical points made by the economists were used by the Liberals in their attack on the government. Pigou spoke on public platforms in support of free trade candidates.
11. By signing his articles, 'An Economist', Hewins deliberately gave the impression that he was speaking for the profession. Indeed, he further maintained that 'the whole trend of economic method and investigation in recent times is in the direction indicated by Mr Chamberlain', *The Times*, 'The Fiscal Policy of the Empire', 20 August 1903.
12. *The Times*, 15 August 1903, p. 4, cols. 2–3. Price's call for a Royal Commission to investigate the matter received support from a variety of quarters, including the King. In a letter written at Marienbad to Balfour, Edward VII asked: 'Would it not be possible to refer the whole matter to a Royal Commission which has been suggested by Mr Price of Oxford?' Sir Sidney Lee, *King Edward VII – A Biography* (London: Macmillan, 1927), vol. II, pp. 173–4. Price was chairman of the Oxford University Tariff Reform League. John Neville Keynes felt the same as Price about the economists' manifesto. He noted in his diary: 'for my part, I think the issue of the Manifesto unwise and likely to injure the authority of professed economists' (J.N. Keynes, Diary, 20 August 1903), quoted in P. Groenewegen, *A Soaring Eagle: Alfred Marshall 1842–1924* (Edward Elgar, 1995), p. 383. As a young enthusiast for Chamberlain's policy, Leo Amery was still resentful of the economists and their manifesto when he wrote his autobiography in 1963. Earlier, in his book, the *Fundamental Fallacies of Free Trade* (London: Love and Malcolmson, 1908, p. 4), Amery wrote: 'The manifesto issued by fourteen professors against Mr Chamberlain in the early days of the present controversy was in its pontifical arrogance a worthy example of the palmiest days of Ricardo and McCulloch.'
13. Foxwell was Marshall's colleague at Cambridge and was well respected in economic circles there. Despite the long and close friendship between the two men, Marshall was apparently upset when Foxwell joined the historical economists' public attack on free trade. Some writers believe that this 'tainted' Foxwell in Marshall's eyes and caused the latter to switch his support to the young Pigou as his successor in 1908. However, Peter Groenewegen in his definitive biography of Marshall finds little evidence for this supposition, citing the fact that there were other longstanding doctrinal differences between the two colleagues (for example, on bimetallism, neoclassical theory, and so on) and that a more pertinent explanation for Marshall's switch to Pigou in the Cambridge election was 'concern for the future of his [Marshall's] Tripos', presumably on the ground that Pigou was judged the stronger and more able of the two for advancing his Tripos. See Groenewegen (1995, p. 625). For his part, Palgrave, noted for his *Dictionary of Political Economy* (1892–94) resented Marshall's indifferent, if not hostile, reaction to his *Dictionary*.
14. According to Coats (1968, p. 192, n. 24), 'Booth subsequently became a member of Chamberlain's Tariff Commission and was regarded by its opponents as the only reputable figure on it.' Booth's social research which found that a third of the people of

London (the richest city in the world) lived in misery, squalor and hopelessness, shocked public opinion. The extent of primary poverty in York, as revealed by Seebohm Rowntree's statistical survey of that city, was another startling social revelation.

15. Earlier, in the mercantilist past, Britain's economic interests were well served by cleverly designed commercial treaties (for example, the Methuen Treaty, 1703, between England and Portugal); and the almost universal acceptance of free trade in the 1860s – except for the United States – was due to the spread of MFN (most-favoured-nation) treaties. But just as the world was being subjected to strong protectionist pressures, Gladstone's abandonment of any tariff negotiation based on reciprocal concessions meant that Britain found itself in a defenceless position. In the words of Lord Curzon (1895), the country entered keen world competition with one hand tied behind its back 'without anything to give, to promise, or to threaten'; Viscount Curzon's speech to the House of Commons, *Parliamentary Debates* 36, 4s. 1272 (30 August 1895), quoted in D.C.M. Platt, *Finance, Trade and Politics: British Foreign Policy 1815–1914* (Oxford: Clarendon Press, 1968), p. 145. Gladstone and the Liberals were not persuaded; for Gladstone, adopting a retaliationist policy was tantamount to following the protectionist precept: 'if somebody smites you on the one cheek, you should smite yourself on the other'. Gladstone's speech at Leeds, 1881. See Platt, cited above, p. 145.

   Free-traders often use such metaphors to suggest the foolishness of autarky or retaliation; for example, 'To say that our government must depart from free trade because other governments are not free traders is like saying that because other countries have rocky shores, we must block up our own harbours' (Krugman 1986, p. 11). Joan Robinson's favourite example of the rationale for reciprocity was: if any nation insists on throwing rocks in its harbour, we must throw rocks at it until it dredges them up (J. Robinson, 'Beggar-my-Neighbour Remedies for Unemployment', in *Essays in the Theory of Unemployment*, London: Macmillan, 1937). In general, it is foolish to add to one harm caused by foreign tariffs a second, self-inflicted harm. If, however, our retaliation has the desired effect and both countries' tariffs are then removed, the net result could be an increase in our welfare above what it would have been in the absence of our retaliatory tariff (since world efficiency gains increase). Of course, if there are any 'distortions' (market failures) to contend with, free trade ceases to be the optimal policy.

16. Marshall, in *Economic Journal*, 11 (1901), p. 265; also Pigou (1925, p. 67).

17. Quoted by Price in his review of Balfour's *Notes, Economic Journal*, 13, p. 567; also Jha (1973, p. 60).

18. *The Times*, 17 October 1908.

19. Giffen (a Scot, born in Strathaven, Lanarkshire) had an early career as a journalist, but became a senior civil servant in 1876 at the Board of Trade with the title of Chief of the Statistical Department. He secured a special dispensation which allowed him to carry on with his journalistic and public-speaking activities touching on all matters economic and political. He was knighted in 1895 and two years later retired from the Board of Trade, but continued to campaign against protection until 1908. It has recently been noted that 'Giffen's intervention in the tariff reform debate was to become a major factor in blocking the move towards trade protection in Britain' (Mason 1996, p. 171).

20. See Wood (1983, p. 167); R. Giffen, *The Recent Rate of Material Progress in England* (London: George Bell, 1887), p. 26. Giffen was a champion of the free trade cause during the earlier Fair Trade controversy. He argued then against any move to aid British sugar producers and refiners by the imposition of countervailing duties against the sale of foreign bounty-fed sugar in the British market. When, however, in 1902 the British government was driven by circumstances to adhere to the Brussels Sugar Convention, Giffen altered his position. He admitted that the state could not ignore a threat to the very livelihood of a section of the community, despite theoretical arguments which showed that consumers as a whole gained from foreign bounties. See Minutes of Evidence, *Report of the Select Committee on Steamship Subsidies*, Parliamentary Papers 1902 (385) IX, Q. 180; also Platt, op. cit. In 1903 the Sugar Convention Act was passed in response to the dumping of subsidised beet sugar in Britain. Marshall himself admitted that 'in fact foreign bounties have never done any considerable harm to any British

industry with the exception of the sugar industry'; but felt that the harm done was much exaggerated . See H.W. McCready, 'Alfred Marshall and Tariff Reform, 1903: Some Unpublished Letters', *Journal of Political Economy*, LXIII (1955), p. 264.

21. Giffen, 'Protection and Manufactures in New Countries', *Economic Journal*, 8 (1898), reprinted in Giffen, *Economic Inquiries and Studies*, vol. II (London; G. Bell & Sons, 1904), p. 159. Giffen challenged Chamberlain's Empire trade figures in letters to *The Times*, but the statistical differences (on time periods, coverage, adjustment for cyclical conjunctures, and so on) – apart from doubts about their reliability – turned on matters of presentation and interpretation. Chamberlain was driven to the point of admitting that even if tariff reform involved a loss of material wealth, that 'would be amply compensated for by the union of the Empire'. As Chamberlain's latest biographer, Peter Marsh notes: 'The debate on tariff reform made him contemptuous of statistics: "The more I deal with the subject . . . the more I distrust all figures – those which tell for us as well as those which tell against us".' 'Ultimately', writes Marsh, 'Giffen was as doctrinaire in his handling of the evidence as was Chamberlain' – an instance of statistics' limited use in economic argument. See Marsh (1994, pp. 588–9).

22. A.L. Bowley, 'Statistical Methods and the Fiscal Controversy', *Economic Journal*, 13 (September 1903), p. 311.

23. Law to Ashley, n.d. December 1904, in A. Ashley, *W.J. Ashley: A Life* (London, 1925), p. 135.

24. Keynes, 'H.S. Foxwell', *Economic Journal*, 46 (1936), p. 593.

25. Peter Cain, 'Political Economy in Edwardian England: The Tariff Reform Controversy', in Alan O'Day (ed.), *The Edwardian Age: Conflict and Stability 1900–1914* (London: Macmillan, 1979), p. 51. For another historical analysis of the political aspects of tariff reform, see A. Sykes (1979).

8. The first era of globalisation and after 1860–1960

8.1 EUROPEAN TARIFF HISTORY

This chapter tells the story of the historical swings or alternating periods between freer trade and protection in Europe over the period 1860–1960: (1) the 'low-tariff' era (1860s to late 1870s); (2) the return to protectionism, or the backlash against free trade in the 1880s and 1890s. It therefore covers the period now commonly characterised as the first major period of globalisation, that is, up to the eve of the Great War (1914–18); followed by (3) the Great Depression of the late 1920s and 1930s, including the problems of postwar adjustment and those arising from the desire to get back to the certainties of the tranquil period before the war; but a period also associated with economic nationalism, protectionism and the collapse of the world economy in the 1930s; (4) post-1945 efforts to get back to an open trade and financial system through multilateral trade negotiations and co-operative world monetary arrangements which resulted in (5) in the second or current phase of globalisation starting from the 1970s.

The Low-Tariff Era

Following this chronological sequence of events, attitudes and policies, we start with the low-tariff era. This came into being in two stages: (1) Britain's unilateral adoption of free trade from the 1840s onwards, famously signalled by the repeal of the Corn Laws in 1846; and (2) the Anglo-French commercial treaty of 1860 which soon afterwards set the pattern for a series of bilateral tariff agreements between the principal European countries, incorporating as a standard feature the 'most-favoured-nation clause' (MFN). Under MFN, in trade negotiations between two countries, the bilaterally-agreed tariff reductions must be extended to all other countries (not originally parties to the negotiations) but which are accorded MFN status by the two countries. If, as many writers claim, Britain's dramatic free-trade policy shift marked by the repeal of the Corn Laws was influential in inaugurating the European 'low-tariff' regime, it is useful to review the impetus behind repeal.

In an earlier chapter (Chapter 6), we discussed the classical economists' involvement in the public debate on the Corn Laws and analysed their contribution to the economic issues involved. But, as we saw there, the economists' direct influence was minimal in securing repeal. In parliamentary debates, the politicians sometimes used the economists' arguments; but as these were often tacked on to buttress more patently polemical or partisan debating points, the strictly theoretical arguments lost their purity, were bowdlerised, misrepresented or simply turned into a defence of populist slogans. The economists themselves were often timid in their advocacy of free trade and, in general, their debating interventions were cautious and uninspiring – perhaps with the singular exception of Torrens' more impassioned arguments.

How then did repeal come about? What were the forces pushing for a radical reform of trade policy, in particular, the removal of that icon of British protectionism, the Corn Laws?

Not surprisingly, old and modern commentators have considered a variety of factors. We briefly discuss two of them relating to (a) 'events' and (b) 'interest-group pressure'. (a) Short-term worries about food supplies after the poor 1845 harvest and the blighted Irish potato crop which raised fears of famine in Ireland during the winter of 1845–6. These critical events coincided with Sir Robert Peel's dramatic 'conversion' to free trade. He resigned after failing to win full Cabinet backing for his abolitionist proposal, but soon returned to power and in February 1846 announced a package of measures abolishing duties on imported grain over three years. The immediate or proximate cause of repeal was then short-term or panic fears over food supplies caused by adverse weather conditions. As John Morley, the biographer of Cobden, remarked: 'It was the rain that rained away the Corn Laws' (Morley 1881, p. 215).

(b) The eight-year campaign by the Anti-Corn Law League, founded in 1838 by Manchester textile manufacturers led by Richard Cobden, a Manchester calico printer (MP for Stockport) and John Bright, a Quaker carpet manufacturer from Rochdale. James Wilson, the Scottish journalist who founded the *Economist* magazine in 1843, was also a leading figure in the League. Agricultural protection, they claimed, meant that workers were being denied the chance to buy cheap food. High British food prices implied lower real wages which depressed workers' living standards and fomented labour unrest. At the same time, since foreign (especially Prussian) grain exporters were effectively shut out of the British market, such potential customers were unable to import British manufactured goods.

As a single-issue pressure group the League, through its propaganda machine, lectures, petitions, public meetings, demonstrations and voter-registration campaign mobilised support for free trade candidates at the forthcoming general elections of 1848. The League, the first ever economic lobby in modern times, has been described as 'the most impressive of nineteenth-century pressure groups, which exercised a distinct influence on the repeal of the Corn Laws' (Howe 1984, quoted in Schonhardt-Bailey 1998, p. 73).

There is no doubt that the League was a formidable public relations (PR) machine, and the political pressure it exerted must have been considerable. Despite the fact that Peel had got rid of duties on raw materials and greatly eased them on manufactured and semi-manufactured goods in 1842 and 1845, the Manchester cotton barons 'acted with the fury of the desperate. They realized that their prosperity was borne on the back of an increasingly mutinous labour force' (Harvie 1998, pp. 497–8) – the evidence for which was plain for all to see in the working class agitation known as the Chartist movement (1838–42). The floods of popular oratory from the Anti-Corn Law League drowned out the cries of the Chartists; thus 'the masterful propagandists of Manchester got the ear of all classes' (Beales [1928] 1967, p. 99). The League gained mass support by showing how cheap imports of corn would benefit consumers and workers, as well as the textile industry. In the clash of economic interests (agricultural vs. industrial) the outcome was predictable: the industrial sector was rapidly expanding relative to agriculture. Later, the propaganda associated with the League gave rise to ideological labels such as 'Cobdenism', 'Manchester liberalism' and the 'Manchester School'.

'Events' and 'interests' were obviously important influences in the policy decision to repeal. Other factors include ideology, pragmatism, and political tactics. The interplay of ideology and interests was obvious in the activities of the Anti-Corn Law League; their activists preached the gospel of Free Trade with great fervour and conviction. Referring to the League's clear and well-defined ideological message, Schonhardt-Bailey writes: 'Arguably, the League so mastered the ideological debate that it was able to use liberal free-trade ideology to shape the interests of the electorate and politicians alike' (Schonhardt-Bailey 1998, p. 77). Ideological conviction also played a part in Peel's decision to get rid of the Corn Laws. Peel, whose wealth came from the calico industry[1] and therefore, perhaps, ideologically predisposed to the League's free trade message was also well versed in the doctrines of the political economists and judged legislative changes not on the basis of class interests but on that of national welfare. Accordingly, when he became convinced (by observing the behaviour of food prices and nominal wages over the previous three years) that there was, in fact, no necessary or fixed relationship between the two, he decided on the abolition of corn duties. He rejected the prevailing 'iron law of wages' – according to which real wages were bound at subsistence level – and adopted the optimistic view that the real wage of labour would, in fact, increase with abolition of protection, that is, he came to believe in the 'economy of high wages' – and hence to accept the central plank of the Leaguers' rhetoric that high wages would be the inevitable result of free trade. The League's propaganda might have furnished Peel with information and stimulus, but in the end he settled the matter in his own mind on the basis of reason and empirical facts. Thus: 'Economic ideas, and not the pressure of interests, were central to Peel's conversion to favor repeal of the Corn Laws' (Irwin 1989, p. 55) and 'Peel was persuaded, not purchased; baptised, not bought' (Bhagwati and Irwin 1987, p. 130).

The question as to which was the dominant motive behind the policy decision to repeal the Corn Laws remains unsettled, and historians continue to debate the matter. In a brief review of the different emphases in the literature, Boyd Hilton mentions one which suggests political manoeuvre on the part of Peel. Another, which he apparently favours, is that Peel was motivated by a different ideology from that of the League, that is, that he was more taken with the gradualist, Huskissonite 1820s approach to economic reform; that he underwent no 'conversion', but that the timing of his decision to repeal was dictated by executive pragmatism (namely, the Irish famine scare) (Hilton 1998, pp. 83–5).

After 1846 Britain moved swiftly along the road to free trade. Earlier, during 1824–5, Huskisson had reduced duties on imports and exports to an average of 20 per cent. Over 1000 Customs Acts were repealed. Revision of the Navigation Acts was initiated by Thomas Wallace, Vice-President of the Board of Trade and continued by Huskisson during 1822–5. In 1849 the second pillar of protection, the Navigation Acts, were repealed by a small majority in the House of Commons, despite Adam Smith's support for the Acts. Supporting the motion for total repeal, Sir James Graham, Home Secretary in Peel's 1841 administration, declared that the principle of reciprocity made 'the interest of others the measure of our interest – I had almost said it makes the folly of others the limit of our wisdom.'[2] In 1860, William Gladstone, Chancellor of the Exchequer, abolished all remaining protectionist tariffs on manufactured goods. The items that remained on the tariff schedule were a few imported consumption goods that either were not produced at home or were already subject to domestic excise taxes (that is, tea, sugar, tobacco, wines and spirits). The duties were maintained to raise fiscal revenue and provided 87 per cent of customs revenue in 1861. Finally, a leftover from the repeal of the Corn Laws, the corn registration duty, was eliminated in 1869.

The Anglo-French Commercial Treaty (1860)

The second stage in the inauguration of the 'low tariff' era came with the signing of the Anglo-French Commercial Treaty on 23 January 1860 (fourteen years after the repeal of the Corn Laws). How did that breakthrough come about? The ground was prepared by Huskisson in 1823 when the Reciprocity of Duties Act was passed which allowed the Board of Trade to negotiate the reduction of duties with individual countries on a reciprocal basis. The previous commercial treaty with France was the one signed in 1786 whereby France reduced duties on British exports of manufactured goods in return for preferential treatment for French wines and luxury goods. Despite their best efforts, British diplomatists failed to make headway in procuring reciprocal treaties in the 1830s (for example, four negotiations with France came to nothing) and such tariff bargaining efforts were abandoned in 1846 owing to the strength of protectionist interests in Europe. What really limited Britain's ability to negotiate more tariff treaties after 1846 was lack of bargaining counters, since tariffs were maintained on relatively few items. But British negotiators might have met with some measure of success had they shown more flexibility on wine duties to revive interest in France, Spain and Portugal and an equal flexibility with respect to spirits duties to attract the German states.

A constraint on governments' willingness or ability to deal with tariff reform was its implication for government revenue. Customs and excise were the traditional mainstays of government revenue, and while income from these sources increased with prosperity (that is, the boom years of the 1850s) so did government expenditure. Yet at the time no one could imagine having it paid for by direct taxation. States therefore continued to look to tariffs. In Britain, Peel's 1842 budget had revived the income tax (abolished in 1815) to compensate for the loss of revenue through tariff reform, and that was a big reforming step, since in 1830 British tariffs provided 43 per cent of government annual revenue; if taken together with the excise, they produced 75 per cent of revenue. In the rest of Europe, however, there was no enthusiasm among the wealthy, propertied classes for any proposal to use the income tax to fill the revenue gap as was done in Great Britain.

The Great Exhibition of 1851 in Hyde Park celebrated Britain's commercial and industrial ascendancy and it was promoted as such by the Whig government, which also used that national showcase to advertise the benefits of free trade. Foreign visitors were suitably impressed, even overwhelmed, by the marvels of British technology and industrial prowess, which (reversing cause and effect) it was easy to attribute to the enlightened policies of the land of free trade and the self-confidence of its entrepreneurs. For many, the British example showed that free trade brought progress, prosperity and national contentment – it was, after all, the start of the boom years of the 1850s. Such admiration encouraged British free-traders to envisage the early inauguration of a 'free trade Europe' and such ideas were actively promoted by the free trade civil servants at the Board of Trade, including Sir Louis Mallett, Cobden's principal official ally, as well as by British diplomatic missions in the capitals of Europe. Earlier, Cobden had believed that Britain's adoption of free trade would be, by its exemplary wisdom alone, the catalyst for European tariff disarmament. Thus he assured his British audience 'there will not be a tariff in Europe that will not be changed in less than five years to follow your example' (Ratcliffe 1975, p. 127). It was with such high hopes that Cobden went in August 1846 on an extended tour of Europe propagating his vision of a free-trade Europe. During the tour, secret negotiations took place in Paris between Cobden and Michel Chevalier, a professor of economics at the Collège de France, converted to free trade by Frédéric Bastiat in 1845. Chevalier played a leading role in the critical negotiations which began in October 1859 and ended in success with the signing of the Treaty (in Paris on 23 January 1860).[3] Working in secrecy, Chevalier was assisted by a small group of free trade enthusiasts (which formerly included Frédéric Bastiat until his death in 1850) with the approval of the Emperor, Napoleon III. Paul Bairoch noted 'a group of theorists succeeded in introducing free trade into France, and thus indirectly to the rest of the continent' (Bairoch 1991, p. 23). But the Emperor was ahead of his people. The Treaty was concluded without the support, indeed, without the knowledge of the business community, the industrialists, the parliamentary deputies (the majority of whom were sup-porters of protectionism) and the public. Industrialists claimed that the Treaty would ruin the economy. Although half of French trade was with Britain, export industry played a far smaller role in the economy (that is, compared with that in Britain); hence, they claimed, there was no synchron-isation of business interests between the two countries. For French indus-trialists, the home market was of paramount importance; their continued prosperity (together with that of thousands of workers) depended on pro-tection of that market which was now threatened by the Treaty's provisions for tariff cuts.

The parliamentary deputies called the signing of the Treaty the new coup d'état, referring to the earlier constitutional coup of 2 December 1851 which established the Second Empire with Napoleon III as Emperor. The protec-tionists were taken by surprise, but 'because the trade treaty did not require legislative approval and because the emperor skilfully diffused opposition by simultaneously putting forth an ambitious public works program – the so-called "Programme de la Paix" – the protectionists had neither the political means nor the popular support to undo it or the other free trade reforms in the early 1960s' (Smith 1980, p. 35; also Dunez 1993, pp. 164–7, 172–5). Although the Treaty was eventually extended, it remained a contentious issue and engendered resentment amongst the bourgeoisie against the dictatorial aspects of the regime that contributed to the decline of the Emperor's popularity. Recording that of all the actions of Napoleon III in the economic sphere, the most hotly disputed was his turn toward lower tariffs, Gordon Wright notes that 'there are Frenchmen still who regard that date as the critical turning point in French economic progress, as the "black day" of the century – just as there are others who see 1892 (the decisive return to high tariffs) as the real disaster.' Undoubtedly, he writes, the imperial regime was the loser, 'for much of its support in business circles was alienated by the brusque turn to freer trade' (Wright 1987, pp. 159–60).

Under the terms of the Treaty (to run for ten years) France abolished all prohibitions (in particular, those on the import of British textiles) and replaced them with import duties not exceeding 30 per cent *ad valorem* (25 per cent after 1865), although in practice most duties were set at 10 per cent or 15 per cent. Britain allowed free entry to a large number of French products with the exception of wine and brandy. Although the duty on wines was reduced by 80 per cent it did not result in any large increase of sales in the British market.

The Treaty was passed by the House of Commons as part of Gladstone's budget of 1860 which, in fact, was designed very much with the Treaty in mind.

The Anglo-French Commercial Treaty was the prototype for all the other bilateral trade treaties entered into by practically all European countries between 1861 and 1866, commonly known as the 'network of Cobden treaties', all incorporating the MFN (most-favoured-nation) clause. In May 1861 a commercial treaty was signed between France and Belgium. During the same period, Great Britain negotiated such treaties with Belgium, Italy, the *Zollverein* (through Prussia) and Austria, with negotiations pending with Spain and Portugal. During the next few years, France made treaties with several of her neighbours, including one with the *Zollverein*. Upon taking office in Prussia, one of Bismarck's first moves was to initiate negotiations with France for a trade treaty which he got other members of the *Zollverein* to accept. The agreement led to a substantial reduction in mutual tariff barriers, for example, an 80 per cent cut on fabricated iron goods, 25 per cent on crude iron, 40–80 per cent on cotton goods, 60 per cent on woollens, and so on. All the increases in the *Zollverein* duties instituted in the 1840s (during the brief protectionist interlude) were removed, and in addition, there were drastic reductions in 160 items, many of which were cut to below 10 per cent. Count Camillo Cavour, a fervent disciple of Cobden, introduced free trade in grains in Piedmont together with other general reductions in tariffs in 1851 and 1859. This liberalised Piedmontese tariff was applied to the whole of Italy on national unification in 1861. Further reductions in tariff levels were made following the Franco-Italian trade treaty in 1863, so that until 1878 Italy was in the front rank of the liberal, free trade European states. Even Russia lowered her tariffs during the twenty years following the great reforms of the 1860s, for example, the tariff reductions of 1868.

Gladstone's vision of a Europe of free trade, prosperity and peace seemed to be realised in those treaties – as he declared at the time, the treaties were entered into not 'for mere increase of trade [but] for those blessings which increase of trade brings with it: peace, security, goodwill'.[4]

The 1860s, when the network of trade treaties was widening, were years of considerable expansion of world trade and of growing European integration. Between 1860 and 1870 European intra-trade (that is, the proportion of European countries' foreign trade directed at other European countries) grew from about 59.5 per cent to 65 per cent. Between 1846 and 1859 the volume of Europe's exports increased by 6.1 per cent per annum. The free-traders pointed to this rapid increase in trade flows as another indication of the need to break down further the barriers to trade, communications and transactions.

Referring to the ideology accompanying this free trade wave inspired by Cobden, James Joll writes:

> In the decade after Cobden's death in 1865 the liberals of Europe regarded his doctrines as axiomatic; and belief in free trade was as essential a part of liberal ideology as belief in national self-determination. (Joll 1973, p. 35)

In retrospect, perhaps the greatest event in the history of the first era of globalisation was the sudden entry of Japan into the global economy under the threat of US Commodore Matthew C. Perry's squadron of black ships in Uraga Bay in 1853 and Edo Bay (now Tokyo) in 1854. Following the treaty of Kanagawa (1854) Japan switched from virtual autarky to free trade in 1858. The domestic prices of Japan's principal exports, silk and tea, rose by 26 per cent and 50 per cent in real terms and the prices of importables fell equally sharply towards world market levels (on average by 39 per cent, again in real terms). By 1863, Japan's foreign trade had risen 70 times to reach 7 per cent of GNP.[5]

8.2 THE RETURN TO PROTECTIONISM: 1880s–1890s

On 12 July 1879 the German Reichstag voted by a majority of 186 to 160 to adopt a new Tariff Act which restored iron and steel duties and introduced a 2-mark levy on wheat, oats and rye. This was after 14 years of relative free trade. In 1881 the French National Assembly adopted a moderate tariff measure which afforded some protection to industry followed by further help for agriculture (sugar in 1884, grains and meats in 1885 and 1887), culminating in the comprehensive Méline tariff of 1892 which provided for broad protective cover for both industry and agriculture. The Méline tariff was the result of compromises between protectionists and free-traders; thus, a blend of free trade and protection. The tariff's two-faced nature was reflected in its structure: 'the minimum-maximum system in essence combined the protectionists' general tariff and the free-traders' conventional tariff. It was reflected even more in the schedule of duties. The Méline tariff effected an overall shift toward protection relative to the conventional duties in operation from 1860 to 1892 but did not entail an increase in all duties . . . By and large, the new schedule of duties struck a balance between what the protectionists wanted . . . and what the free traders wanted' (Smith 1980, pp. 209–10).

Why this turn-round in trade policy after the low-tariff era of the 1850s and 1860s? Many factors contributed to the return of protectionism. The root cause was the grain invasion of Europe, that is, the flood of North American grains which lowered European grain prices from the mid-1870s. Superimposed on that was the world slide into a dip of the Kondratieff cycle, that is, a long downswing in prices, characterised by some writers as the 'Great Depression' which lasted some twenty years. The grain invasion led to an agricultural depression in Europe and the long period of deflation adversely affected business optimism, investment, output and economic growth. To be sure, the fall in world prices, although widespread, was uneven and varied among countries according to the additional financial and industrial problems they faced, ranging from over-speculation in Germany (1873) resulting from the monetary consequences of the French indemnity payments after the Franco-Prussian war (1870–71) to bank failures in Austria, France and Great Britain (the Baring crisis). We touched upon the grain invasion in Chapter 7 in connection with the British Tariff Reform debate, and therefore move on to summarise the course of protectionism in Europe up to the outbreak of war in 1914.

The end of the free trade era in the last quarter of the nineteenth century can be interpreted as a backlash against the integration fostered by the first phase of globalisation. The rise of protectionism was an obvious defensive reaction to the unsettling changes in the economic fortunes of European industrialists, farmers and workers and the sudden, dramatic shifts in income distribution engendered by the process of globalism. Markets became interconnected as a result of improved communications by telegraphs, transatlantic cable, railways, steamships, and so on. There was a dramatic drop in transport costs around 1875 owing to faster and more reliable transport services by rail and ships. The integration of capital markets and the swifter processing of commercial information and increased international flow of goods made economies more open to the transmission of business cycles.

The unsettling nature of the interconnected world that caused immediate bewilderment and resentment was, of course, the sharply falling grain prices faced by European agriculture from the end of the 1870s. In addition to the pressures from outside, governments were presented with new domestic problems arising from the ills of industrial society, a rapidly growing urban population, the stirrings of labour unrest after the boom years, particularly when attempts were made to cut wages. State intervention in economic and social affairs (for example, provision of compulsory education, social welfare schemes, and so on) became more acceptable but involved extra government expenditure which, when added to growing military spending, strained government budgets everywhere.

The change in the economic climate and the practical experience of these varied economic difficulties 'led to the questioning of the principles of liberal economic doctrine and to the abandonment by many liberals, when their own economic interests were threatened, of free trade as an item in their programme' (Joll 1973, p. 36). Exporters in Europe (both industrial and agricultural) in alliance with the ideological liberals were behind the reforms that ushered in free trade in the 1850s. But, two decades later, the reversal of fortunes for some and the unwelcome changes forced on others built up powerful pressures which led to the widespread reversal of free trade policies in the late 1870s to 1890s. Low tariffs had not brought the benefits (or 'payoffs') which had been expected of them. The plight of industry was the same in many parts of Europe. Massive investment in new factories, plant and equipment as well as expansion of existing production facilities during the boom years of the 1850s and 1860s created the effects of a typical investment cycle: the bunching of investments in the race to make profits, leading to over-capacity and a squeeze on profit margins. The rate of return on investment falls, investment spending tapers off and eventually ceases. The end result, though, is that aggregate demand falls and firms that expanded during the boom years were left with excess capacity – idle factories closed for want of customers for their output.

In general, the triumph of the new protectionism was the result of coalitions between agricultural interests and industry. In Germany, for instance, the agricultural estate owners of Prussia east of the Elbe, already disillusioned by the slow growth of wheat sales in Great Britain, were then hit by imports of cheap grain from overseas. The feeling of grievance was compounded by the fact that they had agreed to the total abolition of tariff protection for grain which took place by 1865.

As for industry, some sections of it, the import-competing branches most obviously, had never been convinced of the advantages of free trade. However, heavy industry accommodated itself to reductions in iron and steel tariffs (1873) and the complete abolition of the pig-iron tariff in 1877. At any rate, in 1879 the altered economic conditions prompted the famous alliance or 'marriage of rye and iron' (that is, the political compact between the Junkers and the iron magnates) which was backed by Bismarck, who added his own call for protective tariffs to safeguard German trade. The change of policy was signalled by the resignation of Rudolf von Delbrück, the free trade Prussian minister and chief architect of German economic policy. This policy shift culminated in the Tariff Act of 1879 which, as we noted, marked the end of the free trade era. The united stand on protection between industry and agriculture was strengthened further in the following years (for example, in 1885 and 1887 when tariffs were further increased – the grain duty was raised to 5 marks), although industrial tariffs remained virtually constant. The electrical and chemical industries attempted to stem the protectionist tide in the 1880s by campaigning for the need to regain and expand export markets – perhaps fearful of foreign, particularly American retaliation.

France followed Germany's lead down the road to protection in 1881 as the price of grain kept falling and increasing the pressure for agricultural protection. Protectionist groups in manufacturing industry seized the chance to unite with the farmers' unions in securing tariffs equal to the level granted to agriculture. Agricultural duties were further raised in 1885 and 1887; and in 1892 these tariff changes were consolidated in the comprehensive Méline tariff which remained the basis of French tariff regulation until the 1960s. The reason why the Méline tariff remained in force so long was that it embodied an 'accommodation of interests' which served to bolster and consolidate the capitalist system in France, according to Michael Smith (1980): 'First, it eliminated . . . the split over economic policy between the commercial and industrial wings of the capitalist bourgeoisie and thereby allowed them to close ranks to meet effectively the challenge to "their" Republic emanating from the Left and Right. Second, it restored and perpetuated peasant support for an essentially bourgeois Republic by accommodating the peasants' demand for a return to agricultural protection' (Smith 1980, p. 24). Italy, which had low tariff rates in 1878, became thoroughly protectionist in outlook by the 1890s and Russia reverted to a highly protectionist tariff profile, also by the 1890s. Notable exceptions to the protectionist trend were Holland, Denmark and Switzerland.

In an interesting recent quantitative assessment of the impact of the grain invasion on European countries, using both econometric and simulation techniques, Kevin O'Rourke finds that cheap grain produced different shocks in different countries which explains the differing political responses to the crisis, as described above (O'Rourke 1997, pp. 775–801). An early attempt to explain tariff responses to the European grain invasion was by Charles Kindleberger using a socio-political frame of reference (Kindleberger 1951). He implicitly assumed that all European countries experienced the same shock and that identical price shocks had the same impact on income distribution. O'Rourke, however, found that things were not so clear cut. In fact, the evidence revealed that the severity of the globalisation (price) shock varied from country to country and, depending on the structure of production and trade, these price changes had very different effects on income distribution across countries. O'Rourke was therefore able to present a more realistic, richer picture of the diversity of political responses. In exploring the impact of the globalisation shock (the grain invasion), O'Rourke, to begin with, directs his focus on the grain market and then examines the extent to which protection succeeded in insulating economies from the international commodity market shock. As examples of the differential impacts of the price shocks, we are told that over the period 1870–1913 real grain prices fell less (that is, by only 10 per cent) in traditional grain-exporting countries like Denmark than they did in grain-importing countries like Great Britain – in the latter country real cereal prices fell by 29 per cent and agricultural rents collapsed (declining by over 40 per cent). In Germany land prices were hardly affected and remained roughly the same. Since grain prices fell less in Denmark, land values in Denmark declined only 4 or 5 per cent. At one extreme, Danish and British grain prices converged dramatically while German prices did not – with French and Swedish prices falling somewhere in between. While protection limited the forces making for commodity price convergence, it also hindered convergence between Western Europe and Eastern European granaries (that is, Ukraine). In fact, wheat prices actually diverged between Ukraine and Sweden, Germany and France. As O'Rourke observed: 'Globalization was not a universal phenomenon, even during the comparatively liberal late nineteenth century' (O'Rourke 1997, p. 784). The income-distribution consequences thrown up by the empirical findings are interpreted in terms of the simple Heckscher–Ohlin trade model and the sector-specific factors model. Cheap grain benefited British capital and labour, whereas in countries like France it hurt labour as well as farmers. In Britain (a net importer of food), urban real wages increased by 5 to 6 per cent, since the positive cost-of-living effect of cheap food outweighed the negative labour-demand (or employment) effects stemming from the loss of agricultural jobs, that is, nominal wages might have fallen, but food prices fell even more. Labour would not have gained from free trade in most other parts of Europe (for example, France, Sweden, Germany) since, among other things, agriculture was a much bigger employer, so that the employment effects (the nominal wage) dominated the consumption effects (the cost of living). By 1871 agriculture accounted for only 23 per cent of the British labour force as compared with 68 per cent in Sweden and 50 per cent in France. Consequently, in countries where agriculture loomed large as a proportion of GDP or of total employment, cheap grain lowered workers' cost of living but reduced the demand for agricultural labour and nominal wages fell quite sharply. Where agriculture was a minor employer of labour nominal wages fell only marginally. Such differences may partly explain why Denmark and Great Britain held on to free trade while the French and Germans protected their agriculture. Danish farmers diversified and found their special niche in dairy farming. Globalisation raised the prices of Danish animal products exported to the British market. Denmark therefore had no incentive to impose tariffs on agriculture. Tariffs protected domestic farmers in France, Germany and Sweden, but even so, wheat price convergence on the United States was impressive. Wheat prices in all three countries fell in real terms by roughly 20 per cent (O'Rourke 1997, p. 785). Where tariffs were high enough, they drove a wedge between domestic prices and world prices and therefore to that extent protected agricultural incomes in the protectionist countries. O'Rourke sums up his findings as being 'consistent with an interest-based account of trade policy formation in late nineteenth-century Europe' (O'Rourke 1997, p. 799).

In considering this phase of protectionism during the last quarter of the nineteenth century, one must be careful not to read too much into the large absolute increases in nominal tariff rates registered in the tariff schedules of some countries. One has to be alert to the fact that a rise in nominal tariff levels does not correspond exactly to an increase in the real incidence of protection. In comparing the degree of protection among countries, the use of a simple unweighted averaging of nominal tariff rates can be misleading, since such a measure does not allow for differences in the structure of protection across industries or sectors. In addition, it gives inordinate weight to obscure products and there is a strong upward bias due to the fact that highly protected industries usually have very detailed product breakdowns of dutiable items ('tariff lines'). Only if one country's tariff is uniformly lower on every single item than the other can one confidently conclude that it has the less restrictive tariff structure. Similarly, comparison would be unambiguous if each country had only one tariff rate (for example, 10 per cent) that is applied to all goods entering a country. Weighting the tariff data, however, runs up against the question of on what the weighting should be based. There are various theoretical or ideal weighting methods, one such being weighting the tariff schedule with weights equal to the amount of each product a country would import under free trade; but free trade weights are unavailable since they are not observable in the real world. Other weighting approaches include weighting by shares of world imports and the use of various fixed weights. On account of their simplicity and the ready availability of data, researchers frequently use as a proxy for the height of a country's average tariff one of two measures – the ratio of total tariff revenues to the value of total dutiable imports (that is, weighting by a product's share in a country's own imports) or the ratio of tariff revenues to total imports calculated on an annual basis. Tariff revenue as a share of dutiable imports is a downward-biased indicator of tariff levels, however. As tariffs on a particular commodity increase, the weight of that commodity in the overall index declines. Imports subject to high or prohibitive tariffs receive little or no weight in the index, while goods with low duties have relatively higher weights. Consumers substitute away from commodities subject to higher duties, and of course no revenue is collected in the case of a prohibitively high tariff which therefore carries zero weight. Here we encounter the same index-number problem that arises with the use of a simple unweighted average of nominal tariffs. Average tariff calculations based on dutiable imports are almost always higher than those based on total imports since a proportion of goods imported into a country are assessed no duties, that is, those that enter duty free. Over periods in which tariff rates are adjusted, the changing composition of imports introduces some additional bias. Despite the bias, many studies have used tariff revenues as a share of dutiable imports to measure the height of a country's average tariff. Such a measure gives a reasonable indication of the degree of protection. However, in historical contexts, there are two further problems associated with the average tariff index:

1. Many tariffs were raised for revenue purposes and were not necessarily or directly protective (that is, they did not restrict trade), for example, British duties on tobacco. Very often these revenue tariffs were concentrated on a very narrow range of commodities. Thus in 1840, of the 720 dutiable (and protected) articles, only 17 produced 94.5 per cent of total tariff revenue. If these revenue duties were not included in low-tariff countries like Great Britain and Denmark their calculated average tariffs would be much lower. On the other hand, in some few cases, countries occasionally resorted to quotas and export subsidies (for example, Germany). Of course, the revenue-raising and protective purposes of tariffs conflict: if tariffs are effective in keeping out competitive goods, they bring in little revenue; if they bring in revenue, it means that they are not keeping out competitive goods.

2. Many tariffs were used as bargaining counters in trade negotiations. Before entering into commercial negotiations countries armed themselves with high tariffs which added 'padding' to their tariffs for bargaining purposes. Thus the raising of tariffs was frequently followed by commercial treaties which cancelled their effects. An example of this was the new Swiss tariff schedule of 1890–91 constructed in advance of tariff bargaining with France.

An additional complication to note when interpreting late-nineteenth-century tariffs is that nearly all tariffs in 1879–1914 were specific duties (for example, $2 per ton) and not *ad valorem*, probably because they were easier to collect. However, specific duties imply changes in the incidence of protection when import prices change, for example, in a period of deflation (or falling world prices) the protectionist incidence of such duties tends to increase. For instance, during the period 1874–8 import prices fell by about 40 per cent; the prevalence of specific duties therefore increased the burden of the tariff. Researchers usually convert specific duties to their *ad valorem* equivalents by dividing the specific tariff by a notional world price, set equal to the domestic price *minus* the specific tariff.

Summarising his extensive research in the empirical investigation of tariffs and growth in the nineteenth century, Forrest Capie states: 'This measure [the ratio of duties to imports] reveals relatively little change across the period. The direction is unmistakably upward but its extent is not always large' (Capie 1994, p. 36). By this measure, he finds that French duties increased from 5 per cent to 8 per cent, German duties from 6 per cent to 8 per cent and Italian duties rose from 8 per cent to 10 per cent – hardly stratospheric heights (Capie 1994, p. 36).

This research also indicates that the late nineteenth century in Europe was a period when import duty revenues fell as a proportion of total imports and the ratio of total imports to total output or GDP increased – this latter being taken as a crude index of the degree of 'openness' of these economies. Openness measures are meant to indicate whether a country's commercial policy tends towards free trade or protection. But since there is no generally agreed index of the degree of openness of a nation's trade, the problems of measuring the degree of protection and interpreting the findings of empirical work remain largely unresolved. But these findings of Capie are certainly surprising in view of the marked increase in nominal tariffs during the period and the general perception that it was also a time of 'high protection'.

What was the connection between tariffs and growth during this so-called 'high protection' period? Did tariffs hinder or promote growth? Now, there has always been an impressionistic view that tariffs must have been good for growth, related to the economic development of the United States and Germany – countries which adopted protectionist policies but experienced strong growth. The link between tariffs and growth in the late nineteenth century was not systematically investigated on a quantitative basis until Paul Bairoch's pioneering work reported in 1972 and 1976, which he also summarised in Bairoch (1993). Bairoch compared aggregate growth rates in 'free trade' and 'protectionist' periods for the major European countries and concluded that trade liberalisation was harmful for economic growth, whereas the protectionist periods were associated with faster growth in nearly all countries investigated. He writes: 'in all countries (except Italy) the introduction of protectionist measures resulted in a distinct acceleration in economic growth during the first ten years following a change in policy . . . Furthermore, in Continental Europe the rate of growth reached its peak at the time all countries strengthened their protectionism' (Bairoch 1993, p. 50).

In contrast to Bairoch's finding of a positive relationship between tariffs and late-nineteenth-century European growth, Capie could find no such beneficial effects of tariffs from his work comparing decadal data on the growth of GDP with average tariff levels, as well as from results of country-by-country regressions of growth rates on tariffs for Germany, Italy, Great Britain and Russia. Capie maintains there is no evidence that tariffs boosted growth: 'On the evidence available, tariffs did not improve economic performance in any significant way in the nineteenth or twentieth century' (Capie 1994, p. 94). As noted above, average tariffs (measured by the ratio of duties to imports) were relatively low and their impact was small, weak and even perverse; hence Capie draws the conclusion: 'Protection does not appear to have been sufficiently high to make any significant impact on performance' (Capie 1983, p. 9). Recently, new research has appeared which seems to put the matter beyond doubt. In an impressive econometric exercise, Kevin O'Rourke (2000) estimates the correlation between tariffs and growth (in the late nineteenth century) in the context of two types of growth convergence equations and a factor accumulation model for a panel of ten countries (Australia, Canada, Denmark, France, Germany, Italy, Norway, Sweden, the United Kingdom and the United States) between 1875 and 1914 and finds that tariffs were positively correlated with growth during this period. His data set includes updated purchasing-power parity (PPP) adjusted GDP data consistent across countries and across time, agricultural endowments, school enrolments, capital stocks, average tariff rates,and so on. Average tariffs are conventionally defined as the ratio of customs duties to total imports. Reporting his results, which may come as a surprise to some, O'Rourke himself admits: 'Clearly my prior [assumption] that tariffs should be negatively correlated with growth, is not supported by the data. The data are far more comfortable with the hypothesis that tariffs boosted late 19th century growth' (O'Rourke 2000, p. 468). He goes on to examine various other factors which could be driving the results, but rules them out, in particular the one likely causation route, namely from growth to tariffs. On this he concludes that there is no evidence that the growth effects of tariffs 'are solely due to their impact during recessions' (O'Rourke 2000, p. 472). If tariffs boosted growth it was not only due to the positive effects of tariffs during recessions.

O'Rourke's results confirm the profile of European tariffs reported by Capie, that is, that they ranged from 5.1 per cent in Great Britain to 9.9 per cent for Italy. Also, the results support Bairoch's finding, namely that tariffs were positively associated with growth in late-nineteenth-century Europe. Douglas Irwin (2002) argues that the tariff-growth correlation be interpreted with great care and that it should not be viewed as evidence that protectionist policies were successful during the late nineteenth century. He disputes any casual relationship between tariffs (or trade policy, generally) and economic growth on two grounds: (1) that the two most rapidly expanding, high-tariff countries of the period (1870–1913) – Argentina and Canada – grew because 'capital imports helped stimulate export-led growth in agricultural-staples products, not because of protectionist trade policies'; (2) that many labour-scarce and land-abundant countries imposed high tariffs for revenue purposes (Irwin 2002, p. 165).

But those countries had exceptionally favourable prospects for economic growth quite independently of the influence of tariffs. The link between higher tariffs and higher growth could therefore be spurious and not causal. Briefly, Irwin's point is that the relationship between trade policy and economic performance is 'a complicated issue that cannot be inferred from a simple correlation alone' (Irwin 2002, p. 167). Irwin is probably correct here. Cross-country correlations are liable to produce mixed evidence as to the tariff-growth connection, depending on the sample of countries, the presence of outliers, the tariff measures used, and so on. The best evidence is perhaps to be found in detailed country-studies.

8.3   THE GREAT DEPRESSION

In this section we deal with the interwar Depression. To most people, the interwar years were the 'Dark Ages' in modern economic history; not in terms of the paucity of data, information and details about what actually took place, but as a characterisation of the behaviour of states in response to the succession of economic and political crises ('shocks') that buffeted the international system. For those who entertain a fond, but mythical image of a harmonious, free trade, pre-1914 world, the descent into atavistic mercantilism and the excesses of aggressive protectionism which went with it, deserves the epithet 'Dark Ages'. Free-traders and other defenders of an 'open' international trading system (that is, 'globalism') often raise the bogey of protectionism represented by the US Smoot–Hawley tariff (1930), often resurrected to scare policymakers and the public about the dangers of giving in to protectionist pressures and the log-rolling that goes with it when international trade disputes occur, for example, the 2002 dispute over steel between the USA and the EU.

Equally, on the monetary side, monetary historians and financial experts routinely justify expansionary monetary measures to stave off 'melt-down' in latter-day international financial crises (for example, the 1987 world-wide stock market crash and the Asian currency crisis of 1998) by rhetorical appeals and reference to the 1930s slump. In the section on 'Keynes and Protection' we discuss the impact of the slump on the British economy and the arguments over the appropriate response to the crisis. Here we review more generally the impact on, and the commercial policy responses of the other principal trading countries.

The economic highlights of the interwar years are events and developments like the Wall Street crash (24 October 1929) and the descent into slump, the US Smoot–Hawley tariff (1930), the British return to protectionism (1932) and the collapse of world trade. Each of these have been the subject of exhaustive studies and cannot therefore be easily summarised. Here we offer only an impressionistic survey relevant to our interest in the trade policy developments of the period which can conveniently be divided into two phases: the years before the 1929 Wall Street financial crash and the subsequent period up to the eve of the Second World War in 1939.

Starting with the reconstruction period immediately after the war, the tasks were truly Herculean. The problems to be faced and obstacles to be overcome included the following: (1) Chronic economic instability arising from gyrating exchange rates inviting calls for neutralising changes in tariff rates; (2) war debts; (3) the creation of new states, additional currencies, more customs frontiers; (4) changing trade patterns resulting from wartime disruption of supplies to overseas customers and the desire of many newly-created states to stimulate industrial development through protection; and (5) the isolationism of the United States: the US Senate refused to ratify the Treaty of Versailles and the country declined to join the League of Nations.

Efforts to shorten the reconstruction period (1920–25) were hampered by the widespread floating of exchange rates and consequent currency instability (not only in countries that experienced hyperinflation). Exchange-rate fluctuations increased the demand for protection and resulted in offsetting increases in tariffs through countervailing duties, or (as in France) by the

application of 'coefficients' to the tariff schedules. During the war, governments took extraordinary steps to keep exchange rates from deviating too
far from their prewar parities. As a consequence, the officially frozen
exchange rates lost all touch with reality in respect of the enormous changes
in economic relationships among countries, in particular the differential
changes in the purchasing power of national currencies: in 1919 wholesale
prices were twice as high in the United States as they were in 1913; in Britain
they were two-and-a-half times as high; in France they were more than three
times as high; and in Germany they were eight times as high. These were just
some of the large discrepancies in the movements of price levels in different
countries. But once the artificial pegging of exchange rates was discontin-
ued, inflationary pressures led to the depreciation of most European currencies. Austria, Germany, Hungary and Poland failed to bring inflation
under control and their currencies became worthless. New monetary units
had to be introduced in these countries before hyperinflation could be
brought under control and new parities established. International trade was
severely disrupted or distorted by controls and uncertainties which, added
to the enormous disparities in prices and costs among countries, produced
significant changes in the underlying determinants of comparative advantage and the 'barter' equilibrium in international trade.

In Eastern and Central Europe, the carving up of new states out of old
empires subjected the balance of payments of those states to enormous
strains. Germany and a few countries in Eastern Europe retained import
controls set up during the war. In 1920 Europe had eight new economic territories, thirteen new currencies and 12000 miles of extra tariff frontiers
(often cutting across well-established commercial links). Some of these new
states, like Czechoslovakia and Hungary, embarked on a strategy of import
substitution to speed up their industrialisation. This involved the imposition of high tariffs on import-competing manufactured goods but low
tariffs on raw materials and machine tools.

European exporters lost overseas markets in Latin America and Asia due
to the wartime disruption of supplies. The importing countries turned to
other regional suppliers. Japan, for instance, more than doubled the value
of its exports of manufactures between 1913 and 1929 and replaced Britain
as the principal supplier of manufactured goods to India after the war. The
Poles reoriented their export trade away from the Soviet Union and found
new outlets in Western Europe and elsewhere.

Inter-Allied war debts, international financial flows and reparations
dominated the practice of diplomacy. In 1921 inter-Allied war debts
amounted to $26.5 billion. The United States and Great Britain were the
major creditors, with France the largest debtor. France emerged from the
war owing $4 billion to the United States and $3 billion to Great Britain.

Britain incurred a $4.7 billion war debt to the United States, but was owed $11.1 billion by the other Allies. Britain would repay the United States so long as Britain was repaid by France, which in turn was counting on reparations owed by Germany. Thus emerged the 'reparations/war debt tangle' – the curious debt triangle involving Germany, the European Allies and the United States. The reparation problem in particular bedevilled international relations and impeded efforts to find a cooperative solution to Europe's financial and trade problems.

The United States insisted on payment in gold or dollars for the $10 billion European debt. But the ability of the Europeans to effect payments (in the absence of substantial American loans) was severely circumscribed by the existence of a massive American trade surplus, a consequent dollar shortage and the protectionist Fordney–McCumber tariff of 1922. There was bitter resentment at the size of the debt the Allies owed the United States, a country which was scathingly described as the only one to have made a profit out of the war. The Great War transformed the United States from a net debtor to a net foreign creditor. Unlike Great Britain before 1914, the United States did not provide a ready market for debtor exports and therefore failed in its responsibility as an international creditor. Countries in debt to the United States – particularly France, Italy and Belgium – hoped that the payment of reparations would offset their American debt; but relief only came with the sudden surge (1924) of American investments in Central and South-Eastern Europe (including the $100 million government-to-government Dawes loan to Germany).

Some modern commentators see little merit in the European debtors' argument that they encountered insurmountable obstacles in the repayment of debt to the United States. Kindleberger, for instance, writes about the Europeans' view 'now regarded as fallacious since the macroeconomic impact effects of tariffs on the balance of payments are typically reversed, wholly or in large part by the income changes which they generate' (Kindleberger 1989, p. 171). Quite so! It was fallacious only in the sense that the correct solution to what was, in effect, a 'transfer problem' was discovered only in the late 1920s and early 1930s during the famous debate between Keynes and Ohlin over German reparations. But even so, the theoretical solution in terms of income changes (rather than principally in terms of price changes) effecting a smooth and full transfer of debt obligations through automatic balance-of-payments adjustments rested on assumptions relating to open product markets and an unimpeded gold standard (or other fixed-exchange systems). These conditions did not prevail in the case of the United States and therefore the automatic income–expenditure adjustment mechanism was not available to the Europeans to enable them to effect the real transfer payment to the United

States. The difficulty was that, apart from the high tariffs which partially closed American markets, the US Federal Reserve engaged in a policy of gold sterilisation which prevented reserve flows from affecting US money supplies, and hence US incomes – the effects of which did not come into play, and therefore Kindleberger is wrong in his rejection of the validity of the European complaint.

The network of trade treaties lapsed during the war, and was not restored under their original terms when peace came and reconstruction efforts began. Instead, treaties were renegotiated, providing the opportunity for most countries to raise duty rates. Three World Economic Conferences (1927, 1929 and 1930) sponsored by the League of Nations called upon countries to get rid of their non-tariff barriers (for example, quotas) and to put a stop to further increases in tariff levels. But as modern commentators often point out, nothing was done; and in that sense, these conferences all failed. This observation is, however, not strictly accurate. The recommendations of the 1927 Conference were adopted in some measure, to the extent that customs duties were lowered in almost all developed countries and remained relatively low until 1929–30 (Bairoch 1991, p. 4). For instance, the number of European tariff revisions declined from 10 in 1927 to 5 in 1928 and only 2 in 1929. In the latter year, the German industrial tariff was reduced and the Franco-German commercial agreement of August 1929 included many rate reductions that were passed on via MFN clauses. But it is true that the lack of positive incentives for cooperative behaviour in the international trading system led to the gradual collapse of tariff negotiations during the 1920s. The League of Nations never managed to get countries to actually enter into negotiations with the aim of liberalising world trade from high tariffs. The reasons for failure were quite obvious: (1) the reluctance of countries in a protectionist environment and a world of steady deflation to contemplate any meaningful lowering of their barriers to trade through cooperative unconditional MFN agreements; and (2) the unwillingness of the United States to offer reciprocal concessions when negotiating MFN treaties while at the same time demanding the full MFN benefits normally accorded to third parties, namely the benefits from the tariff concessions made between pairs of other trading partners.

The difficulty was that the United States regarded its tariff levels as autonomous, that is, non-negotiable. Tariff rates would not be reduced in exchange for concessions from other countries. If countries refused to offer unconditional MFN treatment to US exports, the Fordney–McCumber tariff legislation empowered the president to retaliate with duties of up to 50 per cent against such countries. By this tactic the United States did obtain tariff concessions from some countries without offering equivalent concessions (secured through some 29 unconditional treaties by 1929). Such 'free-riding' behaviour was clearly unhelpful and did not encourage other countries to negotiate bilateral tariff reductions, since the benefits would automatically be passed on to third-party countries that had made no concessions. The result was a breakdown of the international trade-negotiating system due to the prevalence of such free-riding behaviour – certainly by the time of the US Smoot–Hawley tariff (1930).

Coinciding roughly with the Wall Street crash on 24 October 1929 and the onset of the depression, US legislators and lobby groups debated (over a two-year period) a tariff bill which became law on 17 June 1930 and known ever since as the infamous Smoot–Hawley Tariff Act. President Hoover ignored a petition signed by 1028 economists and declined to exercise his veto. Smoot–Hawley is a classic example of the success of interest-group lobbying through a political process that encouraged, or at any rate, allowed log-rolling on a massive scale. This was traditional behaviour among Congressmen who provided made-to-measure tariffs for their constituents, but it was a political process of tariff-making which could produce spectacular results that no one might have intended, as in this highly contentious case. Log-rolling was the time-honoured system whereby Congressional legislators promised to vote in favour of protecting industries in other states or districts in return for votes to protect the industries and other economic interests of their own states – 'I'll vote for your tariff if you vote for mine'. The original purpose of the tariff bill was to provide some relief and assistance to American farmers in the face of falling food prices. But against the background of the stock market crash, early signs of a slide into recession, and the desire to benefit special interests, the log-rolling avalanche produced a tariff bill that sharply increased the level of protection all round, including a large general rise in tariffs on manufactures.

The Act raised the average duty on manufactured imports to 60 per cent and froze foreign products out of the American market. Tariffs were raised on over 12000 products. The average duty was in fact near the all-time high of 62 per cent reached in 1830. The impact was immediate and devastating. Within six months 25 nations took retaliatory action. The mutual increases in protection cancelled each other out, and world trade collapsed by 25 per cent. The slide gathered impetus in the following months (falling a further 25 per cent), so that over three years (1929–32) the real value of world trade fell by over 60 per cent – a decline of the order of 35 per cent in volume terms. The world plunged into deep depression (1929–32). The decline in world trade following the depression is illustrated below in a diagram designed by Charles Kindleberger:

The US economy collapsed. GDP fell by 35 per cent and unemployment

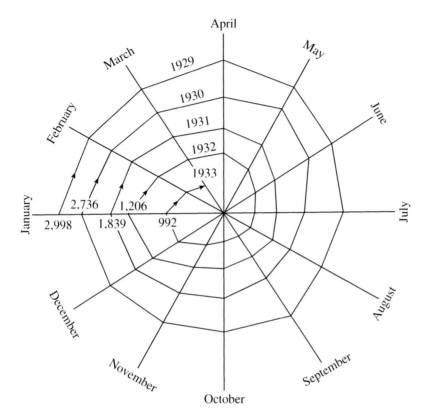

Source: S. Husted/M. Melvin, *International Economics*, 5th edition (figure 6.10 from page 170). © 2001 Addison Wesley. Reprinted by permission of Pearson Education, Inc.

Figure 8.1 The contracting spiral of world trade, January 1929–March 1933

rose to 14 million or 25 per cent of trade union membership. By comparison, the unemployment rate in the previous decade was under 5 per cent – a decade popularly known as the 'Roaring Twenties' when earnings, productivity, stock market prices, profits, GNP and employment soared and the balance of payments was strong. The disintegration of the world economy can be briefly told. Britain's abandonment of the gold standard in September 1931 was followed by the devaluation of the US dollar (by 40.9 per cent in terms of gold) in 1933–4 and the 'gold bloc' currencies in 1936, that is, the currencies of France, Switzerland, the Netherlands and Poland. The rise of the United States to the status of a monetary superpower killed the gold standard. The New Deal legislation in the 1930s converted the United

States from the gold-exchange standard to a managed (or discretionary) fiduciary standard with gold treated just like a commodity, the price of which was fixed by an official support programme. At the new official price of gold, $35 an ounce, the United States began attracting large quantities of gold from abroad which intensified the deflationary pressure on countries remaining on the gold standard – ultimately forcing them off gold.

As the international monetary system collapsed, the world economy fragmented into three competing and hostile blocs: (1) the sterling bloc, (2) the dollar bloc, and (3) the gold bloc, organised around Great Britain, the United States and France, respectively. Trade became bilateral or was increasingly confined to the economic blocs. Germany and several Eastern European countries turned to autarky and imposed exchange controls. The United Kingdom relied upon the system of Imperial Preference introduced at the Commonwealth Conference in Ottawa (August 1932). The United States retreated once again into 'isolationism' and Japan resorted to 'co-prosperity' in South East Asia. By the third quarter of 1932 the trade of European countries had fallen below 40 per cent of its 1929 level. Balance of payments restrictions appeared on a massive scale and in a variety of forms. International capital flows dried up. Protectionism and beggar-thy-neighbour policies flourished, as country after country tried to stimulate their domestic economies by exporting unemployment through competitive devaluations, undervalued currencies and import and exchange controls – at least up to the mid-1930s. At that time, of course, Keynes published his *General Theory* which was to have a profound influence on professional (and public) perceptions of the macroeconomic functioning of a modern capitalist economy, hence on the monetary aspects of international economics.

In some quarters the view is entertained that increased protectionism in the interwar years must share part of the blame for the 1930s depression. Admittedly a minority academic view which still colours popular opinion, it fails to recognise a fundamental difference in trade history between the 1920s and the 1930s. Were the interwar years up to the financial crisis of 1929 a period of increasing protectionism? Did the implementation of the Smoot–Hawley tariff and the foreign reaction to it (that is, regionalism, increased trade barriers, and so on) materially contribute to the depression and the collapse of world trade?

In answer to the first question reference can be made to an oft-quoted calculation which put the weighted average of customs duties on manufactures in Europe as 24.6 per cent in 1913 and 24.9 per cent in 1927 (Liepmann, quoted in Bairoch 1991, p. 4). This figure for the average level of tariffs in 1927 masks variations across countries and commodities, but it clearly suggests that protection did not increase in the 1920s. There was definitely a brief trend towards more liberal trade measures following the successful stabilisation and then restoration of gold convertibility of the major European currencies during 1925–9 as countries came on to the new gold-exchange standard. Referring to this trend, Bairoch points out: 'Therefore, it is incorrect to consider that the 1929 crisis was preceded by increased tariff levels' (Bairoch 1991, p. 4).

Although not an ideal indicator of the trend of protectionist trade barriers, the index movement over time in the volume of world exports is nevertheless widely used. For what it is worth, it shows a decidedly upward trend over the 1924–9 period during which the volume of world exports increased at an annual rate of 6 per cent – 'a rate of expansion that was unprecedented' (Bairoch 1991, p. 5). The prewar level was reached in 1924 until the peak in activity in 1929. Indeed, in that decade, world exports grew more rapidly than output. As calculated by the League of Nations, world trade grew at an annual rate of 4.8 per cent, but the value of trade grew at the much slower rate of 1.6 per cent, obviously reflecting the deflationary trend of the period (James 2001, p. 105).

The hiatus in the link between rising protectionism on the one hand and the depression on the other occurred during 1929–30 when the Smoot–Hawley tariff almost coincided with the 1929 financial crisis.

The real value of world trade fell over 60 per cent between 1929 and 1932, a decline of the order of 35 per cent in volume terms. There was some improvement after 1932; and although by 1938 real output was 15 per cent higher than in 1929, world export volume was roughly 15 per cent below where it stood in 1929. Despite the gradual rise in world exports, particularly after 1934, they did not return to their 1929 level until 1942. Since major 'shocks' converged on the world economy almost simultaneously it is unclear what the precise links were connecting trade flows, increased trade barriers (for example, Smoot–Hawley and the foreign reaction to it) and the depression. Perroni and Whalley (1996) observe that despite extensive discussion of the 1930s in the literature, 'there is a surprising degree of ambiguity as to what actually happened . . . and what was the role of trade policies' (Perroni and Whalley 1996, p. 60). It is certain, however, that the collapse of world trade was not simply the result of increased protectionism as represented by the Smoot–Hawley tariff and the European retaliatory responses to it. The depression was already well under way when Smoot–Hawley was implemented. In fact, the slump had deepened even before the passage of the Tariff Act. Macroeconomic principles suggest that (under fixed exchange rates) the direct or impact effects of tariffs are expansionary rather than contractionary. Tariff increases, by switching expenditure to domestic products, raise aggregate demand and output. But the Smoot–Hawley tariff increases could have had a contractionary effect when the retaliatory increases in foreign tariffs on US exports were taken into account. US imports did fall by more than $1.3 billion (out of a total of $4.4 billion) between 1929 and 1930 and in volume terms, imports fell by over 40 per cent in two years; but as Harold James observes, 'a great part of the decline can be explained in terms of the income effects of the depression, rather than as a consequence of the tariff itself' (James 2001, p. 121). Recent estimates by Douglas Irwin of the trade effects of Smoot–Hawley indicate that the tariff itself reduced US imports by about 4–8 per cent in the period 1930–32. However, the combination of specific duties and deflation in the early 1930s raised the effective tariff and therefore reduced imports an additional 8–10 per cent. These results were obtained from partial and general equilibrium assessments in a strictly microeconomic framework so as to concentrate on the tariff's effects in reducing US imports. Irwin summarises the implications of his results for the issue concerning the likely effects of the tariff on the depression: 'Smoot–Hawley itself appears to have been a very small direct shock to trade and therefore, it is likely, to the economy at large. The additional rise in tariffs due to deflation and higher tariffs abroad intensified the impact of Smoot–Hawley' (Irwin 1998, p. 333). It is reasonable to conclude, therefore, that the fall in income in the United States as well as in Europe (as a result of the depression) was responsible for much of the fall in world trade. Data on trends in US unemployment and tariff rates in the 1930s do not support the argument that the Smoot–Hawley tariff deepened the depression. Reviewing the evidence which showed that an essentially constant US tariff rate from 1932 was associated with rising unemployment up to at least 1938, Raveendra Batra writes: 'From all the evidence, it is ridiculous to conclude that rising tariffs caused unemployment and contributed to the Depression. If anything, the evidence suggests that tariffs generate jobs, not eliminate them' (Batra 1993, p. 151). But, could foreign retaliation against Smoot–Hawley have had a contractionary effect on the US economy which swamped the favourable, expansionary effect? Barry Eichengreen (1989) maintains, contrary to earlier belief, that only Spain clearly retaliated against the Smoot–Hawley tariff, that is, Spain was the only country where the motivation for a tariff increase was Smoot–Hawley (Eichengreen 1989, pp. 31–5). Spain objected to increased duties on grapes, oranges, corn and onions. But what about Canada's reaction to the new US tariffs on many food products, cattle, logs and timber, and so on? Canada, the largest trading partner of the United States, retaliated with substantial increases in their tariffs on American products in September 1930, following the election victory of the Conservative Party under Richard Bennett. In an empirical investigation into whether or not retaliation was indeed the reason for the Canadian tariff increases, McDonald, O'Brien and Callahan (1997) found that the 'evidence . . . is rather convincing that the Canadian tariff increases were largely acts of retaliation' and that any 'analysis of the impact of Smoot–Hawley on the course of the depression in the United States is incomplete if it does not take into account this Canadian reaction' (McDonald, O'Brien and Callahan 1997, p. 824). At least temporarily, Canada loosened its ties with the United States and strengthened those with Britain and the Empire. The US tariff reinforced the argument of those calling for the expansion of trade within the Empire through a full programme of imperial preference, the framework of which was created at the Imperial Conference in Ottawa (July–August 1932).[6]

The general conclusion, therefore, is that 1930s protectionism was not one of the initial or initiating factors in the collapse of the economic system. If anything, the tariff escalation, trade discrimination through regionalism and preferential arrangements, the series of competitive devaluations, exchange controls, barter deals, bilateral clearing arrangements, and so on, were responses to the depression. The depression itself, in the words of Michael Bordo, 'was caused by the egregious policy failure of the monetary authorities in the United States, France and other countries' (Bordo 2002, p. 52). Fundamentally, the Slump was a capitalist crisis. It spread from country to country and was therefore a generalised catastrophe springing from multiple sources or causes. The manifestation of crisis, wherever it originated, transmitted the Great Depression around the world via the gold standard policy regime. The villains of the piece must therefore be sought among the prime suspects – the gold standard, deflation and financial crises. The Great Depression occurred in an international system characterised by intrinsic instabilities and structural flaws – a system which was liable to breakdown or crisis through the adoption of misguided national monetary policies. Despite governments' legal assurances that they were committed to the gold standard, speculators never perceived the terms of the gold parities as immutable, given the inherent instabilities of the system where two reserve assets – gold and foreign exchange – circulated side by side. Speculators' behaviour became adapted to the contingencies of rapid and dramatic changes in interest rates, credit availability and price levels. The system was therefore susceptible to large and sudden inflows and outflows of short-term capital and to destabilising monetary policies. As speculators shifted funds around, motivated by doubts about the stability of reserve currencies, central banks sought to re-establish credibility by scrambling out of foreign exchange and into gold. The liquidation of foreign-exchange reserves and a deflationary switch to gold reserves was an ever-present threat. Indeed, between 1928 and 1932 the value of foreign-exchange reserves of 24 European countries fell from $2520 million to $505 million.

8.4   KEYNES AND PROTECTION

In 1923 Keynes wrote:

> We must hold to Free Trade, in its widest interpretation, as an inflexible dogma, to which no exception is admitted, wherever the decision rests with us . . . We should hold to Free Trade as a principle of international morals, and not merely as a doctrine of economic advantage. (Keynes, *CW*, XVII, p. 451)

Seven years later Keynes advised a government committee:

> My proposal is for a uniform tariff of, say, 10 per cent on all imports whatever, including food, and a bounty of the same amount on all exports whatsoever. (Keynes, *CW*, XX, pp. 416–19)

What accounted for this drastic reversal of attitude to protection vs. free trade was, of course, the worldwide 'Slump' in output and employment which followed the Wall Street crash (October 1929).

Keynes' intellectual and practical odyssey from Marshallian free trade orthodoxy to 'outlandish' protectionism and back again to the vision of an open, free-trading international system, but with in-built, depression-proof safeguards for national economic autonomy is a fascinating story. Here, we can only touch on the highlights of that saga.

Starting out as a staunch, ideologically committed believer in the virtues of free trade, the confrontation with the shock of the slump caused him to reassess the relevance of the intellectual baggage he had inherited from the safe, comfortable Victorian world of his youth. He brought to bear on the many complex problems affecting a great imperial and trading power a sharp, sensitive intelligence combined with a lively political sense.

Commencing with *Indian Currency and Finance* (1913) on the relationship between the Indian rupee and the British pound, through the twists and turns of his response to the crisis of capitalism in the 1930s, up to the wartime Anglo-American plans for a new international economic order and beyond he was a totally engaged internationalist ceaselessly seeking solutions to the world's economic ills. But his plans and remedies were always devised from a perspective that kept Britain's economic interests firmly in view. The international or globalisation element was always present in the many economic problems he faced, and he saw in all of them a common feature: how to resolve the conflict between domestic prosperity and the international economy? As constant as his solicitude for Britain's international economic interests was his abiding concern was to find an answer to the problem of domestic unemployment. However often or abruptly he might have changed his attitudes towards other issues, he never wavered over the question of unemployment. He was determined to crack the problem when it first appeared after the immediate postwar boom fizzled out and Britain experienced one of the sharpest slumps in her history (1920–21). The stagnation of the British economy in the 1920s was patently evident in a level of unemployment that hovered steadily around the 1 million mark (about 7 per cent of the working population), but then climbed to a peak of over 3 million at one point (1931) as the country joined others in the worldwide collapse of 1929–31.

Britain's economic crisis and the response to it was typical of those experienced by the principal late belligerents. The conduct of economic policy in the early interwar years was thrown into disarray as governments tried to cope with the dire monetary, fiscal, industrial and social legacy of the war – inter-allied war debts, the curious debt triangle among Germany, the European allies and the United States of which reparations was one part, swollen public-sector deficits, large stocks of inconvertible currencies, disequilibria in the balance of payments of many countries, differential changes in the purchasing power of national currencies, the loss by European exporters of overseas markets in Latin America and Asia, rigidities in internal cost structures, and so on.

Economic policy shifted from its safe moorings during the war – balanced budgets, adherence to the international gold standard and free trade. It was, however, the attempt to restore the discipline of the international financial and economic order and to get back as soon as possible to the old certainties despite the chaotic state of the world economy that led to fierce disagreements and incoherence over economic policy in many countries. Great Britain was particularly vulnerable and exposed to such tensions – the country was, after all, the 'manager' of the gold standard system, with London as the world's principal financial, gold and produce market; it was also the lone superpower, but already losing ground to the United States, a process which the war accelerated.

The restoration of prewar parities combined with reserve stringency and the undervaluation of gold throughout the 1920s contributed to worldwide deflationary pressure in the late 1920s which eventually led into the severe depression of the 1930s. Monetary restraint kept unemployment high everywhere and exercised a depressive influence on primary product prices. Instability and payments disequilibria were exacerbated by flights of capital motivated by fears of bank failures and currency devaluations.

The international payments difficulties of Great Britain resulting from the overvaluation of sterling (and undervaluation of the French franc) were relieved somewhat owing to the fact that, as a reserve centre, Britain was able to finance part of its deficit by accumulating reserve liabilities and also by attracting short-term funds through high interest rates. But London was no longer the world's leading financial centre. That position had passed to New York, and countries that were on the gold-exchange standard found themselves increasingly under the influence of US monetary policy. The interwar years, and in particular the 1920s, were the period when the transition from the sterling standard to the dollar standard was made. What undermined the attempt to revive the gold standard, however, was, apart from the misalignment of important parities, the unwillingness of several countries, in particular the United States, to allow changes in gold stocks to exert their full effects on the domestic money supply, and hence employment and prices. In deficit countries, prices did not fall in response to tight monetary policies; instead, such countries suffered deflation and unemployment. In the face of an international scramble for gold, restrictive monetary policies after 1928 and weakening confidence in the international financial system caused an enormous increase in the real value of gold which intensified the deflationary trends around the world.

This was the global economic environment in which Keynes grappled with the problem of unemployment and the general malaise of the British economy – a malaise made more intractable by rigidities in internal cost and wage structures and the ill-fated decision to prepare the ground for a return to the prewar exchange parity *vis-à-vis* gold and the US dollar through a savage deflation of internal prices brought about by the retirement of excess paper-money stocks in 1920–21. The actual return to gold at the prewar parity of $4.86 in April 1925 further increased the misery of more deflation, depression and unemployment. But despite all that severe deflationary pressure, prices and wages stubbornly resisted and were still too high relative to US levels so that sterling remained overvalued by at least 10 per cent – this of course further hampered sales of British products abroad and involved a further loss of competitiveness.

Keynes inveighed against what he called the 'deflationary bias' of the gold standard, particularly as the system functioned during the interwar years, on account of the basic asymmetry of the adjustment process noted above: most of the pressure to restore equilibrium in the balance of payments fell on the deficit countries. Noting the lack of elasticity in the social structure of wages and prices, Keynes argued that monetary contraction in deficit countries would facilitate adjustment only by causing unemployment. To insulate the British economy from the pressures of globalisation and remedy the inadequacies of the classical adjustment mechanism, some control over the balance of payments was required. Such control was necessary to ease the pressure for higher bank rates. High domestic interest rates paralysed home investment, but such rates were necessary given the tendency for overseas lending to exceed the surplus on the trade balance.

Keynes' 'flirtation' with protection (as some call it) during 1928–31 was a desperate response to the British situation just described – the stubbornly high level of unemployment and deepening industrial crisis. The rows and disagreements over protection (at least among the economists) occurred over a relatively short period (the two years 1930–31) even though at the political and popular levels protection vs. free trade had remained a contentious issue throughout the interwar period ever since the Conservative leader Stanley Baldwin's announcement at Plymouth on 25 October 1923 that protection was the only cure for unemployment.

Here we focus on the clash between Keynes and the economics establishment on the issue and the response of the policymakers.

As in all urgent national controversies where views, interests, and ideologies become polarised, so in this one (leaving aside 'interests') we can recognise a clear divergence between defenders of orthodoxy and reformers, 'Left' and 'Right', 'hardliners' and 'moderates', the iconoclasts and the dogmatists of old certainties. It was no different among the economists; indeed, when it came to policy, the differences were even sharper, more pronounced than among the public at large. Perceptions, attitudes and prejudices differ among people. Protection (or for that matter, free trade) is just as likely to draw its adherents from the 'Left' as from the 'Right'. The orthodox economists opposed expansionary monetary/fiscal measures. They wanted wage cuts to reduce costs and urged stringency in government expenditure. And, of course, they were appalled by any suggestion of protection. Keynes, on the other hand, contrived to keep an open mind and was prepared to consider any measure that would help to reduce unemployment and stimulate the economy.

Keynes' intuition was better than his current theoretical framework in his diagnosis of the ills of the British economy in the early 1930s. His intuition suggested policy advice more in keeping with the *General Theory* than with the theoretical categories of the *Treatise on Money* (1930) (Keynes, *CW*, V and VI), the book he was then engaged in writing. The latter book, with its emphasis on the 'fundamental equations' whereby macroeconomic equilibrium was determined by the saving-investment relationship via the rate of interest (rather than saving and investment being brought into equilibrium by changes in the level of output as a whole) proved incapable of shedding light on the urgent policy issues of the day.

After a series of conventional remedies or initiatives were considered by Keynes in 1930–31 and found wanting as being too slow-acting, impractical, inexpedient or ruled out by the constraints under which the British economy then operated, Keynes opted for a general revenue tariff as a pragmatic and temporary remedy for unemployment. It struck him forcibly that the free-trade arguments did not apply in a condition of large-scale unemployment and chronic weakness of the balance of trade (such as Britain was in) and made worse by the world slump, since a tariff which switches demand from foreign to home goods increases employment in home industries. That is to say, a tariff could bring about a net increase instead of a mere diversion of domestic productive resources, including labour.

The policy measures suggested by Keynes included: (1) government spending on loan-financed 'public works' projects; (2) subsidising investment in some or all industries to restore profits without reducing wages; (3) tax incentives to business; (4) industrial 'rationalisation' to raise productivity; (5) international cooperation among central banks to pursue inflationary monetary policies; and (6) devaluation of sterling against gold. He later narrowed down these proposals to three policy measures: (1) devaluation of sterling; (2) nominal wage reductions; and (3) tariffs. Of these he selected tariffs as the best practical option in the present policy circumstances. Assuming constant British money wages and costs, the tariff would tend to improve the balance of trade. The resulting surplus in the current account would increase British overseas investment which would in turn have the same positive effect on the unemployment situation as an increase in domestic investment. The export of British capital often resulted in the export of British goods (and the provision of jobs for British workers) since the money lent was usually used to purchase British capital goods. The tariff would leave sterling's international obligations to foreigners unchanged in terms of gold (Keynes, *CW*, XX, p. 296).

Maintenance of sterling's parity was essential if Britain was to 'resume the vacant financial leadership of the world' (Keynes, *CW*, IX, p. 236). He rejected devaluation on the grounds that it would undermine confidence in London's financial markets and hence reduce Britain's invisible earnings; also, it would be necessary to compensate foreign holders of short-term funds invested in London, so that no one would be a loser in terms of the foreign currency value of such investments. In addition, he was concerned about the loss that would be incurred on outstanding sterling-denominated debts. Equally, he dismissed any attempt to force down the real wage through nominal wage reductions (so as to coax employers to take on more labour) claiming that such a direct method would cause 'social injustice and violent resistance' (no doubt having in mind the General Strike of 1926), and might also be ineffective since prices might fall by an equal amount without any stimulus to jobs or output. The second point here is a rejection of the false analogy between the effects of a wage cut by a single employer and economy-wide wage reductions. Output and employment as a whole were bound to suffer from the consequent reduction in the purchasing power of wage earners in the latter case. There was the danger that it would set off an international round of competitive wage-rate reductions which, by reducing world demand even further, would deepen the slump to no country's advantage. If the disequilibrium was really caused by an excess of saving over investment, a reduction of money wages on its own would be of no avail in the restoration of equilibrium and might make matters worse. One has to recognise, he urged, that the modern labour market (characterised by rigidity and institutionalised bargaining) is not 'fluid' (money wages are not flexible): 'we get jammed at the point of un-employment' (Keynes, *CW*, XX, p. 114). The logjam in the labour market persuaded Keynes to think in terms of demand-constrained equilibrium as a feature of modern economies. He persuaded himself (and he hoped, the country) that the tariff (by raising prices) was an indirect but better way of reducing real wages towards their equilibrium level, thereby helping to clear the labour market with the minimum of social strife. Noting that the virtue of free trade is that it does bring money wages down without re-ducing real wages, 'whereas Protection is not so likely to bring down money wages, it is much more likely to bring down real wages. But the virtue of Protection is that it does the trick, whereas in present conditions Free Trade does not' (Harrod 1951, p. 427). In addition, the tariff had several impor-tant advantages:

1. It was the only policy option compatible with the maintenance of ster-ling's gold parity. Moreover, since sterling was currently overvalued (making foreign assets appear relatively cheap), the profitability of the City's foreign investment business would not be disturbed.
2. It would help to restore business confidence by increasing profitability in the traded goods sector, and hence might increase investment rela-tive to saving and so stimulate the economy and promote economic recovery.
3. The tariff would improve the trade balance and possibly also Britain's terms of trade. By reducing the trade deficit it might bolster investor confidence in sterling's gold parity.
4. Since the tariff was not a prohibitive one, it would generate fiscal revenue, help to balance the budget and obviate the need for cuts in government expenditure at a time when tax receipts were falling due to the cyclical downturn of the economy – Keynes estimated the tariff would bring in between £40m and £50m worth of revenue. Keynes' revenue tariff proposal (March 1931) comprised a 15 per cent duty on all manufactured and semi-manufactured goods and a 5 per cent duty on all foodstuffs and some raw materials,

Compare Keynes' approval rating for tariffs just described with that of 1923-Keynes. Then, seven years earlier, at the time of the general election campaign, he was utterly dismissive of Conservative Prime Minister

Stanley Baldwin's call for protection as a cure for unemployment. In magisterial mode, he asserted:

> If there is one thing protection can *not* do, it is to cure unemployment . . . the claim to cure unemployment involves the protectionist fallacy in its grossest and crudest form . . . The proposal to cure the present unemployment by a tariff . . . is a gigantic fraud. (Keynes, *CW*, XIX, pp. 151–2)

At that time (1923), he was calling for cheap money and devaluation of sterling; but he must have known that there was no chance of these being officially adopted, since the objective of national policy as stated in the Cunliffe Report (1918) was to get sterling back to the prewar gold parity through steady deflationary pressure. Yet a general tariff, by putting up prices and reducing real wages, would accomplish precisely the same result. The inference that Keynes failed to see the virtues of a tariff as a practical alternative can perhaps be explained by the assumption that he underestimated the chronic nature of the unemployment.

On 24 July 1930 the Prime Minister, Ramsay MacDonald, appointed a Committee of Economists 'to review the present economic condition of Great Britain, to examine the causes which are responsible for it and to indicate the conditions of recovery' (Harrod 1951, p. 426). With Keynes as chairman, it included Hubert Henderson, Pigou, Sir Josiah Stamp, and Lionel Robbins. At the second meeting of the Committee on 11 September 1930, Keynes circulated a questionnaire to the other members inviting responses to a series of questions dealing with the problems of the stagnating British economy. The replies to the questions, discussed at a weekend session on 26–28 September, revealed widely varying diagnoses and remedies for the ills of the economy. Dissension broke out as Keynes tried to arrive at a consensus. In his own responses, Keynes denied that up to 1929 real wages had grown faster than output per head. Assuming 'abnormal' unemployment to be around 1 500 000 Keynes estimated that only one-ninth of the total was the result of real wages rising in excess of productivity. The unemployment was, in his opinion, overwhelmingly the result of the slump and negative effects flowing from the state of the balance of payments, the high exchange rate, the level of domestic interest rates and the stance of monetary policy. These effects he referred to as the deterioration of the 'equilibrium terms of trade'. Here, Keynes tried to capture in a single phrase the constraints imposed by globalisation on the weak, inflexible British economy. He defined the 'equilibrium' terms of trade as those which prevail 'when the level of money wages at home relatively to money wages abroad is such that the amount of the foreign balance (i.e. of foreign investment) plus the amount of home investment at the rate of interest set by world conditions . . . is . . . equal to the amount of home savings' (Keynes,

CW, XIII, p. 178). Quite simply, Keynes was referring to the problem of 'external balance' under the restored gold standard. For Britain, still attempting to carry its huge pre-1914 international commitments, the maintenance of external equilibrium was becoming ever more challenging. The economy's adjustment to balance of payments equilibrium was, in fact, becoming a threat to domestic prosperity. The difficulties stemmed from: (a) the overvaluation of sterling at the new gold parity which reduced the export surplus available for foreign investment; (b) foreign tariffs which reduced the demand for British goods in addition to the reduction caused by the loss of competitiveness in certain export industries owing to the high exchange rate; and (c) the high bank rate and deflationary monetary policy deemed necessary to protect the gold reserves from capital flight and to hold down overseas investment to the amount that the current account balance permitted. But deflationary monetary policy was discouraging domestic investment and depressing domestic output and employment. Hence the chronic unemployment problem. The latter was the result of forcing the country to meet the requirements of the deteriorating 'terms of trade' (the tightening external constraint). Instead of putting up with that, he proposed to ease the external constraint by enlarging the foreign balance (the current account balance) through protection. The deflationary monetary policy needed for external balance imposed a painful, wrenching process of adjustment on the domestic economy. Unlike the idealised picture of the gold standard automatic adjustment mechanism causing wages and costs to adjust smoothly and automatically to external disequilibria, the modern reality was altogether different and daunting. Resistance to nominal wage cuts meant that a deflationary monetary policy would reduce prices but not wage costs and hence would result in business losses and unemployment.

At the time Keynes came out publicly in favour of tariffs (March 1931) he was something of a celebrity, internationally well known as an expert on economic matters on account of his 1919 bestseller *The Economic Consequences of the Peace* and his subsequent prolific writings on international economic problems. No wonder his fellow British economists were dismayed that a writer of such stature should publicly lend his support to protection.

Keynes' tariff proposals had been known to most of the economists for about a year, ever since his testimony before the Macmillan Committee on Finance and Industry (28 February 1930). His proposal then was for a uniform 10 per cent average tariff on all manufactured imports with provisions for an export bounty to prevent distortion of the conditions of competition among industries. Thus the effect of the proposal would be identical with a devaluation of sterling – presumably, the intention being to

correct for the perceived 10 per cent overvaluation of sterling. He com-
mended his proposal somewhat half-heartedly to the Macmillan
Committee: 'I am frightfully afraid of protection as a long-run policy . . .
but we cannot afford always to take long views, and I am almost equally
clear that there are certain short-term advantages in protection (*CW*, XX,
p. 120). A year later (21 April 1931), even though the slump deepened,
Keynes still regarded the tariff as a *faute de mieux* solution, as he revealed
in a letter to Kingsley Martin, the newly-appointed editor of the *New
Statesman and Nation*. After mentioning the dilemma he faced in choosing
'a definite policy' among 'a tariff, devaluation or an assault on wages', he
judged the last option (that is, 'an adequate reduction of wages') as being
'quite off the map and would . . . have disappointing results. That may be
true of the tariff too. But it is more promising than the others' (Keynes,
CW, XXVIII, pp. 12–13).

At the meeting of the Committee of Economists on 26 September 1930
Keynes raised the contentious issue of tariffs when he submitted for discussion a paper entitled 'A Proposal for Tariffs Plus Bounties'. The proposal
was essentially the same as the one he had suggested in private evidence to
the Macmillan Committee. Although Henderson and Stamp were half sold
on the idea, Robbins, a passionate free-trader, objected most vehemently.
In his discussion paper, Keynes referred more generally to changes in economic conditions which undermined the case for free trade. For instance,
the efficiency gains from international specialisation and trade were not as
great as in the nineteenth century since 'any manufacturing country is probably just about as well fitted as any other to manufacture the great majority of articles' (Keynes, *CW*, XIII, p. 193). Smaller gains from trade imply
smaller losses 'from the obstruction of trade through tariffs. Another
instance: the case for free trade, as regards its connection with the maintenance of full employment, rests on the assumption 'that if you throw men
out of work in one direction you reemploy them in another. As soon as that
link in the chain is broken the whole of the free trade argument breaks
down' (Keynes, *CW*, XX, p. 117). The link in the chain is provided by wage
flexibility and mobility of labour. But, Keynes observed, these were the
very elements that were lacking in the British economy at that time. Free
trade implies the restructuring of national economies, and the dislocation
it causes inevitably involves adjustment costs – in the case of the British
economy at the time, a cut in wages to reduce costs. The efficiency gains
from free trade come at a price. The adjustment costs are less and easier to
bear if wages and costs adjust smoothly and flexibly to shifts in international competitiveness. Keynes understood all this perfectly well, but
judged that the price of flexibility was too high.

Despite some fierce arguments among his colleagues in the Committee

of Economists, Keynes managed to secure majority support for protection
(24 October 1930) to aid economic recovery, create jobs and save the gold
standard. Lionel Robbins refused to sign the final report and attached a dis-
senting report claiming that it was easier to put on tariffs than to get them
removed.[7] The measure would only encourage foreign protectionists and
invite retaliation. But as Donald Winch observes, it was when 'Keynes
made his apostasy public' in March 1931 that he 'brought down upon
himself the wrath of many of his fellow economists' (Winch 1969, p. 150).
Sir Roy Harrod, Keynes's first biographer, felt at the time that Keynes' turn-
about on tariffs was a betrayal of free trade (Harrod 1951, p. 427).

The arguments and disputes raised in the Committee of Economists now
came into the open. Lionel Robbins was Keynes' most persistent and vocif-
erous critic. He belonged to a group based at the London School of
Economics whose members were the principal defenders of free trade
orthodoxy and led the attack on Keynes. Using arguments based on the
standard case for free trade, the conclusions reached by these economists
were not dissimilar to those of Marshall at the time of the 1903 Tariff
Reform debate. Keynes had no quarrel with the standard theoretical argument, but simply wanted his critics to face the real issue, namely the parlous
state of the economy and the necessity for hard policy choices to overcome
the crisis. Instead, the discussion got bogged down with peripheral matters
such as the yield of the proposed duties, the effects on British exports and
imports and flows of foreign investment, and so on, or else degenerated into
dogmatism.

Several critics (Hawtrey, Robbins, Pigou among them) mentioned the
same point: that tariffs are never temporary; once granted, they tend to be
permanent and institutionalised as they become taken over by special interests. Hawtrey, who was not a member of the Committee of Economists,
agreed with Keynes, however, that a tariff had some use as an emergency
measure against the slump, but that Britain should not join in a measure
that would retard worldwide economic recovery.[8] Arthur Pigou, Keynes'
colleague at Cambridge, accepted the theoretical case in certain special
circumstances for a departure from free trade, but did not like Keynes'
actual proposals and rejected the suggestion for bounties on exports.
Hubert Henderson and Sir Josiah Stamp sided with Keynes on the need for
a tariff, but also without the export bounty element. In a memorandum to
the British cabinet on 30 May 1930, Henderson pleaded for a 10 per cent
revenue tariff on manufactured imports: 'I venture to doubt whether a
single economist in the country would dispute that, under such conditions
as now obtain, the effects of a 10 % tariff on manufactures imports would
be beneficial to employment.'[9] In a memorandum on Keynes' draft report,
Henderson coupled his support for tariffs with a declaration calling for

wage reductions, retrenchment in public expenditures, in particular reform of unemployment benefits (the dole).

Keynes' public espousal of tariffs in the *New Statesman and Nation* (7 March 1931) and a popular version in the *Daily Mail* (Keynes, *CW*, XX, pp. 493–512) called forth a flood of replies disputing Keynes' case in language varying from outrage to disbelief – 'the free traders sprang to the defence of their cherished dogma', including 'a passionate and vituperative reply' from Lionel Robbins (Skidelsky 1992, p. 386). Perhaps Skidelsky had in mind Robbins' remark that it was 'a tragedy that he who shattered the moral foundations of the Treaty of Versailles should now turn his magnificent gifts to the service of the mean and petty devices of economic nationalism' (*New Statesman and Nation*, 14 March 1931. Quoted in Winch 1969, pp. 150–51).

Many of the letters concentrated criticism on Keynes' estimate of the yield of the tariff or the effects of it on exports and foreign investment. A number of critical contributions were from economists associated with the London School of Economics (LSE), including Sir William Beveridge, Lionel Robbins, Arnold Plant, Theodore Gregory, Evan Durbin and G.L. Schwartz. In the early 1900s the London academics were in the camp of the Tariff Reformers; now they were the advance guards of the free-traders. Beveridge described Keynes' article advocating tariffs as 'a judgement without reasons', and several other correspondents among the lay public, confronted by the novelty of the tariff proposal, seemed genuinely confused about the isues involved. In an attempt to answer his critics, Keynes followed up his original article setting out the case for a tariff with a series of three short articles in the *New Statesman and Nation* under the heading 'Economic Notes on Free Trade', which 're-read today', wrote Lord Kaldor in 1982, 'show him to be the intellectual master – greatly superior to all his critics' (Kaldor 1982, p. 17). Keynes regretted that 'not a single critic has denied that we need to increase business confidence, to relieve the balance of trade, to raise revenue, and to stimulate employment; and no one has denied that my proposal would have a tendency to do all these things. Resistance to his tariff proposal, Keynes suggested, stemmed from a reluctance to face the uncomfortable facts about the dire state of the British economy and to consider radical, but effective short-term expedients to relieve the situation – expedients that 'will give us a margin of resources and a breathing space, under cover of which we can do other things'. The need for emergency measures such as his tariff proposals were not easy to contemplate, he recognised, since 'we have generally been concerned, not with the problem of how to get out of a very tight place, but with what will be the best long-run policy *assuming conditions of equilibrium*' (see Keynes in letter and article in *New Statesman and Nation*, 21 March, p. 143, and 4 April, 1931, p. 211).

In May 1931 the very same economists who had attacked Keynes' espousal of protection in the columns of the *New Statesman* joined together under the leadership of Sir William Beveridge, Director of the London School of Economics (LSE), to produce a polemical tract forcefully refuting the current wave of protectionist pleas then sweeping the country (including most notably, Keynes' proposal). Three chapters of the book, *Tariffs: The Case Examined* (Beveridge, 1931) were devoted to an explicit rebuttal of Keynes' tariff proposal (chapters VI, VII and XIV). Joan Robinson later ridiculed the effort as a 'now-forgotten volume which represents a low ebb in neo-classical thought' (Robinson 1962, pp. 64–5).

The authors rehearsed the standard free trade arguments against tariffs, such as:

(a) tariffs just shifted labour about from one industry or occupation to another without adding to total employment. Total income must fall with protection, regardless of the state of the labour market. As an empirical fact, the LSE economists referred to the current evidence that countries with high tariff barriers had even higher rates of unemployment.

(b) If tariffs reduced imports, then either exports must fall by an equal amount or foreign investment must increase.

Keynes disputed this second argument (particularly pressed by Beveridge). There was no simple or direct connection between the volume of exports and imports. Beveridge's defence of free trade on that ground must be the result of pure intellectual error about the mechanism of adjustment in international trade. In rhetorical mode, he put the question to Beveridge: 'Does he believe that it makes no difference to the amount of employment in this country if I decide to buy a British car instead of an American car?' (Keynes, *CW*, XX, pp. 508, 509). Beveridge replied in the affirmative, but Keynes tripped him up on logical grounds. Lord Kaldor in 1982 recalled the altercation: '[Keynes] answered Beveridge by a *reductio ad absurdum*. Beveridge's position was that, while a reduction in imports does not help employment because it causes an equivalent reduction in exports, an increase in imports would be bad because it would not cause a corresponding increase in exports!' (Kaldor 1982, p. 17). Beveridge's argument has resurfaced many times in the rhetoric of politically astute free-traders during international trade negotiations under GATT. In everyday parlance, it runs as follows: exports are good, imports are bad, but an equal increase in exports and imports is good. Keynes believed that if the trade balance improved with tariffs, that would allow the bank rate to be lowered. Foreigners would then borrow more from the London capital market so that the capital account would do the adjusting and hence exports might not fall. In fact, if increased British foreign investment stimulated a rise in purchasing power abroad, British exporters might benefit from increased sales. With plenty of spare capacity in terms of idle factories and un-employed workers, increased output, both for home demand and export sales, need not lead to increased export prices and therefore a diminution of foreign sales.

The row about protection was merely symptomatic of a much wider and deeper disagreement between Keynes and his academic colleagues over the appropriate response to the British economic crisis – in terms of both diag-nosis and treatment. The orthodox economists believed that, given time, the unhampered working of economic forces would restore the economy's health. Markets were not clearing (particularly the labour market) because of rigidities, and that was the problem to be addressed by economists and policymakers. The disagreement was basically with Keynes' advocacy of expansionary measures, for example, his call for lower interest rates and 'public works' expenditure, and so on. Keynes, for his part, resisted calls for cutting money wages and for more budget cuts. Despite this, Keynes made concessions to get agreement on tariffs, that is, he was prepared to drop schemes for 'public works' and export bounties. He knew that other econo-mists disliked his policy activism and his refusal to go along with a 'grin-and-bear it' policy – as he satirised the orthodox position of waiting for the slump to run its course, relying on steady deflation to do its work. Referring to the March 1931 newspaper article that carried the tariff proposal, he pointed out that that proposal came at the very end (the last paragraph, in fact) of a lengthy analysis of the country's economic problems. That careful analysis provided the justification for the proposal. Yet, he complained, his critics (described as 'fundamentalists of free trade') chose to ignore that analysis and, instead, rushed to condemn his tariff suggestion. Why, he asked, this wilful refusal to engage with his arguments? 'Is it the fault of the *odium theologicum* attaching to free trade? Is it that economics is a queer subject or in a queer state?' (Keynes, *CW*, XX, p. 505). Referring to a page (p. 74) in *Tariffs: The Case Examined* (Beveridge 1931) to make a general point, Joan Robinson wrote in 1962: '. . . it illustrates how little logic an ideology really needs. The great outcry against Keynes' treachery to the Free Trade cause, which made strong men weep, shows how long an ideology can survive its usefulness; the doctrines that, at least from a patriotic point of view, it was desirable to preach when England was the greatest exporting nation, made precious little sense at any level in the nineteen-thirties' (Robinson 1962, p. 88).

Keynes' protectionism in 1930–31 was formed by the judgement that the tariff was one of several alternative policy measures, none of which were attractive in themselves. It was, as he saw it, 'a crude departure from *laissez faire*, which we have to adopt because we have no better weapons in our hands' (Keynes, *CW*, XX, p. 495). In a recent review of Skidelsky's three-volume biography of Keynes, Martin Daunton remarked that Keynes 'did not think about structural change, or ways in which wages and costs could be less sticky'. Daunton argued that Keynes saw Britain's problem as one of monetary or macroeconomic instability rather than one of deep structural defect. The solution was to avoid policy mistakes and to navigate around problems. 'The "stickiness" of costs was taken as given, rather than as something to be understood and tackled head on' (Daunton 2002, p. 9). In his biography of Keynes, Donald Moggridge summarises some critical comments on Keynes' advocacy of protection (Moggridge 1992). The main criticism centres on Keynes' choice of protection rather than devaluation as the preferred solution for Britain's economic problems. The view of most economists, he believes, is that Keynes was mistaken in making that choice since it was a second-best policy, although, perhaps, one that could have been of some benefit at the time. Keynes failed to recognise that protection, as compared with devaluation, would not do much to improve Britain's invisible earnings, nor would it have remedied the competitive disadvantage of British industry labouring under the handicap of an overvalued exchange rate. In the short run protection might have invited retaliation, so further complicating the position of Britain's export industry – although Moggridge admits that devaluation would also have invited retaliation, he judges that retaliation would have been more pronounced against British tariffs. Finally, Moggridge blames Keynes for refusing openly to advocate devaluation and instead to lend his public support to the protectionist cause on 'an understandably mistaken comparison of the costs and benefits of the two courses of action and of the possibility of sterling being pushed from gold in any case'. Keynes' policy backing for protection 'helped to create the climate of opinion' favourable to the highly protective tariff system Britain got after September 1931 (Moggridge 1992, p. 514). But this latter comment exaggerates Keynes' influence on the decision to turn to protection during 1931–2. It is true, leading Conservatives used Keynes' protectionist views to support their campaign against free trade which resulted in victory with the Import Duties Act, 1932, but, as Garside's research shows, the imposition of protection resulted from the conjunction between a long-term shift in attitude within the Conservative Party, buttressed by growing support for tariffs in labour, business and financial circles by 1930, and the fiscal crisis of 1931–2 (Garside 1998, p. 47). In any case, Keynes' advocacy of protection only became public knowledge in March 1931, long after public protectionist sentiment had hardened, and within six months Keynes promptly rejected the protectionist solution on the abandonment of the gold standard. Writing in 1951, Sir Roy Harrod suggested: 'If the Gold Standard had broken down early in 1930, I have no doubt that Keynes would have remained a Free Trader' (Harrod 1951, p. 431). After all the traumas and dramas of coping with an unsustainable, that is, overvalued, exchange rate and mounting unemployment, sterling was declared inconvertible on 21 September 1931 after being forced off the gold standard. A crisis-of-confidence run on sterling led to a depletion of British gold stocks (a loss of £200 million of gold and foreign exchange reserves since 13 July of that year) and the exchange rate depreciated by 30 per cent over the next three months. Twenty-five countries followed Britain and devalued their currencies in terms of gold – Commonwealth countries and dependencies as well as Egypt, the Scandinavian countries and Portugal. Keynes applauded that development as one freeing Britain from the shackles of the gold standard, leaving her free in future to pursue desirable domestic objectives of stable prices and full employment (internal balance). But, for the present, the lifting of the external constraint on monetary reflation meant that the authorities were now able to stimulate the depressed economy and reduce unemployment by reflating the money supply and price level. That was all along his preferred remedy. Here at last he met on common ground with his erstwhile tariff opponents; for all agreed (including Robbins) that the new monetary freedom had cleared the way ahead towards equilibrium. A week after the suspension of convertibility (28 September 1931) Keynes withdrew his tariff proposal in a letter to *The Times* as he always said he would, should the currency situation change.

However, events moved rapidly on the tariff front. Barely two months after being forced off the gold standard a Conservative-dominated National Government re-introduced protection with a vengeance. In November 1931 the Abnormal Importations (Customs Duties) Act was hastily passed, ostensibly to stem a flood of 'dumped' imports. The Act provided for duties of up to 100 per cent on certain items, although in practice the maximum imposed was 50 per cent. However, the significance of this emergency measure was that it paved the way for the definite abandonment of free trade which culminated in the Import Duties Act of February 1932, with its 10 per cent *ad valorem* tariffs.

The economists were confronted with full protectionism rather than Keynes' temporary, practical variety. In face of that political reality the year-long tariff debate subsided. In that debate the clash between Keynes and his academic controversialists was not, at least on the surface, about fundamental differences. As Donald Winch remarks, the differences were 'mainly of timing, urgency and priorities'; 'Keynes was driven out of the free trade camp by his responsiveness to the pressure of immediate policy

circumstances'. In Winch's view, Keynes' support for a tariff afforded him
a rational escape from all that was 'negative' and 'contractionist' in his
orthodox colleagues' solutions to Britain's economic problems (Winch
1969, p. 151). Keynes' pragmatism and intellectual flexibility, which most
regard as praiseworthy, are seen in a slightly different light by his sternest
critics. On economic policy, they allege, Keynes often looked for soft
options, given the existing constraints. Where the market constraints
proved unyielding, he invariably recommended official intervention
designed to bypass or suppress the undesirable consequences of the
market's discipline. Yet, on all sides it is acknowledged that he could compromise on practical matters relating to political economy, whether on
domestic matters or in international negotiations.

Keynes' pragmatic disposition and diplomatic skills proved to be invaluable attributes when, during the Second World War, he was called upon to
assist in the search for a new international monetary standard or order to
replace the monetary disintegration of prewar days. Keynes influenced the
direction of the quest, both by his copious interwar writings and by his
leadership as head of the British delegation in the round of talks leading
up to Bretton Woods. Although the Bretton Woods agreement (setting up
the IMF and World Bank) included few of the specific proposals advanced
by Keynes, nevertheless it reflected the intellectual consensus later known
as 'Keynesian economics'. Indeed, the wartime economies were run on
Keynesian principles – Keynes was the one who had offered the most convincing interpretation of the interwar experience and it was in light of his
testimony that the (Bretton Woods) Conference participants faced the
tasks of constructing postwar monetary arrangements.[10]

Keynes never fully regained his faith in free trade. Yet such scepticism
never got the better of the liberal spirit that animated his arduous endeav-
ours during those years. On 27 November 1941 Sir Dennis Robertson, a
free trade colleague, wrote to Keynes telling him his feelings upon reading
a revised draft of Keynes's Plan: 'I sat up last night reading [it] with great
excitement – and a growing hope that the spirit of Burke and Adam Smith
is on earth again' (Keynes, *CW*, XXV, p. 66). Sir Roy Harrod noticed as well
how '[h]is [Keynes'] mind reverted to Adam Smith and to the great truths
which he preached' (Harrod 1951, p. 609). Keynes himself, in his posthu-
mous article 'The Balance of Payments of the United States' (June 1946),
declared that he had helped to draft the blueprints for a world economic
order designed 'not to defeat, but to implement the wisdom of Adam
Smith' (Keynes, *Economic Journal*, June 1946, p. 186).

There is an interesting sequel to Keynes' 1930–31 advocacy of a temporary tariff. In a counterfactual exercise with the aid of an estimated econometric model, Foreman-Peck, Hughes Hallett and Yue Ma (1998, pp.

262–86) recently reported results which suggested that Keynes was right in his belief that his tariff recommendations would have created jobs and saved the gold standard; 'We show that he [Keynes] was right and that retaliation would not have offset the potential gains' [p. 268]. Using data on the UK, the USA, France and Germany, the authors first examine the bilateral impacts of the 1930s British and US tariffs on these four major industrial countries through estimates of import-demand equations. The estimated parameters of the import-demand equations are then used to infer the immediate expenditure-switching (or import-volume) effects as British goods, for instance, were substituted for French, German and American products, in the case of the British tariffs. They also took account of monetary repercussions by modelling internal linkages through the calculation of dynamic tariff multipliers which captured the impact of tariffs on GNP, prices, interest rates, gold flows, and so on. Finally, they argued the counterfactual case by simulating what would have happened to British output and gold flows if all tariff barriers by the four countries had been removed by 1930.

According to the authors, an earlier British recourse to tariffs (say, in February 1930, when Keynes first floated the idea) would have improved the trade balance and bolstered speculators' confidence in sterling's gold parity. The gold standard could have been saved. In the absence of sterling devaluation, therefore, there would have been no foreign tariff reaction (or retaliation). Britain could then have used its tariff as a bargaining counter to push through trade liberalisation; consequently the world would have been saved the protectionism and beggar-thy-neighbour policies that flourished, as country after country tried to stimulate their domestic economies by exporting unemployment through competitive devaluations, undervalued currencies and import and exchange controls – at least up to the mid-1930s (Foreman-Peck, Hughes Hallett and Ma 1998, p. 277).

8.5   THE APPROACH TO TRADE LIBERALISATION

The United States emerged from the Second World War greatly strengthened in economic and military might. The country's economic dominance was staggering. The United States held about 74 per cent of the world's stock of monetary gold (and about 60 per cent of the stock of all gold) and accounted for about two-thirds of the world's manufacturing production and for one-third of the world's real GNP and trade. American political and business leaders became conscious of the country's obligations as a world power. That power and influence enabled the United States at war's end to create a liberal international trade regime to complement the monetary arrangements set up at Bretton Woods (namely the IMF and the World Bank).

The US-sponsored postwar open trading system was the culmination of a series of changes and policy shifts begun a decade and a half earlier which shifted American commercial policy from non-negotiable tariffs to support for bilateral trade reductions and finally to the promotion of world-wide trade liberalisation based on non-discrimination and reciprocity.

The point of departure for the future course of US commercial policy was the Reciprocal Trade Agreements Act, 1934. This Act signalled the start of a new approach to tariff policy whereby the United States turned from Republican 'high protectionism' to unconditional MFN bilateral commercial treaties.

With exports making up only 6 per cent of United States GNP in 1929, the relative self-sufficiency of the American economy engendered an attitude of indifference or unconcern on the part of America's leaders about the impact of their trade policies on foreign countries. Angry foreign reactions to Smoot–Hawley came as a jolt to many Americans and gradually changed attitudes with the realisation that after all 45 per cent of the world's production of manufactures was concentrated in the United States and that US exports made up 20 per cent of world exports. The country had grown enormously in economic clout during the First World War and could not continue in the same old ways as far as commercial intercourse was concerned. US tariffs did matter to the rest of the world because the United States was now a big player in world markets and its domestic market (now nearly as large as the British market) was becoming a target for foreign exporters. Equally, the powerfully organised US export interests saw advantages in a reorientation to freer trade, since the prosperity of foreign countries and the enhancement of their capacity to import would provide outlets for surplus US output. The self-indulgent, nationalistic pandering to sectional interests as exemplified in the negative case of the Smoot–Hawley tariff gave way to a pro-trade bias in policy and support for a more open world economy. The stemming of the protectionist tide in the 1930s resulted from the interaction of a jumble of interests, motives and ideology. Let us see how these changes and policy shifts came about.

The US initiative which led to the shift to multilateralism was the reciprocal trade agreements programme stemming from the passage of the Reciprocal Trade Agreements Act, 1934. The newly-elected administration of President Franklin D. Roosevelt, looking for ways to increase output and employment in the slump, saw in the revival of world trade a useful adjunct to the package of domestic expansionary measures comprising the New Deal. Such was the severity of the economic debacle that Roosevelt was prepared to reverse a century-old policy of growth through protectionism in favour of economic revival through freer trade. In addition to the young New Dealers in the Administration, there were some committed free-traders, including Cordell Hull (Secretary of State, with responsibility for commercial policy) who was an ideological, Cobdenite free-trader. Hull, a Southern Democrat, impressed by historical accounts which described the nineteenth-century *Pax Britannica* as being underpinned by Free Trade, was convinced that world peace depended upon the reduction of trade restrictions more than anything else. On behalf of the Administration he persuaded Congress to amend the Smoot–Hawley Act – specifically, to delegate to the President the authority to negotiate bilateral trade agreements based upon the reciprocal reduction of tariffs incorporating the unconditional MFN clause. Convinced of the Administration's argument that no tariff reductions would be made that would injure any American industry, Congress agreed to the transfer of tariff-making powers to the executive branch by passing the Reciprocal Trade Agreements Act. The initiative was promoted as being consistent with the domestic drive to increase output and employment through the New Deal measures. The revival of world trade, it was claimed, could assist American recovery by increasing exports. A remarkable feature of this legislative episode is that Congress, traditionally jealous of its constitutional right to levy taxes (including tariffs) and regulate foreign commerce, meekly ceded that authority to the executive branch. It was not a time for parochial, sectional interests but one calling for a national outlook. Despite their solicitude for the welfare of domestic industries, the legislators were reluctant to stand in the way of a popular president. The delegation of powers to the President was only for three years; but Congress regularly renewed it for periods of one to three years until new arrangements were made under the Trade Expansion Act, 1962, which initiated the Kennedy Round of GATT trade negotiations. In fact, since 1934 US tariff rates have been set by the President, subject to Congressional approval.

A minor precedent of sorts was set by the 1922 Fordney–McCumber Act which contained provisions for 'flexibility' on the part of the executive branch (that is, the Tariff Commission); but flexibility amounted to little more than a requirement to set tariff rates to equalise the difference between American and foreign costs of production. There was no authority to proceed in a liberalising direction.

At any rate, the 1934 Act authorised the President to enter into bilateral agreements to reduce US tariffs by up to 50 per cent in exchange for reciprocal concessions. There was a practical justification for handing over tariff-cutting powers to the President's Office. If the United States was now to be engaged in tariff bargaining with foreign countries, that is, to secure foreign tariff reductions in exchange for US tariff cuts, it was eminently sensible that this should be done by the executive arm with its corps of experts and diplomatists rather than by a large, fractious and unwieldy body like

Congress. To get the hoped for increase in exports, it was necessary to secure tariff concessions by other countries, and these could only be obtained through negotiation and skilful bargaining.

With the delegation of tariff negotiating authority to the president, the free-traders within the government were able to implement their ideas and pursue their objective of trade liberalisation. By the Second World War, the United States had concluded twenty-one reciprocal trade agreements with several foreign countries, mainly in Latin America, but also one with Great Britain in 1938. These agreements provided for tariff concessions on 65 per cent of all dutiable imports into the United States. As a result average US tariffs fell from 54 per cent to 37 per cent. The resulting tariff reductions were extended to a wider network of countries through the MFN principle, that is, even though each agreement was bilateral, the concessions they contained were generalised to all countries, including those that made no concessions themselves. Thus bilateral agreements had multilateral effects as the United States embraced the unconditional (or European) version of bilateral tariff bargaining. In the 1938 trade agreement with Great Britain, the United States agreed to a reduction of duties on about 47 per cent of US imports from Britain; in addition, France, Ireland and the Soviet Union (although not parties to the agreement) also benefited from US tariff cuts via the MFN clause.

How significant were these trade liberalisation agreements? The Anglo-American trade agreement lasted only eight months (that is, it ended when Britain imposed wartime controls in September 1939). Ninety-six items were subject to tariff cuts of 50 per cent, but the total trade involved was a paltry $14 million. Cuts were also made on items which were imported by the United States in insignificant quantities. Commenting on these meagre results of the 1938 agreement, Kindleberger writes: 'the Anglo-American trade agreement was more symbolic than effective' (Kindleberger 1989, p. 193). Patricia Clavin agrees: 'The agreement did little to liberalise Anglo-American trade, never mind trigger a global move to reduce international protectionism', and 'the primacy of politics prevailed' (Clavin 1998, p. 296). The Anglo-American agreement was valued at the time because it advertised the solidarity of the two countries in face of the fascist threat in Europe.

Half the agreements were with Latin American countries and covered non-competitive products which did not in any way threaten American industry in the US market. Referring to Gerard Curzon's work on multilateral commercial diplomacy during the period, Goldstein (1998) notes: 'In general, these agreements did little to increase world trade since American tariffs remained very high and most-favoured-nation status was extended to few countries' (Goldstein 1998, p. 44). John Conybeare (1987) has convincingly argued that the change in US policy after 1934 represented merely a change in tactics rather than in strategy. Trade negotiations instituted under the new policy allowed the United States to 'maintain the hegemonic benefits of high tariffs while systematically reducing the impact of global, foreign retaliation' (Conybeare 1987, p. 251). Through those negotiations the United States was able to exploit its trade bargaining power during the 1930s. Noting that '[Cordell] Hull's vision [of world peace and prosperity through free trade] became the core mythology of American foreign economic policy' after 1945, Conybeare continues: 'the popular idea of the United States leading the world back to free trade from the mid-1930s is little more than an attractive myth' (Conybeare 1987, p. 233). Robert Isaak (1991) neatly summarises the truth of the matter concerning the relevance of the 1930s US-inspired agreements, that they were 'agreements with little overall impact on tariffs but with value as precedents for GATT rules' (Isaak 1991, p. 82). However, the 1934 Reciprocal Trade Agreements Act and the experience gained from the trade agreements resulting from it geared up the United States for the role it played post-1945 – the throwing of its weight behind the establishment of a non-discriminatory international trade regime based on open, multilateral negotiations.

Following the discussion above, we may summarise the factors and events which equipped the United States to play the trade-liberalising role:

1. The sea change in US commercial policy resulting from the 1934 Reciprocal Trade Agreements Act. The transfer of tariff-making authority from the legislative to the executive branch meant that interest groups lost out and the President (standing for the national interest) won. It recognised that the setting of tariff rates should no longer be solely a matter for unilateral national action. National tariff levels and trade policy issues in general were matters of common international concern and should be settled through negotiation.
2. The United States no longer had a single-column tariff schedule. The trade agreements signed under the 1934 Act meant that the US tariff code had to provide for lower tariff rates for all countries with MFN status and higher (Smoot–Hawley) rates for the others. This confirmed that US tariffs were now negotiable.
3. The experience of negotiating over twenty agreements inspired confidence that cooperative solutions could be found for world trade problems, even in the dire conditions of the 1930s. The potential for freer trade was there, and to the US negotiators that suggested how much more could be achieved in more favourable international economic circumstances. Referring to the 1938 Anglo-American trade agreement (despite the paucity of its trade-enhancing results) Douglas Irwin sees

positive long-term gains and considers that it 'set the stage for the great
Anglo-American cooperation during World War II that eventually led
to the Bretton Woods conference in 1944 where the cornerstones for the
postwar economic order were established' (Irwin 1995a, p. 113).

4. Another encouraging experience of what could come from international cooperation was the Tripartite Monetary Agreement, 25
September 1936. Although it was a feeble attempt at international monetary cooperation, it did allow the devaluation of the French franc to
take place under orderly conditions, that is, without inviting American
and British retaliation. It was an agreement to cease competitive devaluations. However, amidst the monetary disintegration of the 1930s it was
seen as a token of what could be accomplished by cooperation.

One blind spot obscuring the vision of the American trade-liberalisation
activists was agricultural protectionism. They made no headway on this for
obvious reasons – the extensive and entrenched agricultural subsidy programmes in the United States which were further extended by the 1933
Agricultural Adjustment Act. Agricultural price support schemes kept
domestic farm prices above the world level, which meant that imports had
to be restricted to protect farm incomes. Such trade restrictions took the
form of import quotas and export subsidies. During the 1930s American
trade negotiators were explicitly mandated not to agree to any international
agreement that would jeopardise the use of import protection for farm
products or undermine the continuation of the US agricultural support
schemes. Indeed, it was at the insistence of US negotiators in the talks
leading up to GATT and the International Trade Organization (ITO)
Charter that an exception for agricultural subsidies was written into the
rules. Consequently, GATT rules allow quantitative restrictions on agricultural products. The irony is that at least from the Kennedy Round of trade
negotiations the United States, with its undoubted comparative advantage
in temperate agricultural products, has been pressing for the liberalisation
of agricultural trade and the opening up of foreign markets for farm products with little or no success. Noting the US negotiators' lack of success in
getting America's trading partners to agree on the agricultural issue,
Goldstein remarks: 'American policies of the 1940s and 1950s were
"coming home to roost"'. (Goldstein 1998, p. 38).

The interwar period demonstrated the need for an international framework that would enable individual countries to follow policies directed
towards domestic objectives of full employment and rising living standards
without creating problems for others. As the Second World War drew to a
close, Anglo-American consensus settled on blueprints for a new international economic order comprising international institutions to deal with:

(a) international monetary arrangements and (b) commercial policy and international trade relations. The monetary institutions were set up at the Bretton Woods Conference (1944), namely the International Monetary Fund (IMF) and the World Bank. Negotiations over the setting up of the institution to deal with trade matters – the International Trade Organization (ITO) – proved more difficult and protracted than was the case with the Bretton Woods institutions. Agreement on the Charter setting up the ITO was finally reached at the Havana Conference in 1948, but the institution never came into being. The complexity and wide scope of its provisions as enshrined in the Havana Charter provoked strong opposition from many quarters and in the United States in particular almost every important group was lined up against ratification. In view of the anticipated overwhelming opposition to it, President Truman never submitted the Charter to Congress. Other governments did the same or failed to ratify it. As Robert Isaak puts it: 'Protectionists opposed the arrangement for being too liberal, and liberals were against it for remaining too protectionist' (Isaak 1991, p. 83).

While the ITO Charter was being discussed, twenty-three countries meeting in Geneva in 1947 signed an agreement (known as the General Agreement on Tariffs and Trade or GATT) enabling them to participate in reciprocal trade negotiations based on non-discrimination and the MFN principle. The protectionists in the United States allowed GATT to proceed because it was a provisional agreement and did not involve any loss of control over American policy to a supranational body, which the ITO would have been. At that first meeting the twenty-three countries (accounting for 80 per cent of world trade) proceeded to bargain on mutual tariff cuts on an MFN basis. The negotiations – known as the first GATT round – were highly successful and resulted in substantial but still undetermined cuts in import duties. Some unofficial estimates put the overall reduction in tariff levels at 20 per cent, but it is known that the United States cut its tariffs by 35 per cent. That early success did much to establish the credibility of GATT and its membership increased. However, for over a decade and a half GATT remained inactive until the Kennedy Round of tariff negotiations (1964–7). That round reinvigorated GATT's bargaining machinery by a new negotiating process that began with an across-the-board cut followed by negotiations of item-by-item exceptions. The next two rounds, the Tokyo Round (1973–9) and the Uruguay Round (1986–94) followed the same successful formula which resulted in a 35 per cent cut in tariffs in the Kennedy Round and another 30 per cent reduction in the Tokyo Round. Difficulties and delays attended the eighth round of GATT negotiations, the Uruguay Round, but the agreement finally came into force in January 1995. However, by the start of the Uruguay Round the cumulative effect of previous rounds resulted in an average tariff rate of about 4 per cent on most industrial products.

The most substantive achievement of the Uruguay Round was the creation of a new international institution, the World Trade Organization (WTO). The WTO replaced GATT as the guardian and arbiter of the rules of trade as well as serving as a host for new talks to liberalise trade. The procedures for dealing with disputes that arise under the rules of trade were strengthened and made the responsibility of the WTO. When the WTO replaced GATT, hopes were high that the successor institution would prove more successful in liberalising agricultural trade and eliminating non-tariff barriers (NTBs) such as voluntary restraint agreements (VRAs).

The successes and failures of GATT are well known and much has been written about its role in creating the conditions for the remarkable expansion in world trade over the last forty odd years. The reduction in tariff levels from an average of 40 per cent at the end of the Second World War to 4 per cent today must be counted a great success, even though a part of the reduction is due to inflation. It provided what was lacking in the inter-war years: (1) a forum for trade negotiations and (2) a set of rules on commercial policy which prevents backsliding by member countries through the 'binding' of tariff cuts once agreed upon. Tariff levels could only go down, except for 'safeguard clauses' built into GATT rules.

But what if there had been no GATT? Douglas Irwin put this counterfactual and asked whether the world would have reverted to the interwar chaos. Referring to the 1930s efforts of bilateral trade liberalisation by the United States described above, Irwin's answer is: 'the United States might have become the central node of a series of bilateral trade agreements, although not necessarily with unconditional MFN as the ruling principle' (Irwin 1995, p. 327). It is true, first, that the forum for negotiation provided by GATT was not dissimilar to the prewar American initiative in arranging bilateral trade agreements; and secondly, that many of the GATT rules were drawn from past commercial practice and were simply codified in the General Agreement of 1947. Aided by the international monetary stability provided by the IMF, Irwin's scenario, *sans* GATT, seems quite plausible, but raises a host of further questions relating to what that would have implied for US hegemony in the postwar world economy, and whether, in the end, the result would have been any different to what actually happened. Would the Bretton Woods system of fixed exchange rates have collapsed earlier than it did? Would there have been a waiver for the setting up of free-trade areas and other preferential arrangements such as the one incorporated in GATT's rules? Would something like the European Economic Community (EEC) have got off the ground? Would the Common Agricultural Policy (CAP) of the European Union (EU) have come into existence?

NOTES

1. Lord Briggs (Asa Briggs) relates that Peel 'was contemptuously dismissed by old-fashioned Tories as "the Spinning Jenny". See Asa Briggs, *Where We Came In: The Industrial Revolution Reconsidered* (London: BBC Publications, 1957) p. 29.
2. *Parliamentary Debates* (Hansard) 3rd Series CIV (1840), p. 662.
3. Cobden, besides conferring with Chevalier and Rouher, the Minister of Commerce, had two audiences with the French Emperor during November and December. Speaking of the Treaty, Gladstone said 'he was more obliged to Cobden than he could express in words – he had done it all – and that no other man could have done it. He considers it a grand success, and its results could hardly be too much thought of, etc.' Quoted in Richard Shannon, *Gladstone, Vol I, 1809–1865* (London: Hamish Hamilton, 1982), p. 406.
4. Quoted in Anthony Howe, 'Free Trade and the Victorians', in Marrison (ed.), *Free Trade and Its Reception* (1998), p. 173.
5. See J. Richard Huber, 'Effects on Prices of Japan's Entry into World Commerce after 1858', *Journal of Political Economy*, 79 (1971), pp. 614–28. Japan made remarkable economic progress over the next four decades.
6. The Smooth–Hawley tariff and the 1932 Ottawa agreements (which raised British and Commonwealth tariffs against the outside world) had a particularly devastating effect on Japan's economic interests, as Johannes Overbeek records: 'Both the Smooth–Hawley Act and the Ottawa Agreement helped to deprive Japan of many of its traditional markets. It paved the way for a military government bent upon imperial expansion that reached its logical conclusion at Pearl Harbor. Thus, in the middle of the Great Depression, the United States chose the course of selfish economic nationalism'. See Johannes Overbeek, *The Modern World Economy: Theories and Policies*, New York, 1933, p. 194.
7. Robbins' dissent from the Committee's report appears in S. Howson and D. Winch, *The Economic Advisory Council, 1930–39* (Cambridge: Cambridge University Press, 1977), pp. 227–31.
8. See R.G. Hawtrey, *Trade Depression and the Way Out* (London: Longmans Green, 1931), pp. 59–60.
9. Public Record Office, CAB 24/212 Unemployment Policy. Quoted in Garside (1998), p. 58.
10. For more on the monetary causes of the 1930s depression and Keynes' principles at Bretton Woods, see Gomes (1993), chapter 4, pp. 170–222.

9. Reflections on globalisation

Globalisation – the buzzword of our age – is a hot topic of debate and controversy among academics, politicians and in the media, which started with the collapse of the Soviet system in 1989. Globalisation, in its economic aspects, refers to cross-border economic integration characterised by increases in flows of goods, capital, and information, as well as labour mobility among countries. As an active global force it is multidimensional and wide ranging and by no means limited to the economic sphere. Apart from its connection with increased international trade and capital flows, globalisation refers also to the increasing speed, ease and extent with which technologies, people, cultures and ideas now cross national borders. It is altering the lives of people across the globe and affecting their culture and values, producing in its wake what some refer to as a 'global culture'. In this chapter we deal only with the economic aspects. Globalisation is condemned by some as a destroyer of jobs and industrial communities in the developed countries and hailed by others as the biggest chance for poor countries to lift themselves out of poverty.

Arguing whether globalisation is 'good' or 'bad' is now seen as irrelevant, although it is the value judgement that, no doubt, provides the ideological prism through which observers appraise the issue. Different vantage points on globalisation, even by economists, account for differences in perception concerning the salient features of the phenomenon. Some writers say there is now a 'consensus' on globalisation. But consensus among whom? The decision-makers, no doubt, the global institutions, the market players, the media, and so on. But perhaps because the process seems unstoppable, inevitable, irreversible, there is growing recognition of the need to 'manage' globalisation so that its benefits are widely shared and its costs kept down – something like the traditional arguments for free trade backed up with compensation, 'adjustment assistance', and so on. This recognition suggests that 'globaphobia' is unjustified; but economists disagree on the relative importance of trade and other factors (such as sound economic policies and institutions) and on how to interpret data on trade, growth, poverty and income inequality within and between countries.

As an economic force in the modern world, globalisation has been around for at least three decades, with trade and capital flows growing significantly faster than output. But globalisation is not a new phenomenon. Forms of globalisation have progressed throughout the course of recorded history, although not in a steady or linear fashion. The geographical spread of globalisation and the number of countries involved have varied from epoch to epoch depending on shifts in the areas of civilisation and the extent and richness of mercantile communities. In modern times, two phases of globalisation have been distinguished: the first phase lasting from around the last three-quarters of the nineteenth century until the outbreak of the First World War in 1914. The integration process was then curtailed by two world wars and an economic depression in between, but was resumed with renewed vigour in the years following the end of the Second World War, including the 'golden years' of the long postwar boom (1948–73) up to the present time – marked as the second phase of globalisation. The period 1948–73 witnessed a global growth rate of nearly 5 per cent – the longest period of sustained growth in the history of capitalism.

Traditionally, historians have seen the big economic changes of the last two centuries as falling into two phases – the first industrial revolution (1760–1850) and its spread from Britain, followed by the second industrial revolution starting from the last two decades of the nineteenth century. Not that historians have neglected episodes of market integration in respect of commodity trade, capital movements and even migration, but the comparative-history treatments were largely related to the economic development of countries in the context of their relationships to the international economy. There was no organising principle such as is commonly understood today by the concept of globalisation; hence some of the important questions raised in today's debate were not addressed by previous historical studies. The contemporary debate on the springs of globalisation, its significance and impact has raised interest in questions such as: what economic and political conditions favour globalisation and the extent of its geographical sway; what factors cause it to go into temporary retreat; what have been its effects in the past, for example on income inequality and convergence or divergence among countries, and so on? No doubt in response to such enquiries, economic historians, with a new focus of interest, have treated us to interesting perspectives on the historical evolution of globalisation, in particular, the first modern phase during the period 1870–1914. The debate on the globalisation issue has benefited enormously from such historical understanding, specifically in respect of questions about what conditions favour spurts of globalism, the extent of its geographical compass and whether the process is irreversible or not.

Karl Marx was the first prominent writer to recognise the significance of the force now known as globalisation. Although in his time it did not cover the globe, he predicted in 1848, accurately, that it soon would:

The bourgeoisie, by the rapid improvement of all instruments of production, by the immensely facilitated means of communication, draws all, even the most barbarian nations into civilisation. The cheap prices of its commodities are the heavy artillery with which it batters down all Chinese walls, with which it forces the barbarians' intensely obstinate hatred of foreigners to capitulate. It compels all nations, on pain of extinction, to adopt the bourgeois mode of production; it compels them to introduce what it calls civilisation into their midst, i.e., to become bourgeois themselves. In one word, it creates a world after its own image. (Marx, *Collected Works*, vol. 6, 1976, p. 488)

He sees capitalism as dynamic and expansionist, remarking on 'the law which gives capital no rest and continually whispers in its ear: "Go on! Go on!"' (Marx, *Collected Works*, vol. 9, 1977, pp. 222–4). And: 'The need of a constantly expanding market for its products chases the bourgeoisie over the entire surface of the globe. It must nestle everywhere, settle everywhere, establish connections everywhere' (Marx, *Collected Works*, vol. 6, 1976, p. 488).

Our reflections on globalisation are organised as follows: a more general review of late-nineteenth-century globalisation, followed by an adversarial account of the contentious pros and cons in the debate, ending with a summing up.

In an impressive synthesis of material on late-nineteenth-century globalisation, Kevin O'Rourke and Jeffrey Williamson summarise and draw conclusions from a large research project in a book entitled *Globalization and History: The Evolution of a Nineteenth Century Atlantic Economy* (1999). The focus is on the Atlantic Economy (Europe and the New World). Globalisation is operationally defined as a reduction in the obstacles to the flows of goods, capital and labour across countries. They analyse the effects of globalisation on convergence in the distribution of income among workers, capitalists and landowners across the Atlantic economy. To test and quantify the impact of globalisation on commodity prices, wages, rents and profits in Europe and the New World, the authors adopt two approaches: in the first place, they estimate a computable general-equilibrium (CGE) model incorporating sector-specific factors and, in the second place, by an econometric approach based on parameter estimation by regression models. The analysis is supplemented by a discussion of the backlash against the changes in income distribution caused by globalisation and the political reaction which resulted in an unravelling of the arrangements that created in the first place the highly interconnected economic world of the late nineteenth century. The O'Rourke and Williamson documentation of late-nineteenth-century convergence, in conjunction with other recent investigations, provides us with a reasonably clear picture of that remarkable historical experience.

Sharply falling transportation costs, reduced tariffs and major inventions such as the internal combustion engine, ocean steamships, telephone and telegraph resulted in a rapid growth in world trade. Distance shrank before the technology of iron and steam – a factor which reduced the natural protection previously afforded by high transport costs. Trade routes were further reduced by marvels such as the Suez and Panama Canals. Goods market integration stemming from the worldwide transport revolution resulted in convergence of commodity prices, especially for bulky primary produce. The reduction in price gaps for many goods continued across the century, resulting in near equalisation of prices by 1913. Wheat and meat prices converged across the Atlantic – for example, British meat prices fell from roughly twice American prices in the 1870s to under 20 per cent higher in 1913. It has been estimated that almost three-quarters of the commodity price convergence was due to declining transport costs and only a quarter can be attributed to the adoption of more liberal trade policies (Lindert and Williamson 2001, p. 7).

Not only goods, but also people moved – and on a massive scale. Between 1870 and 1914, some 36 million people crossed the Atlantic from Europe, two-thirds of them to the United States. A record 1.28 million immigrants poured into the United States in 1907. The remarkable fact was that unskilled labour moved freely with the minimum of government regulation (they did not need passports) and indeed, in the early phase of the exodus, with the aid of government subsidies (like assisted passages). Steamships made transatlantic travel regular, swift and safe. The time of crossing the Atlantic was reduced from a month in the 1830s to about a week in 1900. Travel also became cheaper for people as well as goods. An index of freight rates for the Atlantic trade routes fell by 70 per cent in real terms between 1840 and 1910. According to O'Rourke and Williamson's estimate, immigration increased the New World labour force up to 1910 by an average of some 40 per cent. The US labour force rose by 17 per cent. Argentina's labour force was augmented the most by immigration (86 per cent). The cumulative effect of European emigration between 1870 and 1910 is staggering. Emigration decreased the European labour forces by an average of 13 per cent, but with wide variations: in Ireland, a reduction of 45 per cent, Italy 39 per cent, Norway 24 per cent, Sweden 20 per cent, Britain 11 per cent and France, the least, 1 per cent. The result was to boost the wages of both those who emigrated and those left behind. Stolper–Samuelson reasoning to the effect that free trade increases incomes for abundant factors and reduces incomes of the scarce factors applied to the Atlantic economy during this period, that is, trade increased real wages in Europe. As commodity prices converged, the relative price of exports in each country rose, and since an increase in the relative price of a country's exports tends to increase the price of its abundant factor, the actual result closely followed the theoretical prediction. The abundant factor was land in the New World and labour in Europe. Thus the gainers were landowners in North America and workers in Europe. The losers were the scarce factors in the two regions: the owners of land in previously land-scarce Europe and labour in the previously labour-scarce New World.

The combination of increased trade and labour movements caused prices of locally scarce factors to fall and promoted factor-price convergence as labour markets integrated in the Atlantic economies (Europe, North America and South America). Real wage dispersion declined within the Atlantic economy as a whole by 28 per cent between 1970 and 1910 with Irish wages up by 32 per cent, Italian by 28 per cent. In the New World wages moved in the opposite direction. Argentinean wages fell by 22 per cent and American wages were lowered by 8.1 per cent (O'Rourke and Williamson 1999, Table 8.1, p. 155; also Lindert and Williamson 2001, p. 16). Apparently, the role played by commodity trade was relatively minor. Mass migration can account for practically all of the real wage convergence. Within Europe, convergence was uneven. Real wages in the European core (Britain, France, Belgium, Germany) had been 2–5 times greater than on the periphery (the Iberian countries, Scandinavia, Italy) in 1870, but by 1913 many of the countries on the European periphery had considerably narrowed the gap with the core countries. In 1856 unskilled real wages in urban Sweden were only 49 per cent of those in Britain, but in 1913 equalisation was achieved. But here again, only a very small part (under 10 per cent) of the real wage convergence between the European periphery and either Britain or the United States can be attributed to increases in commodity trade. Sweden experienced mass emigrations and converged towards both the European core and North America by 1913, but Spain and Portugal did not. Low emigration from the Iberian countries kept real wages low. Also Sweden's natural resources attracted foreign capital, whereas Spain, with sparse resources, was not favoured by foreign investors to the same extent.

Migration was the main channel for the relief of poverty in the poorer countries of the Atlantic economy. These countries mostly experienced an increase in incomes and standards of living. Migration provided an escape valve for the unskilled masses. Immigrant labour improved its productivity and income when it was matched with resources of capital and land in the resource-rich countries of the New World.

There was a massive flow of capital from Western Europe to the rapidly developing countries of the Americas, Australia and elsewhere. However, it was natural resource abundance, youthful working-age populations and human-capital abundance rather than low wages that attracted foreign capital to the periphery of the Atlantic economy. European capital built infrastructure such as railways, ports, cities, and so on, and financed traditional investments in mining and other extractive industries. Strong growth prospects overseas attracted European investors, but capital did not flow in a smooth stream. There were waves of lending fuelled by over-optimistic expectations which were followed by speculative collapses. Nevertheless, capital markets (centred in London) became steadily more integrated, reaching a level that peaked in 1913 – reflecting a degree of capital mobility unsurpassed even today. Measured by the size of net capital movements in relation to GNP, both the exports and imports of capital were much greater than today. Compared to today, the share of investment financed by imported funds was greater. Interest rates in different countries moved even more closely together than over most of the Bretton Woods post-1945 years – another confirmation that international capital markets were closely interconnected by 1970 (O'Rourke and Williamson 1999, Figure 11.3, p. 216).

The surprising fact about these massive capital flows taking place in a supposedly integrated world economy was that capital, by and large, did not flow to poor countries; hence, late-nineteenth-century capital mobility was an anti-convergence force. Basic neoclassical capital theory predicts that capital would flow from capital-abundant countries to capital-scarce countries, that is, from countries where the marginal product of capital is low to those where the marginal product of capital is high. Since capital-abundant countries are generally rich countries and capital-scarce countries are poor, the implication is that capital should, in the main, flow from rich countries to poor countries in an integrated world economy. But it did not happen that way. Capital went after countries with abundant natural resources (as mentioned above) and therefore, paradoxically, it drifted towards rich, not poor countries. Michael Clemens and Jeffrey Williamson (2000) confirm this result by a finding that capital inflows and GDP per capita were positively correlated between 1870 and 1913 (Clemens and Williamson 2000; also Lindert and Williamson 2001, p. 19).

In Chapter 8 we discussed the return to protectionism during the 1880s and 1890s – the backlash against globalisation which was generally perceived as harmful. Here we offer some additional observations on the reversal of the globalisation trend. The three channels of globalisation – trade, migration and capital movements – resulted in significant shifts in the distribution of income across the global economy. Those who lost out – workers in North America (through competition from European immigrants) and farmers in Europe (through depressed rents) organised politically to reverse or limit the process of globalisation. The losers joined forces: farmers and capitalists in Europe and workers and capitalists in North

America. Under popular pressure, by 1913, immigration policy became restrictive in the United States. There was a steady drift away from free immigration and towards a more restrictive policy in the form of contract labour laws, Chinese exclusion acts, head taxes, and so on, and Congressional debates on immigration from time to time included calls for more severe restrictions. In the late 1880s the rapid expansion of American manufacturing industry attracted a new wave of immigrants from Eastern and Southern Europe. The existing population, mainly Northern Europeans, felt threatened on two counts: (1) that Anglo-Saxon values, institutions and religion would be undermined by the newcomers; and (2) that with the onset of the depression of the 1890s their jobs would be at risk since the newcomers (accustomed to a lower standard of living) were willing to work for lower wages. President Grover Cleveland had to veto a bill passed by Congress in 1897 which would have excluded immigrants who were illiterate – but which eventually passed into law in 1917. Four years later, the restrictive immigration policy was further tightened when quotas based on ethnic origin were adopted. The surge of immigration from Eastern and Southern Europe which peaked in 1913 was abruptly stopped when the quotas were reduced almost to zero. Also tariffs were on the rise almost everywhere in the economies of the Atlantic periphery and also in parts of the core. The backlash campaign was backed by powerful groups – labour in North America and European landowners. Thus, as soon as its effects were felt, the apparatus of the globalisation project – free trade, unrestricted movements of capital and the gold standard – came under attack by groups who felt threatened by the consequences of the interconnected world. The political reaction to imports and immigration slowed international convergence, but did not eliminate it.

Looking at the practice of globalisation even with a superficial glance, one cannot avoid noticing the ideological element associated with it. The ideological element is even more apparent in the narratives justifying, indeed applauding the onward march of the globalisation project. But the globalising tendency is not identical with the rhetorical and ideological project which, following Steger (2002, pp. 5–9), we shall call 'globalism' – the normative and ideological dimension of the objective, material phenomenon of globalisation. The advocates of globalism seek to incorporate the old ideological twins of 'free trade' and '*laissez-faire*' in a package labelled 'globalisation'. Those who reject globalisation or seek to slow it down, they claim, are really turning their backs on free trade and are therefore protectionists or their apologists.

Ideology has a whole range of meanings and connotations – positive, neutral and negative; but perhaps a working definition derived from the more detailed categories expounded by political and social theorists can be useful in the discussion of economic globalisation. Manfred Steger (2002) defines one such as 'a system of widely shared ideas, patterned beliefs, guiding norms and values, and regulative ideals accepted as fact or truth by some group'. Moreover, an ideology offers its believers a coherent picture of the world 'not only as it is, but also as it should be' (Steger 2002, p. 5). Ideology invariably contains a political dimension, for as Steger notes, it is 'ultimately about the many ways in which power is exercised, justified and altered in society' (Steger 2002, p. 5). The ultimate aim of ideologues is the realisation of their ideas, social beliefs and value judgements into concrete political, social and economic reality. The purpose in identifying the ideology behind globalisation is to distinguish between 'globalism' (the rhetorical, ideological force) and 'globalisation' per se (as a material, visible process), since in much of the discourse on this topic globalism slips in largely unnoticed, riding on the back of globalisation. Thus the debate on globalisation often takes the form of an ideological wrangle among disputants largely on account of the ideological meaning attached to the concept of globalisation. Indeed, globalisation with its embedded component of globalism is seen by many as an ideology itself – perhaps the only ideology left after the end of the Cold War. Yet it is important to recognise that different components make up the globalisation package as commonly experienced. In particular, one must identify the neoliberal market ideology behind the increasing integration of global markets and distinguish it from the objective, material processes we all face from the increasing linkages of national economies brought about by advances in technology and economic development. For instance, technology alone was not responsible for driving the process behind the high levels of integration witnessed over the last two decades. It is misleading to portray globalisation as divorced from all agency (that is to say, policy) and to exaggerate the visible instruments of globalisation. Government policies in the United States (under Ronald Reagan) and the United Kingdom (under Margaret Thatcher), inspired by the rise of neoliberal ideas during the late 1970s, were important influences. The important dimension of globalisation we call globalism, with its complex ideological dynamics, was behind the remarkable process of market liberalisation of those years: privatisation of public enterprises, opening up of capital markets, lifting of state controls through deregulation, massive tax cuts, liberalisation of trade and industry, strict control of organised labour and reduction in the number of public enterprises.

In a book celebrating the past two decades of globalism as a shattering of the twentieth-century 'dream of centralized top-down control over the course of economic development', Brink Lindsey in *Against the Dead Hand* (2002) claims that contemporary globalisation is 'a political event' and has been 'a deliberately chosen response to the worldwide failures of central planning and top-down control.' He claims that there have been champions of free market reforms who made their case in ideological terms, such as Thatcher and Reagan, but they were the exceptions. 'By and large, the worldwide rediscovery of markets has been guided by pragmatism, a rejection of the failed dogma of centralised control in favour of something, anything, that works.' (Lindsey, 2002, p. 8).

In 1997 world merchandise exports amounted to $5.3 trillion. Exports of commercial services amounted to $1.3 trillion. Since the 1950s a remarkable feature of the world economy has been the rapid growth in merchandise trade compared to industrial output. Over the period trade grew at an annual rate of 2.6 per cent while output grew at only 1.5 per cent. This trend of the growth of trade outstripping the growth of output has accelerated since 1984 as indicated in Figure 9.1 which shows the long-term trend in the real volumes of merchandise trade and output.

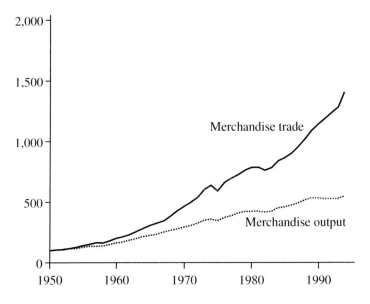

Source: WTO International Trade, Trends and Statistics (Geneva: WTO, 1995).

Figure 9.1   The growth of world trade and production, 1950–94 (volume indices, 1950 = 100)

In popular discussions this feature is often singled out and referred to as 'globalisation'. Trade flows today are certainly impressive by historical standards (meaning by that the levels reached in the decade before 1914) if measured against industrial production, but are not significantly higher in relation to world GDP. If trade in commercial services (which seems to have doubled since 1950) are added to the merchandise trade, total world trade may account for as much as 45 per cent of world GDP. A striking difference with nineteenth-century trade is in relation to the composition of the goods exchanged. Nineteenth-century trade was dominated by the exchange of manufactures for primary products. Today, the bulk of world trade is in manufactured goods and takes place predominantly among the developed countries. For example, in 1996 intra-European Union trade represented 65 per cent of the total trade of member countries. However, much of this trade is in intermediate rather than final goods, that is, intra-industry trade involving similar goods. More than half of all international trade involves the simultaneous import and export of essentially the same products. Several factors account for the growth of trade exceeding growth in world output, and in one way or another they relate to the pace of globalisation:

1. The growth of 'outsourcing' by multinational firms resulting from advances in telecommunications and relatively low transport costs accounts for much of the trade in intermediate goods.
2. The steady reduction in tariffs and other barriers to trade since the 1980s.
3. The shift in development strategies among developing countries towards more export-oriented policies (that is, import liberalisation, export promotion, and so on) first, among the countries of South East Asia and then in Latin America.
4. The transfer of technology and capital which might have increased the capacity for trade in the recipient countries.

The neoliberal supporters of globalisation claim that the universal benefits of market liberalisation (as exhibited by the rapid growth of world trade) would be realised in terms of (a) rising global living standards, (b) economic efficiency, (c) individual freedom and democracy and (d) unprecedented technological progress. Some of these neoliberals, sometimes referred to as 'market fundamentalists', hope to achieve the ideal of big business – the creation of a single global market in goods, services and capital within which production can be shifted, goods traded and where financial, legal, insurance and information services can expand. In fact, a state of affairs representing the realisation of Adam Smith's 'invisible hand' on a global scale. The establishment of transnational networks of production, trade and finance that seek out cost and political advantages, financed by a virtually unregulated system of exchanges of money, credit and equities is referred to by Kenichi Ohmae as projecting a new 'borderless world' (Ohmae 1990). According to an extreme version of this view, the nation-state is becoming irrelevant in the global economy and should only be concerned with providing the legal framework for contracts, defence, and law and order. An influential account of the impact of globalisation along these lines appeared in 1999 in Thomas Friedman's book *The Lexus and the Olive Tree* (Friedman 1999). Friedman, a *New York Times* columnist, says globalisation is not a passing phenomenon; it is inevitable and irreversible. The forward march of technology makes it so. Globalisation is a new technological–economic system based on the microchip. It is being driven by what he terms 'the electronic herd', the anonymous traders of bonds, stocks and currencies, free from any nation-state or power structure, and beholden to none. To retain or attract international investors, countries will need to don the 'golden straitjacket' of neoliberalism. The book contains his famous, but questionable remark that no two nations with McDonald's restaurants have fought each other since the restaurants opened in both. Lindsey (2002) blames the friends of globalisation for starting all the hype about the 'straitjacket' and other binding controls on governments. Much of the hype boomeranged. The critics hurled back the charge that it shows the world is careening out of control in a chaotic 'race to the bottom'. But much of the rhetoric from both sides is gross exaggeration. 'Where are the governments today', he asks, 'that toe a strict laissez-faire line?' (Lindsey 2002, p. 7).

Talk of a borderless world is exaggeration. It may be the dream of the evangelists of globalism, but falls far short of present reality or the foreseeable future – even when the integration talked about is limited only to trade flows. National borders still matter, and so do social networks based on ties of nationality and language. Integration is affected by such historical and customary ties, and so are trade flows. John Helliwell (1998) summarises recent research using very reliable data on trade linkages among Canadian provinces. Adjusting for scale and distance, the results indicate that trade between Canadian provinces was seventeen times as great as between Canadian provinces and equally distant American states in 1988, falling with the implementation of NAFTA (North Atlantic Free Trade Area) to about twelve more recently. Toronto trades more than ten times as much with Vancouver as with Seattle, even though the economy of Washington state is one-third larger than that of Ontario. Using other less satisfactory European data, Helliwell finds very substantial though smaller border effects within the European Union (EU). (Helliwell 1998). The results suggest that the gap between reality and the predictions of the free trade model is still considerable and that globalisation still has a long way to go yet. Trends in trade flows since the 1970s indicate the international transactions are not truly global, but flourish in the developed areas of the world within three regional trading blocs (EU, NAFTA and Asia-Japan). Thus, the trade of developed countries (US, EU and Japan) with developing countries represents only 4 per cent of their GDP.

Moderate pro-globalisers justify their claim that globalisation benefits all, including the poor, by pointing to evidence which shows that countries that have globalised (that is, instituted free-market reforms) and integrated into world markets have done better than those that have not. Such countries have grown the fastest and reduced poverty the most. The developing countries that managed to increase their trade have also attracted the largest share of foreign direct investment (FDI) – China benefited most by having the largest share of FDI over the last decade. Countries with the products, skills and resources that can be marketed worldwide have benefited considerably. Evidence is also cited to the effect that economic growth tends to be highly correlated with poverty reduction. Finally, there is the fact that global poverty has actually decreased over the past two decades. On this last point, it is true that the proportion of the world's poor living in absolute poverty (defined as people living on $1 or less per day calculated at purchasing-power parity exchange rates) fell from 24 per cent to 20 per cent during the 1990s, largely because of rapid income growth in China, India and East Asia generally. In 1980 China and India accounted for about one-third of the world's people and more than 60 per cent of the world's extreme poor. Thus while most countries have experienced lower income growth, these two large countries have had the opposite experience. Rapid growth in exports and high levels of foreign direct investment have boosted economic growth in these economies and lifted 200 million individuals out of absolute poverty in the last two decades. Chinese peasants have become construction labourers and factory workers in the booming coastal cities of China. For the good news on global poverty alleviation, thanks go to China and India, but meanwhile 2.8 billion people in developing countries live on less than $2 a day. If poor countries put into effect the adjustment policies and structural reforms recommended by international institutions such as the IMF, the World Bank and the WTO, then they too can reap the benefits of globalisation.

What is the evidence on trade, growth and poverty? The most widely cited case for the benefits of 'openness', showing that globalisation leads to faster growth and poverty reduction is that put forward by David Dollar and Aart Kraay, two World Bank economists (Dollar and Kraay 2000 and 2002). The econometric evidence is presented in two phases: (1) that trade promotes economic growth and (2) that growth reduces poverty. The authors find a strong positive correlation between globalisation (integration with the world economy) and economic growth. They classify countries into 'globalisers' (24 countries) and 'non-globalisers' (49 countries) according to countries' success in increasing their trade shares in GDP (ratio of exports and imports to GDP at constant prices) during 1977–1997, and found that the globalisers as a group that includes

Argentina, Brazil, China, India and Mexico) experienced per capita growth rates 4 per cent higher than the non-globalisers – a huge difference.

Over the last two decades the globalisers had an impressively large increase in trade relative to income of 104 per cent compared with 71 per cent for rich countries. The non-globalising countries, by contrast, actually trade less of their GDP than they did 20 years ago. Turning to the second link in the empirical evidence, Dollar and Kraay find on the basis of cross-country regressions that on average there is a one-to-one relationship between the growth rate of the income of the poor (the bottom 20 per cent of the income distribution) and the growth rate of overall per capita income, that is, the mean income of the lowest quintile has an elasticity of unity with respect to overall mean income. Thus, the authors' results suggest that the typical outcome of the growth process in developing countries is to leave the income share of the lowest quintile untouched. Across all countries, incomes of the poor grow at around the same rate as GDP, i.e. growth is distribution-neutral. Hence the authors' claim: 'Growth is good for the poor'. The 'trickle down' mechanism is no fantasy: it exists and helps to spread the wealth among the poor. To the authors' evident satisfaction, it appears the syllogism 'increased trade equals faster growth and faster growth equals more rapid poverty reduction' has been amply confirmed by the evidence. It amounts to a ringing endorsement of World Bank and IMF policy packages containing the officially sanctioned rules of openness.

However, the authors' study has been heavily criticised on methodological and theoretical grounds by academics and independent researchers as extremely misleading for being based on 'inappropriate indicators of trade policy', leading to conclusions founded on little more than 'a speculative leap of faith' (see Watkins 2002, pp. 24–7; Lübker, Smith and Weeks 2002, pp. 555–71). What critics decry are not the general results of the Dollar and Kraay study, but their use of inapprpriate measures and methods to assert that growth stimulated by World Bank/IMF policies is good for the poor. For instance, Lübker, Smith and Weeks (2002, p. 570) write: 'To state without regard to a country's economic characteristics, social structure, or political power relations that one specific package of economic and political policies will prove in practice to be universally good for the poor is to move well beyond the boundaries of normative economics into ideology.' In the first place, cross-country correlations between trade and income using ordinary least square regression (OLS) cannot identify the effect of trade, since trade volume as a share of GDP is endogenous and correlates with income – there is a simultaneity problem. The causation between trade and income can run in either direction: countries may trade more simply because they become richer. Secondly, Dollar and Kraay purport to show that trade liberalisation policies result in successful global integration (as registered by increasing trade/GDP ratios), which in turn translates into faster growth and poverty reduction. These empirical links are, however, suspect and cannot be accepted at face value since the authors use changes in trade shares as proxies for measures of trade policy.

But trade volume does not tell us anything about policy. More precisely, trade as a proportion of GDP is not a policy variable; it is a policy outcome – a policy outcome which is only partially determined by policy. Even if suitable measures of trade policy are found and used in the regression, the econometric problem still remains. For example, countries opting for freer trade may also pursue policies geared to macroeconomic stability which, in turn, are likely to affect income. Hence countries' trade policies are liable to be correlated with factors omitted from the income equation. Consequently, the impact of trade policy on income cannot be reliably identified and measured.

Many other factors influence trade as a portion of GDP, including changes in the terms of trade, natural resource endowments, levels of development, country size, countries' geographic characteristics (for example, proximity to major markets or trade routes). In general, the impact of policy on any variable cannot be drawn from a cross-country regression using trade shares as an indicator. As the authors themselves recognise, many countries that liberalised (reduced trade barriers) have not seen increases in trade and growth or a reduction of poverty, and that consequently 'openness' alone is not a 'sure-fire' poverty-reduction strategy. Finally, Dollar and Kraay ignore policies of redistribution as a way of improving the condition of the poor. As Dagdeviren, van der Hoeven and Weeks (2002, p. 391) comment: 'The policy issue is not whether growth is or is not good for the poor (it is, except in a few circumstances) but what policy measures can make it *better* for the poor'.

Now, although the number of people who live on less than $1 per day is slightly down, the number who live on less than $2 is slightly up; and it is well documented that inequality has soared during the last 15 years. For most of the developing world, except China, India, Chile, Vietnam and Uganda, globalisation is failing because it has not produced growth. Recognising that for many countries, integration into the world economy and faster convergence can result in dislocation such as job losses and income reductions which disproportionately hit the poor, the aim of policy should then be to spread the benefits while minimising costs.

Critics of globalisation believe, however, that the costs of integration outweigh the benefits and would like to slow the pace of the whole process. The costs include the loss of national autonomy to carry out egalitarian economic and social policies. In particular, it is alleged, both developed and developing countries have had to cut back on the welfare state and other redistributive safety nets. The main constraint on egalitarian policies in the developed and developing countries has been the excessive pressure put on governments by the IMF and investors to reduce government spending through reductions in the size of the state and the national budget. Notorious among such pressures in the 1980s were the IMF structural adjustment policies and their effects on social spending in developing countries. The impulse towards free markets has tied the hands of less developed countries from using policies such as exchange and price controls in order to affect internal income distribution.

Critics are disquieted by the pace of globalisation in so far as it raises the mobility of capital and makes it harder for governments to tax profits. Skilled and highly-paid workers can flee taxes they do not like. In addition, faster global integration increases competition in the labour market, engendering a fear that wages of low-skilled workers will fall in the markets that face cheap imports and that economic insecurity will increase for almost everyone. The result of such economic changes is a 'race to the bottom' in which workers, communities and whole countries are forced to compete by lowering wages, working conditions, environmental safeguards and social spending. These fears are, however, exaggerated, at least as regards the threat to social spending in the developed countries. The relationship between a country's vulnerability to international markets and the size of its tax-based welfare programme is positive, not negative, as a 'race to the bottom' would imply, according to evidence produced by Dani Rodrik (1997). Although it appears that a country's ability to set tax rates higher than other nations is being put at risk, in practice, tax competition among countries has had only limited effects even on corporate tax. To the extent that capital is more mobile than labour, the incidence of taxes to finance safety nets for those affected by globalisation is shifted to labour.

But fears about job losses among unskilled workers and an increase in income inequality linked to a widening gap between wages of skilled and unskilled labour have some basis in reality. The experience of the 1990s has highlighted what many see as the main effect of globalisation – a rise in income inequality among and between countries. Is globalisation the cause of growing income inequality? Is globalisation to blame for the widening wage gap between skilled and unskilled labour in rich countries? Has globalisation been good for the world's poor? In the developed, OECD countries the gap between rich and poor is widening, despite economic growth and tight labour markets. Particularly noticeable has been the widening gap between the wages of skilled and unskilled workers over the period 1973–98. In the United States, low-skilled workers saw no gain in earnings and perhaps even experienced a slight loss. The relative wage of skilled workers in the United States – defined as those with some college education and above – rose by nearly 20 per cent over the period from 1973 to 1993 despite the fact that the supply of skilled workers rose from 37 per cent of the US labour force to 59 per cent over the same period.[1] Incomes in the United States are now less equal than at any time since the 1930s depression and '[the gap] is now considerably wider than in any other affluent nation'.[2] In the United Kingdom the situation is similar – distribution of income is more unequal than at any time since 1945.

This trend has attracted a huge amount of recent research, but no clear indication of what proportion of the observed widening gap between the wages of skilled workers and unskilled workers is due to globalisation as against other contributory factors. The main factors identified have been the following:

1. Technological change has lowered the demand for the unskilled. Much of the earnings gap is due to the dispersion of skill-intensive technologies. In the US case, it is claimed that the rapid spread of computers after 1980 makes 'skill-biased technological change' a driving force behind rising pay differentials. Technological development raises the relative productivity of the well-trained; therefore the skilled are paid more and the unskilled less.

2. Globalisation increases competition in the labour market resulting from increased imports of lower-cost manufactures. Trade liberalisation has led to greater specialisation in production and the dispersion of specialised production processes (particularly the production of unskilled labour-intensive goods and services) to geographically distant locations. As a result, production of these products in developed countries has come under increased competitive pressure. The effect has been the application of downward pressure on the relative wages of unskilled workers in developed countries. Thus globalisation may lead to sharp short-run changes in the distribution of income as barriers to trade are lowered and the distribution of production is relocated among sectors. Capital flows, including US foreign direct investment (FDI) to emerging countries, that is, 'outsourcing' by US multinationals, added to the competitive pressure in the US labour market. Outsourcing (such as the assembly abroad of components and other repetitive tasks) swells the supply of imports that use unskilled labour more intensively than the rest of the US economy.

3. Decline in union power, and in the United States, an erosion of the real minimum wage.

4. Migrant labour willing to work for significantly less pay. This has particularly affected the US labour market.

Trade and technology are the principal sources of the changes in income distribution, and the interaction between them may have a large impact; but there is no agreement as to their relative importance. They are both obviously involved, to the extent that globalisation and technology make the demand for the services of unskilled and semiskilled workers more elastic. The increase in the elasticity of demand for these kinds of workers signifies that they can be more easily substituted for each other across national boundaries. The outsourcing of industrial activities reduces the demand for unskilled labour in the developed countries in much the same way as replacing these workers with automated production. Pursuing the implications of this analogy, Robert Feenstra writes: 'This means that outsourcing has a qualitatively similar effect on reducing the demand for unskilled relative to skilled labour within an industry as does skill-based technological change'; and he notes further that 'as soon as trade in intermediate inputs is permitted, as with outsourcing, then changes in the demand for labour within each industry can occur due to trade, as well' (Feenstra 1998, p. 41).

Some commentators believe that the role of trade has been exaggerated. They see that globalisation increases competition in the labour markets, but judge that this competition has had little impact on the wages of workers in industrial countries' labour markets. Thus if the impact is small, this implies that the gains from trade are small. For, in a Heckscher–Ohlin–Vanek framework, if the gains from trade were large, then trade would have had potentially large effects on wages (Rodrik 1997). Estimates of the trade impact range from negligible to as much as 50 per cent. Hertel (2000), in a quantitative assessment of the potential gains from trade liberalisation, estimated that the gains in real income for Canada, Mexico and the United States as a whole were around 0.37 per cent. This corresponds closely with most estimates of the static gains from trade as a share of income for the United States.

James Galbraith (2002) recently reported results on global inequality using data from the University of Texas Inequality Project (UTIP) in conjunction with the UN Industrial Development Organization (UNIDO) 2000 edition of Industrial Statistics. The data provide consistent measures of manufacturing pay inequality that can be compared across countries and through time from which inequality coefficients (the Theil statistic) can be derived. The results reveal that over the 1963–98 period manufacturing pay inequality was lowest in Scandinavia, Australia, countries in Eastern Europe, China and Cuba. The regions of highest inequality lie in a broad equatorial belt from Peru and Brazil through central Africa to India. On the whole, the data suggest that 'inequalities of pay within manufacturing tend to be lower in rich countries than in poor', implying that 'inequality almost surely declines as industrialization deepens and as incomes rise'

(Galbraith 2002, p. 17). Galbraith's data show that in the last two decades inequality has increased throughout the world in a pattern independent of national income changes. By the mid-1990s almost the only countries with declining inequality were the booming countries of South East Asia. In general, these trends traced the effects of neoliberalism at the global level. Galbraith concludes with the observation that 'it is not increasing trade *as such* [italics in original] that we should fear. Nor is technology the culprit. To focus on "globalization" as such misstates the issue.' The problem springs from the manner in which integration has been carried out since 1980 under circumstances 'in which wealth has flowed upwards from the poor countries to the rich, and mainly to the upper financial strata of the richest countries' (Galbraith 2002, p. 25).

Only in those countries which have successfully resisted the neoliberal agenda (championed by multinational firms, international organisations and the political leaders of the advanced countries) has growth continued and pay inequality remained under reasonable control. The countries are, notably, China, France, the Scandinavian states and India. Among the developing countries, China and India have done well in terms of economic growth and poverty reduction in the last decade or two. China, in particular, has experienced growth averaging 8 per cent per annum on a per capita basis since the late 1970s. But China's experience, despite the stunning success it is recognised to be, is hardly a good advertisement for neoliberal globalisation. In a recent paper entitled, 'Is Globalization Good for the World's Poor?', Dani Rodrik has put the record straight on how China, India and the so-called 'Tiger Economies' of South East Asia became successful economies. According to his account, these countries' experiences can hardly be trumpeted as shining examples of what globalisation can do for poor countries. For instance, 'China's economic policies violated virtually every rule by which the proselytizers of globalization would like the game to be played. China did not liberalize its trade regime to any significant extent . . . and to this day remains among the most protected economies in the world' (Rodrik 2002, p. 2). China's experience in achieving integration into the world economy despite ignoring the neoliberalisation rules is by no means exceptional. Rodrik refers to the earlier success stories of South Korea and Taiwan: these countries 'made extensive use of import quotas, local-content requirements, patent infringements and export subsidies – all of which are currently prohibited by the WTO'. Rodrik observes: 'Economic development often requires unconventional strategies that fit awkwardly with the ideology of free trade and free capital flows' (Rodrik 2002, p. 2). In the case of Taiwan it is well known that it took the Cold War and strong government policy to bring about Taiwan's economic 'miracle'. Given the island's strategic position for keeping China at bay, it attracted huge amounts of US economic and military aid – a total of $1.5 billion in US economic aid flowed to Taiwan until 1965 – which spurred industrialisation. India's import liberalisation came a decade after the start of high growth (3.7 per cent) in the early 1980s. India has yet to open itself to world financial markets. These countries took advantage of world markets while playing by their own rules. In a well-researched comparative study of industrialisation in several latecomer countries (including China, India, South Korea, Indonesia, Mexico and Brazil) Alice Amsden (2001) reviews their manufacturing experience and documents how these countries managed through well-conceived and executed interventionist state policies to make manufacturing profitable, which provided the basis for rapid growth by 1985. She highlights the key roles of the development state, the development bank, and interventionist state policies more generally in these countries' industrial development. Amsden shows how many of these countries linked their export strategies to import substitution manufacturing and to other strategic policies designed to protect their domestic markets. She catalogues a string of instances of the 'visible' hand of the development state, ranging from local content requirements (for example, for motor vehicles) stipulated in agreements with foreign firms, targeted access to working capital to tax breaks for firms that export. Amsden concludes that only Switzerland and Hong Kong managed to 'achieve high per capita incomes without tariff protection or export promotion' (Amsden 2001, p. 185). Reviewing Amsden's book, Robert Forrant comments on the findings that 'the "magic of the market" does not adequately explain the success of these late-industrializing countries, as many neoclassical economists contend'.[3] With free trade ideology in the ascendant and many of the supports formerly used by the newly-industrialising countries under interdiction by the IMF, WTO and other international organisations it is difficult to see how such paths to development can be followed by other countries. Latin American tariffs decreased from an average of between 35 per cent and 100 per cent (maximum and minimum rates) in 1985 to between 14 per cent and 22 per cent in the early 1990s. Consolidation of tariff schedules has also been effected, resulting in most countries having only three or fewer tariff categories.[4] Despite all this trade liberalisation (and domestic deregulation and privatisation) these countries failed to reap the rewards in terms of export growth. Real economic growth evaporated and income inequality increased.

With respect to developing countries, one expects that increased openness would raise the relative wages of unskilled workers. Given the differences in factor endowments, developing countries' exports are assumed to consist largely of goods whose production involves intensive use of unskilled labour. This is likely to increase the demand for workers of this type and thus decrease the gap between the wages of skilled and unskilled labour. However, the actual experience has been mixed. In the East Asian countries, relative wages of unskilled workers increased in the 1960s and 1970s, but in Latin America they decreased in the 1980s and early 1990s. Wage gaps fell when South Korea, Singapore and Taiwan liberalised, but widened in Latin America when those countries liberalised a decade or more later, despite the fact that in 1980 wage gaps in Latin America were already the largest in the world. By 1997, the wage gap in Latin America was 1.9 times as high as in developed countries and the countries of South East Asia (Klein and Tokman 2000, p. 18). What was the reason for this difference? One plausible explanation is that the Latin American countries' trade liberalisation coincided with the entry of China and other Asian exporters into world markets. When the Latin Americans liberalised, they faced intense competition from less skill-intensive manufactures in all export markets, including their traditional market outlets in the United States. Despite a rise of between 0.4 and 10 per cent in the competitiveness of Latin American countries, their ability to compete with goods from the Asian countries deteriorated. 'Competitiveness gains in these [latter] countries were about 50 per cent – ranging from 20 per cent in Thailand to 60 per cent in Malaysia – while among Latin American countries the largest increase, in Colombia, was about 10 per cent' (Klein and Tokman 2000, p. 11). Latin America adopted the globalisation agenda in the 1990s but experienced inequality and economic growth rates that were less than those enjoyed during the postwar years of 'import substitution industrialization' (ISI). In their careful study of social stratification under tension in a globalised era with reference to Latin America, Emilio Klein and Victor Tokman (Klein and Tokman 2000) conclude that economic liberalisation has placed Latin America under considerable tension: 'it affected social cohesion and introduced greater heterogeneity. As with all processes, there are winners and losers. The difference this time is that the changes are substantial and will have a structural effect on peoples, societies and nations not only today but into the future.' Moreover, the reform measures have 'favoured the relatively rich' (Klein and Tokman 2000, p, 26).

The evidence that global inequality has become more extreme is unequivocal. The most commonly used measure of trends in income inequality is the Gini coefficient with 0 representing perfect equality and 1 representing total inequality. In Latin America, the average Gini coefficient is almost 0.5. In Sub-Saharan Africa it is slightly lower, but there is considerable variation among countries and regions. Average incomes are significantly higher in urban areas than in rural areas. In China, the benefits of trade are concentrated in the coastal cities. The global Gini coefficient (using foreign exchange-adjusted currency) increased from an already high 0.71 in 1964 to peak at 0.80 in 1995 and was 0.79 in 1999. In comparison Brazil, usually considered to be extremely unfair, has a Gini coefficient of little more than 0.60.[5] However, all is not gloom. Apart from Sub-Saharan Africa, most developing countries are still better off in absolute terms than they were twenty years ago.

Free trade has undoubted merits in a globalising world – the market provides signals where profitable opportunities lie within a competitive environment. But the fact remains that 'globalism' in the guise of globalisation restrains the capacity of states to redistribute income and wealth as part of acceptable economic policy. 'Accepting this', writes Francisco Rodriguez, 'is not contradictory with believing in comparative advantage. It simply entails, in the best tradition of economic thought, accepting that globalization has benefits and costs, and that there is no *a priori* reason to believe that the costs cannot outweigh the benefits' (Rodriguez 2001, p. 610). But as Galbraith regretfully notes, 'no mechanism to reverse the policy exists', which policy he later calls 'the appalling disorder of the past twenty years' (Galbraith 2002, p. 25). If these globalising policies are not reversed and current trends continue, could the result be a global backlash against globalisation?

The war of 1914 put an end to the first era of globalisation before the political backlash against it could gather sufficient force and momentum to loosen the global bonds forged over the previous half century. Attempts were made by policy in the mid-1920s to refasten the economic links mainly through the reintroduction of the discipline of the gold standard, but opinions, attitudes and expectations of political leaders, the financial community and the public had changed. The change was in the direction of economic nationalism and away from cosmopolitanism. In the midst of open or latent instability, commitment to the restored global economy was at best lukewarm. The restored system was fragile, the global institutional framework was rudimentary or non-existent. Thus at the first buffeting the design flaws in the system were exposed and it collapsed in the shambles of the Slump. The forces that obstructed the return to the pre-1914 international world economy had their antecedents in the 1880s and 1890s backlash against globalism. Then, as we saw earlier, powerful groups upon whom globalisation had negative effects organised opposition to the free movement of goods, capital and labour. Capital mobility was solidly underpinned by the gold standard managed by the Bank of England. But the losers from globalisation succeeded in making inroads into the other pillars of the system – free trade and free migration. Quotas on immigration based on national origin were introduced in the United States and tariff barriers went up in Europe.

Looking at the collapse of the first era of globalisation in this way shifts one's focus from the systemic faults of globalism to its negative impact effects on economic groups and societies coming within its orbit. Economic groups harmed by late-nineteenth-century globalisation sought protection through the state – a reaction that reappeared with greater force in the 1930s. But both reactions were reflexes to the build-up of a set of common resentment among groups hurt or disadvantaged by the forces of globalisation. The common complaint was about drastic shifts in incomes, increases in inequality and unbearable competitive pressures resulting in job losses and the destruction of whole communities. O'Rourke and Williamson (1999) write: 'History shows that globalization can plant the seeds of its own destruction. Those seeds were planted in the 1870s, sprouted in the 1880s, grew vigorously around the turn of the century, and then came to full flower in the dark years between the two world wars' (O'Rourke and Williamson 1999, p. 93). The authors suggest that the nationalistic backlash would have increased even without the war. The identification of common elements provoking political and social reaction to global integration at different times which can result in the retreat of globalisation has influenced people's attitudes to the future of globalisation. If it is reversible, can it again go into retreat if the same losses and hardships are inflicted on groups and individuals? Can a groundswell of support for the losers become powerful enough to force political action? Are there signs that history might repeat itself? Williamson's short answer is: 'maybe not'. Compared to a century ago the typical industrialised country now has a more diversified spread of wealth and employment across economic sectors and is therefore less vulnerable to the kind of trade backlash seen in the past. Mass migration is a thing of the past. Agriculture is a much smaller proportion of GDP than it was a hundred years ago and governments have various ways of easing the burden of adjustment faced by domestic losers from international competition. Yet despite such grounds for optimism, Williamson concludes that if it happened in the past, it could happen again – a globalisation backlash 'may reappear in our future' (Williamson 1998, p. 70). But financial markets remain fragile and notoriously unstable and could still prove hugely disruptive, as shown by the late 1990s East Asian crisis and the 2001 collapse of Argentina's economy. The fears over immigration in the United States, as articulated by Pat Buchanan, keep resurfacing and European Union leaders, fearing a backlash from supporters of extreme right-wing political parties, have been forced to deal with similar fears over illegal immigrants, refugees and asylum seekers.

In the United States public opinion surveys show that the general public has major reservations about free trade. In fact, there is substantial public opposition to further trade and integration moves. In a 1998 survey conducted by the Chicago Council on Foreign Relations, only 32 per cent of the general public supported the elimination of tariffs and other import restrictions (which would lead to lower prices) even if that meant the loss of jobs in import-competing industries, while 48 per cent were sympathetic to the argument that tariffs were necessary to protect jobs; 19 per cent were unable to express an opinion.[6] Other survey results suggest that 'a majority of Americans think that trade results in fewer jobs and lower wages for some segments of the labour force' (Coughlin 2002, p. 1). Job losses in the United States occur among that broad segment of the population with average skill and education levels where the median voter is located. Over half of the US adult population has achieved no more than a high school education.[7] Thomas Friedman identifies one source of friction when he writes: 'What all the backlash forces have in common is a feeling that as their countries have plugged into the globalization system, they are being forced into a Golden Straitjacket that is one-size-fits-all' (Friedman 1999, p. 269). The 'one-size-fits-all' constraints range from the so-called 'Washington consensus' of the 1980s to the 'Geneva consensus' of the late 1990s represented by the common set of rules of the World Trade Organization (WTO). These constraints clash with the desire to maintain diverse preferences and institutions among countries.

The anti-globalisation street protests in Seattle (1999), Washington, DC, Davos (2000), Gothenburg and Genoa (2001), can, perhaps, easily be dismissed (as the Seattle protest was, by Thomas Friedman) as 'a Noah's Ark of flat earth advocates, protectionist unions and yuppies'.[8] But what is significant as 'straw in the wind' was how such actions, without the violence, were supported by large sections of the population in many countries. What it signifies is that there are real problems out there thrown up by the relentless forces of globalisation to which we referred above – in particular, increasing income inequality and the slow pace of poverty reduction in the poorer countries of the world. The perception of rising inequality is apparent and is most often associated with foreign trade. As a consequence, in some circles the debate is often polarised into free trade versus protectionism; but free trade is not the problem. It can be the solution. The more constructive question is: what kind of free trade? What is required is a global trade system that pays attention to the social costs of adjustment resulting from greater specialisation and integration. For developing countries, freer trade means the ability to import capital equipment and technology necessary for long-term economic growth. But such countries must change the structure of their economies before foreign trade can start to contribute to their development objectives. Forcing developing countries to conform to a free trade, free market orthodoxy is no way to assist them to reach that later outward-oriented stage. They should be allowed the option to adopt development strategies suited to the basic characteristics of their societies and stages of economic development – just as most of the present-day developed countries did during their classic industrialisation periods.

Developing countries, trying to increase their exports of agricultural products and labour-intensive goods such as textiles, complain about asymmetries in market access. Since the conclusion of the Uruguay Round of tariff reductions in 1994, developing countries have reduced by half their average tariffs on agricultural imports, but rich countries have not reciprocated commensurately. Tariff barriers against manufactured goods from the developing countries (leather, footwear, textiles and other products) are, on average, four times as high as those against products from the industrialised world. The rules of the game seem to be summarised in the injunction: 'Do as we say, not as we do'.

Trade negotiations have also been asymmetric: the agribusiness, pharmaceutical and financial services industries in the rich countries have been successful in setting the agenda of multilateral trade negotiations. It remains to be seen whether the new round of trade negotiations launched at Doha in November 2001 will make a difference and whether developed countries will open up their markets in agriculture and textiles and modify intellectual property rights that tend to raise prices of essential medicines in poor countries. At present, the European Union (EU), the United States and Japan subsidize their farmers by about $350 billion a year. The subsidies encourage over-production. The surpluses, sold cheaply to poor countries, depress world prices and bankrupt subsistence farmers in the develoing world. Because of over-supply, the prices of a wide range of staple commodities (coffee, cocoa, rice, sugar, etc.) fell by more than 60 per cent between 1980 and 1990. American officials claim that the United States (set to spend $190 billion supporting American agriculture over the next ten years) is simply providing cheap food for the world's hungry. In sympathy with this view, some commentators fear that many poor food-importing countries might not benefit from the abolition of agricultural protection in the industrialised countries.

Developing countries, for their part, need to look at the anti-trade effects of their own trade barriers against one another – 70 per cent of the tariff barriers that developing countries face are from other developing countries. In another respect, the trade rules also need changing so that the poorest countries can export processed commodities and capture more of the 'value-added' which now accrues to multinational firms in the developed world. Outside East Asia, none of the developing countries that have rapidly liberalised trade and investment in the past two decades have achieved a significant increase in their share of world manufacturing income (value-added), as their exports continue to be concentrated in resource-based, labour-intensive goods.

Unlike in the nineteenth century, mass migration is not an option currently available to labour-abundant poor countries. The market for unskilled labour services has remained untouched by the 1980s liberalising trend. They cannot leave in large numbers and go to lands where capital is abundant. Will capital go to them? The reduced flow of capital from rich to poorer countries is a worrying sign. By 1997, countries in the bottom fifth of income per capita received less than 5 per cent of the total flow of foreign capital.[9]

Commentators from a broad spectrum of opinion have called attention to economic and social fissures opening up in many societies and traceable directly to the effects of globalisation: a rift between those who have skills and mobility to flourish in global markets and those who lack such attributes. In other words, the rise of a 'winner-takes-all' society capable of generating unprecedented inequalities. If too many people doubt that openness works for them, political support for open, integrated economies can ebb away. The nation-state has not withered away. Political sovereignty is still in place to halt or reverse the process.

People will put up with integration brought about by technology, but not with integration through policy. Globalisation is a reality not a choice – that may be true in so far as it refers to technological shifts that are regarded as inevitable and to which they will have to accommodate themselves. But new policy initiatives aimed at deepening integration might be resented. While increased integration harms the economic interests of certain groups (for example, unskilled workers in developed countries) it also creates countervailing groups who have a stake in sustaining open markets. Societies can become fractured by the chaotic world with its combination of great successes and inequalities that globalisation creates.

While the recent spate of corporate scandals in the United States involving the energy giant Enron, World Com, Xerox, and so on, has done nothing to inspire confidence in the American model of capitalism, the international institutions (the IMF and the World Bank) which supervise the progress of globalisation have also come in for their share of criticism from inside sources. Joseph Stiglitz, Nobel laureate and former chief economist at the World Bank has added his criticisms to those of many ordinary people of the policies practised by these institutions in the past decade – in particular, the 'undemocratic' secretiveness and the 'fundamentalist' free-market approach of the IMF (Stiglitz 2002). Besides the voices of the anti-globalisation activists, armchair critics and others have joined in silent literary protest at the pace of globalisation in increasing numbers in the last few years.[10]

As a result, things are beginning to change, or so it seems. World leaders have set themselves the goal of halving by 2015 the share of the world's population living in extreme poverty. The international economic institutions (the World Bank, the IMF, WTO, regional development banks, multilateral development agencies, etc.) have themselves subscribed to a global development agenda whereby progress in globalisation is to be measured against the yardstick of poverty reduction and sustainable development. There is now talk about a post-Washington Consensus – a set of policy measures emphasizing the need for wide-ranging institutional reforms such as property rights, the rule of law, democracy, and so on. Dubbed the 'Augmented Washington Consensus', this ambitious policy reform programme has already attracted criticism from analysts of globalisation. Dani Rodrik, for one, contends that the refurbished Washington Consensus is 'not a helpful guide to promoting development in poor countries . . . It is an impossibly broad, undifferentiated agenda of institutional reform and . . . too insensitive to local context and needs.'[11]

Backlash scenarios for the current phase of globalisation are appearing in greater numbers. One thoughtful account by Harold James (2001) traces the crisis that resulted in the 1930s depression to its roots in the pre-1914 backlash against global integration and warns of the dangers of a similar backlash occurring in the present phase of globalisation. From a different perspective to that taken in the present chapter, James analyses the forces that could produce the next backlash. He sees the beginning of an anti-globalist coalition arising from hostility to immigration, a belief in capital controls and scepticism about global trade. In James' analysis the forces that could produce the next backlash include: (a) Europe's inability to innovate; (b) exclusion of the world's poor nations from the benefits of globalisation; (c) global financial fragility; (d) doubts about the ability of modern politicians and welfare states to soften the impact of economic integration on vulnerable groups; and (e) the political clout of the principal losers in advanced countries – less-skilled labour. Nevertheless, James believes that the anti-globalist coalition is not strong enough at the present time to swing the pendulum against globalism because it lacks: (a) the 'intellectual cement' that can link current resentments to a coherent or credible intellectual package to replace the ideology of globalism and (b) it can point to no specific model of national success based on a repudiation of globalism's tenets. But James gloomily closes with the warning that while the anti-globalists' lack of these two features 'explains why the pendulum is so slow in swinging back from globality . . . it does not and cannot explain why it will not swing' (James 2001, p. 224). Michael Bordo, in a review of James' book, presents a more optimistic vision. He believes that the forces responsible for the backlash a century ago are different from those at work today and suggests that 'now there are more centrifugal than centripetal forces at work to prevent a comparable backlash from occurring' (Bordo 2002, p. 52). Let's hope he is right!

Like James, Brink Lindsey (2002) has expressed similar fears over the chances of globalisation's survival, but like Bordo he is sanguine about the prospects over the long term. He sees the current episode of globalisation as a transitional era in which the 'dead hand' of anti-market forces representing the old forces of negation and obstruction still contend with the 'invisible hand' of free markets. Consequently, globalisation's progress will come in 'fits and starts' and there is always the danger that economic liberalisation will be slowed or even reversed. However, like James, he believes the intellectual climate strongly favours globalisation over 'heavy-handed interventionism'. As a result, 'economic policies and institutions around the world will continue to move in a more or less liberal direction' (Lindsey, 2002, p. 257). Using Biblical imagery about desert wanderings and the Promised Land, Lindsey concludes that 'there is a good reason to believe that we are on our way to somewhere better' (Lindsey, 2002, p. 270).

One can only say 'Amen' to such expressions of optimism.

NOTES

1. See William R. Cline, *Trade and Income Distribution* (Washington, DC: Institute for International Economics, 1997).
2. Christopher Jencks, 'Does Inequality Matter?', *Daedalus* (Winter 2002), p. 49.
3. Robert Forrant's review of Amsden (2001) in *Business History Review*, 35 (Winter), pp. 922–5.
4. See V.E. Tokman, 'The Labour Challenges of Globalization and Economic Integration', in E. Mayobre (ed.), *G-24, The Developing Countries in the International Financial System* (Boulder, Colorado: Lynne Rienner Publishers, 1999).
5. Colin D. Butler, 'Globalization and Health', *British Medical Journal (BMJ)* (25 May 2002), pp. 1276–7.
6. John E. Rielly (ed.), *American Public Opinion and US Foreign Policy* (Chicago: Chicago Council on Foreign Relations, 1999).
7. See US Bureau of the Census, *Statistical Abstract of the United States, 1999*, (Washington, DC: Government Printing Office, 1999), p. 170.
8. See *New York Times* (12 January 1999), Op-Ed page.
9. See *The Economist* (18 May 2002), p. 27.
10. These recent critical writings include George Soros' *On Globalisation* (London: Public Affairs, 2002); Noreena Hertz, *The Silent Takeover: Global Capitalism and the Death of Democracy* (London: Heinemann, 2001); Graham Dunkley, *The Free Trade Adventure. The WTO, the Uruguay Round and Globalism: A Critique* (London: Zed Books, 2000), and Manfred B. Steger (2002).
11. See Dani Rodrik, 'After Neoliberalism, What?' Unpublished version of remarks made at a conference on Alternatives to Neoliberalism, in Washington, DC, 23 May, 2002.

Bibliography

Agarwala, P.N. (1985), *The History of Indian Business*, New Delhi: Vikas Publishing House, PVT Ltd.

Allen, W.R. (1968), 'The Position of Mercantilism and the Early Development of International Trade Theory', in Robert V. Eagly (ed.), *Events, Ideology and Economic Theory*, Detroit: Wayne University Press.

Amery, J. (1969), *Joseph Chamberlain and the Tariff Reform Campaign*, London: Macmillan.

Amsden, A. (2001), *The Rise of 'the Rest': Challenges to the West from Late-Industrialization Economies*, Oxford: Oxford University Press.

Anderson, K. and R. Garnaut (1987), *Australian Protectionism*, Sydney: Allen and Unwin.

Anderson, K.L., (1938), 'Protection and the Historical Situation: Australia', *Quarterly Journal of Economics*, **53** (November), pp. 86–104.

Angell, J.A., (1926), *The Theory of International Prices: History, Criticism and Restatement*, Cambridge, Mass.: Harvard University Press.

Appleyard, D.R., and J.C. Ingram (1979), 'A Reconsideration of the Additions to Mill's "Great Chapter"', *History of Political Economy*, **11** (4), pp. 459–76.

Ashley, W.J. (1904), *The Progress of the German Working Classes in the Last Quarter of the Century*, London: Longman Green

Ashley, W.J. (1905), *Political Economy and the Tariff Problem*, London: Macmillan.

Ashley, W.J. [1907] (1962), 'A Survey of the Past History and Present Position of Political Economy', reprinted in R.L. Smyth (ed.), *Essays in Economic Method*, London: Duckworth.

Bairoch, P. (1989), 'European Trade Policy, 1815–1914', in P. Mathias and S. Pollard (eds), *The Cambridge Economic History of Europe*, vol. VIII: *The Industrial Economies: The Development of Economic and Social Policies*, Cambridge: Cambridge University Press, pp. 1–160.

Bairoch, P. (1991), *Economics and World History: Myths and Paradoxes*, London: Harvester Wheatsheaf.

Ballance, R., J. Ansari and H. Singer (eds) (1982), *The International Economy and Industrial Development: Trade and Investment in the Third World*, London: Wheatsheaf Books.

Barbon, N. (1690), *A Discourse of Trade*, London: T. Milbourn.

Barker, Sir Ernest (1948), *Traditions of Civility*, Cambridge: Cambridge University Press.

Barone, E. [1908] (1935), 'The Ministry of Production in the Collectivist State', in *Collectivist Economic Planning: Critical Studies on the Possibilities of Socialism*, by N.G. Pierson, L. von Mises, G. Hahn and E. Barone, edited by F.A. von Hayek, London: Routledge & Kegan Paul.

Barone, E. (1908), *Principi di Economia Politica*, Rome: G. Bertero.

Bastable, C.F. (1901), 'On Some Disputed Points in the Theory of International Trade', *Economic Journal*, **11**, pp. 227–8.

Bastable, C.F. (1902), 'An Imperial Zollverein with Preferential Tariffs', *Economic Journal*, **12** (December), pp. 507–13.

Bastable, C.F. (1903), *The Theory of International Trade*, 4th edn revised, London: Macmillan.

Batra, R.N. (1993), *The Myth of Free Trade: A Plan for America's Economic Revival*, New York: Scribner's.

Beales, H.L. [1928] (1967), *The Industrial Revolution, 1750–1850*, reprinted by Augustus M. Kelley, Publishers. New York: Kelley.

Beveridge, W. (ed.) (1931), *Tariffs: The Case Examined*, London: Longmans Green.

Bhagwati, J.N. (1988), *Protectionism*, Cambridge, Mass.: MIT Press.

Bhagwati, J. N. (1994), 'Fair Trade, Reciprocity and Harmonization: The New Challenge to the Theory and Policy of Free Trade', in A.V. Deardorff and R.M. Stern (eds), *Analytical and Negotiating Issues in the Global Trading System*, Ann Arbor: University of Michigan Press.

Bhagwati, J.N. and D.A. Irwin (1987), 'The Return of the Reciprocitarians – US Trade Policy Today', *The World Economy*, **10**, pp. 109–30.

Bhagwati, J.N. and H.G. Johnson [1960] (1972), 'Notes on Some Controversies in the Theory of International Trade', *Economic Journal*, **70** (March), pp. 74–93, reprinted in J.N. Bhagwati, *Tariffs and Growth*, London: Weidenfeld & Nicholson, pp. 124–9.

Bickerdike, C.F. (1905), 'Review of Dr R. Schüller's "Schutzzoll und Freihandel"', *Economic Journal*, **15**, pp. 413–15.

Bickerdike, C.F. (1906), 'The Theory of Incipient Taxes', *Economic Journal*, **16** (December), pp. 529–35.

Bickerdike, C.F. (1907), 'Review of A.C. Pigou, "Protective and Preferential Import Duties"', *Economic Journal*, **17** (March), pp. 98–102.

Bickerdike, C.F. (1920), 'The Instability of Foreign Exchange', *Economic Journal*, **30** (March), pp. 118–22.

Blaug, M. (1958), *Ricardian Economics: A Historical Study*, New Haven, Conn.: Yale University Press.

Blaug, M. (1968), *Economic Theory in Retrospect*, 2nd edition, London: Heinemann.

Bloomfield, A.I. (1984), 'Effect of Growth on the Terms of Trade. Some Earlier Views', *Economica*, **51** (May).

Bordo, M. (2002), Review of Harold James, *The End of Globalization*, in *Finance and Development*, **39** (1) (March), Washington, DC: IMF, pp. 52–3.

Boyd, C.W. (ed.) (1914), *Mr Chamberlain's Speeches*, vol. II, London: Constable & Co. Ltd.

Brander, J.A. and B.J. Spencer (1981), 'Tariffs and the Extraction of Foreign Monopoly Rents under Potential Entry', *Canadian Journal of Economics*, **14**, pp. 371–89.

Brander, J.A. and B.J. Spencer (1984), 'Tariff Protection and Imperfect Competition', in H. Kierzkowski (ed.), *Monopolistic Competition and International Trade*, Oxford: Oxford University Press.

Braudel, F. (1984), *Civilization and Capitalism, 15th–18th Century*, vols 2 and 3, London: Collins.

Brewster, Sir Francis (1702), *New Essays on Trade*. Originally published as *Essays on Trade and Navigation* (1695), London: Cockerill.

Brigden, J.B. (1925), 'The Australian Tariff and the Standard of Living', *Economic Record* (November).

Brigden et al. (1929), *The Australian Tariff: An Economic Enquiry*, Melbourne: Melbourne University Press.

Briggs, A. (1959), *The Age of Improvement*, London: Longmans.

Brown, M.B. (1970), *After Imperialism*, London: Heinemann.

Cain, N. (1973), 'Political Economy and the Tariff: Australia in the 1920s', *Australian Economic Papers*, **11–12** (June), pp. 1–210.

Cannan, E. (1953), *History of the Theories of Production and Distribution in English Political Economy from 1776 to 1848*, 3rd edition, London: Staples Press.

Capie, F. (1983), *Depression and Protectionism: Britain Between the Wars*, London: George Allen & Unwin.

Capie, F. (1994), *Tariffs and Growth: Some Illustrations from the World Economy 1850–1940*, Manchester: Manchester University Press.

Caves, R.E. (1960), *Trade and Economic Structure: Models and Methods*, Cambridge, Mass.: Harvard University Press.

Chang, Ha-Joon, (2002), *Kicking Away the Ladder – Development Strategy in Historical Perspective*, London: Anthem Press.

Chipman, J.S. (1965a), 'A Survey of the Theory of International Trade: Part 1, The Classical Theory,' *Econometrica*, **33** (3), pp. 477–519.

Chipman, J.S. (1965b), 'A Survey of the Theory of International Trade: Part 2, The Neo-Classical Theory', *Econometrica*, **33** (4), pp. 685–760.

Chipman, J.S. (1966), 'A Survey of the Theory of International Trade: Part 3, The Modern Theory', *Econometrica*, **34** (1), pp. 18–76.

Chipman, J.S. (1979), 'Mill's "Superstructure": How Well Does it Stand Up?', *History of Political Economy*, **11** (4), pp. 477–500.

Clapham, J.H. [1939] (1967), *An Economic History of Modern Britain*, vol. 1, Cambridge: Cambridge University Press.

Clavin, P. (1998), 'Shaping the Lessons of History. Britain and the Rhetoric of American Trade Policy 1930–1960', in A. Marrison (ed.), *Free Trade and its Reception*, London: Routledge.

Clemens, M. and J.G. Williamson (2000), 'Where Did British Foreign Capital Go? Fundamentals, Failures and the Lucas Paradox 1870–1913', NBER Working Paper 8028, National Bureau of Economic Research, Cambridge, Mass. (December).

Coats, A.W. (1968), 'Political Economy and the Tariff Reform Campaign of 1903', *Journal of Law and Economics*, **17**, pp. 181–229.

Conybeare, J.A.C. (1987), *Trade Wars*, New York: Columbia University Press.

Copland, D.B. (1931), 'A Neglected Phase of Tariff Controversy', *Quarterly Journal of Economics*, **46**, pp. 289–308.

Coughlin, C.C. (2002), 'The Controversy over Free Trade: The Gap between Economists and the General Public', *Federal Reserve Bank of St. Louis Review*, January/February, pp. 1–210.

Cournot, A.A. [1838] (1897), *Recherches sur les Principes Mathématiques de la Théorie des Richesses*, Paris: Hachette. Translated by Nathaniel T. Bacon as *Researches into the Mathematical Principles of the Theory of Wealth*, London: Macmillan.

Cournot, A.A. (1863), *Principes de la Théorie des Richesses*, Paris: Hachette.

Crafts, N.F.R. and M. Thomas (1986), 'Comparative Advantage in UK Manufacturing Trade 1910–1935', *Economic Journal*, **96** (September), pp. 629–45.

Cunningham, W. (1912), *The Rise and Decline of the Free Trade Movement*, Cambridge: Cambridge University Press.

Cunningham, W. (1916), *The Progress of Capialism in England*, Cambridge: Cambridge University Press.

Cunynghame, H. (1904), *A Geometrical Political Economy*, Oxford: Oxford University Press.

Dagdeviren, H., R. van der Hoeven and J. Weeks (2002), 'Poverty Reduction with Growth and Redistribution', *Development and Change*, **33** (3), pp. 383–413.

Daunton, M. (2002), 'On a Sticky Wicket', *The Times Literary Supplement*, 10 May, pp. 6–9.

Davenant, Charles [1696] (1771), 'An essay on the East-India Trade' in Sir Charles Whitworth (ed.), *The Political and Commercial Works of Charles Davenant*, London: R. Horsfield.

Davis, D.R. (1997), 'Critical Evidence on Comparative Advantage? North–North Trade in a Multilateral World', *Journal of Political Economy*.

Davis, R. (1979), *The Industrial Revolution and British Overseas Trade*, Leicester: Leicester University Press.

Deane, P. (1990), 'Marshall on Free Trade', in R.M. Tullberg (ed.), *Alfred Marshall in Retrospect*, New York: Edward Elgar, pp. 113–32.

Deardorff, A.V. and R.M. Stern (eds) (1994), *The Stolper–Samuelson Theorem: A Golden Jubilee*, Ann Arbor: University of Michigan.

Dobb, M. (1973), *Theories of Production and Distribution since Adam Smith*, Cambridge: Cambridge University Press.

Dollar, D. and A. Kraay (2000), *Growth is Good for the Poor*, Washington, DC: World Bank.

Dollar, D. and A. Kraay (2002), 'Spreading the Wealth', *Foreign Affairs*, **81** (January/February), pp. 120–33.

Dorfman, J. (1946), *The Economic Mind in American Civilization 1606–1865*, New York: Viking Press.

Dunez, P. (1993), *Histoire du Libre-Echange et du Protectionnisme en France*, Paris: Editeur.

Edgeworth, F.Y. (1881), *Mathematical Psychics: An Essay on the Application of Mathematics to the Moral Sciences*, London: Kegan Paul.

Edgeworth, F.Y. (1894), 'The Pure Theory of International Values', *Economic Journal*, **4**, (December), pp. 606-38.

Edgeworth, F.Y. (1899), 'On a Point in the Pure Theory of International Trade', *Economic Journal*, **9** (March), pp. 125–8.

Edgeworth, F.Y. (1908), 'Appreciation of Mathematical Theories – III', *Economic Journal*, **18**, pp. 392–403, 541–56.

Edgeworth, F.Y. (1925), *Papers Relating to Political Economy*, vol. II, London: Macmillan.

Eichengreen, B. (1989), 'The Political Economy of the Smoot–Hawley Tariff', in Roger L. Ransom (ed.), *Research in Economic History*, **12**, Greenwich, CT: Jai Press, pp. 1–43.

Elbaum, R. and W. Lazonick (1986), *The Decline of the British Economy*, Oxford: Clarendon Press.

Elmslie, B.T. (1995), 'Retrospectives: The Convergence Debate Between David Hume and Josiah Tucker', *Journal of Economic Perspectives*, **9** (4), pp. 207–16.

Ethier, W.J. (1979), 'Internationally Decreasing Costs and World Trade', *Journal of International Economics*, **9** (1), pp. 1–24.

Ethier, W.J. (1982a), 'National and International Returns to Scale in the Modern Theory of International Trade', *American Economic Review*, **72** (3), pp. 389–405.

Ethier, W.J. (1982b), 'Decreasing Costs in International Trade and Frank Graham's Argument for Protection', *Econometrica*, **50** (5), pp. 1243–68.

Ethier (1986), 'The Multinational Firm', *Quarterly Journal of Economics*, (November), pp. 805–33.

Feenstra, R.C. (1998), 'Integration of Trade and Disintegration of Production in the Global Economy', *Journal of Economic Perspectives*, **12** (4) (Fall), pp. 36–50.

Fetter, F.W. (1962), 'Robert Torrens: Colonel of Marines and Political Economist', *Economica* (May).

Findlay, R. and S. Wellisz (1982), 'Endogenous Tariffs, the Political Economy of Trade Restrictions and Welfare', in J.N. Bhagwati (ed.), *Import Competition and Response*, Chicago: Chicago University Press.

Foreman-Peck, J., A. Hughes Hallett and Y. Ma (1998), 'The End of Free Trade. Protection and the Exchange Rate Regime between the World Wars', in Andrew Marrison (ed.), *Free Trade and Its Reception*, London: Routledge, pp. 262–86.

Forrant, R. (2001), Review of *The Rise of 'the Rest'* by Alice Amsden, *Business History Review*, **75** (Winter), pp. 922–5.

Fortrey, S. (1663), *England's Interest and Improvement*, London: J. Field.

Frank, A.G. (1979), *Dependent Accumulation*, vol. 1, London: Macmillan.

Friedman, T. (1999), *The Lexus and the Olive Tree: Understanding Globalization*, New York: Farrar Strauss.

Galbraith, J.K. (2002), 'A Perfect Crime: Inequality in the Age of Globalization', *Daedalus* (Winter), pp. 11–25.

Garside, W.R. (1998), 'Party Politics, Political Economy and British Protectionism, 1919–1932', *History*, **83** (269) (January), pp. 47–65.

Giffen, R. [1889] (1970), *The Growth of Capital*, London: G. Bell, reprinted 1970 by A.M. Kelley, New York.

Goldstein, J. (1998), 'Creating the GATT Rules: Politics, Institutions and American Policy', in R. Howse (ed.), *The World Trading System: Critical Perspectives on the World Economy*, vol. 1, pp. 22–49.

Gomes, L. (1987), *Foreign Trade and the National Economy*, London: Macmillan.

Gomes, L. (1990), *Neoclassical International Economics*, London: Macmillan.

Gomes, L. (1993), *The International Adjustment Mechanism*, New York: St. Martin's Press.

Graham, F.D. (1923), 'Some Aspects of Protection Further Considered', *Quarterly Journal of Economics*, **37** (February), pp. 199–227.

Graham, F.D. (1934), *Protective Tariffs*, New York: Harper & Bros.

Graham, F.D. (1948), *The Theory of International Values*, Princeton, N.J.: Princeton University Press.

Grampp, W.D. [1952] (1960), 'The Liberal Element in English Mercantilism', reprinted in J.J. Spengler and W.R. Allen, *Essays in Economic Thought*, Chicago: Rand McNally.

Grampp, W.D. (1982), 'Economic Opinion when Britain Turned to Free Trade', *History of Political Economy*, **14** (4).

Green, E.H.H. (1995), *The Crisis of Conservatism: The Politics, Economics and Ideology of the British Conservative Party, 1880–1914*, London: Routledge.

Groenewegen, P. (1983), 'Turgot's Place in the History of Economic Thought: A Bicentenary Estimate', *History of Political Economy*, **15** (4).

Groenewegen, P. (1995), *A Soaring Eagle: Alfred Marshall 1842–1924*, Aldershot: Edward Elgar.

Haberler, G. (1936), *The Theory of International Trade*, London: William Hodge & Co. Ltd.

Haberler, G. (1950), 'Some Problems in the Pure Theory of International Trade', *Economic Journal*, **60**, pp. 223–40.

Hamilton, A. [1791] (1934), *Papers on Public Credit, Commerce and Finance by Alexander Hamilton*, ed. Samuel McKee Jr., New York: Columbia University Press.

Harley, C. Knick (2000), A Review of O'Rourke and Williamson's *Globalization and History: The Evolution of a 19th Century Atlantic Economy*, in *Journal of Economic Literature*, **38** (December), pp. 926–35.

Harnetty, P. (1972), *Imperialism and Free Trade: Lancashire and India in the Mid-Nineteenth Century*, Manchester: Manchester University Press and University of British Columbia Press.

Harrod, Sir Roy (1951), *The Life of John Maynard Keynes*, London: Macmillan.

Harvie, C. (1998), 'Revolution and the Rule of Law, 1789–1851', in *The Oxford Popular History of Britain*, Oxford: Oxford University Press.

Heckscher, E. (1955), *Mercantilism*, trans. M. Shapiro, 2nd edition, London: George Allen & Unwin.

Helliwell, J. (1998), *How Much Do National Borders Matter?*, Washington DC: Brookings Institution.

Helpman, E. (1999), 'The Structure of Foreign Trade', *Journal of Economic Perspectives*, **13** (2) (Spring), pp. 121–44.

Helpman, E. and P.R. Krugman (1985), *Market Structure and Foreign Trade: Increasing Returns, Imperfect Competition and the International Economy*, Cambridge, Mass.: MIT Press.

Henderson, W.O. (1983), *Friedrich List: Economist and Visionary, 1789–1846*, London: Frank Cass.

Herberg, H. and M.C. Kemp (1969), 'Some Implications of Variable

Returns to Scale', *Canadian Journal of Economics*, **2** (August), pp. 403–15.

Hertel, T.W. (2000), 'Potential Gains from Reducing Trade Barriers in Manufacturing, Services and Agriculture', *Federal Reserve Bank of St. Louis Review*, July/August, **82** (4), pp. 77–99.

Hertz, N. (2001), *The Silent Takeover: Global Capitalism and the Death of Democracy*, London: William Heinemann.

Hewins, W.A.S. (1929), *The Apologia of an Imperialist*, London: Constable.

Hilton, B. (1998), 'Comments on Kinealy and Schonhardt-Bailey', in A. Marrison (ed.), *Free Trade and Its Reception*, pp. 82–5.

Ho, P. S.-w. (1996), 'Reappraising Torrens's Contributions to the Analysis of Trade, Growth and Colonisation', *Contributions to Political Economy*, **15**, pp. 1–31.

Hollander, S. (1973), *The Economics of Adam Smith*, London: Heinemann.

Hollander, S. (1977), 'Ricardo and the Corn Laws: A Revision', *History of Political Economy*, **9** (1) (Spring), pp. 1–47.

Hollander, S. (1979), *The Economics of David Ricardo*, Toronto: University of Toronto Press.

Hollander, S. (1982), 'On the Substantive Identity of the Ricardian and Neo-classical Conceptions of Economic Organization: The French Connection in British Classicism', *Canadian Journal of Economics*, **15** (4).

Howe, A. (1984), *The Cotton Masters 1830–1860*, Oxford: Clarendon Press.

Hume, D. [1752] (1955), 'Of Money' and 'Of the Balance of Trade', reprinted in E. Rotwein (ed.).

Hunt, E.K. (1979), *History of Economic Thought*, Belmont, California: Wadsworth.

Irwin, D.A. (1989) 'Political Economy and Peel's Repeal of the Corn Laws', *Economics and Politics*, **1** (1) (Spring), pp. 41–59.

Irwin, D.A. (1995a), 'Multilateral and Bilateral Trade Policies in the World Trading System: An Historical Perspective', in J. de Melo and A. Panagariya (eds), *New Dimensions in Regional Integration*, Cambridge: Cambridge University Press.

Irwin, D.A. (1995b), 'The GATT in Historical Perspective', *American Economic Review*, **85** (2), pp. 323–8.

Irwin, D.A. (1996), *Against the Tide: An Intellectual History of Free Trade*, Princeton, N.J.: Princeton University Press.

Irwin, D.A. (1998), 'The Smoot–Hawley Tariffs: A Quantitative Assessment', *Review of Economics and Statistics*, **80** (2), pp. 326–34.

Irwin, D.A. (2002), 'Interpreting the Tariff-Growth Correlation of the Late 19th Century', *American Economic Review*, **92** (2), (May), pp. 165–9.

Isaak, R.A. (1991), *International Political Economy: Managing World Economic Change*, N.J.: Prentice Hall.

James, H. (2001), *The End of Globalization. Lessons from the Great Depression*, London: Harvard University Press.

Jencks, C. (2002), 'Does Inequality Matter?', *Daedalus* (Winter), pp. 49–63.

Jha, N. (1973), *The Age of Marshall: Aspects of British Economic Thought 1890–1915*, 2nd edition, London: Frank Cass.

Johnson, E.A.J. (1937), *Predecessors of Adam Smith*, Englewood Cliffs, N.J.: Prentice-Hall.

Joll, J. (1973), *Europe since 1870: An International History*, London: Weidenfeld & Nicolson.

Jones, R.W. and J.A. Scheinkman (1977), 'The Relevance of the Two-Sector Production Model in Trade Theory', *Journal of Political Economy*, **85** (October), pp. 909–35.

Kaldor, N. (1978), 'The Nemesis of Free Trade', in Kaldor, *Further Essays on Applied Economics*, London: Duckworth.

Kaldor, N. (1980), 'The Foundations of Free Trade Theory and Their Implications for the Current World Recession', in E. Malinvaud and J.-P. Fitoussi (eds), *Unemployment in Western Countries*, London: Macmillan.

Kaldor, N. (1982), 'Keynes as a Policy Adviser', in A.P. Thirlwall (ed.), *Keynes as a Policy Adviser*, London: Macmillan.

Kemp, M.C. (1960), 'The Mill–Bastable Infant-Industry Dogma', *Journal of Political Economy*, **68** (1), pp. 65–7.

Kemp, M.C. (1976), *Three Topics in the Theory of International Trade*, Amsterdam: North-Holland.

Kennedy, J. (1824), *On the Exportation of Machinery*, London: Hurst.

Keynes, J.M. (1971–89), *The Collected Writings of John Maynard Keynes*, ed. E. Johnson, D. Moggridge and Sir Austen Robinson, London: Macmillan. Cited as Keynes, *CW*.

Kindleberger, C.P. (1951), 'Group Behavior and International Trade', *Journal of Political Economy*, **59** (February), pp. 30–46.

Kindleberger, C.P. (1989), 'Commercial Policy between the Wars', in P. Mathias and S. Pollard (eds), *The Cambridge Economic History of Europe*, vol. VIII, Cambridge: Cambridge University Press, pp. 161–96.

Klein, E. and V. Tokman (2000), 'Social Stratification under Tension in a Globalized Era', *CEPAL Review*, **72** (December), pp. 8–29. (Economic Commission for Latin America and the Caribbean.)

Knight, F. (1925), 'On Decreasing Cost and Comparative Cost – A Rejoinder', *Quarterly Journal of Economics*, **39** (February), pp. 331–33.

Koot, G.M. (1988), *English Historical Economics, 1870–1926*, Cambridge: Cambridge University Press.

Kotwal, A. (2001), 'Globalization – Then and Now'. Review of O'Rourke and Williamson (2000), *Globalization and History*, *Review of Income and Wealth*, Series **47** (4) (December), pp. 549–59.

Krauss, M.B. (1979), *The New Protectionism: The Welfare State and International Trade*, Oxford: Blackwell.

Krugman, P. (1979), 'Increasing Returns, Monopolistic Competition and International Trade', *Journal of International Economics*, **9**, pp. 469–79.

Krugman, P. (ed.) (1986), *Strategic Trade Policy and the New International Economics*, Cambridge, Mass.: MIT Press.

Krugman, P. (1987), 'Is Free Trade Passé?', *Journal of Economic Perspectives*, **1** (Fall), pp. 131–44.

Lindert, P.H. and J.G. Williamson, 'Does Globalization Make the World More Unequal?', paper presented at the NBER *Globalization in Historical Perspective* conference in Santa Barbara, California, 3–6 May 2001, p. 7.

Lindsey, B. (2002), *Against the Dead Hand: The Uncertain Struggle for Global Capitalism*, New York: John Wiley and Sons, Inc.

List, F. (1827), *Outlines of American Political Economy*, Philadelphia: Samuel Parker.

List, F. (1856), *The National System of Political Economy*, trans. G.A. Matile, Philadelphia: Lippincott & Co.

List, F. [1841] (1885), *The National System of Political Economy*, trans. Sampson S. Lloyd, London: Longmans, Green & Co.

Low, J.M. (1952), 'An Eighteenth Century Controversy in the Theory of Economic Progress', *Manchester School of Economic and Social Studies*, **2** (3) (September).

Lübker, M., G. Smith and J. Weeks (2002), 'Growth and the Poor: A Comment on Dollar and Kraay', *Journal of International Development*, **14**, pp. 555–71.

Macintyre, S. (1999), *A Concise History of Australia*, Cambridge: Cambridge University Press.

Magee, S.P. (1978), 'Three Simple Tests of the Stolper–Samuelson Theorem', in P. Oppenheimer (ed.), *Issues in International Economics*, Stockfield: Oriel Press, pp. 138–52.

Magee, S.P. (1987), 'Endogenous Protection in the United States, 1900–1984', in R.M. Stern (ed.), *US Trade Policies in a Changing World Economy*, pp. 145–95, Cambridge, Mass.: MIT Press.

Magee, S.P. (1994), 'Endogenous Protection and Real Wages', in A.V. Deardorff and R.M. Stern (eds), *The Stolper–Samuelson Theorem: A Golden Jubilee*, Ann Arbor: University of Michigan Press, pp. 279–88.

Malthus, T.R. (1820), *Principles of Political Economy*, London: John Murray.

Malthus, T.R. (1826), *An Essay on the Principle of Population*, 6th edition, London: John Murray.

Mandeville de B. [1714] (1924), *The Fable of the Bees: or Private Vices, Publick Benefits*, ed. F.B. Kaye, 2 vols, [London: J. Roberts] Oxford: Clarendon Press.

Maneschi, A. (1983), 'Dynamic Aspects of Ricardo's International Trade Theory', *Oxford Economic Papers*, **35** (March), pp. 67–80.

Maneschi, A. (1998), *Comparative Advantage in International Trade. A Historical Perspective*, Cheltenham, UK: Edward Elgar

Maneschi, A. (2001), 'John Stuart Mill's Equilibrium Terms of Trade: A Special Case of William Whewell's 1850 Formula', *History of Political Economy*, **33** (3), pp. 609–25.

Manger, G. (1981a), 'The Australian Case for Protection Reconsidered', *Australian Economic Papers*, **20** (December), pp. 193–204.

Manger, G. (1981b), 'Summing up on the Australian Case for Protection: Comment', *Quarterly Journal of Economics*, **96**, pp. 161–7.

Manoilescu, M. [1929] (1931), *The Theory of Protection and International Trade*, London: P.S. King.

Marrison, A. (ed.) (1998), *Free Trade and Its Reception: Freedom and Trade*, vol. 1, London: Routledge.

Marsh, P.T. (1994), *Joseph Chamberlain: Entrepreneur in Politics*, London: Yale University Press.

Marshall, A. [1903] (1926), *Memorandum on the Fiscal Policy of International Trade*, reprinted 1926 in J.M. Keynes (ed.), *Official Papers by Alfred Marshall*, London: Macmillan.

Marshall, A. (1919), *Industry and Trade*, London: Macmillan.

Marshall, A. (1920), *Principles of Economics*, 8th edition, London: Macmillan.

Marshall, A. [1923] (1965), *Money, Credit and Commerce*, New York: Augustus M. Kelley.

[Martyn, H.] (1701), *Considerations upon the East-India Trade*, London: A. & J. Churchill.

Marx, K. (1971–7), *The Collected Works of Karl Marx and Frederick Engels*, various volumes, London: Lawrence and Wishart, in association with Progress Publishers, Moscow.

Mason, R. (1996), 'Robert Giffen and the Tariff Reform Campaign, 1865–1910', *Journal of European Economic History*, **25** (1) (Spring), pp. 171–88.

McCloskey, D. (1980), 'Magnanimous Albion: Free Trade and British National Income, 1841–1881', *Explorations in Economic History*, **17**, pp. 303–20.

McDonald, J.A., A.P. O'Brien and C.M. Callahan (1997), 'Trade Wars: Canada's Reaction to the Smoot–Hawley Tariff', *Journal of Economic History*, **57** (4), pp. 802–25.

Meek, R.L. (1965), *Studies in the Labour Theory of Value*, London: Lawrence and Wishart.

Metzler, L.A. (1949), 'Tariffs, the Terms of Trade and the Distribution of National Income', *Journal of Political Economy*, **62** (February), pp. 1–29.

Mill, J.S. (1844), *Essays on Some Unsettled Questions of Political Economy*, London: John W. Parker.

Mill, J.S. [1848] (1920), *Principles of Political Economy*, 7th edition, ed. W.J. Ashley, London: Longman Green.

Mill, J.S. [1865] (1961), *Principles of Political Economy*, Ashley Edition, reprint, New York: Augustus M. Kelley.

Mill, J.S. [1909] (1965), *Principles of Political Economy*, London: Longmans Green, reprint New York: A.M. Kelley.

Mill, J.S. (1963), *Collected Works of John Stuart Mill*, vol. IV, Toronto: University of Toronto Press.

Misselden, E. (1622), *Free Trade. Or the Meanes to make Trade Flourish*, London: J. Legatt.

Moggridge, D. (1992), *Maynard Keynes. An Economist's Biography*, London: Routledge.

Morley, J. (1881), *The Life of Richard Cobden*, New York: Macmillan.

Mun, T. [1664] (1959), *England's Treasure by Forraign Trade*, Oxford: Blackwell.

Myint, H. (1977), 'Adam Smith's Theory of International Trade in the Perspective of Economic Development', *Economica*, **44** (September), pp. 231–48.

Negishi, T. (1989), *History of Economic Theory*, Amsterdam: North-Holland Publishing.

Nicholson, J.S. (1897), *Principles of Political Economy*, vol. II, London: Macmillan.

North, D. [1691] (1952), *Discourses Upon Trade*, London: T. Basset; reproduced in J.R. McCulloch (ed.), *Early English Tracts on Commerce*, Cambridge: Economic History Society Reprint.

O'Brien, D.P. (1970), *J.R. McCulloch: A Study in Classical Economics*, London: Allen & Unwin.

O'Brien, D.P. (1975), *The Classical Economists*, Oxford: Oxford University Press.

O'Brien, D.P. (1981), 'Ricardian Economics and the Economics of David Ricardo', *Oxford Economic Papers*, **33** (3).

Ohlin, B. (1933), *Interregional and International Trade*, Cambridge, Mass.: Harvard University Press.

Ohmae, K. (1990), *The Borderless World: Power and Strategy in the Interlinked World Economy*, New York: Harper Business.

O'Rourke, K.H. (1997), 'The European Grain Invasion, 1870–1913', *Journal of Economic History*, **57** (4), pp. 775–801.

O'Rourke, K.H. (2000), 'Tariffs and Growth in the Late 19th Century', *Economic Journal*, **110** (April), pp. 456–83.

O'Rourke, K.H. and J.G. Williamson (1999), *Globalization and History: The Evolution of a 19th Century Atlantic Economy*, Cambridge, Mass.: MIT Press.

Pangariya, A. (1981), 'Variable Returns to Scale in Production and Patterns of Specialization', *American Economic Review*, **71** (March), pp. 221–30.

Pareto, V. [1906] (1972), *Manual of Political Economy*, ed. A.S. Schwier and A.N. Page, London: Macmillan.

Pareto, V. (1935), *The Mind and Society (Trattato di Sociologia Generale)*, New York: Harcourt Brace.

Perroni, C. and J. Whalley (1996), 'How Severe is Global Retaliation Risk under Increasing Regionalism?', *American Economic Review*, **86** (2), pp. 57–61.

Pigou, A.C. (1906), *Protective and Preferential Import Duties*, London: Macmillan.

Pigou, A.C. (1907), 'The Incidence of Import Duties', *Economic Journal*, **17** (June), p. 90.

Pigou, A.C. (ed.) (1925), *Memorials of Alfred Marshall*, London: Macmillan.

Playfair, W. (1805), *An Inquiry into the Permanent Causes of the Decline and Fall of Powerful and Wealthy Nations*, London: W. Marchant.

Pomfret, R. (2000), 'Trade Policy in Canada and Australia in the Twentieth Century', *Australian Economic History Review*, **40** (2), pp. 114–26.

Porter, B. (1987), *Britain, Europe and the World 1850-1986: Delusions of Grandeur*, 2nd edn., London: Allen and Unwin.

Porter, R. (2000), *Britain and the Creation of the Modern World*, London: Allen Lane, The Penguin Press.

Poulett Scrope, G. (1831), 'The Political Economists', *Quarterly Review*, **44**.

Poulett Scrope, G. (1833), *Principles of Political Economy*, London: Longman, Rees.

Price, L.L. (1904), 'Economic Theory and Fiscal Policy', *Economic Journal*, **14** (September).

Price, L.L. (1906), 'The Fiscal Question: Retrospect and Prospect', *Economic Review*, **16**, pp. 129–55.

Ratcliffe, B.M. (1975), 'The Origins of the Anglo-French Commercial Treaty of 1860: A Reassessment', in B.M. Ratcliffe (ed.), *Great Britain and Her World, 1750–1914: Essays in Honour of W.O. Henderson*, Manchester: Manchester University Press.

Raymond, D. (1823), *Elements of Political Economy*, vol. II, Baltimore: Johns Hopkins University Press.

Reitsma, A.J. (1958), 'Trade and Redistribution of Income: Is There Still an Australian Case?', *Economic Record*, **34** (August), pp. 172–88.

Ricardo, D. (1951), *The Works and Correspondence of David Ricardo*, various volumes, ed. P. Sraffa, Cambridge: Cambridge University Press. Cited in text as (Ricardo, *Works*, 1951).

Robbins, L. (1952), *The Theory of Economic Policy in English Political Economy*, London: Macmillan.

Robbins, L. (1958), *Robert Torrens and the Evolution of Classical Economics*, London: Macmillan.

Robbins, L. (1968), *The Theory of Economic Development in the History of Economic Thought*, London: Macmillan.

Robinson, J. (1962), *Economic Philosophy*, London: C.A. Watts & Co. Ltd.

Robinson, J. (1979a), 'Reflections on the Theory of International Trade', in *Collected Economic Essays*, vol. 5, Oxford: Blackwell.

Robinson, J. (1979b), *Collected Economic Essays*, various volumes, Oxford: Basil Blackwell.

Rodriguez, F. (2001), Review of *Globalization and Progressive Economic Policy* by D. Baker, G. Epstein and R. Pollin, Oxford: Oxford University Press (1998) in *Economica* (November 2001), pp. 608–10.

Rodrik, D. (1997), *Has Globalization Gone Too Far?*, Washington, DC: Institute for International Economics.

Rodrik, D. (1998), 'Symposium on Globalization in Perspective: An Introduction', *Journal of Economic Perspectives*, **12** (4), pp. 3–8.

Rodrik, D. (2002), 'Is Globalization Good for the World's Poor?', unpublished paper, May.

Rotwein, E. (ed.) (1955), *David Hume: Writings on Economics*, London: Nelson.

Rybczynski, T.M. (1955), 'Factor Endowment and Relative Commodity Prices', *Economica*, **22** (November), pp. 336–41.

Samuelson, M.C. (1939), 'The Australian Case for Protection Re-examined', *Quarterly Journal of Economics*, **54** (1), pp. 143–9.

Samuelson, P.A. (1938), 'Welfare Economics and International Trade', *American Economic Review*, **28** (June).

Samuelson, P.A. (1969), 'The Way of an Economist', in Paul Samuelson (ed.), *International Economic Relations*, London: Macmillan.

Samuelson, P.A. (1972), *The Collected Scientific Papers of Paul A. Samuelson*, ed. R.C. Merton, vols 2 and 3, Cambridge, Mass.: MIT Press.

Samuelson, P.A. (1981), 'Summing Up on the Australian Case for Protection', *Quarterly Journal of Economics*, **96** (1), pp. 147–60.

Samuelson, P.A. (1986), *The Collected Scientific Papers of Paul A. Samuelson*, vol. 5, ed. Kate Crowley, Cambridge, Mass.: MIT Press.

Say, Jean-Baptiste (1821), *Letter to Mr Malthus on Several Subjects of Political Economy, and on the Cause of the Stagnation of Commerce*, trans. John Richter, London: Sherwood, Neely & Jones.

Scheve, K.F. and M.J. Slaughter (2001a), *Globalization and the Perceptions of American Workers*, Washington, DC: Institute for International Economics.

Scheve, K.F. and M.J. Slaughter (2001b), 'What Determines Individual Trade-Policy Preferences?', *Journal of International Economics*, **54** (2), pp. 267–92.

Schonhardt-Bailey, C. (1998), 'Interests, Ideology and Politics: Agricultural Trade Policy in Nineteenth-Century Britain and Germany', in Andrew Marrison (ed.), *Free Trade and Its Reception*, pp. 63–81.

Schüller, R. (1905), *Schutzzoll und Freihandel: Die Voraussetzungen und Grenzen ihrer Berechtigung*, Vienna: Tempsky.

Schumpeter, J.A. (1954), *History of Economic Analysis*, London: Allen & Unwin.

Semmel, B. (1970), *The Rise of Free Trade Imperialism: Classical Political Economy, the Empire of Free Trade, and Imperialism*, Cambridge: Cambridge University Press.

Senior, N. [1830] (1931), *Three Lectures on the Cost of Obtaining Money*, LSE Reprints of Scarce Tracts, etc. 1931.

Senior, N. (1843), 'Free Trade and Retaliation', *Edinburgh Review*, **78** (July), pp. 1–47.

Shelton, G. (1981), *Dean Tucker and Eighteenth Century Economic and Political Thought*, London: Macmillan.

Sideri, S. (1970), *Trade and Power: Informal Colonialism in Anglo-Portuguese Relations*, Rotterdam: Rotterdam University Press.

Sidgwick, H. [1883] (1901), *Principles of Political Economy*, 3rd edition, London: Macmillan.

Siriwardana, M. (1996), 'The Economic Impact of Tariffs in the 1930s in Australia: The Brigden Report Re-examined', *Australian Economic Papers* (December), pp. 370–87.

Sked, A. (1987), *Britain's Decline: Problems and Perspectives*, Oxford: Blackwell.

Skidelsky, R. (1992) *John Maynard Keynes: The Economist as Saviour, 1920–1937*, vol. 2, London: Macmillan.

Sleeman, W. (1829), *On Taxes, or Public Revenue*, London: Elder & Co.

Smith, A. [1776] (1976), *An Inquiry into the Nature and Causes of the Wealth of Nations*, ed. R.H. Campbell, A.S. Skinner and W.B. Todd, vols 1 and 2, Oxford: Clarendon Press.

Smith, M.S. (1980), *Tariff Reform in France 1860–1900: The Politics of Economic Interest*, Ithaca and London: Cornell University Press.

Steger, M.B. (2002), *Globalism: The New Market Ideology*, Oxford: Rowman & Littlefield Publishers, Inc.

Stigler, G.J. (1941), *Production and Distribution Theories*, New York: Macmillan.

Stigler, G.J. (1958), 'Ricardo and the 93 Per Cent Labour Theory of Value', *American Economic Review*, **48**, pp. 357–67.

Stigler, G.J. (1976), 'Do Economists Matter?', *Southern Economic Journal*, **42** (3), pp. 347–8.

Stigler, G.J. (1982), 'Nobel Lecture: The Process and Progress of Economics', *Journal of Political Economy*, **91** (4).

Stiglitz, J.E. (2002), *Globalisation and Its Discontents*, London: Allen Lane.

Stolper, W.F. and P.A. Samuelson (1941), 'Protection and Real Wages', *Review of Economic Studies*, **9** (November), pp. 58–73, reprinted in A.V. Deardorff and R.M. Stern (eds) *The Stolper-Samuelson Theorem: A Golden Jubilee*, Ann Arbor: University of Michigan Press, pp. 36–61.

Sykes, A. (1979), *Tariff Reform in British Politics, 1903–1913*, Oxford: Clarendon Press.

Taussig, F.W. (1892), *The Tariff History of the United States*, New York: Putnam.

Theocaris, R.D. (1983), *Early Developments in Mathematical Economics*, 2nd edition, London: Macmillan.

Thweatt, W.O. (1976), 'James Mill and the Early Development of Comparative Advantage', *History of Political Economy*, **8** (2), pp. 207–34.

Tinbergen, J. (1945), 'Professor Graham's Case for Protection', Appendix 1 in *International Economic Cooperation*, Amsterdam: Elsevier.

Tomlinson, J. (1981), *Problems of British Economic Policy, 1870–1945*, London: Methuen.

Torrens, R. [1808] (1857), *The Economists Refuted*, reprinted in R. Torrens, *The Principles and Practical Operation of Sir Robert Peel's Act of 1844 Explained and Defended*, 2nd edition, London: Longmans.

Torrens, R. (1815), *Essay on the External Corn Trade*, London: J. Hatchard.

Torrens, R. (1821), *Essay on the Production of Wealth*, London: Longman, Hurst, Rees, Orme, and Brown.

Torrens, R. (1827), *An Essay on the External Corn Trade*, 4th edn, London: Longman, Rees, Orme, Brown and Green.

Torrens, R. (1833), *Letters on Commercial Policy*, London: Longman.

Torrens, R. (1837), *A Letter to the Right Honourable Lord John Russell*, London: Longman.

Torrens, R. (1844), *The Budget: On Commercial and Colonial Policy*, London: Smith, Elder.

Torrens, R. (1852), *Tracts on Trade and Finance*, Nos. I and II, London: Chapman & Hall.

Tucker, J. [1774] (1973), *Four Tracts together with Two Sermons on Political and Commercial Subjects* (Gloucester, 1774), Tract 1. Extracts reprinted in R.L. Meek (ed.), *Precursors of Adam Smith, 1750–1775*, London: Dent, pp. 173–96.

Viner, J. (1929), 'The Australian Tariff: A Review Article', *Economic Record*, **5** (November), pp. 306–15.

Viner, J. [1937] (1955), *Studies in the Theory of International Trade*, London: Allen & Unwin.

Viner, J. (1951), *International Economics*, Glencoe, Ill.: The Free Press.

Watkins, K. (2002), 'Making Globalization Work for the Poor', *Finance and Development* (March), pp. 24–7.

Watkins, M. (1986), *The Idea of Free Trade: Reflections on a Canada–United States Free Trade Arrangement*, London: Canada House Lecture Series, No. 33 (December).

Whitaker, J.K. (ed.) (1975), *The Early Economic Writings of Alfred Marshall 1867–1890*, vol. II, London: Macmillan.

Williams, J.H. [1929] (1949), 'The Theory of International Trade Reconsidered', *Economic Journal* (June 1929), reprinted in American Economic Association, *Readings in the Theory of International Trade*, ed. H.S. Ellis and L.A. Metzler, Philadelphia: Blackiston.

Williamson, J. (1998), 'Globalization, Labour Markets, and Policy Backlash in the Past', *Journal of Economic Perspectives*, **12** (4), pp. 51–72.

Winch, D. (1969), *Economics and Policy. A Historical Study*, London: Hodder and Stoughton.

Wood, J.C. (1983), *British Economists and the Empire*, London: Croom Helm.

World Trade Organization (1995), *International Trade, Trends and Statistics*, Geneva: WTO.

Wright, G. (1987), *France in Modern Times*, 4th edition, New York and London: W.W. Norton.

Young, K. (1963) *Arthur James Balfour*, London: G. Bell and Sons.

Index

The Economics and Ideology of Free Trade

Unless Recalled Earlier
DATE DUE